God's Appointments

50 Years Of Soul Winning

Gloria (Vermaas) Goering

"Like a tree planted by streams of water that yields its fruit," bloom for Christ where you are planted!
Psalm 1

God's Appointments

50 Years Of Soul Winning with Gloria (Vermaas) Goering

"Like a tree planted by streams of water that yields its fruit," bloom for Christ where you are planted!
Psalm 1

[1]Blessed is the man (or woman)
    who walks not in the counsel of the wicked,
nor stands in the way of sinners,
    nor sits in the seat of scoffers;
[2]but his delight is in the law of the LORD,
    and on his law he meditates day and night.
[3]He is like a tree
    planted by streams of water
that yields its fruit in its season,
    and its leaf does not wither.
In all that he does, he prospers.

Psalm 1:1-3

Copyright © 2011 by Gloria (Vermaas) Goering

God's Appointment
50 Years Of Soul Winning
by Gloria (Vermaas) Goering

Printed in the United States of America

ISBN 9781613790595

All rights reserved solely by the author. The author guarantees all contents are original and do not infringe upon the legal rights of any other person or work. No part of this book may be reproduced in any form without the permission of the author. The views expressed in this book are not necessarily those of the publisher.

Unless otherwise indicated, Bible quotations are taken from The Holy Bible, English Standard Version. Copyright © 2001 by Crossway Bibles, a publishing ministry of Good News Publishers. Used by permission.

To order additional books, call 1-866-909-2665.

www.xulonpress.com

CONTENTS

Dedication xix

Acknowledgements xxi

Forward xxiii
    Rhonda Moore.. xxiii
    Dr. Hal Miller xxiv
    Bernice Vermaas.. xxiv
    Pastor David Moore xxv
    Sue Hoven xxv

Introduction xxvii

SECTION 1: BEING BORN AGAIN

Chapter 1   Do You Know for Certain You Are
Going to Heaven?...................................... 31
A Conversation with Jesus....................... 34

SECTION 2: GOD'S APPOINTMENTS

Chapter 2   1959-1969 54

1959	September	God changed my life 54
1959	October	Protection during a storm 58
1960	June	Volunteer for life 61
1964	July	Seven happy campers 62
1964	September	Special neighbors 63
1965	September	Prescription for pain.................... 66
1966	October	Fire escape conversion................. 67
1967	March	Invalid hesitations 70
1967	October	Traveling by faith........................ 71
1968	January	Identity search 73
1968	March	Jogging partner 73
1968	April	Dead religion............................... 74
1968	September	Study, then decide 75
1968	October	Bible "errors"............................... 76
1969	September	Whirlwind summer...................... 77
1969	December	Snowy winter 78

Chapter 3   1970-1974 80

1970	September	The Christian horse 81
1970	October	White witch................................ 82
1971	May 5	Thanks.. 86
1971	May	Sorrowful life turned glorious..... 86
1971	June	Choosing a mentor 89
1972	July	Teaching the Word 91
1972	December	Searching hearts.......................... 91
1973	May	Fruitful ministry.......................... 91
1973	June	Our Father's care......................... 92
1973	December	Long way from home 93
1974	January	Can't explain it............................ 94
1974	March	Need to build............................... 96
1974	December	Picture in the mail....................... 98

Chapter 4   1975-1978 100

1975	July	Foreboding dreams	100
1975	August	Lawyer on the bridge	102
1976	June	Hit by a car	103
1976	September	Rejoicing in Heaven	104
1977	July	Moving day	106
1977	August	Vacation Bible school	107
1977	September	Changed destination	108
1977	October	First time visit	109
1977	October	*The Burning Hell*	110
1978	January	No longer afraid	111
1978	May 19	"Hope so" becomes "know so"	112
1978	June	At our doorstep	114
1978	September	State fair	114
1978	October	On a porch	116
1978	December	Demonstration turned real	117
1978	December	Visiting Grandma	118

Chapter 5   1979 120

1979	January	Thanks to a flat tire	120
1979	February	Trip to the Middle East	121
1979	March	Rescued girls	122
1979	March	Baptism for two	123
1979	April	New church	124
1979	April 8	Crumbled tract	125
1979	April	Second film showing	125
1979	May	Child's example	126
1979	June	Substitute teaching	126
1979	July	Last in the family	127
1979	August	Drinking everlasting water	128
1979	September	Ripple effect	129
1979	October	From emptiness to joy	130
1979	October	Grace finds God	131

Chapter 6 1980-1981 133

1980	February	Skeptical young woman	133
1980	April	Special reunion	134
1980	May	Praise or panic	134
1980	June	Spiritual baby	135
1980	September	God blessing His work	136
1980	October	Spiritual birthday for two	140
1980	November	Younger leading the older	141
1981	May 7	Kristi's decision	143
1981	June 5	In the garden	143
1981	August 5	Young people searching	144
1981	August 28	Needing more prayer	145

Chapter 7 1982 147

1982	January	Life of earnest service	147
1982	February	"Will they laugh?"	148
1982	March	Persistence paid off	149
1982	April	Shared connection	150
1982	May 23	Offer not refused	150
1982	June	Wedding bells	151
1982	June	Time for VBS	153
1982	July	Providentially not home	153
1982	July 4	New life	154
1982	July 7	Key to tomorrow	155
1982	August 8	Pain with purpose	155
1982	August 15	Knock, knock	157
1982	August 29	"Oh, no—the preacher!"	157
1982	September	Generations apart, same needs	158
1982	September	Birthday gift	160
1982	October	Need a lift?	161
1982	October	Not according to plan	161
1982	October	Finding the one?	162
1982	November	Yard sale treasure	164
1982	November	"But I was a deacon!"	165

| 1982 | November | Brother and sisters on Earth, in Heaven .... 167 |

Chapter 8 1983 169

1983	January	Like a lost boat 169
1983	March	Attempted suicide 171
1983	March 6	Praying for Mom 172
1983	April	Finding the Jewish Messiah 173
1983	April	Free things 175
1983	May 1	From out of town 176
1983	May 8	Humble faith of a child 177
1983	May	Icebreaker 178
1983	May 10	Place to stay 179
1983	May 31	Testimony by daughter Angela 180
1983	June 9	Tragic wedding dance 182
1983	July	Better than fireworks 183
1983	August 7	Making it personal 184
1983	August	Time preparing hearts 184
1983	September	Clean rugs, clean heart 186
1983	September	Timed just right 187
1983	September	"I want to listen." 188

Chapter 9 1984 190

1984	March	Wife in hiding 190
1984	May	Spiritual twins 191
1984	May 23	Testimony by daughter Victoria 192
1984	June	Lame will walk 195
1984	July	Blind will see 196
1984	September	Right place, right time 197
1984	September	Tragic fire 198
1984	November	Deathbed vigil 199
1984	November	High-speed crash 200

| 1984 | December | Testimony by daughter Jessica...204 |

Chapter 10   1985-1986 207

1985	January	Spiritual heart surgery 207
1985	January	Worth a second visit...................208
1985	April	Daughter of the King 209
1985	May 27	Broken dryer 210
1985	June	Living in a church bus 213
1985	September	Cattle Congress interview 214
1985	December	Family's cry for help...................218
1986	March	Tears of deliverance 220
1986	May	Jesus thrills my heart..................221
1986	June	Life-changes, in an instant 221
1986	July 4	Firecracker convert....................222
1986	December	Copier problems, again...............225

Chapter 11   1987-1989 227

1987	February	Hell is worse than jail! 227
1987	May	Little trouble-maker 229
1987	August	"Jungle Jim"...............................230
1987	September	Newspaper boy 231
1987	October	Bingo..232
1988	June	Eager learner...............................233
1988	August	Not too late................................234
1988	August	Looking for a hand-out...............235
1988	August	Not by good works 237
1988	September	Daring to stand alone.................239
1989	April	Paralyzed 241
1989	May 14	Freedom from Satan 243
1989	August 6	Visiting New Brunswick 245
1989	September	Hand-delivered from Oregon....246
1989	September	Religion, not the answer 247

Chapter 12   1990-1994 250

1990	April	Testimony by son, Josiah 250
1990	May 10	Road trip 252
1990	June	Appointments with the teacher 253
1990	September	Celebrating in style 254
1991	February	7 Videos for rent 256
1992	March 10	"Come to Lincoln" 258
1992	October	At John's store 260
1993	April	Hope, not lost 261
1993	March	Students from around the world 262
1993	May	Twins with different birthdays 264
1993	September	No coincidence 265
1994	May 19	Vietnam vet 267

Chapter 13   1995-1999 270

1995	August	Rabbits and everlasting life 270
1995	August 4	YMCA 273
1995	December	High school volunteer 273
1995	December	Baby bunnies 274
1996	January	Brown mouse 275
1996	June	Cousin Mike 275
1996	September	"Farmers for Christ" booth 276
1997	August 18	Missing Mother 276
1997	September	Understanding Scripture 277
1997	October	Amiga computer parts 278
1999	December	Honorary Grandma 279

Chapter 14   2000-2004 281

2000	December	Christmas gift for Jesus 281
2001	March 10	The next step 283
2001	June	"Cattle Congress Lady" 284

2001	July 10	Little charmer	285
2001	July 25	Practice pays off	286
2001	September	Visiting Dorothy	287
2002	March 6	Inaudible voice	288
2002	May	Happy Birthday	289
2003	April 21	Thank you, Jesus	291
2003	June	Adam fixes my tire	293
2003	July	Phone call from Brandon	294
2004	May	Missing Grandma	295
2004	July 16	Car trouble	297

Chapter 15   2005-2006 299

2005	February	Right there, ready!	299
2005	May 23	Letter to Bradley	299
2005	September	Cattle Congress	301
2005	December	"Rebel"	303
2006	January 2	Child of the King	305
2006	September	Needing battery cables	306
2006	September	On assignment	307
2006	December	"Home last, please?"	311
2006	December	Teamwork	312

Chapter 16   2007 314

2007	January 4	Touch of love	314
2007	January	The lady who takes us to church	315
2007	February	Public access TV	316
2007	March 2	Trying to wait	319
2007	March 6	Two birthday gifts	323
2007	March 9	Missed appointment, God's appointment	325
2007	March 14	Sandra in Germany	326
2007	May 26	Graduation open house	328
2007	May 28	"Got Jesus?"	329
2007	June 1	Anna from the Ukraine	330

2007	June 6	VBS at Washburn 331
2007	July 4	Fun in the "Son"..........................332
2007	September	Church booth at Cattle Congress..334

Chapter 17   2008-2010 338

2008	February	AWANA Club time 338
2008	April 16	Silver coins..................................339
2008	June 24	Spiritual and physical birth 340
2008	July 3	Jumping on the bed....................341
2008	November	Writing on the wall 342
2008	December	No longer a pagan 344
2009	January	Eternal Life insurance................346
2009	January	Need a vacuum cleaner? 348
2009	March 19	Spring break................................350
2009	June	Twenty years later......................351
2010	June 15	The last breath............................352
2010	August	A slow day...................................354
2010	September	Our mechanic 356
2010	November	Something good from cancer? ...358
2010	December	A Chinese lunch..........................359

In the future..362

SECTION 3: A GUIDE TO SOUL WINNING

Chapter 18   *Tips on Soul Winning   1-7* 364

Personal Preparations

1	Focus on eternity 365
2	Be willing to try 366
3	Study the Bible 367
4	Have a Bible handy 368
5	Be the third party...369
6	Practice..370
7	Be in prayer 371

God's Appointment

Chapter 19   *Tips on Soul Winning   8-25* 372

Personal Attitudes

8	See the need	372
9	Visualize Hell	373
10	Volunteer for harvesting	374
11	Be confident in Christ	375
12	Avoid "class" consciousness	376
13	Be involved	377
14	Lift up Christ	378
15	Attract others with joy	378
16	Notice people	379
17	Learn to love	380
18	Avoid prejudging	381
19	Let God be in control	382
20	Overcome shyness	383
21	Be obedient	383
22	Purify your lives	384
23	Let problems position	386
24	Recycle the Gospel	386
25	Avoid "missionary" dating	386

Chapter 20   *Tips on Soul Winning   26-41* 388

Approaches

26	Reach children	388
27	Avoid defensive reaction	391
28	Find receptive people	392
29	Use the buddy system	393
30	Exercise caution in mixed company	393
31	Be one-on-one	394
32	Use fair booths	395
33	Watch for home deliveries	398
34	Talk to telemarketers	399
35	Look for points of connection	400

36	Practice role playing	405
37	Remember the experience	405
38	Know their standing	407
39	Be patient with multiple decisions	409
40	Discern between religious and "born again"	410
41	Hear explanations	414
42	Reach people in cults	414
43	Win people in other religions	417

Chapter 21   *Tips on Soul Winning   44-51* 419

Various Observations

44	Use available time	419
45	Pray for the unsaved	419
46	Take people	421
47	Watch for Satan's interference	421
48	It's all about God	422
49	Use names	423
50	Consider the age of accountability	424
51	Build a strong foundation	424

Chapter 22   *Tips on Soul Winning   52-62* 426

Different Methods

52	Make the Gospel clear	426
53	Use "The Romans Road"	427
54	Use Jesus' conversation	428
55	Distribute tracts	432
56	Utilize the internet	434
57	Share your personal testimony	436
58	Avoid hypocrisy	436
59	Be careful of tricky emotions	438
60	Use courtesy on the job	440
61	Know the evidence	441
62	Repeat often	442

Chapter 23 *Tips on Soul Winning   63-75* **444**

Bringing to a Conclusion

63	Expect results	444
64	Follow through to a conclusion	445
65	"Get ready"	447
66	Prevent "pleasing you" decisions	449
67	Reconfirm commitments	450
68	Use a salvation prayer	451
69	Avoid just saying the words	452
70	Give control to God	453
71	Beware rejection of the messenger	454
72	Take step to future	455
73	Come just as we are	456
74	Avoid coercion	457
75	Realize "No" can change to "Yes"	458

Chapter 24 *Tips on Soul Winning   76-84* **460**

After a Decision

76	Introduce assurance of salvation	460
77	Encourage Christians to grow	461
78	Share helpful literature	464
79	Do multiplication	465
80	View results	465
81	Acknowledge the help of others	466
82	Enjoy the harvest	467
83	Follow up	468
84	Be cautious	469

DEDICATION

After winning people to Christ through the years, I've joyfully shared many of the experiences with my parents. It was the testimony of their lives that originally sparked my own desire to discover what they had found in Christ. Any spiritual fruit that I may have in my life, I believe is also credited to their account. Through the years, they have encouraged me to write a book sharing these experiences and giving soul-winning tips. God burdened my heart to make their suggestion a reality. I lovingly dedicate this book to my parents, Bernice and Martin Vermaas.

ACKNOWLEDGEMENTS

My thanks go to those who helped get this book ready for publication. My abilities run in the area of verbal rather than written communication. It has taken the hard work of many gifted people to give me advice on the rules of English. I marvel that God gave so many capable people a desire to come along side me in this project. Grammar has been a giant obstacle to me. Writing this book became a challenge to face this giant. I seek to avoid being a poor testimony to the readers. It has taken the hard work of many to get me to the point of publication. Also, I appreciate the fact that God burdened the hearts of individuals to cover the cost of printing the book in advance giving me the determination to finish the job. I deeply appreciate all the helpful suggestions and accept responsibility for any errors. This has been a labor of obedience. It will be interesting to see God's purpose for it, and how He intends to use this book.

FORWARD

~Rhonda Moore
Hostess of the TV Public Access Program, *Words Of Life Ministries*

Gloria Goering loves Jesus. Her heart is after the heart of God. Her passion is sharing His love with as many people as opportunity affords. She is a true "Ambassador for Christ," representing His cause respectfully, honestly, and directly, in whatever situation and to whomever she comes in contact.

Knowing that His Truth brings freedom, she lives with urgent expectation of helping to bring God's salvation into reality for people on a daily basis.

Watching Gloria "in action" is exciting. Whether at the fair, in a restaurant, with neighbors, or speaking to a group, she is able to introduce Jesus and bring people to make eternal decisions, without pressuring them. Asking poignant questions or utilizing practical examples, she causes people to think and respond. Gloria is the best, most successful witness with whom I have worked.

May you be challenged as you read of her "appointments." You will be inspired as you apply her encouragement and helps to your life.

~Dr. Hal Miller
Consultant, *Campus Bible Fellowship* with Baptist Mid-Missions

I am excited about Gloria's writing this book. I know that God's hand has been on her life, and He will use these accounts for His glory.

From the campus ministry, I have learned that there are people uniquely qualified by God to experience subjectively His hand in their lives. Others, equally qualified, have had to obtain evidence objectively to answer their questions and understand God. Though I am of the latter, Gloria is of the former. She came to work with us in campus ministry, *Campus Bible Fellowship*, just as we were getting started. We learned together. I watched many times as God worked experientially with Gloria, in an amazing fashion, reaching young intellectuals for Him. I could explain some of those exhilarating experiences, but will leave that to her.

Her accounts are not exaggerated. The events happened the way she explains. Readers will appreciate the enthusiasm with which Gloria relates accounts. May that excitement become contagious in their own lives. Gloria is very devoted, completely sold out to the Lord. May her compilation and handbook of tips be used of the Lord in many lives, as has been true of her life and witness.

~Bernice Vermaas
Gloria's mother

I have been watching Gloria all of her life. She came to know the Lord as her Savior shortly after I did; we grew in the knowledge and love of the Lord together.

After high school, Gloria attended Omaha Baptist Bible College. After graduation, she was commissioned as a missionary to college students by Lighthouse Baptist Church in Omaha, Nebraska. She served with Hal Miller, director of *Campus Bible Fellowship* under Baptist Mid-Missions in Iowa. Later, Gloria married Pastor James Goering, and has helped him in the ministry of the radio program

Family Altar Broadcast, as well as several churches in the area. Gloria and James have four children, all of whom know the Lord as their Savior. Their son is a youth pastor.

A devout Christian lady, Gloria lives her faith every day and is not fearful of speaking to others about her Savior.

Seeking to introduce others to her beloved Lord and friend, Jesus Christ, Gloria is a soul winner. Calvary Bible Church in Washburn, Iowa, recognizes and supports her as one of their missionaries.

~Pastor David Moore
Emeritus Pastor, *Walnut Ridge Baptist Church*, Waterloo, IA

There's a beautiful, powerful simplicity about this book. The author relentlessly encourages us to go for the harvest of souls. It is refreshing to read these real-life experiences of people who step right out of these pages into our hearts. Here's the reality of God's grace bringing people to Himself in a forever salvation. These testimonies cannot be read without feeling a renewed passion for the God who so loved the world that His Son did it all, so that we could have eternal life.

~Sue Hoven
Retired English teacher working with final editing of book, Waterloo, IA

Getting to know Gloria was instantaneous for me. The Holy Spirit rides shot-gun with her, and the love of Jesus radiates in her smile. We met and our hearts became eternally attached as Christian sisters. I'm the sister full of doubt, fear, and all the reasons something isn't possible. Gloria sees the possibility of everything.

First hand I've seen the powerful tool of Gloria's witness. The story of Nicodemus in John Chapter 3 explains in Our Lord's own words how we gain entrance to heaven. Perhaps Gloria will soon put together a DVD demonstrating her loving approach. Trust me; it is beautiful!

Get convicted to become a soul harvester. Increase you love of God's word in the Bible and enjoy using this book.

Introduction

As a young Christian, I was challenged by the story of a terminally ill nine-year-old boy who asked the Lord to allow him to influence as many people for eternity as he was years old. At his funeral, nine people, including several doctors and nurses, said that they had met the Savior because of the boy's life and witness; they would spend eternity with Jesus in Heaven. The story inspired me to do the same.

What a joy it was when I led my first soul to Christ. It was as if I was on a team, like a nurse assisting the best doctor in the world, the Holy Spirit. I saw the transformation of a soul reaching out for God, accepting His redemption, and being born again, literally born from above (John 3). I remember saying to the Lord, "This is awesome; I want to do it again."

After leading as many to Christ as I was years old, I heard the song *"Oh, for a Thousand Tongues to Sing."* The Holy Spirit prompted me to seek a new goal of influencing a thousand souls for Christ. These individuals would join me singing praises before the throne of God. None of us can take *things* with us to Heaven, only *those* we have influenced for Heaven. Not having tabulated the number of soul surgeries I have scrubbed for—only God can keep track of something like that. I do believe that I have reached my first two goals and am now just seeking to win as many for Christ as God enables.

Through the years, people close to me have suggested that I write a book to encourage others in their soul winning and to share how

I make a conversation turn into a soul winning experience. Since there is no way I am going to be able to handle the need in my own strength and realizing that when we help others, we multiply our influence, I do want to share anything that might be of any help to others. Jesus said, ***"Look, I tell you, lift up your eyes, and see that the fields are white for harvest"*** (John 4:35b). My mother has been the most persistent as she seeks to be more bold in her own witnessing. James, my husband, has been supportive as have our children who are now adults. My sisters and brothers kindly encouraged me, as have numerous friends. A teenage niece said, "Aunt Gloria, you ought to write a book about your experiences."

Reading testimonies of how people have come to know Christ as their personal Savior has been an inspiration and challenge to me. Experiences of soul winners such as Dwight L. Moody, John R. Rice, Jack Hyles, Billy Graham, Mark Cahill, Ann Kiemel, and Walter Lewis Wilson, M.D. and others are motivating.

This collection of stories is the result of my response to God's work in my life. Leading people to Christ has been a spiritual high for me. Through the years, I found that jotting down notes and recording details helped me to come down from that high. Later, when the Lord laid it on my heart to write this book, those notes became essential. No other way could I have recounted these experiences. If sharing challenges believers to consider opportunities available to them, praise the Lord. Since God is the author of each incident, the honor and glory is His.

When James and I married in September of 1974, James was publishing a monthly newsletter for the Family Altar Broadcast. I began contributing a short soul-winning column, "God's Appointments." Some accounts in this book are taken from those articles. Many "appointments," which never got recorded, have been forgotten. By God's grace, I joyfully look forward to many more "appointments," until the Lord calls me home.

Obviously, not everyone I talk to about Christ makes a decision for salvation. More say, "No," or "I'm not ready right now," than say, "Yes." Sadly, even during Jesus' earthly ministry, many rejected His message. The Apostle John recorded that because of peoples' unbelief, ***"Jesus wept"*** (John 11:35). Praise the Lord, God has given me the privilege to see many people come to know Christ. In this book, for the most part, I have shared accounts of individuals who said, "Yes." My prayer is that others will have that same joy. Jesus promised his disciples, saying, *"Follow me, and I will make you fishers of men"* (Matthew 4:19). Having first made certain that we ourselves are on the way to Heaven, let us endeavor to take others with us.

This book is divided into three sections. The **first section**, Chapter 1, provides insight into what I try to share when talking to people about how to become a Christian. The focus is primarily on the conversation between Jesus and Nicodemus found in the Gospel of John, Chapter 3. It shows how I explain the plan of salvation. The **second section** of this book, chapters 2-17, recount over fifty years of soul-winning experiences. The **third section**, chapters 18-24, contains a number of practical tips for witnessing.

The goal of this book is to encourage others to win souls to Jesus. Let us look for opportunities, not only to witness, but to lead people to follow through and accept Christ. Some fishermen fish for the fun of fishing while others fish to catch fish. Our main objective in soul winning is to see decisions made for salvation. We need to pick the spiritual fruit which is ready for harvest in everyday opportunities. We must pray that God will increase the number of laborers in His field. Jesus taught His disciples, *"The harvest is plentiful, but the laborers are few. Therefore pray earnestly to the Lord of the harvest to send out laborers into his harvest"* (Luke 10:2). God receives the glory when He uses those who understand that they cannot succeed on their own. Jesus explained, *"I am the vine; you are the branches. Whoever abides in me and I in him, he it is that bears much fruit, for apart from me you can do nothing"* (John 15:5). No spiritual endeavor should begin without fervent prayer. Experience the assignment, *"Sing to the LORD, bless his name; tell of his salvation from day to day"* (Psalm 96:2). What a joy it is to tell others about salvation.

In the accounts included in the second section, the names of some individuals have been changed to protect their privacy. Since Heaven, Earth, and Hell are specific places like Chicago, New York, Waterloo, or Iowa, I have chosen to capitalize the references to them. The first chapter of this book is available in pamphlet form for your use.

As long as God gives strength, I would love to be available to tutor those who desire to develop their witnessing skills. Feel free to contact us if you have any questions or comments: Gloria Goering, P.O. Box 4185, Waterloo, IA 50704, gloriagoering@hotmail.com, or www. familyaltarbroadcast.com.

CHAPTER 1

Do You Know for *Certain* You Are Going to Heaven?

The issue, "Am I going to Heaven?" is vital for each of us to consider. It would be horrible at the end of life to learn one had missed Heaven and had to go the other direction. We want the answer to be from a reliable source. Jesus was and is the most reliable source on the subject!

Who is Jesus? The Scriptures tell us, *"And the Word became flesh and dwelt among us, and we have seen his glory, glory as of the only Son from the Father, full of grace and truth"* (John 1:14 NKJV). The phrase, "became flesh and dwelt among us" clearly describes Jesus taking on human form and living here on the earth with us. A person can be described by different names: son, husband, father, or brother. Jesus is described with many different terms. One name; among many used in the Bible for Jesus is "the Word." Jesus is referred to as *"clothed in a robe dipped in blood, and the name by which he is called is The Word of God"* (Revelation 19:13). Jesus is called, God's Word. Placing the name *Jesus* along with *Word*, we read, *"In the beginning was the Word* [Jesus], *and the Word* [Jesus] *was with God, and the Word* [Jesus] *was God. He was in the beginning with God. All things were made through Him* [Jesus], *and without Him* [Jesus] *nothing was made that was made. In Him* [Jesus] *was life, and the life was the light of men"* (John 1:1-4). The Bible states that Jesus is God and that He is the creator of life, and He came from Heaven to rescue His creation.

Nicodemus was described in the Bible as being a ruler of the Jews. History gives the added information that he was a Pharisee; a member of the Sanhedrin, and his full name was Nakdimon Ben Gurion. He was one of the three richest nobles in Jerusalem at the time of Jesus. His distinguished family was highly respected and even today passengers flying into Israel, land at Ben Gurion International Airport! (www.jewishjewels.org, January 2010).

One night Nicodemus came to Jesus asking Him how one gets to Heaven. The conversation between them was recorded in twenty-one consecutive verses in the Bible. (John 3:1-21) Looking at Jesus' answer we can discover what He would say to us if we were able to have a one on one discussion with Him. So, how does one get to Heaven? Let us study what Jesus said!

God's Appointment

Jesus and Nicodemus in conversation
Entretien de Jésus et de Nicodème
Artist: James Tissot
French, 1836-1902

A Conversation with Jesus
John 3:1-21

Let's take a close look at how Jesus explained one gets to Heaven.

Now there was a man of the Pharisees named Nicodemus, a ruler of the Jews. This man came to Jesus by night and said to him, "Rabbi, we know that you are a teacher come from God, for no one can do these signs that you do unless God is with him." Jesus answered him, "Truly, truly, I say to you, <u>unless one is born again he cannot see the kingdom of God.</u>" Nicodemus said to him, "How can a man be born when he is old? Can he enter a second time into his mother's womb and be born?" **(John 3:1-4)**

Nicodemus knew that Jesus was from God, and he came to Him wanting an answer to his concern. Jesus understood his unspoken question and said that a person must be "born again," literally born from above (John 3:3) in order to see the kingdom of God. Nicodemus was not familiar with the term and asked if Jesus meant one had to go back into the womb and come out a second time. No, once a child comes out they do not go back into the womb. A pregnant woman carries the baby in a sack of water, the amniotic fluid. Once the water breaks, the baby will soon be born. Jesus clarifies "born of water" as being "born of flesh." He was not saying we need to be born over and over but explained that one must be born twice, needing both a physical and a spiritual birth.

The Problem

Jesus answered, "Truly, truly, I say to you, unless one is born of water [physical] and the Spirit [spiritual], he cannot enter the kingdom of God. That which is born of the flesh is flesh, and that which is born of the Spirit is spirit." (John 3:5, 6)

Jesus repeated the fact that two births were needed. To understand the solution to a problem one must first understand what the problem is. Nicodemus was familiar with the account of how God originally created the human race and the tragic separation that followed. He had extensively studied Genesis, the Hebrew book of beginnings, which documented how God had created Adam and Eve perfect in body, soul, and spirit. The three—God, Adam and Eve had walked and talked together in the Garden of Eden. It was a place without thorns, pain and death. They experienced a beautiful relationship. God warned them, *"Of the tree of the knowledge of good and evil you shall not eat, for in the day that you eat of it you shall surely die"* (Genesis 2:17).

Something went terribly wrong; the first man and woman chose to disobey God. They were tricked by Satan into doing that which they had been instructed to avoid. Sin was introduced to the human race. Adam and Eve were immediately overcome with a sense of guilt and were uncomfortable in the presence of God, their Creator. God had declared what the consequence of disobedience would be, *"You shall surely die."* (Genesis 2:17). While physical death is separation from the body, spiritual death is the result of separation from God. Adam and Eve's relationship with God was broken. They became spiritually dead. Because of God's holiness and our sinfulness we can not go directly to God without Jesus. God is a God of love, but He is also a Holy God and cannot ignore sin. King David wrote, *"Your way, O God, is holy. What god is great like our God?"* (Psalm 77:13).

Spiritual Death

A rose plucked from its root (source of life) begins to wilt and die. So too, the human race cut off from God by sin died spiritually and became mortal. Adam and Eve had children and each child, though born physically alive, was born with a sin nature and spiritually separated from God. *"In Adam all die,"* (1 Corinthians 15:22a). On top of that, we have added our own disobedience to the original sin. Scriptures tell us, *"All have sinned and come short of the glory of God,"* (Romans 3:23). What Adam and Eve lost we need to regain. We need to have that relationship restored, to be reunited with God. We need to be born again spiritually!

God loves us and wants us to come to Heaven but not with our sin. If we went to Heaven as we are, with unrepentant sin we would mess up Heaven. Look at the mess we have made down here. God says yes He loves us and wants us to come to Heaven, but our sin has to be dealt with first. Heaven is God's home and He has the right to set standards.

The Remedy

Adam and Eve repented and sought God's forgiveness, but, their disobedience was serious and could not just be ignored. God promised that He would provide a remedy. In the mean time, they were instructed to make a yearly blood sacrifice to show their confidence in God's promise. They accepted God's promise and expressed their faith by performing the offering; *"For on this day shall atonement be made for you to cleanse you. You shall be clean before the LORD from all your sins"* (Leviticus 16:30). *"Indeed, under the law almost everything is purified with blood, and without the shedding of blood there is no forgiveness of sins"* (Hebrews 9:22).

Through the years that followed, Adam and Eve had children, and their children had children. Some chose to follow God and trust Him for His provision, others rejected the concept of blood being necessary and tried to find other ways to appease God. Many rebelled and sought to live their lives as they saw fit. Cain, the first child born to Adam and Eve, tried to offer God fruits and vegetables instead of a blood sacrifice and God rejected his sacrifice, just as He will any substitute.

God's Payment

Years later, John the Baptist saw Jesus coming towards him and identified Him, *"Behold, the Lamb of God, who takes away the sin of the world"* (John 1:29). God affirmed Jesus as being the Son of God, *"And behold, a voice from heaven said, 'This is my beloved Son, with whom I am well pleased"* (Matthew 3:17). God's Son, Jesus Christ, satisfied all the Biblical laws required of the blood sacrifice (Hebrews 7:27, 28; 10:12-18).

Because we have sinned, we cannot produce a sacrifice that would be acceptable to God. Only a perfect sacrifice could be accepted. Jesus was without sin. When Jesus died on the Cross, he died in our place; He was the sacrifice for our sins. He is our substitute. His death was the payment for our sin. (Hebrews 9:11-15) A comparison would be of a courtroom where the judge finds the defendant guilty and makes a judgment. The guilty individual is unable to pay the fine. The judge leaves the bench and pays the fine for the guilty party. Jesus took the punishment we deserve and offered us His righteousness. When trusting Christ for our salvation, we are trading our sin and its death penalty for His righteousness and life. God has pure eyes and cannot even look at evil without having to judge it. *"But the LORD of hosts is exalted in justice, and the Holy God shows himself holy in righteousness"* (Isaiah 5:16). *"The blood of Jesus Christ his Son cleanses us from all sin"* (1 John 1:7).

Spiritual Life

How was God going to restore spiritual life to Adam and Eve and their descendants? The Bible tells us: *"For as in Adam all die, so also in Christ shall all be made alive"* (1 Cor. 15:22). *"For God so loved the world, that he gave his only Son, that whoever believes in him should not perish but have eternal life"* (John 3:16). *"I came that they may have life and have it abundantly"* (John 10:10). Why would Jesus Christ choose to become human? C. S. Lewis said it well, "The Son of God became a man that men might become sons of God."

Our physical freedom has been purchased for us by the blood of many soldiers on the battlefield. Only Jesus Christ was qualified and able to pay the price for our spiritual freedom. Christ was the only one who could help us, the promised Messiah of the Old Testament, the Passover Lamb. *"But he was wounded for our transgressions; he was crushed for our iniquities; upon him was the chastisement that brought us peace, and with his stripes we are healed. All we like sheep have gone astray; we have turned—every one—to his own way; and the LORD has laid on him the iniquity of us all"* (Isaiah 53:5,6; 1 Corinthians 5:7b).

The prophecy came to pass. Jesus was condemned to the death penalty. He was whipped so severely that the flesh was torn from His body. He was beaten so horrific that His body was shredded and his beard was ripped from His face. A crown with thorns, two to three inches in length, cut deeply into His scalp. He endured the humiliation and strain of carrying His cross, estimated to be 400 pounds. The crowd spat in his face and threw stones. Nails six to eight inches long were driven into His wrists. Both of His feet were nailed together. Forced to alternate between arching His back and using his legs just to breathe, He endured it for over three hours. Finally, a Roman guard pierced His side with a spear. Only water poured out as He had no blood left. Jesus endured this so that sin could be "washed" away and free access to God made possible. JESUS CHRIST died for you and me! If it were not necessary for Jesus to pay this price, God would never have required it. If there was any other way... but there was not, JESUS IS THE ONLY SALVATION FOR THE WORLD.

The innocent Lamb of God promised in the Garden of Eden came to deliberately die in our place. His physical death was not the end of the story. The Apostle Paul gave this testimony,

> *Christ died for our sins in accordance with the Scriptures, ... he was buried, ... he was raised on the third day in accordance with the Scriptures, and that he appeared to Cephas, then to the twelve. Then he appeared to more than five hundred*

brothers at one time, most of whom are still alive, though some have fallen asleep. Then he appeared to James, then to all the apostles. Last of all, as to one untimely born, he appeared also to me" (I Corinthians 15:3-8).

Victory

The crowning point of Christ's death and burial is the fact of His resurrection! In all of human history, only Jesus Christ was able to pronounce victory over death. (I Corinthians 15:54-56). Such a blessed hope, *"that I may know him and the power of his resurrection,"* (Philippians 3:10). Jesus arose and once again is in Heaven, and He is interceding for us before His Father's Throne. God's original design for mankind was interrupted but not destroyed. The Apostle John tells us that one day those who have been born again will enjoy an unhindered relationship with God for eternity (Revelation 21:3-7).

You Must Be Born Again

Do not marvel that I said to you, "You must be born again." The wind blows where it wishes, and you hear its sound, but you do not know where it comes from or where it goes. So it is with everyone who is born of the Spirit (**John 3:7, 8**).

Jesus compared being born again to the wind. Although it is invisible, it can be undeniably powerful. Spiritual birth may be difficult to explain; but when individuals experience the new birth, they know it and others can see a change in their lives. A new, *divine* power is at work through Christ; we can be born again.

Throughout Scripture from Genesis to Revelation, the need for a second birth is emphasized.

"Everyone who believes that Jesus is the Christ has been born of God" (1 John 5:1a).

"This is he who came by water and blood—Jesus Christ; not by the water only but by the water and the blood. And the Spirit is the one who testifies, because the Spirit is the truth" (1 John 5:6).

"And this is the testimony that God gave us eternal life, and this life is in his Son. Whoever has the Son has life; whoever does not have the Son of God does not have life. I write these things to you who believe in the name of the Son of God that you may know that you have eternal life" (1 John 5:11-13).

Authority of Jesus

Nicodemus still had difficulty understanding. Jesus again affirmed both His authority and message as He stated to him that what he was telling was the truth.

Nicodemus said to him, "How can these things be?" Jesus answered him, "Are you the teacher of Israel and yet you do not understand these things? Truly, truly, I say to you, we speak of what we know, and bear witness to what we have seen, but you do not receive our testimony. If I have told you earthly things and you do not believe, how can you believe if I tell you heavenly things? No one has ascended into heaven except he who descended from heaven, the Son of Man" (**John 3:9-13**).

Jesus had illustrated the power of God in the natural world by relating to the miracle of physical birth and the invisible force of the wind. He asked Nicodemus, a well-educated Jewish religious teacher, how he explained spiritual truth to others since he himself did not understand. Apparently Nicodemus had to use abstract words like: maybe, might, could be, possibly, we can speculate, assume, and think. As the Son of God, Jesus spoke with Divine authority. What a contrast this was, and is to so-called spiritual authorities who could not and cannot with clarity or conviction, explain how to get to Heaven. Since Heaven was Jesus' eternal home, He was not just offering religious speculation or human reasoning but rather, facts.

And as Moses lifted up the serpent in the wilderness, so must the Son of Man be lifted up, that whoever believes in him may have eternal life (**John 3:14-15**).

Jesus referred Nicodemus to the account of Moses and the Israelites in the desert. An Old Testament scholar, Nicodemus knew how Moses had led the Israelites out of Egypt only to see his people wander in the desert because of their unbelief. The Israelites complained:

> *Why have you brought us up out of Egypt to die in the wilderness? For there is no food and no water, and we loathe this worthless food." Then the LORD sent fiery serpents among the people, and they bit the people, so that many people of Israel died.*
> *And the people came to Moses and said, "We have sinned, for we have spoken against the LORD and against you. Pray to the LORD, that he take away the serpents from us." So Moses prayed for the people.*
> *And the LORD said to Moses, "Make a fiery serpent and set it on a pole, and everyone who is bitten, when he sees it, shall live."*
> *So Moses made a bronze serpent and set it on a pole. And if a serpent bit anyone, he would look at the bronze serpent and live* (Numbers 21:5-9).

Each person had the choice of life or death. Those who would not look at the serpent and seek God's forgiveness, died. Those who obeyed and looked at the serpent on the pole and called upon God to save them from their snake bite lived. The people's hearts needed to be humble enough to trust God for help and to obey His directions. Would they follow his simple instructions, could they learn to trust God?

Jesus identified that wilderness experience as a picture of His coming role on the Cross. In a clear prophecy concerning His death on the cross, Jesus explained to Nicodemus that it was God's will for Him to be crucified in order that those who look to Him might be given new life. Jesus would die on a Cross so that everyone bitten by the "snakebite" of sin could look to the Cross and be saved.

We cannot work our way, or slide into salvation; it takes a definite step of acknowledging sin in one's life and calling upon Jesus Christ to apply His shed blood to pay for our sin. Jesus says that all who call upon Him for His help He will respond to with a "yes." He's just waiting to be asked. *"And it shall come to pass that everyone who calls upon the name of the Lord shall be saved"* (Acts 2:21).

Believe "in" Christ

In what can be identified as the most familiar passage of Scripture, Jesus explained to Nicodemus it was because of love that He came to die.

For God so loved the world, that he gave his only Son, that whoever believes in him should not perish but have eternal life. For God did not send his Son into the world to condemn the world, but in order that the world might be saved through Him. Whoever believes in him is not condemned, but whoever does not believe is condemned already, because he has not believed in the name of the only Son of God (**John 3:16-18**).

We are to believe <u>in</u> Jesus Christ, not just <u>about</u> Him. Jesus chose the expression **"believes <u>in</u>"** three times, including *"whoever believes <u>in</u> him should not perish but have eternal life."* Jesus repeated the promise of eternal life to all who would believe in Him. *"Whoever <u>believes in</u> the Son has eternal life; whoever does not obey the Son shall not see life, but the wrath of God remains on him"* (John 3:36). *"I am the way, and the truth, and the life. No one comes to the Father except through me"* (John 14:6). What is the difference between **in** and **about**?

For years, I believed <u>about</u> Jesus. Knowing that Jesus Christ had died on the Cross and that His blood paid for all sin, I assumed that my sin was automatically forgiven. I did not understand that we all must individually accept Christ's payment for our sin debt (Isaiah 53). Trying to do what I thought was good did not make me a Christian and did not grant me forgiveness or eternal life. I had not personally believed <u>in</u> Him and accepted His life-giving covering for my sins.   A personal commitment is needed. A simple illustration may help. Believing that Jesus is the resurrected Son of God but not accepting Him personally would be like receiving a check made out by Him for the full payment of sin with our name on it, but never cashing it. Believing <u>about</u> the check is fine, but to get to Heaven we need to receive the check and present it as our payment. If we were to try to write our own check, our funds would be insufficient.

All Have Sinned

None of us can stand before a righteous, holy God and feel acceptable. The Apostle Paul wrote, *"All have sinned and fall short of the glory of God"* (Romans 3:23). I am a sinner; there are things I should not do that I do, as well as things I should do but do not. We are all in the same situation. Paul describes our predicament, *"For I know that nothing good dwells in me, that is, in my flesh. For I have the desire to do what is right, but not the ability to carry it out. For I do not do the good I want, but the evil I do not want is what I keep on doing"* (Romans 7:18, 19). Feeling sorry does not help us get rid of sin. We must see sin as God sees it and repent. Jesus gave the urgent invitation, *"The time is fulfilled, and the kingdom of God is at hand; repent and believe in the gospel"* (Mark 1:15).

The Bible teaches that God has *"raised us up with him and seated us with him in the heavenly places in Christ Jesus"* (Ephesians 2:6). In order to reach a destination, one must get on board an airplane, not just believe about airplanes. Only in Christ can we reach our destination of Heaven. Christ alone is worthy; those who accept Christ's message are in Christ and Christ is in them (Colossians 1:27). The followers of Jesus Christ were called Christ-i-ans / Christ-in, the origin of the term *Christian* (Acts 11:26b). When we believe in or on Jesus, not just about Him, right then and there, God has promised to provide us with everlasting life.

Jesus reminded Nicodemus that God loves and desires to have fellowship with us, but since the time of Adam and Eve, our inherited sin nature has prevented that fellowship. We need to accept His offer of forgiveness and eternal life.

Christ stands interceding for us before His Father in Heaven. By the Father's acceptance of Jesus' finished work, He accepts those who are in His Son. Christ is *"able to save to the uttermost those who draw near to God through him, since he always lives to make intercession for them"* (Hebrews 7:25; also Romans 6:9-10). Christ does intercede for us, perhaps like this:

"Father, I love Gloria, I have fulfilled the requirements to pay for her sin. I have asked her to allow me to come into her heart and be her Savior. She has agreed to receive me, and I received her. I am in her, and she is in me. We are now one. As you love me, Father, I ask you to love her and receive her as your daughter."

As you read this, you can insert your name. Isn't it beautifully simple? That is the invitation of love found in John 3:16, 17.

Jesus did not come to condemn us: we were already condemned and on "death row." He died in our place, giving us an opportunity to be pardoned, to choose eternal life. The Apostle Paul said, *"For the wages of sin is death, but the free gift of God is eternal life in*

Christ Jesus our Lord" (Romans 6:23). Jesus can save us from the death penalty of sin. He brings light into a dark world.

Jesus concluded his conversation with a stern warning, followed by a promise to those who choose the light:

And this is the judgment: the light has come into the world, and people loved the darkness rather than the light because their works were evil. For everyone who does wicked things hates the light and does not come to the light, lest his works should be exposed. But whoever does what is true comes to the light, so that it may be clearly seen that his works have been carried out in God **(John 3:19-21).**

Jesus made clear to Nicodemus that He is the "light." Jesus repeated this truth later, *"I am the light of the world. Whoever follows me will not walk in darkness, but will have the light of life"* (John 8:12). Knowing the human heart, Jesus Christ identified two types of people; some believe what they want to believe and live the way they want to live. They do not want to be confused by the facts. Others seek the truth and to the best of their ability, try to live accordingly. As with Adam and Eve, Moses and the children of Israel, we are provided a choice. We can choose the Light of the World or choose darkness.

A New Relationship

In one of the saddest verses in the Bible, Jesus reveals that He *"came to his own, and his own people did not receive him"* (John 1:11). God allowed individuals and nations throughout history the liberty to choose. In Jesus' day, as today, people choose to crucify Him. Not all rejected Christ as John affirmed, *"But to all who did <u>receive</u> him, who believed in his name, <u>he gave the right to become</u>*

God's Appointment

children of God" (John 1:12). Think of that—the right to become a child of God, born again into God's family.

The marriage relationship can illustrate how we may become children of God. Years ago, James asked me to marry him. At our wedding, the preacher asked James, "Do you take this woman to be your lawfully wedded wife?" James said, "I do." Then the preacher asked, "Gloria, do you take this man to be your lawfully wedded husband?" If I had not responded to that question, or had said, "No," we would not have been married, but I said, "I do." When we were pronounced husband and wife, we were considered one. Our relationship changed from dating to being married. At this point in time, James' father called me his daughter. I became a daughter of Jacob Goering by receiving his son as my husband. Likewise, we become a child of God by receiving His Son, Jesus Christ, as our Savior. The way to the Father is through His Son. Jesus has already said on the Cross, "I do" to us—"I do want to be your Savior." He simply waits for us to respond to Him. We need to choose Jesus as our Lord and Savior.

What qualifies us to be called God's children: riches, beauty, intelligence, athletic abilities, power, prestige, our own good works, religion, or penance? Absolutely not; natural attributes, internal qualities, or dead works cannot bring life. From Genesis to Revelation, the basis for salvation has always been simply receiving Jesus' payment for our sins. Jesus was the Lamb of God who sacrificed His life so that we can become children of God. God's plan of salvation is the same throughout the ages. The only difference is that before the Cross, people were looking forward in faith to the coming promise. After the Cross, they looked back in faith at the accomplished promise. Although it is true that everyone is God's creation, He does not call everyone His son or daughter. It is when we receive Jesus and believe in His name that God pronounces individuals His child. God does want us to come to Heaven. He made the arrangements in Christ for us to be able to go to Heaven. It is understandable that He has stipulations for admittance to Heaven. If I went to Heaven with my sin not forgiven by Jesus and others did as well, we would mess up Heaven. Look at what we have done here on this earth. God is not able to be in the presence of sin because of His holiness. Look at what we have done here on this earth. God's right in that our sin first has to be dealt with properly before we can come to Heaven. It has been said, "God loves you the way you are but He refuses to leave you that way!"

When we believe in Jesus and that the blood of Christ has paid for our sins, God Himself declares that we are born into His family. We are "born from above" (John 1:12). At this time, God calls each of us His child. When He pronounces that our relationship has been changed, it truly has happened.

Our Debt Paid

We all have a sin debt that must be covered. The Apostle Paul, having trusted Christ shared: *"Blessed are those whose lawless deeds are forgiven, and whose sins are covered; blessed is the man against whom the Lord will not count his sin"* (Romans 4:7, 8).

When we recognize our sin and invite Jesus Christ to apply His blood as payment for our personal sin account, He will. He has promised, or covenanted with us, that our sin is covered by His blood. When God sees the blood of the perfect Lamb, His own Son, applied to our sin, God declares that our sin debt—past, present, and future—is paid in full. Having entered into a covenant with Christ, Jesus promised that we will live where He lives: *"In my Father's house are many rooms. If it were not so, would I have told you that I go to prepare a place for you? And if I go and prepare a place for you, I will come again and will take you to myself, that where I am you may be also"* (John 14:2-3). For the individual who believes in Jesus, the lost fellowship with the Creator has been restored; God assures the Christian a place with Him forever, where the dead are alive, the blind can see, and the lame can walk. Jesus explained the necessity for God to work in our lives; the new birth through the blood of Christ gives those who choose eternal life. After the discussion between Jesus and Nicodemus concluded, Nicodemus was mentioned twice in the Bible, giving evidence that he had indeed become a believer (John 7:50-51; 19:38-42).

As a young person, I sincerely believed that I loved God. It was not until September 20, 1959, that I personally asked Jesus Christ to apply His blood payment to my sin. I simply received His open invitation to choose Him. That day, for the first time, I trusted on Christ's finished work on the Cross. I had not earlier realized that I needed to request that my debt of sin be paid by the blood of Christ. Many are in that same situation, trying to please God, but with their sins yet unforgiven. Is that your situation? We all have a sin debt that must be covered. The Apostle Paul, having trusted Christ shared: *"Blessed are those whose lawless deeds are forgiven, and whose sins are covered; blessed is the man against whom the Lord will not count his sin"* (Romans 4:7, 8).

Have You Been Born Again?

When reflecting on Jesus' conversation, where do you consider yourself to be in your spiritual journey? Having a consciousness of God and a desire to please Him does not provide anyone with eternal life. Over and over the Bible teaches the necessity of new birth in Christ: *"But to all who did receive him, who believed in his name, he gave the right to become children of God, who were born, not of blood nor of the will of the flesh nor of the will of man, but of God"* (John 1:12-13).

GOD IS REACHING TOWARDS US

Before Birth — **At Birth** — **After Birth**

1. We are trying to reach God.
2. We connect with God.
3. We have an established relationship with God!

Before a child is born, a mother can feel her baby move around until ultimately it gets into the position to be born. Our human responses to God, stimulating our spirit, helps us get into position for spiritual birth—head first, heart second, feet last. I thought that I loved God and tried to live for Him, but like Nicodemus, I was not yet born into His family. Then God moved my heart toward Him and brought me to the point of spiritual birth. God can show you what your spiritual position is with Him. Are you <u>before spiritual birth</u>, <u>at the point of spiritual birth</u>, or <u>have you already been born again</u>? You need to ascertain where you are in your spiritual journey.

If you know you are "born again," that is great. If you do not know, then realize your need to be "born again." Simply tell God that you want Jesus Christ to come into your life, apply the blood that He shed on the Cross to your sins, and really mean it with all your heart. According to Jesus' promise to Nicodemus, you will be forgiven and be born into His family, giving you everlasting life, *"For God so loved the world, that he gave his only Son, that whoever believes in him should not perish but have eternal life"* (John 3:16). It is your choice. Do you want life, or do you want to continue in death? Only you can make the decision—the sooner, the better.

If you wish, you can become a Christian; wherever you are you can humbly receive Jesus Christ right now. Pray something like this:

"Dear Jesus Christ, I am a sinner and in trouble. Please help me. I realize you died on the Cross for me, for my sins so that I may have everlasting life. I invite you to come into my life and forgive my sins."

The only thing left to do then is say, "Thank you."

God knows your heart attitude. One individual in the Bible prayed simply, *"'God, be merciful to me, a sinner!' I tell you, this man went down to his house justified"* (Luke 18:13b, 14a). Another prayed, *"I believe; help my unbelief!"* (Mark 9:24). It is not our choice of words, but our heart attitude that matters to God. Jesus has promised that God the Father will not turn anyone away who truly comes through Him. If this is something you know you have done in the past—great. If at this point you just sincerely asked Him to pay for your sin, did He? What just happened? Let us look again at John 1:12 where it says, *"But to all who did receive him, who believed in his name, he gave the right to become children of God."* Did you just receive Him? If you did, then God calls you a son or daughter. If God calls you a son or daughter, then what are you? You are indeed a child of God! You are "born again." Nothing could be more marvelous! At what point in time are you "born again?" It is when you receive Jesus as your personal Savior. If you right now received Jesus, then right now would be your second birth, just as He promised. I have two birthdays, a physical one and a spiritual one. They are fifteen and a half years apart, and I celebrate both of them.

Do you think that you may have received Jesus already but are not completely certain? Why live in doubt? You can "confirm your reservation" for Heaven. Just tell the Lord you want to make sure, **"If I haven't before today, I am now asking you to come into my heart. Thank you for dying in my place so that I may be forgiven."** Why not know for certain that you are God's child? Remember His promise: *"But to all who did receive him, who believed in his name, he gave the right to become children of God, who were born, not of blood nor of the will of the flesh nor of the will of man, but of God"* (John 1:12, 13). It is important to confirm our eternal reservation before death, making certain that our reservation for Heaven is secure.

If you do not wish to ask the Lord to save you right now, that is your choice. There are no guarantees about the future, and the decision is all-important. Please do not wait! How awful to miss Heaven and spend all eternity in Hell. Jesus took the opportunity to tell Nicodemus how to get to Heaven because He knew how crucial it was. Jesus Christ died making that gift of eternal life possible. Do not dismiss His message.

If you have made a decision to accept God's offer to become His child, I would enjoy hearing from you. If you are considering your position with God and desire further help or if you have questions, feel free to contact Gloria Goering, P.O. Box 4185, Waterloo, IA 50704, gloriagoering@hotmail.com, or www.familyaltarbroadcast.com.

A Growing Christian

After accepting God's rich gift of salvation, we need to grow in our Christian lives. God instructs us how. According to the Bible, God nurtures us when we are involved in the following activities:

Prayer: Prayer is simply talking to, and listening to God. Christ wants to lead us, to direct us in things we should or should not do and tells us to, *"Pray without ceasing"* (1Thessolians 5:17). There are things we should do as well as things we should not do. Christ our Shepherd wants to lead us. In fact, the Bible calls believers, sheep. Jesus observes that *"the sheep follow him: for they know his voice"* (John 10:4). Jesus will give guidance. The Lord's Prayer, Matthew 6:9-13, is a prayer that we should model.

Bible Reading: As we prayerfully read the Bible, we will grow in our understanding. A person could pray something like this: "Lord Jesus, as I read the Bible now, help me to understand what it says and apply it to my life. Thank you."

In the New Testament, the Apostle Paul encouraged Timothy, *"Do your best to present yourself to God as one approved, a worker who has no need to be ashamed, rightly handling the word of truth"* (2 Timothy 2:15). We can ask Jesus to help us understand the Bible. When considering doing something that contradicts the Bible, prayerfully choose to follow the Bible. It is to be the final authority for what we believe and do. God empowers the Christian who prays and obeys God's teaching.

Attend Church: The Apostle Paul encouraged Christians to attend church regularly, *"not neglecting to meet together, as is the habit of some, but encouraging one another, and all the more as you see the Day drawing near"* (Hebrews 10:25). We can ask Him for direction about which church to attend. Some churches do not teach the Bible; some deny its' truth, and some are only social clubs. There are churches that really mean business for Christ. Recognize a good church as one where people usually bring their Bibles and know more about the Bible when they leave than when they came.

They often get together for study and fellowship, more than just on Sunday mornings. A good church is a place full of love for God, for His word, and for others. It is a place that emphasizes sharing with others how to get to Heaven.

Certainly no church, pastor, or denomination is perfect, but going to church is God's design, and command. God instructs Christians to search the Scriptures and discern truth from error. God wants us individually to understand and obey the truths of Scripture and not blindly follow what others may expect of us. Paul complimented the church in Berea for just that effort: *"Now these Jews were more noble than those in Thessalonica; they received the word with all eagerness, examining the Scriptures daily to see if these things were so"* (Acts 17:11). We also need a place where we can actively serve God, not just a place where we are entertained.

Baptism: Baptism has nothing to do with being saved, or obtaining eternal life; Scripture consistently includes the practice of believers being baptized as an outward sign of their salvation. Jesus obeyed God and was baptized (Matthew 3:13-16). Baptism is included in Jesus Christ's last instruction to His disciples as part of the Great Commission: *"Go therefore and make disciples of all nations, baptizing them in the name of the Father and of the Son and of the Holy Spirit"* (Matthew 28:19).

A letter by the Apostle Paul to believers in Rome explains the meaning of baptism, *"We were <u>buried</u> therefore with him by baptism into death, in order that, just as Christ was raised from the dead by the glory of the Father, we too might walk in newness of life. For if we have been united with him in a death like his, we shall certainly be united with him in a resurrection like his"* (Romans 6:4, 5). Consider the fact that it takes more than three spoonfuls of dirt to be buried. Sprinkling and pouring do not portray the same picture as immersion does. God wants us to tell the world by public baptism that we have received Christ as our Savior and are not ashamed of Him. We need to be obedient in baptism, showing our submission to God. It has been my observation that those who follow the Lord in baptism are strengthened in their Christian life.

Share: Someone shared with us, and as God leads, we should tell others how to get to Heaven. Jesus said, *"I am the way, and the truth, and the life. No one comes to the Father except through me"* (John 14:6). He *is* the only way to Heaven. Everyone must come through Jesus Christ, *"the Lamb of God, who takes away the sin of the world"* (John 1:29). Let's not go to Heaven alone—let's take others with us. Jesus promised His disciples, *"Follow me, and I will make you become fishers of men."* (Mark 1:17). We can love others as God loves us and spread the good news.

Lordship: Paul fervently encouraged believers in Rome, saying,

> *I appeal to you therefore, brothers, by the mercies of God, to present your bodies as a living sacrifice, holy and acceptable to God, which is your spiritual worship. Do not be conformed to this world, but be transformed by the renewal of your mind, that by testing you may discern what is the will of God, what is good and acceptable and perfect* (Romans 12:1, 2).

We need to allow the Lord to be in control of our lives every day. After all He has done for us; the least we can do in return is to give Him our faithful service. God promises many blessings and rewards in this life, and in the life to come—for those who serve Him, as Psalm 23 teaches, *"Surely goodness and mercy shall follow me all the days of my life, and I shall dwell in the house of the Lord forever"* (Psalm 23:6). But regardless the benefits we may or may not receive, He is worthy of our full-hearted love and service.

A suggested prayer: **"Lord Jesus, I want you to be Lord of my life. Please take control. I give you your rightful place as King, Lord, Master, and God in my heart. Take the pieces of my existence and put them together, as only You can. Make something beautiful out of my life to bring honor and glory to Yourself."**

[This conversation is available in pamphlet form. Request **"Do You Know for Certain You Are Going to Heaven?"** Contact us at Gloria Goering, P.O. Box 4185, Waterloo, IA 50704, gloriagoering@hotmail.com, or www.familyaltarbroadcast.com.]

CHAPTER 2

1959-1969

❋

Gloria, age 15, with a young cousin.

September 20, 1959 ~ God changed my life

My parents, high-school sweethearts, married young. World War II separated them as Dad joined the Marines, and I was born while he was in boot camp. Wounded in the battle of Iwo Jima near Japan he received a purple heart. Later, Steve joined our little family and then my sister Sue.

As the years passed, stress increased between my Mom and Dad culminating in their divorce when I was ten. Mother and the three of us children moved to a housing project in Omaha, Nebraska. At times, I had to prevent my little sister from being used as a football by gangs terrorizing the playground. One day I even had to intervene when a girl wanted my brother's swing and tried to stab him because he wouldn't relinquish it. Eventually I came to believe that the less we had to do with people, the better. Gradually avoiding conversations, I stopped trying to communicate with people.

As a young person, I attended church regularly, was baptized, took communion, read my Bible, and prayed. Loving God, I tried to do what was right. Within me, however, frustration increased. I didn't realize I was not a Christian, and I didn't know how to become one. Jesus was preparing my heart, and I would soon realize His promise, *"Ask, and it will be given to you; seek, and you will find; knock, and it will be opened to you. For everyone who asks receives, and the one who seeks finds, and to the one who knocks it will be opened"* (Matthew 7:7, 8).

Several Bible verses were a concern to me one of which was: *"I know your works: you are neither cold nor hot. Would that you were either cold or hot! So, because you are lukewarm, and neither hot nor cold, I will spit you out of my mouth"* (Revelation 3:15, 16). I did not consider myself "cold" as I tried to live like a Christian to the best of my ability, but my internal struggles made me quite certain that God would not consider me to be "hot." That left only "lukewarm." Why does God want to spit "lukewarm" people out of His mouth?

Dissatisfied during my freshman high school year, our family began visiting various churches. Every Sunday morning we would board a bus or take a taxi to a different church, until we visited Temple Baptist Church. We were fascinated that people there brought their Bibles to church and opened them to study along with the message. Pastor Herb Anderson preached clearly from the Bible and we knew more about the Scriptures after the service then when we came.

Temple Baptist Church, Omaha, NE

Herbert Anderson, Pastor

Theresa Moore, Director of Christian Education

Weeks later during a Saturday evening Temple Baptist youth rally; a 1955 Billy Graham film *Wire tapper* was shown. The film was about a man trapped into working for a mob. After hearing Billy Graham preach, the wire tapper made a decision for Christ. The film showed not only how he connected with God but also the change in his life that resulted. That night I realized that I had taken for granted that the Blood payment Christ had made on the Cross was automatically applied. I had not realized that I needed to personally "believe in", "on", "receive Christ's Blood" individually. I had not asked Jesus Christ to come into my heart and life.

It seemed as if God was speaking directly to me: "Gloria, how about it? Will you receive Me?" Afraid of "trusting Christ," and not fully understanding what was involved, I felt that the worst-case scenario would be to leave the way I had come. I decided not to pass up this opportunity. Christ was the answer to my loneliness, frustration and emptiness.

That evening I finally received His blood as payment for my sin and became God's child, *"But to all who did receive him, who believed in his name, he gave the right to become children of God"* (John 1:12); in Jesus' words, I would be "born again" into His family: *"Truly, truly, I say to you, unless one is born again he cannot see the kingdom of God.... That which is born of the flesh is flesh, and that which is born of the Spirit is spirit. Do not marvel that I said to you, 'You must be born again'"* (John 3:3, 6, 7).

I whispered, "Yes Jesus, be my Savior and pay for my sin!" It was a mystery to me that He could love me, but I marveled that He did and decided to trust Him. While He was at it, I also told Him I needed Him to be my friend. He took me up on that invitation. We are not saved by feelings, but I experienced deep emotion as the empty hole in my heart was filled, and the heavy weight of sin was lifted from my shoulders.

Before, I thought that acting like a Christian made me a Christian. Now, according to His written Word, God Himself gave me the gift of salvation and declared me "Born Again."

On the way home, I decided not to tell my family about the experience, being concerned that I would not be able to live up to people's expectations. To my surprise, as soon as I walked into the house, my mother looked at me and exclaimed, "Gloria, what happened to you?"

"Why?" I responded.

"Your face just seems to be lit up. I haven't seen you smile for a long time."

When I explained to her my decision, Mom was pleased. She had trusted Christ a couple of years earlier, but had been unable to explain to me how to accept God's salvation. She had been praying that I, too, would somehow come to know Christ as my Savior. The following week I was baptized at the church, giving public testimony of my decision to trust Christ.

A song expresses my new happiness:

HAPPINESS IS THE LORD
by Ira F. Stanphill

Happiness is to know the Savior,
Living a life within His favor,
Having a change in my behavior,
Happiness is the Lord.

Happiness is a new creation,
"Jesus and me" in close relation,
Having a part in His salvation,
Happiness is the Lord.

Happiness is to be forgiven,
Living a life that's worth the livin'
Taking a trip that leads to heaven,
Happiness is the Lord.

Refrain:
Real joy is mine, no matter if teardrops start;
I've found the secret—it's Jesus in my heart.

Robert Boyd Munger in his pamphlet *MY HEART CHRIST'S HOME* so eloquently described:

Jesus Christ came into the darkness of my heart and turned on the light. He built a fire in the cold hearth and banished the chill. He started music where there had been stillness and He filled the emptiness with His own loving, wonderful fellowship. I have never regretted opening the door to Christ, and I never will—not into eternity!

I can say "Amen," to those sentiments.

*   *   *   *   *

October 1959 ~ Protection during a storm

At age fifteen, I worked as a babysitter for Bob and Rosie. Bob was tall, thin, and quiet—a sergeant at Offutt Air Force Base in Omaha, Nebraska. His wife, a taxicab driver, was boisterous, heavy set, and warm. Five days a week, I cared for their four children after school. Cleaning, washing, and cooking, I was grateful for many valuable learning experiences and the wages of $15.00 a week.

Thankfully, they were patient and did not get angry with me even the time I mistakenly added bleach to their wash!

During the time that I first became a Christian, discovering God's love was such a thrill. Paul explains, ***"But God shows his love for us in that while we were still sinners, Christ died for us"*** (Romans 5:8). I wanted to share with others what I had found in Christ. Rosie was my mother's friend, and we had many interesting conversations about what it meant to be saved. Together we read the Bible, including where the Apostle Paul said, ***"If you confess with your mouth that Jesus is Lord and believe in your heart that God raised him from the dead, you will be saved"*** (Romans 10:9). Mom and I urged Rosie to come with us to church. If she didn't have a customer Rosie would sometimes give us transportation to church in her taxi cab, and at times even came in with us wearing her uniform.

One Sunday evening, both Rosie and Bob came to church. Rosie trusted Christ as her Savior. Seeing the change in her life, Bob observed, "It was like seeing champagne bubbles, starting in her toes and working up to the tip of her head." Rosie's decision for Christ was genuine and life-changing.

While I was babysitting Rosie and Bob's children one night, a tornado tore through the neighborhood. A huge tree was pulled straight out of the ground and laid neatly between their house and the neighbor's. None of us was injured; we marveled at the power of God and His protection. As months passed, several of their children also came to know Christ.

Bob & Rosie McClain, Gloria, Bobby, Bernice (Mother), Deanna, Joey, Wesley, Steve (brother), Sue (sister)

Discovering God's love as a new Christian was a thrill. Paul explains, *"But God shows his love for us in that while we were still sinners, Christ died for us"* (Romans 5:8). I wanted to share with others what I had found in Christ.

A lesson I had to learn early in my Christian walk was that even Christians can fail. A couple of influential Christians in my life made immoral choices that broke up their families. My first reaction was disbelief. I remember thinking, "If this is Christianity, stop—I want out!" God spoke clearly to my heavy heart, gently rebuking me for looking at people instead of Him. He affirmed that Christians may disappoint and fail, but He never will. Instead of having my eyes on man, I need to keep my eyes on Christ. We can take the good that people have to offer, while understanding that they are not perfect, none of us are. Only God is perfect.

* * * * *

June 1960 ~ Volunteer for life

One night as I talked with God in my heart I asked, "Lord, what can I do for you that would please you best?" In gentle tones of love this is what He shared with me.

"You asked what you could do for me that would please me best, so this I'll share with you. There are others I died for that yet needs to be won. Share my burden for the yet unsaved souls for which my heart yearns."

In my heart I knew the love He had for me, and understood in a small way, the love He had for the souls of others. I prayed, "Yes Lord, I desire to share this burden with you. Give me a measure of your love for souls that need to be won, and I will seek with you their souls to win." By sharing with Him this burden dear to His heart I could return in a small way His love! *"Jesus wept"* (John 11:35). *"And I heard the voice of the Lord saying, 'Whom shall I send, and who will go for us?' Then I said, 'Here am I! Send me'"* (Isaiah 6:8).

When our church needed a counselor, I volunteered. The guest speaker that week was a missionary home on deputation from Germany. The missionary's daughter was in my cabin. One evening she asked me to help her receive Jesus as her Savior, and I led my first soul to Christ. What a thrill! God promises that the person *"who goes out weeping, bearing the seed for sowing, shall come home with shouts of joy, bringing his sheaves with him"* (Psalm 126:6). I told the Lord, "This is awesome. I want to do it again." My passion in life became leading others to Christ.

Subsequent attempts at explaining God's offer of eternal life were not as effective. With a pillow damp from tears, I agonized with God about how to tell others of Christ. The gifts of love, peace, and joy that Christ had brought into my life were marvelous; I wanted to share it: *"For God so loved the world, that he gave his only Son, that whoever believes in him should not perish but have eternal life. For God did not send his Son into the world to condemn the world, but in order that the world might be saved through him"* (John 3:16, 17).

At camp that summer, my brother Steve trusted Christ. My father, who had been a backslidden Christian, had started attending church and serving the Lord following my parent's divorce. A wonderful thing happened. God brought my parents together again and after six years of being divorced they were remarried. On January 13, 1961, when I was sixteen, my parents remarried. Our home was put back together, not the way it was before—this time with Christ as the center. On August 21, 1963, my brother Tim was born; and two years after that, November 24, 1965 my sister Carol. Amazingly, God took our family's broken pieces and put them together beautifully.

During this time, our family continued attending church, studying the Bible, and seeking God's leading in our lives. I worked my way through high school, helping in the school office, babysitting, waitressing, and doing janitorial work. In 1962, I had graduated from Central High School and then enrolled in the Omaha Baptist Bible College (OBBC). Wanting to learn more about the Bible and Christian living, I selected classes that interested me in addition to the required courses. The first two years of college I lived at home, working first on campus and then at the Mutual of Omaha Insurance Company.

* * * * *

July 1964 ~ Seven happy campers

There was again a need for counselors at our church camp. Unable to arrange vacation time to help at camp in the summer of 1964, I decided to use the money I earned working that week to send several cousins and a number of neighbors to the Raccoon River Bible Camp in Nebraska. Although that decision seemed expensive at the time I was writing out checks for each of the seven campers, it was a thrill when all seven made decisions for Christ. Even though I had been unable to go to camp, I could send others.

Jesus Christ instructed His disciples to invest for eternity: *"Do not lay up for yourselves treasures on earth, where moth and rust destroy and where thieves break in and steal, but lay up for yourselves treasures in heaven, where neither moth nor rust destroys and where thieves do not break in and steal"* (Matthew 6:19, 20). A song expresses this desire, "May I do each day's work for Jesus, with eternity's values in view." It is important for us who know the Lord as our Father to pray and consider areas where God would have us invest our money, lives and energy for eternity.

*   *   *   *   *

September 1964 ~ Special neighbors

With few Christian young people being in our neighborhood, Mother was concerned that my brother and sisters wouldn't have good Christian friends. In order to reach our neighborhood kids for Christ, we invited many to attend church with us. We also held weekly Child Evangelism (CE) classes in our home, as well as a Bible study for women. The memories from those years are precious.

God did indeed give my brother and sisters Christian friends. Kids would stop at our house on their way to school so that they could join my mother and siblings for family devotions, and then walk to school with Sue and Tim.

One neighbor, Chip, attended those CE classes and trusted Christ as his Savior. When Chip began asking his parents questions, his mother was interested in looking for answers. Mim decided to attend the ladies' Bible study in our home even though she knew some neighbor ladies mocked the study. She became involved and eventually trusted Christ.

Mim became a great blessing to our family. An ex-army nurse, she often commented with a smile, "I wish I had a nickel for every baby I've delivered." When Mom became pregnant with Carol, Mim appointed herself Mom's private nurse.

After she received Christ, Mim's life changed as she grew in the Lord. For example, she sought to be more submissive to her husband, allowing him take more leadership in the family. Interestingly, Phil didn't appreciate the change at first. Mim told me that on one occasion, Phil raised his fist to hit her, but she diverted the action by quickly putting a coffee cup in his hand. Phil slammed the cup into the refrigerator, leaving a dent in the door.

At OBBC chapel services, I often asked for prayer for Phil's salvation. Later, Phil joked that he hadn't stood a chance of rejecting God's salvation with the college praying for him. Both Mim and Phil experienced the change God promised when one accepts Christ in their lives. The Apostle Paul writes to the believers in Corinth, **"Therefore, if anyone is in Christ, he is a new creation. The old has passed away; behold, the new has come"** (2 Corinthians 5:17). Our families became close friends; Mim and Phil's family also became active in church, serving the Lord.

Along with this family, God worked a miracle in our lives. Nine of us were on a highway in Mim and Phil's new car, heading to a youth roller skating party. Suddenly, rain came in torrents and washed our car along with others off the road in a flash flood. Water rose inside the car, leaving us with little air. Phil read from a Bible that he had with him, **"God is our refuge and strength, a very present help in trouble. Therefore we will not fear though the earth gives way, though the mountains be moved into the heart of the sea, though its waters roar and foam, though the mountains tremble at its swelling"** (Psalm 46:1-3). We claimed God's promise; my prayer was "Lord, I'm coming home to Heaven now, unless you intervene."

God was not finished with us. My teenaged brother, Steve, rolled down the window behind the driver. The water current was so strong that it flowed past the car without coming in. We did not know what was on the outside, but we knew that staying inside the car was certain death. Steve bravely went out the window first, and the rest of us followed. All nine of us miraculously escaped the flooded car. Numb from the cold water, I bumped into a barbwire fence. Steve, climbing on top of a partially submerged car, called directions to me to follow the fence to the nearest hill.

Washed downstream a distance by the current, Phil was trying to work his way back toward the car. He felt something soft bump against his leg, reaching down he grabbed and pulled up his six-year-old daughter who was submerged under the water. Taking her to the nearby hill he began working his way again towards the car. He experienced a second underwater bump, it was Mim. Unable to swim she too was wonderfully rescued from the murky water. A difference of inches could have been fatal. Phil's wife and daughter both could have swept past him into eternity.

When we finally got out of the water and on solid ground, in a phone call, I reported to my parents, "We went swimming instead of roller skating!" The following day, we returned to the car. The police at the scene didn't believe that we had been in the car after it was swept off the road and stated that if had we been in the car, they believed that we would still be in it—dead. What a magnificent and powerful God we have.

Mim, Phil, Beth Ann & Chip Bell

During this stage in my life, I felt the Lord leading me to consider full-time Christian service. Feeling inadequate, I argued with the Lord. Understanding that influencing people for eternity was a valuable life goal I agreed to do His will, no matter how the Lord would direct.

* * * * *

September 1965 ~ Prescription for pain

A summer missionary apprentice program offered by Baptist Mid-Missions was of interest to me. The main hindrance was that as a part-time employee at Mutual of Omaha, I would have to quit with no guarantee of a job in the fall. After bathing the situation in prayer, I decided to go ahead and enroll by faith in the apprenticeship program. That summer in Bledsoe, Kentucky, In had the privilege of working with veteran missionaries, Lola Robinson and Mr. and Mrs. Bill Patterson. When the Patterson's asked about my arrangements for returning home, I confessed that I didn't have any. Having come by faith, I believed that if I obeyed the Lord in going, God would make a way to return. Shortly later, at the end of the summer, the Vacation Bible School kids' offerings were divided among the missionary apprentices helping, in appreciation for their work. The portion given to me was just enough to purchase a bus ticket home. God did indeed provide.

That fall I moved into the dormitory at Omaha Baptist Bible College. Since Mutual of Omaha had filled my job position, I applied for a position as a nurse's aide at the County General Hospital. Immediately after I started work there, Mutual of Omaha, valuing my work contacted me offering a job with a higher salary. Appreciating their offer, but interested in developing new skills, I chose to keep my commitment to the hospital.

One day at the hospital, a new patient named Leonard arrived. The teenager had associated with the wrong crowd and fallen into trouble. He and his friends had rammed their car into a tree while trying to escape from police. His legs were broken in numerous places, and Leonard was in a full body cast. In intense pain, Leonard received morphine shots every four hours. The shots would ease his pain for the first hour; after that, Leonard cried pitifully until the next injection. We heard his cries, but there was nothing we could do. One of my tasks was to change his position in bed to prevent pressure sores. Leonard was beside himself with pain, especially when he was moved.

One night after work, I went to Leonard's bedside and whispered, "Leonard, we can't give you pain medication sooner than the doctors allow, but there is one way that I can offer you help. The pain may be easier to bear if someone shared the pain with you." That night, I explained how he could invite Jesus to come into his life. God would forgive his sins and be his Lord, Savior and Comforter; he would not be alone. "He knows what you are going through, and He cares," I added, referring to God's promise, *"Casting all your anxieties on him, because he cares for you"* (1 Peter 5:7).

Leonard did just that. Immediately, his lonely, helpless confrontation with pain was eased. The next time I came to work, I learned that fellow employees had noticed that Leonard's desperation was gone, though he was still in pain. Leonard was not facing his pain alone any more.

At Thanksgiving, because of his full body cast, Leonard's parents removed a door from their home and brought it to the hospital. They used it to transport him in their station wagon, taking him home for the weekend. Months later, Leonard's family took him home in a wheelchair; only his legs were still in a cast.

* * * * *

October 1966 ~ Fire escape conversion

Lonny was in isolation because of a staph infection. Having shot and killed a bartender who gave him incorrect change for a twenty-dollar bill, he was under police guard. Just before dying, the bartender had shot Lonny in the stomach. The wound was infected.

A horrible patient, no one wanted to care for Lonny. He was in the same room as Joe, my favorite patient. Joe and his son had touched their metal ladder against a power line. The electricity had shot through Joe's body, leaving his hands and feet severely burned. While I rubbed cocoa butter on his wounds and then rewrapped them, I would talk with Joe, quoting Bible verses that I was memorizing. Joe had a sense of humor; he called me his "Christian Nurse." After treating Joe, I would care for Lonny. He demanded constant attention, requesting his pillow be fluffed, more ice in his water pitcher, and a myriad of other demands.

One evening, Lonny's room light came on requesting help. Since no one else wanted to go, I walked down the long hallway to check on him. Lonny insisted that he wanted a preacher to come and talk with him. Surprised, I reported his request to the head nurse. She didn't know who to contact, but directed me to find a pastor. I called a pastor I knew who came that evening.

Lonny had overheard me talking with Joe about being born again and informed the pastor that he wanted to get saved. That night, the pastor led him to the Lord. The next time I worked, I expected Lonny to be a better patient, but he was not.

When the pastor stopped again, I shared my concern that perhaps Lonny had not been sincere and had prayed only a "fire escape" prayer. The pastor insisted that I tell Lonny that I didn't think he had really been saved; I believed that his profession was insincere since I had not seen any change in his life. Fearfully, I went with the pastor and confronted Lonny with my suspicions. I was thankful we did.

Lonny just laughed. I'll never forget what he said. "Gloria, before, if I'd seen you on the street, I'd as soon shoot you as not. Now, I wouldn't shoot you."

Well, that was a change! Perhaps he had been so far down that the change was not visible. Lonny was sent to prison for a long time, but I heard that he continued to grow in the Lord. The pastor later led Lonny's wife to Christ.

* * * * *

Having selected a smorgasbord of college courses over the span of four years, I was surprised to discover that by staying one extra semester, I could graduate with a double major in Bible and Christian education, and a minor in missions. During that final semester, Rev. Hal Miller came to Omaha Baptist Bible College to recruit workers for Campus Bible Fellowship (CBF), a campus ministry that he was starting under Baptist Mid-Missions. He invited me to come to Iowa and join his team.

Although I did not feel qualified to work with college students, God continued tugging on my heart strings until I said, "Yes." Since I could not possibly do the work in my own strength, God had to do the work through me; He would get the credit. I claimed the verse, *"He who calls you is faithful; he will surely do it"* (1 Thessalonians 5:24).

That winter, with college bills paid in full, I stepped out on faith, committing to go to Iowa to help Hal and Patty Miller. Only a fool would go to an unfamiliar state without a paying job. I had met Hal Miller for only a few minutes. With no place to stay and only ten dollars to my name, I believed God was leading. This was the time to trust God to care for me as I obeyed Him. Scripture provided courage: *"For I know the plans I have for you, declares the LORD, plans for welfare and not for evil, to give you a future and a hope. Then you will call upon me and come and pray to me, and I will hear you. You will seek me and find me, when you seek me with all your heart"* (Jeremiah 29:11-13).

My church, Lighthouse Baptist Church in Omaha, Nebraska with Pastor Ray Johnson, commissioned me as a missionary to college students. By the time I picked up the bus ticket, my funds had increased to one hundred dollars. The Millers met me at the bus depot in Iowa Falls; I stayed in their home a short time while we prepared the campus house for college girls. That fall, I became the dormitory mother for the CBF campus house in Iowa Falls, Iowa. As, I helped out in the office and activities on the campus.

* * * * *

Enjoying a Bible study with a college student

March 1967 ~ Invalid hesitations

In March, Baptist Mid-Missions accepted me as a missionary with Campus Bible Fellowship. God was richly blessing the campus ministry with Iowa college students from Ellsworth Jr. College in Iowa Falls, The University of Northern Iowa in Cedar Falls, Iowa State University in Ames, Northern Iowa Area Community College in Mason City, and Marshalltown Community College.

During the fall of 1967, when I was talking to a number of college students in the Ellsworth girls' dormitory lounge, one of the girls at the table told me that she had *never* heard the name of Jesus spoken in the reverent tone that I used. How my heart ached for her, and others who had heard my precious Lord's name only in anger and swearing. She had no idea that Christ had come to earth to die for our sins so that we might have access to Heaven. As a team, Hal and Patty Miller and I saw many decisions for Christ. Even today I meet students with whom we worked who are now strong Christians serving the Lord—pastors, teachers, missionaries, and others in many walks of life as God has led.

Previous personal hesitations about my work with college students were disappearing, proving invalid. Students were not necessarily looking for me to be highly intelligent, fashionable, famous, rich, or beautiful; they were looking for someone in whom they could see God working. As Jesus told Nicodemus, **"Whoever does what is true comes to the light, so that it may be clearly seen that his deeds have been carried out in God"** (John 3:21). Since I lived in close proximity with the students, they observed my life. The word *coincidence* just could not explain the many ways God was working.

Interestingly, the Apostle Paul also found an educational campus a fruitful mission field when he **"withdrew from them and took the disciples with him, reasoning daily in the hall of Tyrannus. This continued for two years, so that all the residents of Asia heard the word of the Lord, both Jews and Greeks"** (Acts 19: 9, 10).

* * * * *

October 1967 ~ Traveling by faith

Five students came to know the Lord that semester—two girls living in the campus center, a school athlete and a young Catholic student and her fiancé. The Lord also worked in many other students who were close to making decisions for Christ.

Toward the end of September, we sponsored a college fall retreat, the first of three retreats planned for the '67-'68 school year. Approximately fifty college students attended from eight different campuses. With testimonies around the campfire, students expressing their desire to know and serve the Lord, it was a tremendous time.

Nine girls rented space to live upstairs with me in the campus center, the Green House. They certainly kept life interesting. Remodeling the inside of the house was complete except for a few small projects here and there. One pressing need remained, we needed a working vacuum cleaner. Picking up particles by hand and sweeping the rugs with a broom was not adequate. Praise the Lord, an individual gave us a brand new vacuum cleaner.

We continued praying that the Lord would work in a mighty way. We prayed that the Holy Spirit would increase the spiritual longing in students' hearts for God and that new Christians would grow in their faith. Additionally, we prayed for boldness to proclaim the Gospel, for spiritual and physical strength, and for more workers to join us in this vast outreach.

We were building a basketball court in the backyard of our campus Green House. Before pouring the concrete, we were cutting and laying down wire mesh, trying to finish before the cement truck would come. Not having the proper tools, I did it the hard way.

While opening a letter from home, I remember thinking, "Would my parents approve of my being here if they were to see my bleeding hands from cutting the wire?" But it was worth it all, that basketball court was almost constantly in use, drawing students to our campus facilities and contributing many coming to know Christ.

Though working with the college students kept me busy, the mission board also needed help raising financial support from churches, groups, and individuals. Not having a car made deputation difficult, but God wonderfully provided transportation.

One Sunday evening, I was scheduled to speak at Laurens Baptist Church in Iowa. Buses and trains did not service that area and airline service was not available to the rural community. I prayed, "Lord, how do I get to Laurens?" A friend who had planned to attend Clear Lake Baptist Camp for a ladies' retreat that weekend was unable to go; she suggested that I take her place. Since the retreat was in the same direction as Laurens, I caught a ride with the local Iowa Falls church group.

At the camp, I noticed a lady's name tag which read "Laurens, Iowa." In fact, she was a member of the church I was trying to reach. When she learned that I was scheduled as a guest speaker that Sunday evening, she suggested that I stay overnight at her home, then ride to church with her the next day. I took her up on the offer. God provided.

The next morning I met the pastor who had been away the previous week for a funeral. Over lunch, the pastor and his wife inquired about my arrangements to return home. They generously offered to drive me home the next day; but knowing it would require a two-way trip for them, I prayerfully declined. Surely, I thought, the Lord could provide a different way. God's promises can be put to the test in our lives, as the Psalmist wrote, *"The steps of a man are established by the LORD, when he delights in his way"* (Psalm 37:23).

After the slide presentation of the campus work that Sunday evening, a couple approached me from Hampton, a town close to Iowa Falls where I lived. They attended the same church as I in Iowa Falls. The couple had come to celebrate the husband's elderly father's birthday. They offered to drive me to their home that night; the husband could drop me off at the campus house Monday morning on his way to work. The Lord delivered me neatly to my destination and back home again.

Explaining to the Lord that it would be much easier for Him and for me if He would provide me with my own car, I waited on God. Without a guaranteed monthly income, I did not qualify to buy a car from a dealership. An elderly couple sold me their 1952 Dodge for fifty dollars, with the agreement that I would pay for it as I was able. God supplied that need. Then another problem surfaced—I had never driven a stick shift. The car bucked and stalled all the way home. What an experience! I learned two lessons for the price of one: living by faith and learning to drive a standard transmission. Before long, the car was paid in full and getting from place to place became much easier.

* * * * *

January 1968 ~ Identity search

On January 6, we launched a program of Campus Bible Fellowship (CBF) leadership training. Twenty key students from various campuses met in Iowa Falls for a day of challenge. After that, we met twice each month to provide them with materials and discuss different methods of teaching so that the students could form small group Bible studies on their campuses.

The University of Northern Iowa (UNI) had recognized CBF as a student organization; we were in the process of receiving recognition at the Fort Dodge campus.

Eleven new girls moved into our Green House campus center. The previous semester had provided many opportunities to talk with the girls in our house; we prayed that the same would be true with these girls. We were learning that college students were open to considering the claims of Christ in their lives.

* * * * *

March 1968 ~ Jogging partner

One of the Ellsworth students wanted a jogging partner. Having already spoken with Janet about the Lord, I was happy to spend time with her. She could jog much better than I. Out of breath most of the time, I didn't say much while we jogged. Nonetheless, we bonded through the exercise routine. Physical conditioning became an inroad to spiritual training. Janet eventually trusted Christ as her

Savior and became more than my jogging partner; she became a sister in Christ.

Janet's decision to trust God was similar to the experience of ten men, according to a published report, who were trapped while fighting a forest fire. After several unsuccessful attempts to rescue the men, a helicopter pilot dropped a note, instructing them to follow him. The men did so. They followed a narrow path lined on both sides with fire to the only safe exit. The men did not argue about the note or try to escape on their own. They believed that the pilot was showing them the only way out; he alone could view the whole scene from above. They put their faith in the pilot, and their lives were saved.

We talked about our human condition. Without Christ, we also are lost. We must put our faith in the One who can see the whole situation from above and knows that His plan is the only way out. As the Bible teaches in the Book of Proverbs, *"In all your ways acknowledge him, and he will make straight your paths"* (Proverbs 3:6). Janet discovered that she could trust the Pilot of the universe to guide her, though she herself could not see the future.

* * * * *

April 1968 ~ Dead religion

Rev. Hal Miller led many students to the Lord. Others were clearly beginning to understand truths of the Gospel and considering a decision for Christ. God also gave me tremendous conversations with students; I was hopeful that the Holy Spirit would open their understanding of spiritual things. Many were already engrossed in false philosophies and unscriptural religious practices; others were sick of religion, an attitude not difficult to understand. If all we had to offer them was more dead religion, we might as well not waste our time or theirs. But I knew that the living Savior, Jesus Christ, saves from sin and gives peace, joy, and purpose in life. In speaking to the Samaritan woman at the well, Jesus authoritatively said, *"But whoever drinks of the water that I will give him will never be thirsty again. The water that I will give him will become in him a spring of water welling up to eternal life."* (John 4:14). That message is worth sharing.

*   *   *   *   *

September 1968 ~ Study, then decide

College students often came to visit in the office of our campus house. In one conversation, Steve told me that he didn't believe that the Bible was accurate or that there was a God. When I asked Steve for an example, he explained that he had attended Sunday school for a time as a child and remembered the Bible story about Noah's ark that held all those animals. It had always bothered him that later in Scripture, that same Ark was carried by four men across a river. He did not believe that feat possible.

"But there are two arks in the Bible," I explained. "One was a large, barge-like boat, capable of carrying the animals, as well as Noah and his family. The other, the Ark of the Tabernacle, was the size of a table with rings on the two sides for poles to be placed for the four priests who would carry it." Steve was surprised.

"You need to do more study before you make such a serious decision about dismissing the Bible and God," I urged. "Having studied the Bible, I am confident that the author is indeed God and that He is revealing to us what He wants us to know. How to get to Heaven is one of the things He wants us to know."

Before the end of that school year, Steve had not only gained confidence in the Bible as the Word of God, but also trusted Christ as his Lord and Savior. What the Apostle Paul said is true, *"For since, in the wisdom of God, the world did not know God through wisdom, it pleased God through the folly of what we preach to save those who believe"* (1 Corinthians 1:21).

*   *   *   *   *

October 1968 ~ Bible "errors"

A skeptical student answered my knock. Informing her that we were having a Bible study on campus, I invited the student to attend. She made a face. "Why should I want to study the Bible? I have a typed, single-spaced page, listing errors in the Bible that I need to study for a test in my class. The Bible is full of inaccuracies and mistakes."

Requesting permission to see the page of Biblical "inaccuracies," I looked over the material. One of the listed "mistakes" included a reference to Jesus telling his disciples to cast their net on the *left* side of the boat; in another, He told them to cast their net on the *right* side of the boat. Hence, the study sheet claimed that the Bible contradicted itself. When I asked if we could look up those references, she agreed. We turned to one passage, then the other. Clearly, there were two different fishing experiences. Why couldn't Jesus fish from the right side one day and the left side on another day?

Curious at that point, we looked up a number of the other references. It became obvious to both of us that whoever had collected the list of Bible "errors" had not seriously studied the Bible. That day the girl decided to come to our Bible study on campus; eventually she trusted Christ as her Savior. The Bible is very powerful and changes lives: *"For the word of God is living and active, sharper than any two-edged sword, piercing to the division of soul and of spirit, of joints and of marrow, and discerning the thoughts and intentions of the heart"* (Hebrews 4:12).

* * * * *

1969 Minnesota Camp

September 1969 ~ Whirlwind summer

During the summer of 1969, I spent a few weeks in Bible camps in Minnesota and Illinois, serving as a counselor, missionary speaker, and teacher. I also worked with handcrafts, helped at the waterfront and taught archery. The sore muscles, head cold, sprained shoulder, rope burn, bruises, and mosquito bites were worth the blessing of seeing young people make life-changing decisions for Christ. What a summer—what a privilege! The girls and I tearfully parted. Altogether at the two camps I dealt with five for salvation, six for assurance of salvation, and ten for dedicating their lives to the Lord.

Acquainting people with our work and helping to raise necessary financial support, I scheduled speaking engagements in Iowa, Nebraska, Minnesota, and Illinois that summer. In the churches, I met potential students interested in Bible study groups and other Christian activities on campus; we anticipated a good nucleus of Christian students on all of the campuses. The goal of Campus Bible Fellowship was to see many souls won to Christ established in the Word and directed into Bible-believing churches. We were thankful that God was still bringing people to Himself, as He had in the early church: ***"And day by day, attending the temple together and breaking bread in their homes, they received their food with glad and generous hearts, praising God and having favor with all the people. And the Lord added to their number day by day those who were being saved"*** (Acts 2:46, 47).

As the school year approached at The University of Northern Iowa, renters were lined up for the CBF campus house. Interviewing with each student prior to the school year had already resulted in my sharing about Christ with four students. Moving into our Cedar Falls campus house were Susan, Penny, Sharon, Mary Ann, Kathy, Marianne, Maria, Debbie, and Sandi.

* * * * *

December 1969 ~ Snowy winter

During a record-breaking snowstorm that winter, the Millers and I wondered if we should try to return home to Iowa Falls after a visit to Cedar Falls. Since the schedule was full for the next day, we decided to go ahead and travel. Hal suggested that I leave first; he and Patty would be able to help me if I had trouble. God gave us peace. I felt confident that He would make the trip possible.

There was no traffic. The wind blew fiercely; snow drifted across the road forming barricades. It was difficult to keep the car going fast enough to plow through the drifts and still be able to watch for the road. Where was the road, I wondered more than once. Was that a drift across the road or the bank along the side? "Lord, give me wisdom," I kept praying. Bright or dim lights—neither seemed to help. Then I noticed that along the side of the road, I could see the telephone poles. Aiming the car between the poles, I put my foot on the gas, plowed through drifts and stayed on the road.

Finally arriving home, I thanked God for His safety. A call to the Millers proved that they had also made it home safely. Hal said seriously, "We were certain that you were alongside the road in a ditch; but with the blinding snow, we could never have seen you." Our two cars were the last permitted to leave town before the highway department declared the highway totally impassable. I had to live down the kidding from the Millers and the college students about my "aim and plow" snow-driving technique. Once again, I had experienced that with God all things are possible. When we trust Him, He looks after His own.

Frequently, I was asked about my ministry as a single woman working on college campuses. One concern people mentioned was safety: "Do you really travel all by yourself?" My answer before and still is, "No, I'm never alone—God is always with me." What a comfort, knowing we can trust God who gives His children safety when they follow in His will. The shepherd Psalmist wrote, *"Even though I walk through the valley of the shadow of death, I will fear no evil, for you are with me; your rod and your staff, they comfort me"* (Psalm 23:4). Christianity is a walk, both exciting and fulfilling, with a living God.

* * * * *

CHAPTER 3

1970-1974

Misty and Gloria

September 1970 ~ "The Christian Horse"

Leaders of a Bible camp in Minnesota invited me to work with them. When one of the counselors invited me to her family farm in Blue Earth between the weeks of camp, I gladly accepted. Her family had horses, and we went riding. Horses had always been a passion of my life. When she mentioned her plan to sell a horse, the thought crossed my mind, "I would love to have a horse." I prayed about that possibility.

Surprisingly, when I called my parents for advice, even my common-sense, logical father agreed. For two hundred fifty dollars, I purchased a large, gentle Appaloosa gelding—saddle, bridle, and delivery included. His name was Misty.

The reaction of the college students was indescribable. They loved Misty. Sometimes I would ride him to the campus house where students would ride Misty; many of the students had never been on a horse. Big, strong football players rode Misty behind the CBF campus house where we had built a basketball court for athletes. They held onto the saddle horn for dear life, as I slowly led them around.

Amazingly, God provided a wonderful place for Misty. An older couple who kept a pony for their visiting grandchildren made Misty welcome. There Misty had everything he needed—a field with grass, water, protection from the wind, even companionship. In return, the couple requested that I ride their pony to keep him tame.

Often one of the college girls came with me to ride Misty while I rode the spirited pony. The pony loved to run; Misty preferred to walk and gallop. But when I rode the pony, Misty would follow me jealously, matching the pony's speed; he would not let me out of sight, regardless of his rider. Since Misty was a big horse, sixteen hands tall, girls could ride double with me. We would stop somewhere along the way, have Bible studies and heart-to-heart talks. The Bible study I frequently used was called *The John Series*. We claimed the promise in the Gospel of John, ***"In him* [Jesus] *was life, and the life was the light of men"*** (John 1:4).

The Greek Orthodox couple who owned the pony and pasture had observed our activities. One day when I came out to ride, they requested that I have a Bible study with them. Both trusted Christ. The couple nicknamed Misty "The Christian Horse." God can reach out through whatever means to bring individuals to new birth in Christ—even a horse! And while Misty was God's instrument which brought the couple to Christ, we must understand that it is entirely God's work that saves us. The Apostle John explained how we become His children, *"Who were born, not of blood nor of the will of the flesh nor of the will of man, but of God"* (John 1:13). The new birth is not achieved by family heritage, our good intentions, or other people trying to make us good. God can use any dynamics to bring us to the point of salvation, but we become His child only when we are born "of God."

* * * * *

In 1974, I sold Misty to finance my wedding. A good horse trader, I traded Misty for James. Our children that God later gave us joked that I should have kept the horse—but then, they never would have been born and never ridden Misty anyway. I made the right choice.

October 1970 ~ White witch

A student at UNI, Pat was a practicing "white witch." She explained that white witches seek to do "good" with the "power" they have. Pat, her mother and her grandmother—all practiced fortunetelling. She attended one of our Bible studies and listened but was not ready to trust Christ as her Savior. One day, I had a particular burden to visit her. After a bit of conversation, I asked if she was ready to make a decision for Christ.

"Yes, I am." Pat replied.

Thrilled, I shared Scripture with her, and then asked if she would like simply to tell the Lord what she wanted Him to do for her.

She prayed softly, "Jesus, I know that I am a sinner and need to claim your blood as payment for my sins. Right now, I invite you to come into my life, pay for my sins, and give me everlasting life. Be my Savior forever." As we talked and shared Bible verses about what she had just done, the fire alarm sounded. Student rules required putting a towel around their heads and exiting the building by way of the stairs. On the twelfth floor, Pat and I went down the stairs with the other students.

On the packed stairway, at the top of her voice, Pat enthusiastically said, "Praise the Lord. I'll never again have to be afraid of the fire of Hell." By the expressions on the faces of those around us, it was clear that they had no clue what had gotten into her. But I understood that the direction of her life had just changed from Hell to Heaven and that she was rejoicing. Later, a loudspeaker announced that the fire drill had been set off accidentally. Pat and I both knew that the fire drill had not been an accident. Satan had tried to prevent her from making a decision for salvation, but God had delayed that alarm until she was finished.

After trusting Christ as her Savior, Pat was under tremendous pressure to continue her involvement as a white witch. Late one night, I received a frantic phone call. She was crying and terribly afraid. Pat had awakened suddenly and found bite marks up and down her back, neck, and arms—many in places she could not possibly have reached. Her frightened roommate had left, saying she wanted to move out. Pat didn't know what to do and asked me for help.

"It is not possible to play both sides of the fence," I explained. If she wanted to continue to dabbling with witchcraft, she was inviting trouble. I inquired if she was serious about giving up all involvement with Satan and the occult lifestyle.

"Yes," Pat replied soberly, "Satan's price is too big."

With one condition, that she was serious and willing to stop playing around with Satan completely, I invited Pat to my apartment. I cried in prayer, "Lord, help!" I realized the seriousness of challenging Satan. At the same time, I knew that Jesus is stronger than Satan and that the Almighty God could help Pat.

Sitting on the floor in my living room, we opened our Bibles to Ephesians, chapter one. I read a few verses, explaining the meaning; then she read a few, commenting on what she understood. Finally, with our hands on the following passage, I said that her decision to stop dabbling with witchcraft pleased God, but cautioned that she had to choose, once and for all, whether she would serve Satan or God. Pat could not be double-minded.

> *Paul, an apostle of Christ Jesus by the will of God, To the saints who are in Ephesus, and are faithful in Christ Jesus: Grace to you and peace from God our Father and the Lord Jesus Christ.*
>
> *Blessed be the God and Father of our Lord Jesus Christ, who has blessed us in Christ with every spiritual blessing in the heavenly places, even as he chose us in him before the foundation of the world, that we should be holy and blameless before him. In love he predestined us for adoption as sons through Jesus Christ, according to the purpose of his will, to the praise of his glorious grace, with which he has blessed us in the Beloved. In him we have redemption through his blood, the forgiveness of our trespasses, according to the riches of his grace, which he lavished upon us, in all wisdom and insight making known to us the mystery of his will, according to his purpose, which he set forth in Christ as a plan for the fullness of time, to unite all things in him, things in heaven and things on earth.*
>
> *In him we have obtained an inheritance, having been predestined according to the purpose of him who works all things according to the counsel of his will, so that we who were the first to hope in Christ might be to the praise of his glory. In him you also, when you heard the word of truth, the gospel of your salvation, and believed in him, were sealed with the promised Holy Spirit, who is the guarantee of our inheritance until we acquire possession of it, to the praise of his glory,* Ephesians 1:1-14).

When we finished reading, Pat said, "I choose God." Then I encouraged her to tell God that she realized the power she had been playing with were Satanic and sinful. She wanted His forgiveness for that sin. Pat also needed to ask Him to take away this power and any of Satan's strongholds in her life. Finally, I encouraged her to give the power to Jesus, asking Him to remove it from her, never to return to that sin.

Pat prayed earnestly, confessing her sin of witchcraft. Acknowledging the generational curse passed on by her mother and grandmother who also practiced witchcraft, she asked God to break the bondage, to free her and protect her. Pat had a great sense of relief and said that she wanted nothing to do with her former power. When family and peers pressured her to come back into the satanic fold and use her former powers, Pat refused, declaring, "I gave it to Jesus, and it is gone."

Pat soon followed the Lord in believer's baptism at Cedar Heights Baptist Church in Cedar Falls, Iowa. Through Pat's personal witness, her mother also eventually came to a saving knowledge of Jesus Christ. In Acts is recorded a promise for us even today, ***"And it shall come to pass that everyone who calls upon the name of the Lord shall be saved"*** (Acts 2:21).

Pat married a fine Christian, moved to Wisconsin, and reared a family. They serve the Lord in their local church, working with youth. The last time I received a letter, Pat sent a family picture; she rejoiced that each of her children had trusted Christ and were living for Him.

* * * * *

Gloria Vermaas

May 5, 1971 ~ Thanks

The girls in the Monday small-group studies at UNI told me, "Gloria, we really appreciate your spending time with us in these Bible studies. They have meant much to us. We do not know what we would have done without them." I had held studies in three of the six dormitories. Eager to learn and participate, the girls had grown spiritually and appreciated my coming to them. Paul's words also encouraged me, *"How beautiful are the feet of those who preach the good news!"* (Romans 10:15). Desiring to expand the ministry the next year, several students and I began praying for a handful of girls willing to open a Bible study in the other three dormitories.

Activities that year included my traveling with Gospel teams, taking two car loads of students out East to visit several U.S. mission endeavors under Baptist Mid-Missions, visiting the Baptist Bible Seminary campus in Pennsylvania and conducting banquets and retreats. Twenty students made decisions for salvation, ten for dedication, and several for Bible school training. God gave eternal results that school year.

* * * * *

May 1971 ~ Sorrowful life turned glorious

While Dad was in the service during World War II, Mother and I lived for a while with Grandma and Grandpa, Aunt Mary and Aunt Dottie. A baby photo shows Aunt Mary holding me on the back of the old farm horse. As years passed, Mary married, moved quite a bit, and had her own children. Life for her was full of sorrows, disappointments, and poor health.

But Aunt Mary was a survivor; she kept going when others would have quit. Many times my mom and I talked with her about the Lord. Aunt Mary was polite, but God was just not a priority in her life. She encouraged her children to go to Sunday school and church on the church bus or with us when we were in town, but she herself never went.

God's Appointment

One night, I received a telephone call from Aunt Dottie. Aunt Mary was in critical condition, the result of complications following surgery—she was one of the first people to receive a kidney transplant. Mary was asking for me.

At her bedside, I talked frankly and openly; my burden was that she be ready to meet the Lord. Mary asked questions and spoke about her spiritual condition. Needing to return to Iowa the next day, I made one request, "Mary, please turn to Jesus. Ask Him to be your Savior, forgive your sins, and be born again into God's family soon."

She nodded. The next day, further complications took her to the edge of despair. She wanted to talk with me again, but I had already left. In God's appointed time, however, a pastor poked his head in the door and greeted Aunt Mary, "Hi! Can I be of help to you this morning?"

"Only if you can show me how to be born again," replied Mary.

The pastor did show her. Mary was saved that morning. God's promise to the Philippian jailer proved true also in our family, ***"Believe in the Lord Jesus, and you will be saved, you and your household"*** (Acts 16:31).

The next time I visited Aunt Mary, she was different. A personal relationship with the Lord Jesus Christ made her eager to grow in the understanding, knowledge, and grace of our Lord. The rest of her life, Aunt Mary was in and out of hospitals. She became one of the longest surviving of those first kidney transplant patients. Side effects of the medication swelled her little four-foot-tall body like a balloon; she could hardly look in a mirror without tears. Gradually, the medications caused the loss of her hearing and she was no longer able to walk very well. Her world became smaller; but her spirit soared as she spent more and more time alone with the Lord and her Bible.

The last time I visited Aunt Mary she was in her home in Lincoln, Nebraska. James and our three daughters were with me. Mary enjoyed watching the girls play. Letters from Grandma had kept us informed of Mary's progress and of her hospitalization again—this time with cancer. Blisters in her mouth and throughout her body, side effects of her cancer treatment, made her unable to talk or eat. When the hospital sent Mary home, terminally ill, Grandma converted her bedroom into a hospital room and cared for her.

One day, Mom called. She was flying from Virginia to Nebraska to be with Grandma and Mary. "Pray that I get there in time," was her request. Mom had called Mary and begged her to wait for her arrival before leaving this world.

Mom arrived at Mary's bedside June 13, 1983, stroked her face and talked with Mary for a short time. Mary had struggled to hold on, but then gradually her breathing slowed, and she slipped from this world into the presence of her Savior. Mom called me that night to tell me of Mary's home-going, and to share a note that Mary had written to her a few days earlier. Here is what she wrote.

Dear Becey,

Well, honey, I hope you get here on time to see me in August. I may just have to give you a rain check and see you in Heaven. Won't that be something?

We talked about this before, because that's where I am headed without any regrets. Take care now. Love to all.

Mary— Now sisters also in Christ.

Finally released from her pain and suffering, Aunt Mary was safe in the arms of her Savior.

Aunt Mary

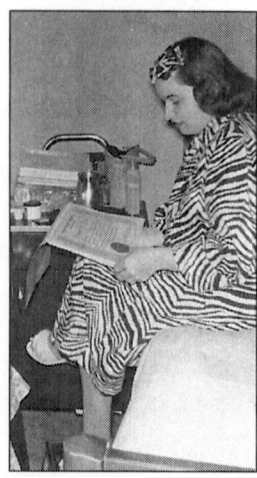

* * * * *

June 1971 ~ Choosing a mentor

Ruby arranged for me to come to her home for a Bible study. Without my knowledge, she also had invited a Jehovah's Witnesses teacher. Highly intelligent and inquisitive, Ruby intended to hear from both of us and then choose a mentor. The Jehovah's Witnesses teacher started; I listened. When it was my turn, the Jehovah's Witnesses lady became extremely upset when I shared my personal testimony of salvation. I explained that I knew I was going to Heaven because of the finished work of Christ on the Cross.

The Holy Spirit triumphed. Ruby chose to continue future Bible studies with me. We read passage after passage affirming the Deity of Jesus Christ and His finished work for mankind. One day, Ruby trusted Christ as her Savior; she led her younger brother to Christ and eventually her three children. God still leads His people to witness, just as He did for Philip and the Ethiopian eunuch:

Now an angel of the Lord said to Philip, "Rise and go toward the south to the road that goes down from Jerusalem to Gaza." This is a desert place. And he rose and went. And there was an Ethiopian, a eunuch, a court official of Candace, queen of the Ethiopians, who was in charge of all her treasure. He had come to Jerusalem to worship and was returning, seated in his chariot, and he was reading the prophet Isaiah. And the Spirit said to Philip, "Go over and join this chariot." So Philip ran to him and heard him reading Isaiah the prophet and asked, "Do you understand what you are reading?" And he said, "How can I, unless someone guides me?" And he invited Philip to come up and sit with him. Now the passage of the Scripture that he was reading was this:

"Like a sheep he was led to the slaughter and like a lamb before its shearer is silent, so he opens not his mouth. In his humiliation justice was denied him. Who can describe his generation? For his life is taken away from the earth."

And the eunuch said to Philip, "About whom, I ask you, does the prophet say this, about himself or about someone else?" Then Philip opened his mouth, and beginning with this Scripture he told him the good news about Jesus. And as they were going along the road they came to some water, and the eunuch said, "See, here is water! What prevents me from being baptized?" And he commanded the chariot to stop, and they both went down into the water, Philip and the eunuch, and he baptized him. And when they came up out of the water, the Spirit of the Lord carried Philip away, and the eunuch saw him no more, and went on his way rejoicing. (Acts 8:26-39)

* * * * *

1972 Iowa Falls Campus Bible Fellowship Staff

July 1972 ~ Teaching the Word

With the help of church ladies from the Waterloo/Cedar Falls area, we conducted 145 small group studies in the girls' dormitories at the University of Northern Iowa (UNI) during the '71-'72 school year. A number of small group Bible studies were also held at Ellsworth Junior College.

The large group studies which Hal Miller taught at UNI, attracted between 60 and 70 students. There were many opportunities for sharing the Word with students on campus; the Lord opened doors and hearts.

* * * * *

December 1972 ~ Searching hearts

While I visited with several students in one of the girls' dormitories, Linda trusted Christ. As I left her room, she said, "Thanks for caring enough to talk with me." The same evening, another girl told me that she had trusted Christ the previous day, following Bible study at the Union building.

Students with searching hearts were asking questions. "Can you go to Heaven if you do not believe in a Hell?" "How can you prove that there is a moral God, who is involved with individuals?" "What does the Bible really teach about what is going to happen in the future?" "What is truth?"

Throughout His ministry, Jesus affirmed, ***"Your word is truth"*** (John 17:17). The Bible is *truth* for every generation. When answering questions from the Bible, God gave me real confidence.

* * * * *

May 1973 ~ Fruitful ministry

Having grown to love the students, I hated to see the school year end. When they left, I never knew if I would see them again this side of Heaven. Unless the Lord broke through spiritual barriers and they received Christ, some students I would never see again, even in eternity.

Several students in 1973 had trusted Christ as Savior; others were growing in the things of Christ. Many had decided to participate in believer's baptism and joined evangelistic local churches—churches which preached the good news of the Gospel and tried to lead people to Christ. Seven students had decided to transfer to Bible school because they were considering full-time Christian service. Praise the Lord for young people desiring to invest their lives for the Lord.

Nine students from five Bible colleges came to the CBF headquarters for a three-week apprenticeship program. Our goal was to teach them effective communication with secular campus students. Several stayed for the entire summer to help us develop college ministry activities.

* * * * *

June 1973 ~ Our Father's care

When my family moved from Nebraska to Oakland, California, I was unable to visit them as frequently. But when I did, my little sister Carol would line up her friends to meet me, requesting that I talk to them about Jesus and how to get to Heaven. It was precious of her to care for their souls, and I felt honored.

When I recently asked Carol what she remembered about those conversations, she said that she could not remember how many had received Christ, but she knew that her friend Kathy had. When Carol moved to Virginia, she lost track of Kathy. Years later, Carol learned that at the time we had known her, Kathy had been in a difficult situation. The unconditional love of her Heavenly Father could not have come into Kathy's life at a more needed time. The Lord's Prayer tenderly points to *"Our Father in heaven"* (Matthew 6:9); so do verses in the Old Testament, as the Psalmist wrote, *"As a father shows compassion to his children, so the Lord shows compassion to those who fear him. But the steadfast love of the Lord is from everlasting to everlasting on those who fear him, and his righteousness to children's children"* (Psalm 103: 13, 17).

* * * * *

Two friends: Koyoko with Gloria

December 23, 1973 ~ Long way from home

    A graduate student at UNI, Koyoko came to America to improve her mastery of the English language. She had been a teacher in Japan. Separation from her husband in Japan was difficult; Koyoko and I often talked. In a foreign culture, she needed someone to talk to, someone who cared. At first, the concept of Christ and Christianity was difficult for Koyoko. She politely listened, but gave no indication of a curiosity about the subject.

    Over Christmas break, almost everyone was off campus, most home with their families. So, when I invited Koyoko to go with me to Wednesday evening choir practice at Hagerman Baptist Church, she agreed. During rehearsal, Koyoko listened intently. We had talked often about how Jesus Christ loves and cares for everyone, and how a person can become a Christian. She had never been interested. But as she watched us practicing the songs, I thought perhaps her attitude was changing. That evening, something did "click" for her: she understood the message of Christmas. Jesus Christ had come to die so that she might live in Heaven.

After practice, I sat next to her in the pew and asked, "If I showed you again tonight how to trust Jesus Christ as your personal Savior, would you want to?"

After a pause, she said, "For me, I think it is very necessary." Koyoko prayed a prayer of acceptance that must have thrilled her Heavenly Father's ears. As we left the church, she eagerly shared with those around her, "I accepted Jesus, and He has given to me the very best Christmas gift ever, eternal life."

We talked often after that. The next summer, she returned to Japan, where she teaches English. Jesus Christ is with Koyoko, in her heart forever.

* * * * *

January 1974 ~ Can't explain it

Another UNI student, Marilyn, regularly taught Sunday school. One day as we visited, I asked, "How do you explain to the children in your class the way they can get to Heaven?"

"I can't," Marilyn replied, "I'm not sure myself."

"Would you be interested in how I explain that important Bible truth?"

"Yes."

Opening our Bibles, we studied the first three chapters of the Gospel of John, where Jesus conversed with Nicodemus. Jesus told the ruler of the Jews, ***"Unless one is born again he cannot see the kingdom of God"*** (John 3:3).

Then I asked Marilyn if she had ever been born again.

"I think so," she replied.

"You may be like me—I was religious, but not really born again," I remarked.

"Yes, that is where I am," she nodded thoughtfully.

Marilyn decided that day to accept the Savior's offer of new life in Christ. She prayed. With a warm smile, Marilyn exclaimed, "It is different. I can feel it inside. Thank you for showing me the way to have Christ as my own Savior."

* * * * *

Major Life Change!

During this academic year, Rev. James E. Goering, a radio pastor, and his brother Dwight from the Family Altar Broadcast, headquartered in Waterloo, began attending the campus Bible studies. They enjoyed the college students and appreciated the CBF ministry. James and I began dating in February. Our first dates were Valentine Banquets, three weeks in a row: Cedar Heights Baptist Church's banquet, the Campus Bible Fellowship banquet, and James' Family Altar Broadcast banquet.

The next month was busy. In March, I traveled to the state of New York to take part in the North American Field Council, Baptist Mid-Missions' Tri-Annual Missionary Conference business sessions; I had been elected Secretary-Treasurer. Considering a transfer to the New York CBF team to work with Betty Wallin, I also visited the Campus Bible Fellowship work in New York for a week.

Returning to Iowa, I thought that God had brought James into my life temporarily, perhaps to soften the fact that I was turning thirty and still unmarried. Busy and content, I told the Lord that if He wanted me to marry, He would have to "hit me over the head" to get my attention. Through the years, I had dated only Christians, and I was happy being single.

James says that he knew God wanted him to marry me, even before he asked me out for our first date. It's a good thing James didn't tell me that bit of news before God did some earnest work in my heart.

Our relationship turned more serious. After much prayer and searching for the Lord's will, I knew that God was preparing me for a **Major life change**.

March 1974 ~ Need to build

Sherry Bernot became my roommate and co-worker early in 1974. Across from the high-rise dormitories at UNI, our apartment was a regular student stopover for fellowship and counseling. My couch had stains from the tears of many students who knelt with me there in prayer, addressing serious life decisions. At our large campus Bible studies, a number of students were saved. Many made other spiritual decisions. Five students who felt called to full-time Christian service, transferred to a Bible college.

My small group Bible studies were in the girls' dormitory; I began a new series entitled "Created a Woman," which was well received. Another study for professional ladies also was well attended; that study group included a physical education teacher at the University and a high school counselor. Not certain of the personage of God, the ladies indicated that they were interested in exploring the question, "God: He, She or It?"

We began studying Scripture to understand better the personhood of God. Regardless of the popular woman's movement claims, we learned that the Bible is consistently clear about the Fatherhood of God and Jesus Christ, the Son of God. We noted, for example, that in the Lord's Prayer, Jesus refers twice to God as "Heavenly Father": *"Our Father in heaven"* (Matthew 6:9) and later in the same prayer, *"For if you forgive others their trespasses, your heavenly Father will also forgive you"* (Matthew 6:14). The studies created a bond of fellowship among us, and the ladies grew in the things of the Lord, even visiting church with me.

With continued growth in the ministry, and the need to build an addition to the Cedar Falls campus house became apparent.

* * * * *

Rev. & Mrs. James E. Goering

In June, 1974, James Goering asked me to marry him. As I prayed, the Lord gave me peace. I accepted James' proposal, believing that God was leading us.

James was the third radio pastor for the Family Altar Broadcast, begun in 1932 by Anton Cedarholm, succeeded by his brother, Hilmore Cedarholm. At the time, James considered joining the CBF staff and developing a radio ministry for the college campus. My desire was that James would become a CBF staff member, but that was not a condition for my marrying him. God could be guiding me into something entirely new. No matter, we would become a husband and wife team in full-time Christian service, teaching and seeking to win people to Christ.

Eventually, James was not led to start a radio ministry for CBF. Leaving Baptist Mid-Missions became one of the most difficult things I had ever done; nevertheless, just because God had greatly blessed me in the campus ministry did not mean that He would continue to bless if I stopped being obedient to His will.

Two days before our wedding, we celebrated James' thirty-third birthday; I was thirty. James and I married on September 7, 1974. It was the first marriage for both of us. Together we continued the Family Altar Broadcast ministry in Waterloo, Iowa.

December 1974 ~ Picture in the mail

We received the following letter in the mail, which included a young boy's picture:

Dear Gloria,

I'm sending you a picture of Jerry. Thank you for giving him the plan of salvation. May the Lord continue to use you and bless you.

In Christian Love,

Signed, his grandparents

I do not remember the details of talking with Jerry, but this letter touched my heart. It made me reflect on those instrumental in my own life, which brought me to trust Christ as my Savior. Indeed, I owe a debt to those who have faithfully shared the Good News of salvation, beginning with the disciples of Jesus, down through the centuries to those who led me to Christ. Following that golden chain of communication from one person to the next, would make an interesting movie or book. In Heaven, I look forward to learning how that message traveled from one person to the next, until it came to me.

We all need to ask God for a grateful spirit for that rich gift we have received and keep passing it on to others. Paul characterized the richness of the gift in Romans, *"For I am not ashamed of the gospel, for it is the power of God for salvation to everyone who believes, to the Jew first and also to the Greek. For in it the righ-*

teousness of God is revealed from faith for faith, as it is written, 'The righteous shall live by faith'" (Romans 1:16, 17).

* * * * *

CHAPTER 4

1975-1978

Gloria and James Goering

July 1975 ~ Foreboding dreams

Ruby trusted Christ in 1971; she wanted me to help her friend Roma, who had been diagnosed with cancer. Roma was experiencing terrible dreams about Hell and the torment awaiting her. Of course, I agreed. We set a time to visit her in Otterville, Iowa later that week. When the day came, I was sick. James believed that it was important for us to keep the appointment. While he drove, I lay down in the back seat of the car.

By the time we arrived at her home, I was feeling much better. James and I sat down with Roma, her husband, and their ten-year-old son. Roma shared her deep-seated fears of death and a horrible future waiting in eternity. Since Jesus Himself spoke about Hell and its eternal torment, I could not tell her that there was no Hell since Jesus himself spoke of its torments. He described the rich man who cried in vain for mercy and a drop of water, in Hades (Luke 16:22-24). Roma needed to understand why people are in danger of Hell and that there is a way of escape so that we do not need to live in fear.

Beginning with the "bad news," I explained that we all have a terminal disease of sin, but quickly followed with the "good news," that there is a cure. The prescription is the blood of Christ applied to our sin. As her cancer medication would avail nothing unless she took the pills and followed the directions on the bottle, so we must take the prescription Christ gave us: *"For God so loved the world, that he gave his only Son, that whoever believes in him should not perish but have eternal life"* (John 3:16). We must believe in His finished work on the Cross.

The Bible assures us that there are "great seats" still available on the plane to Heaven. Roma could reserve her place, I explained, by calling on the Lord Jesus Christ to apply His blood as payment for sin to her account. Tickets, however, are NOT available at the gate; that choice must be made before we die. The Gospel of Matthew warns, *"Enter by the narrow gate. For the gate is wide and the way is easy that leads to destruction, and those who enter by it are many. For the gate is narrow and the way is hard that leads to life, and those who find it are few"* (Matthew 7:13-14).

If Roma would accept Christ as her personal Savior, I explained, God would deliver her from the devil as she sought God's strength. The Bible promised Divine power to believers, *"Submit yourselves therefore to God. Resist the devil, and he will flee from you"* (James 4:7). Roma did trust Christ that evening. She experienced relief from Satan's oppression immediately and menacing dreams of Hell.

Her life changed dramatically. Both her husband and son also decided to become Christians because of her vibrant testimony. The three were baptized and became active in their local church. Later, when Roma passed on from her cancer, she was looking forward to being reunited with her family in Heaven.

* * * * *

Norman Seeman

August 1975 ~ Lawyer on the bridge

As James walked across the Fourth Street Bridge on an errand for Family Altar Broadcast (FAB), he struck up a conversation with Norman, a trial lawyer. Norman wanted to know more about tape duplication since he also had a radio program and seminars about police science. That meeting was the beginning of a special friendship. Through the months, James and I talked about spiritual things with him and his wife, Janie; we went to meetings together where the Gospel was preached. Norm began to think seriously about his personal relationship with God.

While listening to his car radio, Norm heard a song on the local Christian radio station, KNWS, which at that time also carried the FAB program. The song touched Norm's heart that day, convicting him of his need to get right with God. Norm pulled to the side of the road and asked Jesus Christ to be his personal Savior. He developed a strong desire to reach others for Christ and help Christians grow.

Norm spent many hours counseling us in areas of business and participating as advisory board member for FAB, as well as board member for KNWS. A dynamic man of vision and enthusiasm, Norm became an active witness for the Lord and a personal soul winner, developing a specialized tract ministry and speaking to Christian groups. We praise the Lord for God's appointment on the bridge with Norm. What a help and encouragement he became for both us and FAB. Words of Solomon accurately describe our friendship, *"As iron sharpens iron, so a man sharpens the countenance of his friend"* (Proverbs 27:17, NKJV).

* * * * *

June 1976 ~ Hit by a car

As newlyweds, James and I lived in a small apartment on East Fifth Street in downtown Waterloo, right next to the bridge. The Family Altar Broadcast office was adjacent to our apartment.

Ruth worked with us in the office. She was a good worker as well as a warm, sweet-spirited lady. One day when Ruth left work, as she crossed the street to her vehicle, she was hit by a car. The young driver had not seen her. I rode with Ruth in the ambulance to the hospital. In considerable pain, her concern was for the young man who had hit her. Ruth was afraid that the accident would be traumatic for him.

James and I made an appointment with the young driver and his parents. He was distressed about hitting Ruth. When I explained that Ruth wanted him to know that "accidents happen" and that she was not angry or bitter against him, he was surprised at both Ruth's attitude and ours.

By explaining that Ruth was a Christian who loved the Lord and was praying for him, James and I were able to comfort him. Ruth believed that the Bible is true when it encourages us to trust in God. Together, we read a few verses. The Apostle Paul said, ***"We know that for those who love God all things work together for good, for those who are called according to his purpose"*** (Romans 8:28). A few verses later, Paul explained that Jesus is personally concerned with us all the time: ***"Who is to condemn? Christ Jesus is the one who died—more than that, who was raised—who is at the right hand of God, who indeed is interceding for us"*** (Romans 8:34). Jesus was interceding for him, and this situation could be God's bringing something good into his life.

That night, the young man did trust Christ as his Savior. Ruth was pleased to know that her accident had been used by God to bring about the young man's salvation.

* * * * *

September 1976 ~ Rejoicing in Heaven

Family Altar Broadcast decided to sponsor a booth at the Iowa State Fair in Des Moines, Iowa in order to promote the ministry. Overwhelmed by the opportunities, we expanded our vision to include a soul-winning outreach since thousands of people attend the fair. Earnest sessions of prayer and careful planning brought heartwarming blessings.

James and I spent most fair days at our booth with three volunteers. Two other ladies from Des Moines also helped us, Geneva Nell and Margie Cunningham. Geneva and Margie had a special boldness from the Lord for soul winning. Not content to sit behind the table and distribute literature, they were on their feet, asking people if they knew for certain that they would go to Heaven. Many individuals came into the booth where we shared familiar Scripture with them about receiving Jesus Christ as their personal Savior. A passage we shared many times was *"God so loved the world, that he gave his only Son, that whoever believes in him should not perish but have eternal life. For God did not send his Son into the world to condemn the world, but in order that the world might be saved through him"* (John 3:16, 17). From our booth, we gave out thousands of pieces of literature.

Many people were interested. In our FAB booth, we shared from the Bible how individuals, upon death, can enter Heaven. Using a tract that looked like a check, Geneva would smile and say, "This is the best check you'll ever receive." Many asked for extra copies of the tract to share with others. We also had colorful balloons with a Cross printed on them. A Gospel tract which explained the simple terms of God's gift of salvation accompanied each balloon. Many parents who perhaps would have rejected the literature permitted their children to take the balloons with the tracts. Grandmothers asked for balloons and children's tracts for their grandchildren.

We worked in teams of two; one handed out literature and cared for the booth while the other visited with people, answered questions, and led individuals to the Lord. So many prayer warriors spent hours with us in preparation, praying that God would bless the booth ministry. Praise the Lord that over one hundred individuals made professions of coming to know Jesus Christ.

Dear to the heart of God is spreading the Good News; Jesus said, *"There is joy before the angels of God over one sinner who repents"* (Luke 15:10). Jesus offered up His own life to provide that gift, and God the Father allowed His Son to suffer that pain and public shame for our sake. I can only imagine the rejoicing in Heaven as souls were saved at the booth.

****** * * * ****

On March 17, 1977, God gave us Angela Ruth. She was not only our first child, but also the first Family Altar Broadcast baby. Anton Cedarholm had started FAB back in 1932 after his children were older. Hilmore Cedarholm remained a bachelor all the years he was the radio pastor; now James was the radio pastor. Angela always accompanied us to the office. With Angela, God fulfilled the promise to me, *"He gives the barren woman a home, making her the joyous mother of children"* (Psalm 113:9).

Gloria with baby Angela our youngest secretary.

July 1977 ~ Moving day

Having outgrown our apartment, we prayed for God to lead us to the place where He wanted us to live. After weeks of looking and praying, we finally bought a home. Moving day brought aching muscles but also an opportunity to witness for Christ.

A man came to install our telephone. While he fixed the wiring, we talked to him about eternity and God's requirements for getting there. He was open to the conversation. When I shared one of our tracts, "What If I Gave You a Million Dollars?" he commented that he "could sure use a million dollars!"

We continued talking while he worked. I explained that God gives eternal life to those who accept His Son, a priceless gift worth more than even a million dollars. When James joined the conversation, he helped to answer many questions. When the installation was finished, I asked if he would have time for prayer. He responded, "Yes."

James asked if he would like to pray, accepting Christ as his personal Savior, relying on God's promise that *"everyone who calls on the name of the Lord will be saved"* (Romans 10:13). A little surprised but willing, the man asked Jesus Christ to be his Savior, to pay for his sins and give him eternal life. As the repairman left, he expressed deep thanks for showing him what he had been seeking for so long. We praised the Lord for the opportunity to talk with the former Jehovah's Witness.

Two things we found attractive about the location of our home: there was a park across the street and a cherry tree in the back yard. The tree was brimming full of cherries and children. We met most of our neighborhood children who climbed the tree that summer. We were happy to share the fruit with them since I was too busy to do any canning that year. The children even picked some cherries for us.

* * * * *

August 1977 ~ Vacation Bible School

The Washburn church asked me to direct Vacation Bible School. Each day, I presented a Bible story lesson on the overhead projector. Then we invited the young people to go to the back of the auditorium if they wanted to know for certain that they had received Jesus as their Savior. They could have their reservation for Heaven confirmed.

A young person named Bryan came up to James and said, "I want to ask Jesus to be my Savior."

James talked with him and led him in a prayer of salvation, "Yes, Lord Jesus, I do know that I am in trouble and ask you to pay for my sin right now so that I may have eternal life."

The next day after class and the invitation, Bryan walked up to me and said "That's what I did yesterday, and now *I'm* a Christian."

Billie Jo, a teen-ager and one of our neighbors who came with us to the meetings, asked me to help her ask Jesus to be her Savior. That week we saw over twenty young people trust Christ as their Savior. The Bible documents the importance of God's work in children's lives. For example, the child King Josiah influenced a nation for God: *"In the eighth year of his* **[King Josiah's]** *reign, while he was yet a boy, he began to seek the God of David his father, and in the twelfth year he began to purge Judah and Jerusalem of the high places, the Asherim, and the carved and the metal images"* (2 Chronicles 34:3). Reaching children for Christ is so important because they have their entire lives ahead of them.

* * * * *

September 1977 ~ Changed destination

Specific prayer went up for the FAB booth ministry before the 1977 Iowa State Fair in Des Moines. Praise the Lord, many trusted Christ.

* *

Two boys from Iowa City said, "We do not go to church anywhere, but we have been talking together these past few days, thinking that we should get saved." They trusted Christ.

* *

A sixty-three-year-old Sunday school teacher in a Christian church received the Lord. She took many pieces of literature to share with her students, stating that she would be "a more effective Sunday school teacher now."

* *

A boy from Belmond, Iowa said, "You know, sometimes I can't sleep. I just worry about not knowing how to get to Heaven." He also trusted Christ.

* *

Two young teens that were smoking marijuana, stopped to talk. After they had trusted Christ, they put out their joints and then emptied their pockets of drugs. When we asked how they got the drugs, they replied, "Our parents smoke pot, and they do not care if we do."

* *

Men in charge of the foosball games on the other end of the floor trusted Christ.

* *

No doubt during the days of the fair, many walked by our booth on their way to Hell, but 153 individuals professed to trust Christ as their Savior, changing their destination to Heaven. Just as Jesus had compassion on the multitudes in Matthew 15, He still has compassion for people today: *"Then Jesus called his disciples to him and said, 'I have compassion on the crowd because they have been with me now three days and have nothing to eat. And I am unwilling to send them away hungry, lest they faint on the way'"* (Matthew 15:32).

Letters were written, correspondence courses sent out, and local pastors contacted to follow up those who had trusted Christ at our booth. A promise we can claim as we seek to serve Him: *"He who goes out weeping, bearing the seed for sowing, shall come home with shouts of joy, bringing his sheaves with him"* (Psalm 126:6).

* * * * *

October, 1977 ~ First time visit

Many Sundays we had the opportunity to minister in churches. There, too, James and I rejoiced when individuals came to a saving knowledge of Jesus Christ.

One Sunday morning, James preached on the subject, "Why Good People Go to Hell." The Holy Spirit touched hearts. When James gave the invitation, Opal, a lady in her sixties, came weeping down the aisle. Feeling that God was talking straight to her, she wanted to make certain that she was going to Heaven. James asked me to talk with her. When I explained how she could ask Christ to be her Savior, Opal bowed her head and without hesitation prayed, asking God to save her. Opal accepted Christ. How radiantly she shared her new assurance of eternal life with me and others while still at the church. Opal claimed the wonderful promise,

I write these things to you who believe in the name of the Son of God that <u>you may know that you have eternal life</u>. And this is the confidence that we have toward him, that if we ask anything according to his will he hears us. And if we know that he hears us in whatever we ask, we know that we have the requests that we have asked of him. (John 5:13-15)

That Sunday morning, both Opal and her husband had felt like attending that particular church for the first time. Opal's husband was fighting cancer. We talked with him for a while, explaining how he, too, could have assurance of eternal life. He wanted more time to think about that decision. We were glad that God had led them and us, to that morning service. It is marvelous how God connects people for His honor and glory—another of God's appointments. What a blessing to be led by God, day by day.

* * * * *

October 1977 ~ *The Burning Hell*

A family in Le Grand, Iowa was burdened for neighborhood teens to be reached for Christ. They invited us to come for a Halloween party and show the film, *The Burning Hell*. Promoting the film as "so scary that only the strong-hearted could sit through it," they kept the title a secret. Enthusiasm was high as they invited neighborhood teens by word of mouth.

Approximately twenty teenagers came to the party. The group enjoyed fun games and then watched the film. The teens were introduced to the seriousness of facing a real Hell unprepared to face God, their sins not forgiven through the blood of Christ.

After the film, James invited the teens to make certain of where they stood with God in terms of their eternal soul. He explained how Jesus Christ gave a brief glimpse into the torments of Hell, His words recorded in the Gospel of Luke:

The poor man died and was carried by the angels to Abraham's side. The rich man also died and was buried, and in Hades, being in torment, he lifted up his eyes and saw Abraham far off and Lazarus at his side. And he called out, "Father Abraham, have mercy on me, and send Lazarus to dip the end of his finger in water and cool my tongue, for I am in anguish in this flame." (Luke 16:22-24)

Three teens decided that they wanted to trust Jesus Christ as their Savior that night. James talked to the one teen; I talked to the others. All three trusted Christ. Afterwards, they shared their testimonies with the other teens and the host family; they were glad that they had come and that they would no longer have to worry about going to Hell.

* * * * *

Gloria, James, and Angela

January 1978 ~ No longer afraid

The Lundstrum family presented a Christian musical concert at Traer, Iowa. State Auditor Lloyd Smith, a Christian friend of ours, was one of the sponsors. James and I volunteered to be counselors. Halfway through the presentation, our baby Angela became restless, adding her voice to the music. I decided it would be wise to leave.

When I left the auditorium, I saw a young man sweeping up broken glass. I had noticed the same fellow earlier in the hall with a group of young men, laughing and playing. When a couple of ushers had asked them to be more orderly, the fellows made light of the meeting. One of the friends jokingly had asked this young man, "Why don't you become a Christian?"

"I'm afraid" was his response.

Because of having overheard that bit of conversation, I had prayed that he would come to know the Lord that evening. Amazingly, God had brought about one of "His appointments." When I struck up a conversation with him, he said that he was helping with the janitorial work in the building that evening. He had recently lost a parent and was quite concerned about death. When I asked if he knew whether or not he would go to Heaven when he died, he quietly answered that he did not.

"Would you like to know how you could?"

"Yes" was his reply. We read verses in the Gospel of John, including, *"And as Moses lifted up the serpent in the wilderness, so must the Son of Man be lifted up, that whoever believes in him may have eternal life"* (John 3:14,15). Then he bowed his head and prayed, asking Jesus to be his Savior.

As we returned to the auditorium, the speaker was just beginning the invitation. The young man went down the aisle to take a public stand, letting all know of his personal decision to accept Jesus as his Lord and Savior. Jesus confirmed the joy in Heaven, *"Just so, I tell you, there will be more joy in heaven over one sinner who repents than over ninety-nine righteous persons who need no repentance"* (Luke 15:7).

* * * * *

May 19, 1978 ~ "Hope so" becomes "Know so"

Audrey Wee asked me to team teach a seminar with her in the Waterloo/Cedar Falls area. The theme *Christian Attitude Enrichment* was based on the Biblical command for Christians to be *"transformed by the renewal of your mind"* (Romans 12:1). We hoped that the seminar would provide helpful instruction about how to "renew the mind" daily and establish a personal relationship with God. I thoroughly enjoyed this opportunity to work with Audrey.

At one seminar, a distressed lady requested personal counseling. Audrey and I talked with her. When we asked the lady if she had trusted Christ as her personal Savior, as Christ had instructed, she said, "I think so—I hope so."

Opening Scripture to John 3:1-21, we talked about the necessity of being born again. In an attempt to illustrate the truth, I asked the lady whether or not she was married. Of course, her answer was "Yes," not "I hope so," or "I think so."

"Likewise, our relationship with Christ is clear," I explained. "If we are His children, we can know it—not just hope so. Knowing our standing with God is the foundation for going forward in Christian growth."

Bowing her head, she prayed a simple prayer, telling the Lord that if she had never done it before, she was now asking Christ to be her Savior, to pay for her sins and give her eternal life. Just as the Philippian jailer long ago listened to the Apostle Paul when he said, **"Believe in the Lord Jesus, and you will be saved"** (Acts 16:31), that lady also believed and was saved.

That evening she exclaimed with a smile, "How wonderful to know for certain that I have received Christ and am going to Heaven." Confident that she was born again, the lady expressed joy in her salvation. Being religious is not the same as having a personal relationship with Jesus Christ. She avoided the terrible situation of some who will stand before God on Judgment Day, not having accepted Jesus' provision of salvation.

In the Gospel of Matthew, Jesus said, **"On that day many will say to me, 'Lord, Lord, did we not prophesy in your name, and cast out demons in your name, and do many mighty works in your name?' And then will I declare to them, 'I never knew you; depart from me, you workers of lawlessness'"** (Matthew 7:22, 23).

In contrast to many who attempt to establish their own "fig leaf" righteousness, as Adam and Eve did first (Genesis 3), this lady accepted Christ's blood covering. Mercifully, God has provided His perfect remedy for sin. When we ask God to save us from our sin, He alone does that work. At the beginning of the Gospel of John, he identifies Jesus as the answer, *"All who did receive him, who believed in his name, he gave the right to become children of God"* (John 1:12). She discovered that we cannot pull ourselves up to Heaven in our own strength; God reaches down and lifts us up.

* * * * *

June 1978 ~ At our doorstep

Children attract children. When Angela was fifteen months old, neighbor children began coming to our house to play. Several of the neighbor girls began to say, "God bless you," and "We love you," when they left our house, parroting phrases that I frequently used with them. It was delightful seeing Christian principles influence their lives.

One ten-year-old became like an adopted daughter. She regularly went to church with us. One morning during the invitation, she whispered, "May I go forward?" That day I had the privilege of helping her trust Jesus Christ as personal Savior. Tammy reminded me that the mission field is at our doorstep. A continual prayer in my heart is that every neighbor will come to know and love our wonderful Lord Jesus.

* * * * *

September 1978 ~ State fair

Arriving at the Des Moines State Fair again, we worked together to unload the car and set the booth in order. Our five-member group—James and I, Angela (1½ years), Margie, and Geneva—began to pass out tracts, inviting people to let us show them from the Bible how to know for certain that they would go to Heaven. People walked by, many on their way to a Christless eternity as far as we knew. But we talked with hundreds of people in those eleven days; some prayed with us, trusting Jesus Christ to forgive their sins and give them everlasting life.

* *

A complete family—husband, wife, and two daughters—stopped by the booth. James led the husband to the Lord; his wife and daughters I was blessed to bring to the Savior. They were so glad to know that Christ would be the center of their family life, helping them overcome problems.

* *

Two other girls paused at the booth, listened carefully, and then trusted Christ. Later, they returned, bringing their brother. He, too, desired to have Christ as his Savior.

* *

A pastor and his wife stopped to visit. As the pastor talked with James, the pastor's wife joined me, passing out tracts and inviting people to stop and visit. Two girls stopped to talk with her. Working with elephants at the fair, the girls were on break. Both became believers. We encouraged them to bring their friends so that they also might trust Christ. The next day, the girls came back with a friend who, praise God, did ask Jesus to save them. While I spoke with their friend, they took care of little Angela.

* *

One grandmother, a Christian, waited while her grandson made his decision to become a Christian.

* *

During the 1978 Iowa State Fair, we saw over 260 individuals profess to trust Jesus as their Savior. Our prayer is that they, in turn, will share the good news of salvation with others, and receive the promised reward, ***"And those who are wise shall shine like the brightness of the sky above; and those who turn many to righteousness, like the stars forever and ever"*** (Daniel 12:3).

Gloria and Angela Traveling home.

* * * * *

October 1978 ~ On the porch

After returning from a trip, we learned from neighborhood children that Lisa, one of the girls who played with Angela, had been in the hospital for an appendectomy. Saturday morning, I awoke with a burden to visit twelve-year-old Lisa.

The day was fully scheduled, but the burden was strong. James was recording his regular FAB radio program in our home and needed the house quiet. Preparing a plant gift, I left a note for James, put Angela and the Bible in her stroller, and walked the several blocks to Lisa's house. She answered the door, delighted to see us, and joined us on the porch. After we had talked for a while about her operation, I asked Lisa if she knew for certain whether or not she would go to Heaven when she died.

She quietly answered, "No."

"Let me show you in the Bible," I suggested, "how you can know today you're ready to go to Heaven." Getting the Bible, I sat with Lisa on the stairs and began showing her from Scripture how she could become a child of God.

At that point, Angela became fascinated by the white puppy next door. While "Mommy" was occupied, she went visiting, walking fearlessly up to pet "the nice doggie." Praise the Lord, the puppy was friendly. But a seventeen-month-old toddler needs supervision. In the process of showing Lisa how to receive Jesus Christ as her Savior, I retrieved Angela from the "doggie" several times.

When I asked Lisa if she was ready to pray and have Jesus come into her life, forgive her sins, and give her everlasting life, she replied, "Yes." There on her porch steps, she prayed aloud, requesting that God would give her everlasting life. She received Jesus as her Savior and, as the Bible clearly teaches in John 3:1-21, was born again: *"Jesus answered him, 'Truly, truly, I say to you, unless one is born again he cannot see the kingdom of God'"* (John 3:3).

Soon after we had prayed, Lisa's mother drove up. I visited with her, explaining what Lisa had just done, showing her the verses in the Bible that I had showed Lisa. She was friendly and asked many questions.

Just as I was ready to leave and perfectly timed, as God's appointments are, James came to pick us up to go to the office. We rejoiced together that because of Angela's making friends in the neighborhood, Lisa was now prepared for eternity.

* * * * *

December 1978 ~ Demonstration turned real

A listener to our radio broadcast on KNWS in Waterloo telephoned to ask if we would come to her home. She wanted us to show her how to share Jesus with her neighbors. We scheduled a visit.

A cold, snowy night, we bundled up twenty-one-month-old Angela. Then James and I, with Angela, drove to Mary's home. We enjoyed a good time, visiting about the things of the Lord; James answered many questions from the Bible. Eventually, the conversation turned to the subject of *how* to lead someone to the Lord. Mary

God's Appointment

called her twelve-year-old daughter Cassandra into the room and said, "Demonstrate on someone who really needs it."

Explaining that we were doing a demonstration of how to show someone from the Bible how to get to Heaven, I asked Cassandra if she would be willing to participate. She consented and sat next to me on their couch. Then I explained (1) *who* needed to be born again—everyone; (2) *why* we needed to have Jesus pay for our sin personally—the penalty for sin is death; and (3) *how* to believe *on* the Lord Jesus rather than just *about* Him—by personally appropriating His blood payment. Cassandra listened seriously.

When I asked if she was ready to trust Christ to forgive her sin, she responded, "Yes." That morning Cassandra prayed, receiving Christ and His payment on the Cross for her sin. Then I asked her where Christ was now. She said, "In my life, as He said He would be."

A demonstration had become the real thing. God makes salvation so simple a child can understand. We can turn on the light by flipping the wall switch without having to know all about electricity and how it works. In the same way, we can put a key in the ignition of our car and turn it on, without knowing all the details of how a car works.   Likewise, we do not have to understand the intricacies of salvation when we first accept Christ. God knows what He is doing and He offers it as a free gift to all who will receive it. I understand salvation better now than I did the night I trusted Christ as my Savior. Acting on faith in the finished work of Jesus Christ is sufficient. The Apostle Paul writes to the church in Ephesus, *"For by grace you have been saved through faith. And this is not your own doing; it is the gift of God, not a result of works, so that no one may boast"* (Ephesians 2:8, 9).

* * * * *

December 23, 1978 ~ Visiting Grandma

Over the holidays, we visited my grandmother's home in Lincoln, Nebraska. One afternoon, my cousin left his six-year-old son, Lee, for Grandma to watch while he and his wife did some shopping. Grandma told us how much Lee loved to sing songs and listen to her read from the Bible. She had taught him many spiritual things while taking care of him.

Visiting with Lee, I found him serious and open to the things of the Lord. Telling him that I enjoy talking with people about Jesus I said, "Let me show you how Jesus got us out of trouble and how He paid for our sins." Opening the Bible, I explained how sin started in the Garden of Eden. "Because of sin, we can't get to Heaven. The Bible tells us that Jesus died for our sins. We need to tell Him how sorry we are for doing wrong, ask Him to pay for our sins, and invite Him to come into our life." As I explained Scripture, I sensed that he understood.

"Would you like to pray?"

He nodded affirmatively, bowed his head, and prayed a sweet, simple prayer. How happy he was to have his spiritual birthday two days before we celebrate Jesus' birthday.

* * * * *

CHAPTER 5

1979

January 1979 ~ Thanks to a flat tire

One chilly, rainy day we worked in our office. A young woman came in, requesting to use our telephone. Her van had developed a flat tire just outside. She made a call and left. A little later, she returned to call again. This time the Lord led me to talk with Diane; I invited her to wait inside until help arrived.

As we visited, Diane mentioned that she missed her fourteen-month-old son whom she hadn't seen for nine months. Her ex-husband had left, taking their son with him. Since then, she had been unable to locate them. Assuring her that God knew where they were and He could help in her dreadful situation, I then asked if she knew for certain that she was going to Heaven.

Thoughtfully, Diane responded, "No." Opening the Bible, we read together about God's plan for forgiveness of sins. All of us need to ask Christ to pay for our sins. If we ask, He has promised to give us everlasting life.

With a voice soft and tears in her eyes, Diane prayed, asking Jesus Christ to pay for her sins and come into her life. We also prayed that God would help her to locate her son and that she would grow in the things of the Lord. Peter encourages believers to *"grow in the grace and knowledge of our Lord and Savior Jesus Christ"* (2 Peter 3:18). As Diane grows in Christ, He will be with her and meet her needs. Because a flat tire brought her to our doorstep, she could claim God's wonderful promise that she was now His child— He would certainly care for her.

* * * * *

Grandma Hazel & Gloria in Athens Greece.

February 1979 ~ Trip to the Middle East

God gave us the opportunity to lead a group tour to Israel for the Family Altar Broadcast. At the time, I was expecting our second child; she went with us, in hiding, as we traveled to the Netherlands, Italy, Greece, Jordan, Israel, and Egypt. It was a marvelous trip. We were able to see with our own eyes the places we had read about in the Bible. It made Scripture even more alive to us. As we traveled, we secured the service of many local tour guides.

In Egypt we came in contact with a Muslim guide named Muhammad. As we traveled, we visited with him. At one point, he laughed and said, "Christians are so foolish. Jesus Christ did not really die on the Cross at all. Christians are misinformed. God removed Jesus from the Cross; it was Judas who died."

With a prayer in my heart, I softly answered, "There is a major problem with that theory. If I were to stand before the holy God right now, I would be very self-conscious in His presence. With sin and impurities in my life, I would feel unworthy of Heaven. How would you feel, Mohammad, if you were suddenly in God's presence?"

"The same as you," he admitted.

Prayerfully, I continued, explaining that it was important for Jesus Christ to be the one on the Cross, shedding His blood to pay for sins—my sin, your sin. Without that payment, sin comes between us and a holy God. In order for our sin debt to be paid, Christ purposely took the penalty for sin, which is death. When we have received Christ's blood payment to be applied to our sin, then, and only then, can any of us stand before God. We are accepted in Christ, not on our own merits.

He appeared to be thinking about what I had said about the Gospel message. Reaching into my purse, I gave Mohammed the only tract I found, "The Blood on the Door," dealing with the importance of the blood of Christ being shed for sin. Although Mohammed did not accept Christ, I understood why God had led me to bring the tract. This conversation was another of God's appointments.

* * * * *

March 1979 ~ Rescued girls

Returning from Israel, we picked up little Angela who had stayed with my parents in Winchester, Virginia. There we had the privilege of helping with Sunday school and junior church at Shenandoah Valley Baptist Church. When the pastor gave an invitation for the young people to trust Christ, a number came forward for counseling. I spoke with two young girls, Julie and Roslyn, both were experiencing problems at home. They eagerly asked Jesus Christ to forgive their sins, come into their lives, and give them everlasting life. Jesus became their Shepherd.

How wonderful to know that He will take care of them and meet their needs, as the Shepherd Psalm promises, ***"The LORD is my shepherd; I shall not want.*** **He *makes me lie down in green pas-***

tures. He leads me beside still waters. He restores my soul. He leads me in paths of righteousness for his name's sake" (Psalm 23:1-3). Through all our years, we can trust our Shepherd, Jesus Christ, to care for us (John 10).

* * * * *

March 1979 ~ Baptism for two

Cedarloo Baptist Church invited me to speak to the Thursday ladies' group at Bishop's Buffet, a local restaurant in Cedar Falls. Twenty-four ladies gathered for food and fellowship.

"Created Beautiful: Insights from the Bible on God's Design" was the topic. After the meeting, a lady expressed appreciation for my devotional and requested prayer for herself and her husband, Daryl. Lei had looked for an apartment that morning, intending to leave her husband. But while listening to the message at the ladies' group, Lei had decided to invite Christ into her life to be her Savior. She had renewed desire to stay with her husband, "for better or for worse," she explained, as she had promised in her wedding vows.

Later that week, Lei contacted me by telephone and asked about being baptized. Encouraging her to follow the Lord in believer's baptism, I suggested that she call her pastor. She made plans with Pastor Dave Holm to be baptized the next Sunday evening. That Sunday, however, her husband forbade her to go to church. Lei later shared her sentiments, "It was hard for me to be nice to him that day because he knew how much that meant to me."

A few days later, when her pastor visited, Daryl commented that his wife was different. Since the Thursday Bible study, Lei had demonstrated a new peace; he also wanted to trust Christ. The following Sunday, the couple was baptized together. The power of God allowed a ladies' Bible study to facilitate their salvation. How glad I am that Lei and Daryl allowed God to change their lives and their marriage.

* * * * *

Beginning the work in Tama, Iowa.

April 1979 ~ New church

James became ill, unable to leave the house for a period of time. We needed to move the Family Altar Broadcast recording studio into our home; there James could continue recording and do other work. When he finally felt better, we continued with scheduled plans for a trip to Israel.

Upon returning home, the reality of our home office became overwhelming—it was crowded. Each room served a dual function, depending on the time, office hours or home time. Our bedroom was the recording studio; Angela's bedroom, the secretary's room; our living room, the reception area; and the kitchen, our work area for folding and assembling monthly newsletters. Added to those pressures was the nearing arrival of our second child. We deeply appreciated the help of our secretary. We could not have handled the responsibilities without her.

During this time, Bob Mason asked us to start a Gospel-preaching church which we prayerfully considered. James and I agreed that we could commit part of each week to starting a church in Tama, Iowa;

the remainder of the week we would continue to spend in Waterloo with the FAB ministry. We bought a "fixer-up" house in Tama and started the Tabernacle Baptist Church in a building on Main Street. God had hungry hearts waiting, and we saw a rich harvest of souls.

* * * * *

April 8, 1979 ~ Crumbled tract

Our friend from Des Moines, Geneva Nell, sent us this encouraging little note: "A young man attending our church found a tract that you had passed out at the Iowa State Fair, all crumpled up and thrown away. Since it looked like a check, he picked it up. After he had unfolded and read that tract, he trusted Christ as his personal Savior." One man's trash is another man's treasure.

* * * * *

April 1979 ~ Second film showing

Attending our church in Tama, a family asked us to suggest a film for them to show in Toledo, Iowa, where they lived. James recommended *The Burning Hell*. They requested that James introduce the film and at the end, give an invitation for individuals to trust Christ.

The film was spiritually challenging. When the invitation was given, five youngsters came forward, desiring to become Christians. I had the privilege of talking with a ten-year-old girl and her seven-year-old brother; someone else talked with three other boys.

Suzy's prayer was definite and touching; her brother's prayer was indefinite and vague. As we talked, it was clear that Suzy truly had just accepted Jesus as her Savior. Her seven-year-old brother, however, had not that evening fully understood the Gospel message, but wanted to do what his sister was doing.

Afterwards, I suggested that they tell their parents about having received Christ into their hearts. Suzy easily did so; her younger brother seemed shy and uneasy. I assured him, "That's all right. You should think about it some more and ask questions and trust Jesus later. But be sure you do ask Jesus to save you because it is important." He smiled, relieved that he didn't have to deal with it all, right then. The parents happily promised to follow up with their son and to help their daughter to grow in the things of the Lord.

Jesus' instruction, by example, shows us how important it is to bring children to Christ. The Great Teacher said to His disciples, ***"Let the children come to me; do not hinder them, for to such belongs the kingdom of God.*** (Mark 10:14b)

* * * * *

May 1979 ~ Child's example

We had counseled with twelve-year-old Tracy who became a Christian. Now he desired to follow the Lord's command to be baptized. Wishing to talk with his mother about his desire to be baptized at the Tama church, James and I went to their home. His mother willingly gave her permission.

As we visited, I broached the subject of her salvation. "Dee, do you know for sure you're going to Heaven when you die?"

"No," she answered thoughtfully.

"Would you like to have a Bible study?"

"Yes," she nodded.

Together, we read Scriptures explaining the origin of sin (Genesis 3), the dilemma of not being able to go to Heaven because of sin (John 3), and Christ's payment for that sin (Romans 6:23).

Finally, Dee exclaimed, "It seems so clear to me now." That evening, she asked Christ to come into her life, forgive her sins, and give her everlasting life.

* * * * *

June 1979 ~ Substitute teaching

When a Sunday school teacher was unable to teach, I agreed to substitute. There were six young people, ages nine through eleven, that morning. We began class with prayer, asking God to teach us something from the Bible that would help us live for Him.

The young people participated beautifully. When I asked how many could remember asking Jesus to be their Savior, only one boy responded affirmatively. Speaking to the class, I said, "If you do not remember such an occasion, perhaps you have not yet asked God to save you. How many of you would like to ask Christ to come into your life and forgive your sins?"

Four hands went up.

"If you want me to show you from the Bible how to have Jesus forgive your sins and get you out of the trouble caused back in the Garden of Eden, you're welcome to stay here after class."

Two boys, Jeff and John, stayed behind. We read together from the Gospel of John the wonderful promise, ***"But to all who did receive him, who believed in his name, he gave the right to become children of God, who were born, not of blood nor of the will of the flesh nor of the will of man, but of God"*** (John 1:12-13). One at a time, each boy prayed and became a child of God. I was thankful for the privilege of substitute teaching.

* * * * *

July 1979 ~ Last in the family

When Eddie's mother and sister trusted Christ at the kitchen table, fifteen-year-old Eddie was in and out, but not interested. Later, when his dad trusted Christ in the living room, Eddie was gone. When his youngest brother trusted Christ at church, Eddie was not present. When his youngest sister trusted Christ in the living room, Eddie listened from a distance, but said nothing.

Regularly stopping to pick up any family members who wanted to go with us to the Tama church, James and I were happy when one Sunday, Eddie was dressed and ready to go. After the services, I asked Eddie if he was ready to ask Jesus Christ to be his Savior.

"Yes," he answered, "I would like that."

James prayed with him, and we all rejoiced when Eddie excitedly told me that now Jesus Christ was his Savior, too.

The Scripture promises that entire families can become Christians: *"Believe in the Lord Jesus, and you will be saved, you and your household"* (Acts 16:31). The refrain of a century-old Gospel song says,

*Will the circle be unbroken
By and by, by and by?
In a better home awaiting
In the sky, in the sky?*
(Habershon/Gabriel)

* * * * *

August 1979 ~ Drinking everlasting water

At the Central Iowa Fair in Marshalltown, we met Larry who worked nearby in a booth of his own, selling water conditioning supplies. Several times we felt impressed by the Lord to talk with Larry. An agnostic, Larry had known people during college who had been "Jesus Freaks," but never felt that kind of life would work for him.

Day after day, we talked about the Scripture with Larry. The Holy Spirit was giving him a hunger for "truth." One day when traffic was slow, I decided to visit Larry in his sales booth. As we talked, he finally smiled and said, "I think I'm going to do it." Bowing his head, he prayed aloud, inviting Christ to be his Savior. A peace came over his countenance. "It is real" was his response.

The following week, James and I decided to visit Larry at his home. His wife and nineteen-month-old son were home; Larry was not. Pleased to see us, Diane invited us to come in. Larry had told her about talking with us at the fair. I asked about her reaction to her husband's trusting Christ.

"I couldn't believe it," she exclaimed. "It's like being married to a different man. His attitude has changed—we get along so much better now. We didn't even get married in a church because Larry didn't believe in God."

"Would you like me to show you what we shared with Larry?"

"Yes," she said, "please do." That night Diane bowed her head, also receiving Christ as her personal Savior. Both Diane and Larry had the same Savior.

The water conditioning salesman and his wife drank of the water of everlasting life, as Jesus told the woman of Samaria: *"Whoever drinks of the water that I will give him will never be thirsty forever. The water that I will give him will become in him a spring of water welling up to eternal life."* (John 4:14).

* * * * *

Several converts at the Fair.

September 1979 ~ Ripple effect

At the National Cattle Congress, we had a table full of literature, a colorful background on the back wall to greet passers-by, and a circle of chairs for people who wished to sit down. There we read the Bible with those interested in knowing for certain that they were going to Heaven.

To thousands of those passers-by, Family Altar Broadcast staff and volunteers handed out tracts and asked questions like "Do you know if you are going to Heaven when you die?" We received a variety of responses.

Two sixteen-year-old girls passed our booth. I engaged them in a conversation. Laurie said she knew that she was going to Heaven because she was "born again"; her friend, Dee, was uncertain. When I asked Dee if she wanted to make certain that she was saved, Laurie encouraged Dee, "Go on, you should."

Both girls came in and sat down. Taking the Bible, I explained how we can be born into the family of God. Dee listened to God's Word carefully, and then prayed, trusting Christ as her Savior. In that instant, the girls became more than friends: according to the Gospel of John, they became sisters in Christ (John 1:12). With joy in their hearts, they thanked us for talking with them.

Dee returned later that day with another friend; she wanted Tammy to accept the Lord, too. Tammy listened and prayed, receiving Christ as Savior. What a joy to see one Christian friend lead another to the foot of the Cross, and that friend then bringing another lost soul to the same redeeming place. The Bible records that the Apostle Peter was brought to Jesus Christ by his own brother: *"One of the two who heard John speak and followed Jesus was Andrew, Simon Peter's brother. He first found his own brother Simon and said to him, 'We have found the Messiah.' He brought him to Jesus"* (John 1:40-42). Later Peter led many to the "Messiah," Christ.

* * * * *

October 1979 ~ From emptiness to joy

Bob invited Howard to attend the Sunday service at our church in Tama. Though quite Howard was quite friendly, he nervously backed away each time the things of the Lord were mentioned.

After a particularly difficult time in Howard's life, he and Bob had a long talk. The next morning, Howard was in church. The instant James gave the invitation, Howard came down the aisle. I invited him to kneel at the platform and accept Jesus Christ as his personal Savior. Howard had already made up his mind. He was ready to leave his old life, including alcohol, for a new life of service for Christ.

Desiring to follow Scripture, Howard requested baptism at the nearby lake, taking a public stand that he wanted to follow the Lord. Howard's zeal reminded James and me of the Ethiopian's desire, following his salvation, to be obedient in baptism:

Then Philip opened his mouth, and beginning with this Scripture he told him [Ethiopian] *the good news about Jesus. And as they were going along the road they came to some water, and the eunuch said, "See, here is water! What prevents me from being baptized?" And he commanded the chariot to stop, and they both went down into the water, Philip and the eunuch, and he baptized him.* (Acts 8:35-38)

* * * * *

October 1979 ~ Grace finds God

At the Nebraska State Fair in Lincoln, we sponsored a soul-winning booth. Down the hall, two ladies sold handmade crafts. When one of the ladies, Grace, walked by our booth, James asked if she knew that she was going to Heaven. Responding that she did not, James invited her to spend a few minutes in our booth, and learn more. I showed Grace from the Bible that we can know for certain our final destination—Heaven or Hell.

We read about God's wonderful provision for eternal life in Heaven through the blood of Jesus Christ. He has already paid for our sins and wants to give us everlasting life. How happy she was to hear the Good News. She prayed, claiming Christ as her Savior. For the next eleven days of the fair, whenever Grace passed our booth, she had a radiant smile for us.

* * * * *

During the Nebraska State Fair, I was nearing the end of my second pregnancy. On Monday, October 20, Jessica was born, making us a family of four.

Happy sister Angela & baby Jessica.

CHAPTER 6

1980-1981

February 1980 ~ Skeptical young woman

Visiting homes in the neighborhood, I invited people to join us at church. In one home, I met Kim and her friend. Kim had been studying with the Jehovah Witnesses, but recently had decided to leave their study group. I sensed that she was searching for something that I had found, a personal relationship with Jesus Christ.

When I asked if she would like to see in the Bible how God says we can get to Heaven,

Kim skeptically answered, "First, I'd like to know if there is something you believe that I should know about up front, instead of later?"

Assuring Kim that I was not a member of a cult, I said that we should try to understand what the Bible says, in context, rather than trying to prove what we want it to say. "I want to know what God meant when He wrote the verses. What the Bible says, I believe. And I believe that we need to ask God to be our Teacher, and then read the Book humbly, seeking to know the truth."

She agreed.

Opening my Bible to John 3:1-21; we read together Jesus' instructions that we need to be born again. Soon Kim was praying, trusting Jesus Christ to pay for her sins.

* * * * *

April 1980 ~ Special reunion

One afternoon James and I, with our two young daughters, visited a lady who recently had been widowed. She and her husband had known the Lord; now she was determined to get back into the habit of attending church. Her eleven-year-old granddaughter, Gina, was staying with her, keeping her grandmother company.

As Gina sat quietly beside her grandmother, I felt burdened to ask Gina if she had asked Jesus to be her Savior yet.

"No, not yet," she replied seriously.

"You'd like to, wouldn't you?"

"Yes, I would," she replied.

"Why don't you come over here by me," I offered, "and I'll show you how the Bible tells us that we need to trust Jesus Christ to pay for our sins."

Carefully, I explained that God's program of salvation is for everyone. Reading together in the book of Romans, we saw God's plan for saving us: ***"Sin came into the world through one man [Adam], and death through sin, and so death spread to all men because all sinned"*** (Romans 5:12); we turned the page to another verse, ***"The wages of sin is death, but the free gift of God is eternal life in Christ Jesus our Lord"*** (Romans 6:23).

Gina bowed her head and opened her heart, trusting Jesus Christ to be her Savior. How happy she and her grandmother were that she, too, would be reunited one day with her grandfather in Heaven.

* * * * *

May 1980 ~ Praise or panic

The telephone rang. A young man identified himself as Jimmy Jo. He asked for a listening ear. Having located the number for Family Altar Broadcast in the telephone directory, he requested prayer that God would help him "push the praise button instead of the panic button." Jimmy Jo was handicapped and recovering from drug abuse. As a part-time student at the University of Northern Iowa, Jimmy Jo was trying to "put things together" again. He talked much about politics and a coming world government.

On the telephone, we talked about how people get to Heaven by believing on the Lord and trusting Jesus Christ to apply His blood payment to their sins. We read the promise, as well as the clear warning in the Gospel of John: *"Whoever believes in the Son has eternal life; whoever does not obey the Son shall not see life, but the wrath of God remains on him"* (John 3:36). Individuals can be saved from God's wrath for man's not believing on the work of the Son on the Cross. Jimmy Jo suddenly began to pray, trusting Jesus Christ and accepting Christ's blood as payment for his sins. I asked if he had ever prayed that prayer before.

"No, not like this," he replied.

To help him become better equipped for growth in his Christian life, I gave him several Bible references, many included in Chapter 1 of this book. Suggesting that Jimmy Jo jot down the references, I believed that he needed to look them up later. It was a special blessing to visit with someone over the telephone and direct him to God, preparing him for his entrance into eternity. Jimmy Jo praised God that his future was secure in God's hands.

* * * * *

June 1980 ~ Spiritual baby

An opportunity arose to hold Bible studies at the Allen Hospital student nurses' dormitory. Lynn decided to attend because of the inspiring life-style of her friend, who already attended the study. Lynn sought answers to her own spiritual questions.

When I explained God's provision for sin by Jesus' death on the Cross, and the wonderful gift of everlasting life that He offers to all, Lynn understood God's offer, and was ready to accept Christ as her personal Savior. In the nurses' dormitory, Lynn called on Jesus Christ to be her Savior. That evening, Lynn began a new life in Christ—a new spiritual baby was born.

* * * * *

September 1980 ~ God blessing His work

Picture with me the fun and excitement of going to a fair. Each summer, tens of thousands of people attend fairs all over the country. Entertainment, games, food, cotton candy—so much to see and do. Attendees can learn: how to cut and dry food, redecorate their homes and how to get to Heaven. Wait a minute—did I say, "How to get to Heaven"? Yes.

At the Family Altar Broadcast booth, our goal was presenting Christ to the thousands of people who walked by, as well as encouraging Christians to grow in their spiritual lives. We were following Christ's example: Jesus went where the people were and let them know that He cared about them. Inviting those interested to read with us in the Bible, many learned how they could know for certain that they would go to Heaven. We shared Bible verses, precious promises for all who believe: *"This is the testimony that God gave us eternal life, and this life is in his Son. Whoever has the Son has life; whoever does not have the Son of God does not have life. I write these things to you who believe in the name of the Son of God that you may know that you have eternal life"* (1 John 5:11-13). What a wonderful promise to those who ask God for the faith to believe His truth of salvation.

Almost all interested in listening to Jesus' clear and simple explanation of how to get to Heaven, decided at that time to trust Christ as their Savior. It was beautiful to see individuals bow their heads in the hubbub of fair life and hear their voices rise to Heaven, asking Jesus to forgive their sins and give them everlasting life.

* *

Two teen-agers, Shari and Karen, trusted Christ as their Savior. Later the same day, they brought Shari's nine-year-old brother, Mike. Wishing to do what the girls had done, he also trusted Jesus Christ as Savior.

* *

Brenda was walking a friend's puppy on a leash when we invited her to come into our booth. She was visiting from Indiana. We

God's Appointment

explained the plan of salvation to her, including the promise that *"in him [Christ] we have redemption through his blood, the forgiveness of our trespasses, according to the riches of his grace"* (Ephesians 1:7). Brenda asked Jesus to be her Savior.

* *

A family came by—Leonard and Anita; their daughter Cheri, age seven; Lisa, five; and a three-year-old. From our conversation, we sensed that they were spiritually hungry. James talked to Leonard, while I talked with Anita and Cheri. All three asked Jesus Christ to be their Savior. Since the two younger ones did not understand the Gospel yet, we encouraged the parents to start family devotions, so that they could teach their family about the Lord.

* *

A young married couple, Dave and Diane, from Waterloo, just back from their honeymoon asked Christ to be their Savior.

* *

A grandmother stopped. When I asked if she knew that she would go to Heaven when she died, she answered, "Yes."

"Wonderful." I replied, "I wish everyone coming past here could say the same." Her grandson Brian was by her side. "How about your grandson?" When she didn't know, I turned to Brian. "How about it, are you going to Heaven when you die?"

He replied, "I hope so."

With his grandmother's approval, I invited him to come into the booth and showed him from God's Word, how he could know *for certain* that he was going to Heaven. While his grandmother watched and prayed, Brian accepted Christ as his Savior.

* *

Jill stopped and very carefully listened to the plan of salvation; I believe she understood. We were just getting ready to pray when her parents came; she needed to come immediately. My heart ached as I saw Jill leave, but she turned and smiled, "On the way home, I will ask Jesus to be my Savior." My prayer is that she did. What a blessing that God hears our prayers from every corner of the globe—even in a quiet, dark corner anywhere.

* *

Eddie, eleven, and his friend Eric, twelve, both from Des Moines, enjoyed the fair together. When my husband talked with them, Eddie explained that he was Jewish—"It's not for me."

James quickly explained, "Oh, yes, God's gift of salvation is for Jews, too. If you want to come into this booth, my wife will show you how to ask Christ to be your Savior."

* *

Both Eric and Eddie sat down. After I had explained God's simple plan for all of us to be saved, they bowed their heads and trusted Jesus Christ. Eddie recognized Christ as his Messiah and Lord, cherishing the verse from the Old Testament prophet, *"All we like sheep have gone astray; we have turned every one to his own way; and the LORD has laid on him the iniquity of us all"* (Isaiah 53:6).

* *

Age fifteen, Brian and a friend were enjoying a skate-board race down the aisle. The boys from Des Moines stopped just beyond our booth. When I offered to show them how to get to Heaven when they died, Brian was interested; his friend scoffed. As his friend stood waiting, Brian sat down, listened, and then asked Christ to be his Savior. When they left the booth, one was a new child of God and the other, still a child of Satan. Throughout the rest of the fair, Brian tried to convince his friend to return to our booth. It was obvious that the friend was under conviction, but he never did come and talk with us. My prayer is that one day he will come to know Christ as his Savior.

* *

Another young man, whose father was sick and in the hospital, was concerned about life and death. Rick wanted to be prepared for the time that he himself would face death. After trusting the Lord, he inquired about how to tell his father about Christ. We shared some helpful literature and prayed with him for his father's salvation.

* *

The Lord blessed His work. In the summer of 1975, we saw over 50 souls profess to trust Christ as their personal Savior; in 1976, over 100; in 1977, about 150; in 1978, over 260; in 1979, over 250; and in 1980, over 250. Others who heard the Gospel wanted to wait and think more about Jesus' offer of eternal life. We distributed lots of literature for people to read later.

Each year, we scheduled between one to five fairs, each lasting from three to eleven days. For professions of salvation, we recorded the person's name and address so that we could send them helpful literature. Additionally, we attempted to contact a fundamental, Bible-believing, soul-winning church in their area, requesting that those churches encourage the new believers to become involved in church activities, helping them to grow in their new Christian lives.

Jesus desires all of us believers to become good disciples, as He clearly expressed in the Great Commission: ***"Go therefore and make disciples of all nations, baptizing them in the name of the Father and of the Son and of the Holy Spirit, teaching them to observe all that I have commanded you. And behold, I am with you always, to the end of the age"*** (Matthew 28:19, 20). The role of older believers in helping new believers to learn "all" that God has "commanded" is an important responsibility.

*   *   *   *   *

Visiting Aunt Donna in Houston, Texas.

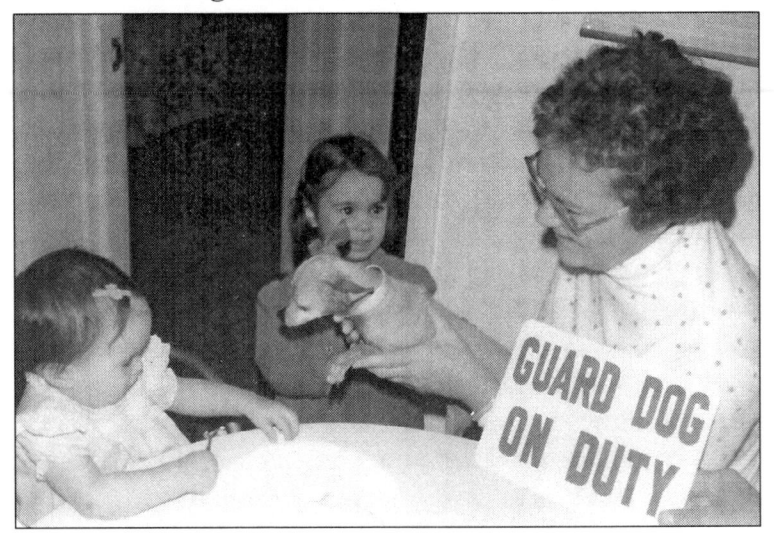

October 21, 1980 ~ Spiritual birthday for two

In the fall, we returned to working full-time at Family Altar Broadcast, having finished our work with the Tama church. We also drove Grandmother Hazel to Texas so that she could live with my Aunt Donna in Houston.

When we arrived, Aunt Donna was entertaining a friend who was visiting overnight while her husband was away on business. Cookie was friendly and talkative. As we visited, I mentioned that James was a radio preacher. Both of us enjoyed telling people that Jesus taught how we can get to Heaven when we die. Cookie was interested.

There in the guest room, I opened the Bible to John and began explaining Jesus' wonderful plan of salvation. First, we need to reestablish the relationship with God that Adam and Eve lost when they sinned. Cookie had many concerns—a nervous breakdown, using the Lord's name in vain, cigarette smoking, and living in a common-law marriage. I explained that it was neither so much what we did, nor did not do that determines our eternity. All of us mortals need deliverance from the Devil's power.

"We are *all* sinners, including me," I repeated. "No one deserves or is good enough to enter Heaven." The Bible clearly declares, **"For by grace you have been saved through faith. And this is not your own doing; it is the gift of God, not a result of works, so that no one may boast"** (Ephesians 2:8, 9). Heaven is not earned. Eternal life in Heaven is a free gift from Jesus Christ. He paid the price for us, and all we need to do is accept that gift. We sin because we are sinners. Jesus died for all our sins, and He wanted her to receive Him as Lord.

It was supper time. When I asked if she would like to resume the visit later, Cookie quickly said, "Yes, of course. This is really interesting. I'm so glad you're sharing it with me."

After supper, I continued showing Cookie in the Bible that God wanted her to be His daughter, born into His family: **"But to all who did receive him, who believed in his name, he gave the right to become children of God"** (John 1:12). When I asked if she would like to receive Jesus as her Savior, she replied that she would.

First, I prayed, and then she prayed, pouring out her heart, "Yes, Jesus, I do want to trust you. I want you to apply your blood to pay for my sins and give me everlasting life."

Happily we had traveled with an extra Bible which I gave to Cookie, writing her name and spiritual birthday on the front page.

Concerned about her husband Waldo, Cookie asked if I would also tell him about the Lord. When Waldo arrived, I began talking with him about spiritual matters. Receptive to the Gospel, he also prayed, accepting Christ into his heart. Husband and wife were born again on the same day, hours apart. God's appointments—what a blessing!

* * * * *

November 1980 ~ Younger leading the older

James was invited by Faith Baptist Church of Belle Plaine, Iowa to fill the pulpit. We met a warm and friendly congregation of believers. For the next two months, while the church was between pastors, we enjoyed the Christian fellowship of those fine people. Gerry, Marge, and their teenage son, James, often invited us to stay in their home between the morning and evening services. One day when I shared our enthusiasm about soul winning, we discovered that they also desired to see people come to Christ.

They were especially concerned that Marge's parents accept Christ as Savior, and were thankful that we would partner in prayer for them. When they asked advice about witnessing to relatives, I mentioned that parents often do not appreciate when their children try to tell them something. Grandchildren often find a soft spot in hearts; people often listen to their grandchildren.

The following week, when young James visited his grandparents, he expressed concern that they might not be ready to go to Heaven. At first, they were indignant. "We're just as good as you are. Do not worry, we will go to Heaven," was their response. When James opened his Bible, they both listened. He read from the Gospel of John, which plainly states the necessity for the new birth, ***"Truly, truly, I say to you, unless one is born again he cannot see the***

kingdom of God" (John 3:3). After reading together a number of other verses, the grandparents understood that James was talking about a new birth which they had never received. They humbly prayed for God's forgiveness of sins and asked Christ to save them. Their grandson, through the power of the Holy Spirit, had reached their hearts.

The family reached other souls for Christ. Praise the Lord for people who become excited about soul winning.

* * * * *

Family Altar Broadcast sponsored an Israel trip.

In February, 1981, we sponsored a trip to Israel through Family Altar Broadcast. Once again, we enjoyed walking where Jesus walked and seeing firsthand the location of many Biblical accounts. On this second trip, I was again expecting; our third daughter traveled with us, in hiding.

May 7, 1981 ~ Kristi's decision

One week, while I substitute taught a Sunday school class, we talked about God's sending Philip to speak with the Ethiopian eunuch. We read together how Philip obeyed God's leading, *"the Spirit said to Philip, 'Go over and join this chariot'"* (Acts 8:29); then Philip was able to teach the eunuch how to trust Jesus as his Savior. When I asked the children if they had ever trusted Jesus Christ as had the eunuch, only three replied, "Yes." I suggested to those who could not say "yes," that they needed to decide soon.

Six-year-old Kristi said that she wanted to do it, right then. After I had explained the reason that Christ had to die, Kristi bowed her head and prayed, "Jesus, I trust you to put your blood on my sins so that I can go to Heaven."

Following the examples that Scripture gives us, like Philip and the Ethiopian eunuch, provides a good foundation for teaching others.

* * * * *

June 5, 1981 ~ In the garden

During breakfast on a Friday morning, we heard a quiet knock. Sherry, a six-year-old neighbor, worried that she had missed going with us to VBS.

Smiling, I assured her, "No, Sherry, Vacation Bible School starts Monday. We'll come pick you up at your house—not tomorrow or the next day, but the next."

She paused. "May I wait for Angela to come out and play?"

While we finished breakfast, Sherry waited, then joined us for family devotions and eagerly talked about church.

"People who go to church are happy, aren't they?"

"It's not just that people go to church—but yes, Sherry, people who have Jesus in their hearts are happy because they are going to Heaven."

Sherry fingered our piano while I kissed James good-bye as he left for the office. Then Sherry and my two girls went outside to play. While I pulled weeds from the onions in our garden, Sherry came over to me with more questions.

There in the garden, I explained that she was a sinner, just like me—and everyone else in the world; she needed Jesus to help her because He has paid for our sins. If she would trust Him to forgive her sins, she would live in Heaven with Him when she died. After a few more questions, she said she would do that, at church. Explaining that she didn't have to wait until church time, I invited her to pray right there, beside our garden. Bowing her head, Sherry trusted Christ. Afterwards, she had many questions and shared many of her thoughts.

Children attract other children. My prayer was that, when neighborhood young people came to our house, they would find more than just a good time playing with our girls.

* * * * *

August 5, 1981 ~ Young people searching

We attended the Jones County Fair in Monticello, Iowa on August 5-7. Pastor Dick Marscau and his people from Bible Community Church in Central City had scheduled a booth for Family Altar Broadcast and invited us to come and talk with people attending the fair.

It was a blessing to work with Pastor Marscau and his congregation. At the fair, we met many people, including Christians in every stage of growth. Some people were not interested in anything that had to do with God. We met many who hoped that they were on their way to Heaven and many who just did not want to talk about spiritual things.

Most heart-warming were conversations with over fifty teenagers and pre-teens. One or two at a time, they listened to what the Bible says about God's pathway to Heaven and prayed, trusting Christ to be their Savior. God brought these young people into our booth whose hearts were already prepared, hungry for answers about how to get to Heaven. Those teenagers listened intently and marveled at the way Jesus Christ, the Son of God, displayed the greatest love ever known, died to pay for their sin and to give them everlasting life. With people continuously walking by, we heard simple, earnest prayers in that booth, individuals unashamedly inviting Jesus into their hearts.

What a joy to witness their gratitude and hear them say, "Thanks for being here at the fair to share this wonderful news with us." Throughout each day, we saw flashes of warm smiles as the young people passed again by the booth. Many times, young people who only hours before had trusted Christ, returned with friends, asking us to tell them the Good News we had shared with them earlier.

* * * * *

August 28, 1981 ~ Needing more prayer

The Nebraska State Fair in Lincoln was unique. Booths around us were staffed with many Christians. When we dealt with people about their salvation, Christians around us joined in prayer rejoicing with us when a decision was made.

Still, we felt hardness in the hearts of people attending the fair, greater than at any other fair. The week was a reminder to us of the importance of prayer ahead of time, necessary to prepare hearts for outreach. Twelve individuals prayed, asking Christ to forgive their sins and be their Savior.

One evening, since two young women were helping at the booth, James and I decided to leave an hour early. Expecting our third child, I was feeling the strain of standing too long. Passing displays we walked toward the car, we stopped to visit a booth on solar energy. Since the salesman, Wilber in his late fifties, seemed open to talking, I shared with him how he could know that he was going to Heaven. As the crowd at the fair ebbed and flowed around us, Wilber bowed his head, trusting Christ.

When we prepared to leave he said, "Wait a minute." Fishing two one-dollar bills from his billfold, he said, "Let me give you a little something for sharing the Bible with me." The gift was an expression of his appreciation.

* * * * *

1981 we became a family of five.

On October 12, 1981, God blessed us with our third daughter. We named her Victoria Joy.

CHAPTER 7

1982

January 1982 ~ Life of earnest service

On January 4, 1982, Reverend Sarge Lusthoff announced to the congregation at Calvary Bible Church of Washburn that because of his health, he was retiring as pastor. That kindly saint ended a ministry of shepherding his flock for forty-five years.

In the early 1930s, Sarge and Trina Lusthoff attended an evangelistic meeting at Burton Avenue Baptist Church in Waterloo where Anton Cedarholm, founder of the Family Altar Broadcast, ministered. There Sarge and Trina trusted Christ as their Savior, beginning a life of earnest service for their Lord. Saved under the ministry of the FAB's founders, Pastor Sarge Lusthoff had a special place in his heart for the broadcast ministry that James and I were continuing and often was an encouragement to us

Pastor Lusthoff was highly respected as an active soul winner. Wherever Sarge went: hospital, grocery store, or in homes, hungry souls found Christ. We were drawn to his evangelistic zeal and served at Calvary Bible Church under Sarge's pastoral care. James frequently had filled the pulpit for Sarge. When he requested that James be called as the next pastor of the church, James accepted, adding pastoral duties of the church to his FAB ministry.

* * * * *

February 1982 ~ "Will they laugh?"

While visiting a young lady from the church hospitalized for foot surgery, James and I met Debbie, her roommate. Debbie was friendly and open to our conversation. As James continued speaking to our parishioner, I went over to Debbie's bed to ask if she knew whether or not she would go to Heaven.

"I hope so" was her reply.

"Yes, Debbie, that is where we would want to go, isn't it? I don't like the other place. But how do we get there?"

"I don't know," she responded.

Sitting next to her bed so that she could read along with me, I opened the Bible, reading Jesus' conversation with Nicodemus about how to get to Heaven (See John 3:1-21). When she understood that Christ had died to make possible her getting to Heaven, she talked to God and received Christ as her Savior. Then I asked her to share with others in the room what she had just done.

"But they will laugh at me," she said.

Overhearing her concern, James promised, "No, we won't. What did you do?"

"I asked Jesus to be my Savior."

"And did He?"

"Yes," she smiled, "He did."

Because Debbie didn't have a Bible there in the hospital, we promised to bring her one. Returning the next day, we rejoiced to see that Debbie had a good understanding of her decision for Christ the day before and was interested in studying the Bible with us. Hallelujah, one more entered Christ's fold. Jesus said, *"I am the door. If anyone enters by me, he will be saved and will go in and out and find pasture"* (John 10:9). The Shepherd rejoices over every sheep safely in His fold.

* * * * *

March 1982 ~ Persistence paid off

While driving on a residential street in Washburn, we saw several children playing. James stopped the car so that I could ask the children if they would like to come with us to Sunday school.

Shyly, they nodded.

"Where do you live?" we asked.

They pointed to two homes nearby. Jotting down their names, we promised to ask their parents for permission. Knocking at the first door, James asked the father. A negative response met us there.

"No, we have our own church."

At the second home, the mother answered. She was busy and could not talk, but we could come back another time.

The following week we again found her too busy. On our third attempt, however, persistence paid off. With a smile, she said that she would ask her husband.

When I later telephoned them, she explained that her husband thought it would be all right, but that they were having company from out of town Saturday. Their daughter Candy might be too tired Sunday morning. I promised to stop in the morning to see if she could go—if that would be okay.

Sunday morning, I stopped. Candy would not be going, her mother said. So, I promised to return in a week. As I pulled into the driveway the following Sunday, out of the house popped Candy, all smiles and dressed prettily for church.

After introducing her to the Sunday school teacher, I invited Candy to sit with our family during church if she would like. She listened carefully as James preached, joined in the singing and followed with me, reading Scripture. At the close of the message, when James gave the invitation, I asked Candy if she knew she was going to Heaven. She shook her head, "No." When I suggested that she go forward for counseling, she was too shy. After the service, when I asked her if she would like me to show her in the Bible how to get to Heaven, she nodded, very interested. Handing four-month-old Victoria to a friend, I took Candy to the pastor's office. After we had read Scripture together, she trusted Christ as her Savior.

Candy eagerly told several of the church ladies and James that she had trusted Jesus. Giving her a New Testament to keep and read, I took her home, promising to stop again the next Sunday. The following week, nine-year-old Candy was ready, waiting to go to Sunday school and church and excitedly participated in her first communion service. The Sunday after that, Candy said her brothers wanted to come along. Our prayer was for the whole family to come to Christ. God can use children for His honor and glory and our persistence to help bring individuals to the Lord.

* * * * *

April 1982 ~ Shared connection

A father and two daughters from out of town visited our Washburn church. Years before as a young lad, he had attended the church. After the service, James spoke with the three of them. Having noticed that the two girls seemed under conviction while he was preaching, James encouraged me to talk with them. I asked the girls if they would like to talk with me about knowing for sure if they were prepared for Heaven; the girls, ages ten and eight, went with me to a quiet room where both received Christ as their Savior. Both girls eagerly told their father and James about their newfound relationship in Christ.

Tears came to their father's eyes. "There is something special about this church," he said: "I was saved here many years ago; and now both my girls have trusted Christ here, too."

* * * * *

May 23, 1982 ~ Offer not refused

We came in contact with a couple from North Carolina who had eleven children. They were friendly and I enjoyed their Southern drawl.

While visiting in their home, James and I offered to bring any interested family members to church. The next Sunday morning, three of the children—ages eight, nine, and ten—came with us. On the way home, I talked with them about Jesus' sacrificial payment for sin and how important it was for us all to accept His blood as payment for sin. Explaining that this free gift of salvation is the only way that we can experience eternal life in Heaven with Christ Jesus our Lord, I was happy to see the conversation sparking their interest. They asked many questions about how a person can become qualified to get to Heaven, reflecting considerable thought about eternity. They listened intently as I showed them Scripture passages answering their questions.

As James drove, all three young people bowed their heads and accepted Jesus' offer to pay for their sins, giving them everlasting life. When we arrived at their home, they were rejoicing in their new relationship with God, illustrating again the truth that the Apostle Paul wrote, *"For everyone who calls on the name of the Lord will be saved"* (Romans 10:13). They did not refuse God's offer of salvation.

* * * * *

June 1982 ~ Wedding bells

A young couple stopped to visit with us about their upcoming marriage. A sweet and somewhat shy couple, they were getting ready to make one of the most important decisions of their lives. Casey was certain that he had trusted Christ as his Savior as a young man; Dianne was religious, but did not understand what we meant by "knowing for certain that they were on their way to Heaven," or being "born again."

Diane and I went to a separate room where we could talk privately. There I showed Dianne what Jesus said about being born again:

"Truly, truly, I say to you, unless one is born again he cannot see the kingdom of God." Nicodemus said to him, "How can a man be born when he is old? Can he enter a second time into his mother's womb and be born?" Jesus answered, "Truly, truly, I say to you, unless one is born of water and the Spirit, he cannot enter the kingdom of God. That which is born of the flesh is

flesh, and that which is born of the Spirit is spirit. Do not marvel that I said to you, 'You must be born again.'" (John 3:3-7)

Writing to believers, Peter also spoke of that new birth in Christ that all may receive, *"You have been born again, not of perishable seed but of imperishable, through the living and abiding word of God"* (1 Peter 1:23). We also looked at John 1:1, where the Apostle identified Jesus as "the Word."

Dianne listened. When she understood the work of Christ and His promises, in simple faith she received Jesus as her Savior. Returning to Casey and James, Dianne shared with them that she had just received Jesus as her Savior. Casey was delighted. When they left, they thanked us. A few weeks later there was a happy day when we saw them exchange vows. James and I rejoiced that they both knew the Lord and would be "yoked" in Christ from the beginning of their marriage as Scripture commands: *"Do not be unequally yoked with unbelievers. For what partnership has righteousness with lawlessness? Or what fellowship has light with darkness"* (1 Corinthians 6:14). When problems come, and they do for all, Casey and Diane can pray together—what a blessing.

*   *   *   *   *

Teaching at Vacation Bible School, 1982

June 1982 ~ Time for VBS

When school lets out for the summer, children naturally look for interesting activities. Every year at Washburn, we planned a special week to reach children for Christ. With singing, games, crafts, missionary stories, Bible lessons and delicious snacks, Vacation Bible School always added up to a spiritual blessing and challenge for young people. This year, as every year, decisions were made for salvation and Christian growth. Praise the Lord.

*   *   *   *   *

July 1982 ~ Providentially not home

One day, James and I stopped to visit, but no one was home. Next door, a teen-ager diligently scraped peeling paint off her house. She informed us that the people who lived next door were gone and had not returned. Admiring her hard work, I visited with sixteen-year-old Jodi.

"Could I ask you a question?" I inquired. "Do you know for sure, if you were to die today, that you would go to Heaven?"

Looking down self-consciously Jodi said, "I'm not sure, but I hope so."

"God loves us all and wants us to come to Heaven," I replied. "In fact, He explains in the Bible how to get there."

Jodi sat down with me in our car in the driveway. We read together from my Bible how to trust Christ as Savior: *"And this is the testimony, that God gave us eternal life, and this life is in his Son. Whoever has the Son has life; whoever does not have the Son of God does not have life. I write these things to you who believe in the name of the Son of God that you may know that you have eternal life"* (1 John 5:11-13).

When Jodi's neighbor drove into his driveway, James visited with him while Jodi and I finished our conversation. Jodi prayed, receiving Christ as her Savior. She rejoiced in the wonderful yet simple way to get to Heaven God had provided her, through Christ's sacrifice on the Cross.

"Now, do you know that you are going to Heaven?" I asked.

"Yes, because I have now accepted Christ as my Savior."

What a providential meeting this turned out to be, certainly not planned by us or by this young woman. This was God's appointment, indeed.

* * * * *

July 4, 1982 ~ New life

After the morning service, a lady approached me. "Gloria, my nephew is in the pastor's study. He wants to get saved. Will you talk to him?" James was speaking with another young man, so I agreed and asked one of the ladies to watch our girls.

Her nephew, Mike, explained that he was on probation; he knew that the only way "to turn his life around" would be with the Lord's help. We studied Scripture for a while, turning to the passage where Jesus explained to Nicodemus in the Gospel of John 3:1-21, how we must be born again, literally born from above. Mike bowed his head and received Christ as Lord and Savior.

Afterwards, we continued our conversation. For eighteen years he had only the sin nature that all of us inherit from Adam, but now Mike had a new nature that would empower him to obey God: *"Therefore, if anyone is in Christ, he is a new creation. The old has passed away; behold, the new has come"* (2 Corinthians 5:17).

"Since your new nature is young, Mike, it needs to mature. On a daily basis, Christians need to read the Bible prayerfully, asking God to help us to learn and live it; we need to pray regularly, go to church, and choose the company of other Christians (Psalm 1). You'll also need to be baptized soon, to show your obedience to Christ." I showed Mike where the Apostle Paul instructed believers in Rome the meaning of baptism: *"We were buried therefore with him by baptism into death, in order that, just as Christ was raised from the dead by the glory of the Father, we too might walk in newness of life. For if we have been united with him in a death like his, we shall certainly be united with him in a resurrection like his"* (Romans 6:4, 5).

Mike expressed his desire to become strong in the things of the Lord, choosing to claim the promise, *"For to this end we toil and strive, because we have our hope set on the living God, who is the Savior of all people, especially of those who believe"* (1 Timothy 4:10). We all need to live with eternity in view.

* * * * *

July 7, 1982 ~ Key to tomorrow

On the last day of our Daily Vacation Bible School, James invited those that wanted to know how to get to Heaven to meet with me in the pastor's study. Three girls and one boy came forward, sat around the open Bible with me, and listened carefully. Just watching their faces was fascinating as they absorbed Scripture and caught a glimpse of Jesus and the power of His presence. His Word penetrated their minds and traveled down into their hearts.

The disciples on the road to Emmaus experienced the power of the Gospel of Christ and marveled, *"They said to each other, 'Did not our hearts burn within us while he [Jesus] talked to us on the road, while he opened to us the Scriptures?"* (Luke 24:32). Three prayed, wanting to receive Christ right then. Not ready yet, one girl wanted to wait.

Young people are our key to tomorrow—it is important that we present to them Christ and His transforming power.

* * * * *

August 8, 1982 ~ Pain with purpose

The reality of cancer came too early for one man in our church. Jim returned from the military after receiving life-altering news: bone cancer had invaded his body. While battling for his physical life, he also fought a spiritual battle. Jim had trusted Christ as his Savior while in the service. In that way, he was ready to die; he knew his destination was Heaven. As the Apostle Peter wrote, *"Since you have been born again, not of perishable seed but of imperishable, through the living and abiding word of God"* (1 Peter 1:23). Jim regretted leaving his wife and young family struggling to commit their lives to God's care.

James and I spent considerable time with Jim, but the Lord also made us aware of his extended family and their spiritual needs as they watched this young man embarking on his journey through the "Valley of the Shadow of Death" (Psalm 23). Death becomes real when we watch it experienced by a loved one. That event causes many to examine their own life and destiny.

One day we felt the Holy Spirit prompt us to call on one of Jim's uncles. When we did, only his wife and daughter were home. Because of Jim's cancer, they had been considering the inevitability of death. Both Teresa and her daughter Shelly, listened carefully as I shared with them the importance of preparing for eternity in Heaven where no one will ever again be sick or die. After considering Scripture concerning their personal need of being rescued from the consequence of sin, both decided to call upon Christ for His salvation.

Jim did lose his battle with cancer, but his life impacted others. It was amazing that God, through Jim's intense suffering and pain, had touched others for eternity. As we travel the paths of life that God has planned for us, let us remember that people are watching our lives; they need to see the difference between one who is prepared for Heaven and one who is not.

> *Blessed be the God and Father of our Lord Jesus Christ, the Father of mercies and God of all comfort, who comforts us in all our affliction, so that we may be able to comfort those who are in any affliction, with the comfort with which we ourselves are comforted by God. For as we share abundantly in Christ's sufferings, so through Christ we share abundantly in comfort too. If we are afflicted, it is for your comfort and salvation; and if we are comforted, it is for your comfort, which you experience when you patiently endure the same sufferings that we suffer. Our hope for you is unshaken, for we know that as you share in our sufferings, you will also share in our comfort.* (2 Corinthians 1:3-7)

God may plan our natural pains in life for the eternal benefit of others.

*****

August 15, 1982 ~ Knock, knock

An Old Testament promise teaches that God can use our feet to deliver His Good News: *"How beautiful upon the mountains are the feet of him who brings good news, who publishes peace, who brings good news of happiness, who publishes salvation, who says to Zion, 'Your God reigns'"* (Isaiah 52:7).

James and I determined to walk through Washburn, inviting people to church and sharing with them from God's Word if they were willing to listen. One day, a young man from Georgia who was visiting his grandparents for the summer, answered our knock. The grandparents providentially gone for a doctor's appointment, I asked Denny if he was going to Heaven when he died; he "hoped so," but didn't know. Sitting down and opening the Bible, I showed Denny how God has provided salvation for him through Jesus Christ. The Apostle John wrote, *"Behold, I stand at the door and knock. If anyone hears my voice and opens the door, I will come in to him and eat with him, and he with me"* (Revelation 3:20). This good news met the need of his hungry heart; he humbly prayed, receiving Jesus Christ as his Savior.

*****

August 29, 1982 ~ "Oh, no—the preacher!"

When I asked Cindy, one of the church teenagers, if she knew anyone who needed to trust Jesus Christ as Savior, she replied, "Yes, my parents." We began to pray for her parents regularly. One day, it seemed the right time to visit.

Knocking at their door, we heard Cindy's mother say with dismay, "Oh, no. It's the preacher and his wife!"

Nevertheless, Donna kindly answered the door. Tired from babysitting and in the middle of a project, Donna invited us to come in. Ken, Cindy's father, had experienced a serious accident at his worksite. He was undergoing extensive physical therapy and was in considerable pain. Both Ken and Donna sat in their living room and visited with us; Cindy quietly listened and prayed. Explaining that we appreciated Cindy's coming to our church, we invited them to come, too.

"Ken never has liked going to church. I would like to go," Donna explained, "but since Ken is Lutheran and I am Catholic, we don't go anywhere."

Rather than discussing differences in denominations, I asked if we could show them from the Bible how God says people get to Heaven. They were interested in seeing from Scripture how Christ made it possible for us to be reunited with God. We shared familiar Scripture with them, including John 3:16, *"For God so loved the world, that he gave his only Son, that whoever believes in him should not perish but have eternal life."* After answering a few questions, I asked if they would like to receive Christ as their Savior.

"Yes," Ken said.

"I would, too," Donna enthusiastically replied.

First Ken, then Donna prayed aloud, appropriating the blood sacrifice that Christ made on the Cross for our sin. Looking on, Cindy beamed happily, rejoicing with us that her parents had trusted Christ. A daughter burdened for her parents' eternal salvation was able to witness the answers to her prayers, right before her eyes.

* * * * *

September 1982 ~ Generations apart, same needs

Inside the Family Altar Broadcast fair booth during Waterloo Cattle Congress, we placed a large sign across the back: "Jesus says, 'You must be born again.' Stop and visit with us." Decorated with random articles of baby clothes, the focus of the sign was a colorful picture of a little boy and girl praying beside their bed. People smiled in agreement, appeared puzzled, or frowned in disagreement.

God's Appointment

Three young men stopped, one of them, Ken. "What does that mean?" he asked the others with him. The two understood the meaning and tried to explain what it meant to be born again. Overhearing their conversation, I invited seventeen-year-old Ken to come into the booth so that I could help explain being born again from the Bible. He did so. Ken bowed his head receiving Christ into his life to pay for his sin and give him a home in Heaven.

When he rejoined his friends, they smiled. "Ken, we didn't think you would ever really do that. How wonderful—now you are a Christian, too."

"Right," Ken responded.

What a blessing to see Christian young people so concerned about their friends that they witness to them.

An older gentleman stopped to ask if we knew where to find the booth that sold polished rocks. As we talked, I casually asked if he knew where he was going when he died.

"I don't know," Sydney said. "I have a lot of questions."

When he began asking questions, I invited him to sit down and visit. As so often, I turned to the Bible (John 3:1-21), where Jesus explains to Nicodemus how a person becomes born again. Tearfully, Sydney told me of his Christian mother who had given birth to nine children. On her deathbed, she had talked to each child. Sydney promised then he would be saved and join her in Heaven. Now, at seventy-nine-years-old he asked, "Don't you think after this long, it's about time to get born again?"

"Yes," I replied, "seventy-nine years is about time. You wouldn't want to wait much longer."

Right there, no longer delaying his decision, he asked the Lord to pay for his sins and be his Savior. "It is such a comfort to know that this is finally settled," Sydney declared. He had fulfilled his mother's prayers and was ready to join her and his Savior in Heaven.

* * * * *

September 20, 1982 ~ Birthday gift

On September 20, 1959, at the age of fifteen, I had come to know Christ as my personal Savior. Twenty-three years later in 1982, I lifted up my heart in prayer, asking the Lord to give me a birthday gift: I wanted to talk with twenty-three people about trusting Christ as Savior. God answered that prayer. That day, I was in a booth at the National Dairy Cattle Congress Fair and had a perfect opportunity to witness. I did talk with over twenty-three people about trusting Christ as Savior, and a number made decisions for Christ.

My heart especially soared when two fifteen-year-old girls responded to my offer to show them how they could be born again and be on their way to Heaven. After they trusted Christ, I told them that this particular day was also my spiritual birthday, and I considered their openness to God a birthday present. "When we trust Christ as our Savior," I explained, "it is a relationship that lasts." Jesus promised, *"I am the light of the world. Whoever follows me will not walk in darkness, but will have the light of life"* (John 8:12). After we have received that light of Christ in our lives, Jesus said we need to tell others about it: *"No one after lighting a lamp puts it in a cellar or under a basket, but on a stand, so that those who enter may see the light"* (Luke 11:33). "I shared with you, and my desire is that you will in turn share with others and be a light for God in a dark world."

Jesus told a parable of a farmer who sowed seed. Some seeds fell by the wayside, some on stony ground, some among thorns, and others on good ground. Even though much of the seed fell fruitlessly on unproductive soil, the remnant still brought an abundant harvest. (Luke 8:5-15) It was a perfect example of witnessing at the fair, many would not listen; others listened but did not respond, while others believed.

* * * * *

October 1982 ~ Need a lift?

As was typical on Sunday, we stopped for a family on the way to church. They were unable to go with us that week. Also, they were hosting a young man who was sleeping on their couch. Jeff, about 27 years old, was interested in visiting with us. Jeff was a former radio announcer who had met James a few years earlier. James had taped a FAB program at the station where Jeff had been working.

Rubbing his eyes, Jeff exclaimed, "I should go to church—my life sure needs turning around." His paycheck had been stolen the night before at a bar while he was drinking, and Jeff had no way to get home. Somehow he had made connections with this family, and they had invited him to stay overnight at their house.

James offered to return after church and give him a ride home. Jeff said that he would appreciate our help. We returned after the church services and picked him up. While James drove, I visited with Jeff about how trusting Christ would be the first step in "getting turned around." James parked in a shopping center so that we could finish the discussion and have a time of prayer. Jeff asked Jesus Christ to forgive his sins and become his Savior.

After we had delivered Jeff to his home, we stopped at a nearby church to ask the pastor to make contact with Jeff. The church did and helped him to grow and become established in the Lord. The institution of church is God's plan to be the means of fulfilling the Great Commission. Jesus instructed: *"Go therefore and make disciples of all nations, baptizing them in the name of the Father and of the Son and of the Holy Spirit, teaching them to observe all that I have commanded you. And behold, I am with you always, to the end of the age"* (Matthew 28:19-20).

* * * * *

October 17, 1982 ~ Not according to plan

Asking for counseling, Gene called from a nearby community. When he arrived, we visited. Discouraged, Gene felt that life was "passing him by" and that God was not doing anything about it.

"I'm not asking too much," he commented, "I don't need to be rich, but I would like to have a job, get married, and have a family." When we asked about his relationship with God, Gene sharply said, "I know all about *that*."

During subsequent visits, we were able to share with Gene about the need for a real relationship with a living God. A person's faith can be misguided when it is based solely on intellectual perception. Faith needs to have a solid foundation which is God's promises, revealed in His Holy Word. In Acts 16:31, the Apostle Paul told the jailor in Philippi to believe in Christ and he would be saved.

The times we spent with Gene were moments of planting seeds. Gradually, he became interested in finding out more about a personal relationship with Christ—even visiting our church several times. One Sunday evening after the service, Gene asked James to show him how to be born again, literally born from above, as Jesus said in John 3. That night, Gene trusted Christ as his Savior.

Gene's attitude slowly matured. As he grew in the Lord, he became an altogether different person. Resting in the truth of John helped him: *"Jesus said to him, 'I am the way, and the truth, and the life. No one comes to the Father except through me'"* (John 14:6). Truth found in Scripture changes lives. It sets a person free from the power of the great Deceive who makes many believe that they can work their way to Heaven: *"And you will know the truth, and the truth will set you free"* (John 8:32).

* * * * *

October 24, 1982 ~ Finding the one

After Gene trusted Christ, he continued coming to church and often came to our home. He met a girl he liked and asked us if she could be the right one for him.

"It is hard to tell, without meeting her," James replied; "but a good rule of thumb is to find a girl who loves the Lord and fits the description in Proverbs 31."

"But she doesn't know the Lord yet," Gene countered.

God's Appointment

"Well, then," James replied, "she needs to come to know the Lord as her Savior, as you did. Have Gloria talk to her, and we'll see how she responds to the Gospel."

The next day, Gene came to our office to introduce his girlfriend, Debbie. He wanted me to talk to her about the Lord. Debbie was open, and we sat down to talk.

"Can I get to Heaven even if I have done terrible things in my life, like trying to commit suicide?" she asked.

"Trying to commit suicide is not what determines whether we go to Heaven or not," I answered. "But, there is another point to consider—are you ready to die?" It is not that suicide keeps one from Heaven, but sin will. No one can enter with any sin. The reason Jesus Christ had to die on the Cross was to pay for sin. Without that sin payment being applied personally to our account, no one can get to Heaven (John 3).

The Old Testament recounts the story of King Saul, anointed by God as the leader of Israel, who fell on his sword, committing suicide. The previous day, the prophet Samuel in a vision had said that Saul would die and be with God the next day: *"Moreover, the LORD will give Israel also with you into the hand of the Philistines, and tomorrow you and your sons shall be with me"* (1 Samuel 28:19). Can you imagine people committing suicide and then trying to explain to God why they arrived in Heaven early? People who are on drugs, depressed, or not in their right minds might commit suicide, but it is wrong, and we should never do it. Rather, the giver of life should also be the taker of life. Only God knows when our time on earth should be finished.

We do not know the spiritual health of people who commit suicide, but many may not be prepared for eternity. If they have not accepted Christ's provision of sin to be forgiven, they are not on their way to heaven, but rather Hell. Jesus told us of a rich man that died and went to a terrible place called Hell. (Luke 16:22-24) Can you imagine anything worse than going from a difficult situation here, to a horrible situation, forever in Hell?

We turned to Paul's letter to the people in Rome, *"For all have sinned and come short of the glory of God"* (Romans 3:23). "We have all sinned, Debbie. I have sinned, and so have you. We all deserve to go to Hell because of our sins, but none of us has to go there: Christ died for our sin so that we can go to Heaven" (John 3:16). After studying Scripture together, I asked Debbie, "How about it? Are you ready to tell Jesus that you want to belong to Him, that you want Him to pay for your sin, come into your life, and give you a home in Heaven? Places are still available, and you can make a reservation. It is important to do it today; tickets are NOT available at the gate. We simply accept God's gift to receive a place in Heaven." I read to Debbie the words of the Apostle Paul, ***"For the wages of sin is death, but the free gift of God is eternal life in Christ Jesus our Lord"*** (Romans 6:23).

Bowing her head, Debbie earnestly trusted Christ to forgive her sin and give her eternal life.

* * * * *

Home with our three girls

November 1982 ~ Yard sale treasure

Through our daughter's birthday party, we became acquainted with Chastity who began to attend church with us. Although I wanted to talk with her about salvation, interruptions always came. Following one Sunday morning service, while I was talking with two other young ladies, Chastity told James that she wanted to be saved. James directed her to go to the room where I was counseling others; he knew I would gladly speak with her.

Quietly knocking, Chastity came in and listened intently while I spoke with two other girls about receiving Christ as their Savior. All three girls asked the Lord to apply His blood as payment for their sin and give them a new birth into God's family. Later, when we brought Chastity home, we heard her happily greet her mother, "Guess what I did today, Mom? I got saved."

Chastity regularly came to church to learn more about the Bible; she also brought her younger sisters. But one day she announced, "We are soon moving to Minnesota." Since I had been praying for her mother to come to know Christ, I was concerned. I needed to check with her mother immediately. Stopping by their home, I found Sharon, Charity's mother, conducting a yard sale in the rain in preparation to move. In spite of her yard sale, Sharon did indeed desire to understand Charity's decision to be saved. Right there in her yard, she bowed her head and asked Jesus to be her Lord and Savior.

They did move, but their new eternal relationship with Jesus Christ went with them.

* * * * *

November 14, 1982 ~ "But I was a deacon!"

Don, in his early thirties, commented that he had "as good a chance as anyone" to get to Heaven; after all, he had even been a deacon in his church.

"But church work is not the way to Heaven," I replied. "Remember Jesus' telling the thief on the Cross that soon he would be with Christ in Heaven? (Luke 23:43) He didn't have an opportunity to do anything to earn his way; it was strictly on the basis of Jesus' invitation. As a result of his believing that Jesus was the Son of God, the thief asked for forgiveness." Jesus' invitation did not depend on participation in religious activities. I asked permission to show him from the Bible how Jesus explained to Nicodemus the way a person gets to Heaven. We read Jesus' statements in the third chapter of the Gospel of John where Jesus said we must be born again, literally born from above (John 3).

Don was interested. Explaining the importance of believing *on* the Lord Jesus rather than believing *about* Him, I used a helpful illustration. Believing *about* airplanes does not transport us anywhere; we must put that belief into action and board the airplane. Likewise, believing *about* Jesus is fine but does not get us into Heaven. Each individual must believe *on* Jesus and receive Jesus' payment of sin personally. We read more in John 3, where Jesus carefully explained:

> *That whoever <u>believes in</u> him [Christ] may have eternal life. For God so loved the world, that he gave his only Son, that whoever <u>believes in</u> him [Christ] should not perish but have eternal life. For God did not send his Son into the world to condemn the world, but in order that the world might be saved through him [Christ]. Whoever <u>believes in</u> him [Christ] is not condemned, but whoever does not believe is condemned already, because he has not <u>believed in</u> the name of the only Son of God.* (John 3:15-18)

Don understood the difference between being religious and being born again and decided to trust the work of Jesus Christ on the Cross so that he could have a home in Heaven.

Many others, like Don, believe that doing good and serving God is the way to Heaven. Our good deeds will never get us to Heaven. Each of us must accept Jesus' blood as the payment for our sins. Jesus spoke with a stern warning to the religious in His day, as well as today:

> *Not everyone who says to me, "Lord, Lord," will enter the kingdom of heaven, but the one who does the will of my Father who is in heaven. On that day many will say to me, "Lord, Lord, did we not prophesy in your name, and cast out demons in your name, and do many mighty works in your name?" And*

then will I declare to them, "I never knew you; depart from me, you workers of lawlessness." (Mathew 7:21-23)

Honestly trying to love God and do the best we can to please Him by good works, according to the Bible, is not the way to Heaven; we must be born again. Having heard the term *born again* used improperly, some people wonder why being born again is so important. It is important because it is the term Jesus used. Instead of trying to earn our way into the pearly gates, the good news is that the work has already been completed on the Cross. Christ eagerly awaits our decision to enter into that personal relationship with Him. The Apostle Paul reiterated this teaching of Jesus when he affirmed, *"For by grace you have been saved through faith. And this is not your own doing; it is the gift of God, not a result of works, so that no one may boast"* (Ephesians 2:8-9). By acknowledging our own personal sin to God, anyone can ask for His forgiveness and become born again into the family of God. We then become His children.

* * * * *

November 1982 ~ Brother and sisters on Earth, in Heaven

When we went to visit a young lady who had trusted Christ at the fair, her seventeen-year-old brother answered the door. "She'll be back soon," he said, and invited us to come in and wait for her.

James and I visited with him and their older sister, explaining about our booth at the fair and how we ask people if they know whether or not they are going to Heaven when they die. "We receive various reactions to that question," I commented. "But we truly care and think many people would like to talk to someone about the subject, especially when they learn that Jesus' answer to such a question is recorded in the Bible for us to study."

Both Todd and Angela were interested in talking about how a person does get to Heaven. Taking advantage of the opportunity, I showed them Jesus' answer in the third chapter of John. At that point, Debbie returned. Sitting across from us, she gladly listened as we explained to her sister and brother what we had shared previously with her.

Then I asked Todd and Angela, "Would you be embarrassed to pray in front of Debbie and ask Christ to come into your life and apply His blood as payment for your sin?"

"No, not at all," they both responded.

They prayed aloud, first one and then the other, asking Christ to be their Savior, pay for their sins, and give them a home in Heaven. The three were thrilled to share a mutual trust in Christ as their Savior.

It is not unusual for one family member, when they discover Jesus as their Savior, to lead others in the family to Christ. The Bible records many such circumstances, including the account of Philip and Nathanael, two of Jesus' disciples: *"The next day Jesus decided to go to Galilee. He found Philip and said to him, 'Follow me.' Now Philip was from Bethsaida, the city of Andrew and Peter. Philip found Nathanael and said to him, 'We have found him of whom Moses in the Law and also the prophets wrote'"* (John 1:43-45). It is natural to want to share our new found relationship in Jesus with loved ones and friends.

* * * * *

CHAPTER 8

1983

January 1983 ~ Like a lost boat

Dee was undergoing treatment for cancer. We had been asked to visit her in the hospital. Dee was friendly, delightful, and concerned about others. She was also a deep thinker and stated, "I don't think church denomination is important."

"When we approach the gate to Heaven, God will not ask us the name of our church but rather, what we have done with His Son." I responded. Asking permission to read Scriptures with her, I turned in my Bible, and we read together the conversation between Jesus and Nicodemus. Jesus' had told Nicodemus that he must be "born again," literally, "born from above," in order to get to Heaven. (John 3:1-21) Jesus explained that the blood He shed on the Cross was to deliver us from sin's death sentence. Just as during the time of Moses in the Old Testament, the Israelites in Egypt were instructed by God to put a lamb's blood on the top and sides of their doorways, *"Then they shall take some of the blood and put it on the two doorposts and the lintel of the houses in which they eat it* [the Passover lamb]*"* (Exodus 12:7). The Death Angel did not enter the homes where the doorways were sprinkled with blood, but in the homes where the doorways were not, they experienced the death of their first born. Today we need the blood of Jesus Christ, our Sacrificial Lamb, applied to the door of our hearts.

To illustrate, I told her the story of a little boy who painstakingly made a small boat. Placing it in the river, he watched with joy its graceful movements. One day the current carried away the boat. As much as he tried to recover his boat, it became lost. Tearfully, he returned home without his prized creation. Sometime later, while walking past a store window in town, he saw his boat displayed for sale. The youngster rushed into the store and explained to the storekeeper that the boat in the window was a boat he had made and lost. The owner insisted that the boy would have to pay the posted price. Determined to buy his boat back, the boy toiled for some time at small jobs to earn money, then finally emptied his piggy bank and returned to the store. Placing his money on the counter, he redeemed his lost boat from the shopkeeper. This time he left with a smile. Clutching his beloved boat he exclaimed, "I made you, lost you, and bought you back. I'm never going to lose you again."

This touching story illustrates Christ's creating us, losing us to the power of sin, and then buying us back with His own blood on the Cross. That Divine work of love is the redemptive work of Christ.

Dee exclaimed, "I sure wish I knew for certain that I have been bought back, never to be lost again."

Taking her hand, I suggested that we pray. First, I thanked God for the opportunity to talk with Dee about the serious subject of how we can get to Heaven, and asked God to help Dee receive His gift of everlasting life. Pausing, I looked up and said, "Dee, would you like to trust Jesus to apply His blood to your sin and buy you back, never to be lost again? Why don't you ask Him right now?"

With a quiver in her voice and tear in her eye, Dee acknowledged her sin and called upon Christ to pay for her sin. "Dear Jesus, buy me back, never to be parted from you again." Smiling, she claimed the promise in the Bible that He would be with her forever, ***"For God so loved the world, that he gave his only Son, that whoever believes in him should not perish but have eternal life"*** (John 3:16).

* * * * *

March 1983 ~ Attempted suicide

"Please come to the hospital," pled a frightened young woman late one Sunday night. "My husband has taken a lot of pills. The doctors have him on a respirator, and I'm so scared."

James and I hurried to the hospital where we quickly located Doug's wife. Together we went to see her husband. Doug was resting quietly, but he was gravely ill. Medical equipment was keeping his heart beating. We visited with Doug's wife and a friend who had accompanied her. They both desperately wanted Doug to recover.

After a while, I asked, "Here's an important question to consider—Doug almost died today. If *you* were to die, would you go to Heaven?"

Each answered, "I hope so."

"Everyone hopes so," I responded gently. "Heaven is the better of two choices. Let me show you from the Bible how you can *know*." I showed the young ladies the Scripture that tells how to be born again as Jesus, centuries before, had instructed Nicodemus, ***"Truly, truly, I say to you, unless one is born again he cannot see the kingdom of God"*** (John 3:3). They both invited Christ into their lives to be their Lord and Savior.

The next day, James spoke with Doug, whose condition had improved considerably. "I won't ever try that again!" he declared emphatically. The couple promised to come to church the next Sunday to "put their lives together," with God's help.

This situation was resolved favorably. Not all end so well. Suicide is never a good solution. Trusting Christ as Lord and Savior is the answer. No life is free from problems, and some face greater difficulties than others. But every person chooses whether to ask God for help or not. As God's children, we have His all-sufficient help through the storms that come (Philippians 4:19-20). He makes life worth living, as Jesus explained:

Whoever believes in him may have eternal life. For God so loved the world, that he gave his only Son, that whoever believes in him should not perish but have eternal life. For God did not send his Son into the world to condemn the world, but in order that the world might be saved through him. Whoever believes in him

is not condemned, but whoever does not believe is condemned already, because he has not believed in the name of the only Son of God. . . . Whoever believes in the Son has eternal life; whoever does not obey the Son shall not see life, but the wrath of God remains on him. (John 3:15-18, 36).

In the last book of the Bible, the Apostle John also writes, *"Behold, I stand at the door and knock. If anyone hears my voice and opens the door, I will come in to him and eat with him, and he with me"* (Revelation 3:20). Life is precious. Each of us, individually, needs to open the door of our hearts to Jesus Christ. We need to make wise decisions, first to become His child, then to trust His wonderful leading the rest of our lives. God's blessings follow those who obey His word.

* * * * *

March 6, 1983 ~ Praying for Mom

A teenager requested that we pray for his mother to be saved. Although Rosie had allowed Scott, as well as his brothers and sisters, to attend church activities, she had never come with them. After praying for Rosie, we felt that it was the right time to visit her.

Rosie was friendly and interested. Together we read verses from God's Word that spoke of sin, Christ's sacrificial atonement, and the importance of accepting His gift personally. And we rejoiced that Rosie prayed, receiving Jesus' payment for her sins. Scripture proved true again:

For the word of the cross is folly to those who are perishing, but to us who are being saved it is the power of God. . . . For since, in the wisdom of God, the world did not know God through wisdom, it pleased God through the folly of what we preach to save those who believe. . . . But God chose what is foolish in the world to shame the wise; God chose what is weak in the world to shame the strong. (1 Corinthians 1:18, 21, 27)

How wonderful that God can use children to help reach their parents for Christ.

* * * * *

April 1983 ~ Finding the Jewish Messiah

A teenage friend called requesting a ride to the roller skating rink. Unable to find another way, she and her girlfriend were hoping we would take them. James and I picked them up. As we drove, I talked with Gail, a lovely Jewish girl. She said that she was not comfortable in the Jewish faith. When she had told her parents, they had not responded in a supportive manner, concerned that she was changing religion as an expression of a rebellious attitude.

"I don't want to rebel," Gail explained, "but I am not happy."

When I asked what she thought of Jesus Christ, and if she had ever accepted Him as her Lord and Savior, she answered, "Oh, I love the Lord, but I don't know if I have done that."

Opening the Scriptures, I explained that we need to believe on the Lord Jesus Christ in order to have everlasting life. The Old Testament speaks of Jesus prophetically:

Surely he [Jesus] *has borne our griefs and carried our sorrows; yet we esteemed him stricken, smitten by God, and afflicted. But he was wounded for our transgressions; he was crushed for our iniquities; upon him was the chastisement that brought us peace, and with his stripes we are healed. All we like sheep have gone astray; we have turned—every one—to his own way; and the* LORD *has laid on him the iniquity of us all.* (Isaiah 53:4-6)

When we arrived at their destination, Gail wanted to bow her head and heart and to trust the Promised Messiah, Jesus Christ, to come into her life. As Abraham trusted God, so Gail in faith accepted God's provision, the blood of Jesus' sacrifice on the Cross, to cover her sins. She claimed the promise of a home in Heaven. I urged Gail to continue studying Scripture, reading more of the Old Testament prophecies concerning Christ.

We look forward to visiting with her parents, explaining that we greatly respect the Jewish people and their Scriptures as being God's Holy Word. We hope that they will also be open to learning how the Jewish Messiah can be their personal Lord and Savior. Born a Jew, the Apostle Paul, after his conversion, clearly affirms the life-changing power of the Gospel: *"For I am not ashamed of the gospel, for it is the power of God for salvation to everyone who believes, to the Jew first and also to the Greek"* (Romans 1:16).

Whether Jewish, Christian, Muslim, Hindu or followers of any other religion—the pathway to God is the same. It has to be God's way, not our way. The Apostle Paul, a converted Jew stated, *"There is salvation in no one else, for there is no other name under heaven given among men by which we must be saved"* (Acts 4:12). Salvation is only through Christ's blood atonement. If individuals believe that they love the Lord but are uncertain if they have received Him as their own Lord and Savior, they can pray anytime, anywhere. Here is a simple prayer:

Dear Jesus, I know I am a sinner and that I am in trouble. I know that you died to pay for sin, and I recognize that you are alive now in Heaven. I may have already asked you to save me; but if I haven't, I am asking now, because I want to be certain. Please apply the blood that you shed on the Cross to my account and give me a home in Heaven.

There is no reason to live in doubt when God has made salvation so simple. We need to make certain of our eternal destiny. When going on a trip, it is wise to confirm ones reservation before arriving and expecting transportation to a desired location. This is even more important concerning the trip into eternity.

* * * * *

April 1983 ~ Free things

A salesman responded to a card of interest we had filled out. First introducing us to his inventory with a free demonstration, Mike returned on a number of occasions to show us his office products. At one point, when talking about spiritual matters, I gave him a tract. One day

Mike stopped to let us know that he was changing jobs; he had given our name to a new salesman. That day, I asked Mike if he knew that he was going to Heaven when he died.

"No," he answered, "I don't."

"May we show you how you can know?"

"Sure, why not?" was his reply.

Taking the Bible, James explained that God's Word instructs us to call upon the name of the Lord for his gift of salvation: ***"Everyone who calls on the name of the Lord will be saved"*** (Romans 10:13). After reading a number of passages, including that all-inclusive promise, Mike bowed his head and prayed aloud, trusting Jesus Christ to be his Savior, forgive his sin, and give him a home in Heaven. We continued visiting. Mike mentioned that he had not read the tract we had given him but promised he would. When Mike left, we had the distinct impression that he had come hoping we would talk to him again about the Lord.

We pray that individuals stop "just thinking" about God, Heaven, and the meaning of life. Talking to God and accepting His free gift of salvation is so important and so simple. We need only to ask God to help us. That important decision should not be postponed. Throughout the Bible, from the story of Adam and Eve through all the ages, all of us have needed to ask the Lord to be our Savior. Paul's letter to the Romans communicates how to make that step:

> *As it is written, "None is righteous, no, not one"* (3:10). *For all have sinned and fall short of the glory of God* (3:23). *For the wages of sin is death, but the free gift of God is eternal life in Christ Jesus our Lord* (6:23). *If you confess with your mouth that Jesus is Lord and believe in your heart that God raised him from the dead, you will be saved. For with the heart one believes and is justified, and with the mouth one confesses and is saved.* (Romans 10:9, 10)

Mike came to know the Lord as a result of a free demonstration of office equipment. Salvation provides believers free access to God's promise to take care of all their needs, both in this life and for all eternity (Psalm 23).

* * * * *

May 1, 1983 ~ From out of town

A lady in Iowa wrote that she appreciated the Family Altar Broadcast newsletters, which a friend had passed along to her. She enjoyed reading about people coming to know Jesus. For a long time, she had wanted to know if she herself was going to Heaven and requested an opportunity to meet us. Of course, we wrote back immediately that we would love to meet her.

Traveling by bus to Waterloo, she checked into the YWCA and then called to tell us that she had arrived. In her mid-eighties, she was not completely certain of her eternal destination. Opening the Bible, I shared Scripture about salvation including these verses by the Apostle Paul, *"For by grace you have been saved through faith. And this is not your own doing; it is the gift of God, not a result of works, so that no one may boast"* (Ephesians 2:8, 9).

After our study, she humbly bowed her head and prayed, "If I haven't already, I am now asking you to forgive my sins and give me a home in Heaven." She was relieved, having gained complete assurance of salvation by claiming God's promises. We were thrilled to be present when she became a child of God. She followed the instructions written clearly in the Bible. Returning to her home the next day, the elderly lady later wrote a sweet thank-you note.

If there had been any doubt about how human beings could be reconciled or "made right with" God, it would have been a fearsome responsibility to advise this lady about the destiny of her soul. At her own expense, she had come quite a distance by bus to find the truth about one thing: She wanted to know what the Bible teaches about how to get ready to die. She wanted to have an eternal home in Heaven. The Apostle Paul tells us that *"If while we were enemies we were reconciled to God by the death of his Son, much more, now that we are reconciled, shall we be saved by his life"* (Romans 5:10). I am glad that God has made it clear in Scripture that we can be confident about salvation.

God's concern is that the good news of reconciliation reaches the entire world. According to the Great Commission, the spreading of that good news needs to be our concern. The Lord sent laborers into the fields to share the good news of reconciliation with others. Paul communicates that message, *"All this is from God, who through Christ reconciled us to himself and gave us the ministry of reconciliation"* (2 Corinthians 5:18).

*   *   *   *   *

May 8, 1983 ~ Humble faith of a child

The wonder of going to Heaven was the focus of our preschool class at church. "Our very best day will be the day that we see Jesus," I told them. "That day will be better than a birthday and better than Christmas." We sang "Jesus Loves Me," then played with a few toys.

A serious-minded young fellow had started to come with his grandmother to church. Four-year-old Christopher was interested in this "very best day." His parents did not yet love Jesus; neither did his grandfather nor aunts and uncles, but his grandmother did. And so, when his grandmother prayed at the dinner table, Christopher would bow his head and say, "I pray to Jesus, too, Grandma." He often asked his grandmother to read him Bible stories. One day, when she read about the crucifixion, he exclaimed, "I'm glad Jesus died for me, but I'm sad it hurt Him so much."

In his grandmother's car after church, little Christopher asked, "How do I trust Jesus?"

"You just pray and tell Him that you are sorry for your sin," his grandmother answered. Tell Him that you are glad that He died for you. Tell Him you are glad that He has risen and is alive in Heaven. Trust Jesus to pay for your sin and give you a home in Heaven. He will." Little Christopher prayed as his grandmother suggested.

The next Sunday he sat beside me in church. "Christopher, have you trusted Jesus yet?" I asked.

"Yes, Teacher, I did!" He smiled widely.

"That's great—when?" I asked.

"When I was in the car with Grandma last Sunday."

How wonderful the faith of a young child. According to Jesus, all who come to Christ in simple faith as that of a little child, God receives: ***"Whoever humbles himself like this child is the greatest in the kingdom of heaven. Whoever receives one such child in my name receives me"*** (Matthew 18:4-5). With God's help, grandparents can live their Christianity so that their grandchildren can see and desire the same relationship with God in their own lives.

* * * * *

May 1983 ~ Icebreaker

On the way home from the FAB office, James needed to visit a man in the hospital. Since our girls were along, I took them to the hospital snack machines while James went upstairs. The three girls were disappointed when I did not have the right change. Several nurses' aides who were eating their brown-bagged lunches, noticed our predicament and offered to make change so that we could use the machines. Selections agreed upon, finally we sat around a table, enjoying our snacks.

Wishing to express my appreciation, I took a couple of tracts from my purse and sent three-year-old Jessica with a "thank you" for the ladies. Glancing at the title, one of the nurses' aides said, "I sure do hope I go to Heaven." She seemed serious. When I asked if I could show them from the Bible where Jesus explained how to get to Heaven, they invited me to join them at their table. While the girls played, I showed from Scripture in the Gospel of John, chapter 3, that people can receive Christ by believing <u>on</u> His name, not just <u>about</u> Jesus. After reading several more Scripture passages, both ladies prayed and received Christ as their Savior. Just as they finished praying, James came back from his visit, and it was time for us to go home. The nurses' aides had finished their break and went back to work, rejoicing in a new-found relationship with Christ.

God can use us all in His plan, to open hearts and communicate God's loving message. James' visit upstairs, the candy machine, our children, and the tracts in my purse—all were important in God's plan. In this case, children served as real icebreakers, used of God to make contacts. Recognizing that another of God's appointments had been timed perfectly, I thanked God for everything. I recalled the wonderful verse of the Psalmist, *"This God—his way is perfect"* (Psalm 18:30a).

* * * * *

May 10, 1983 ~ Place to stay

While I visited a friend, nineteen-year-old Gina walked in. Staying temporarily with her friend, Gina had been looking for a place to rent.

"Don't ask how things turned out," she lamented. "Everything went wrong. I can't get a place to stay for a couple of months."

The two then began talking about problems she was encountering. Gina had recently lived through several near-death experiences. Quietly I asked, "Gina, do you know where you will go when you die?"

"I don't—" Gina answered, "I hope Heaven, but I don't know."

"Could I show you in the Bible how you can know that you have a place in Heaven?"

"Sure, I'd like that," Gina responded.

Sitting on the couch, we read together in Scripture how Christ died on the Cross for sin. We can receive His payment in full for our sins and have a home in Heaven if we personally call upon Christ for His help. Sensing her readiness to make a decision, I invited her to pray. She bowed her head and prayed, receiving Jesus as her Savior.

Just as Gina finished her prayer, her friend's husband came home from work. A bit embarrassed and thinking he was interrupting us, he almost left. We quickly assured him that we wanted him to stay. My friend spoke with deep emotion. "Calvin, listening to Gloria talk to Gina, and now having you come in the door, makes my heart really burdened. I know that you are not a Christian and that you need to be saved, too." Again Calvin appeared uncomfortable.

Prayerfully, I asked Calvin if he would like me to show him what I had just showed Gina in the Bible about how to get to Heaven. I needed to see if he was open to the Gospel.

"Yes," he answered.

Trading places with Gina, Calvin watched closely as I showed him first one verse, then another. When I invited Calvin to pray, trusting Jesus to pay for his sins and give him a home in Heaven, he prayed sincerely, asking Christ to forgive his sins and be the Lord of his life. What a time of rejoicing as two people trusted Christ, one right after the other.

* * * * *

May 31, 1983 ~ Testimony by daughter Angela

For a school assignment, our oldest daughter wrote this testimony about how she came to know Christ.

My name is Angela Goering. I was a little tomboy who, one day, couldn't wait to get outside and run around freely. I had just turned six years old in March. We lived across the street from a park, but my mother thought I should stay inside because it was still chilly outside, and she didn't want me to catch a cold. I kept begging my parents to let me go, but they had plans that night and I was to go with them.

Little did I know that we were going to church to hear a special speaker who was coming to town. It was not just a normal Sunday when we always went to church to hear my daddy, the pastor, preach. Instead, it was a Saturday night and that meant that it was very special.

I remember sitting in the very back where I always sat; this time I actually listened and sat quietly. The speaker was talking about Jesus and how He came to earth to die for me. I had heard the same story before, but this time it seemed different. I began to understand more fully that Jesus cared especially for me and loved me so much that He gave His life for me. Tears started to roll down my face. I looked up to my mother and said, "Mother, Jesus loves me, and I know that he will always take care of me. Mom, would you take me to Jesus? I need a friend like Him to help me." My mother's face lit up and sparkled so heavenly.

I remember walking down that aisle with Mom by my side that memorable Saturday night. On May 31, 1983, at 8:35 p.m., I trusted Jesus. Ever since that day, Jesus has been the best friend I could ever have. Thank you, Jesus.

The next Sunday at church I asked if could take part in communion. Mom told me it was just for those who had trusted Jesus to pay for their sin. The Bible clearly instructs believers to partake in communion. As the Apostle Paul explains, ***"For as often as you eat this bread and drink the cup, you proclaim the Lord's death until he comes"*** (1 Corinthians 11:26).

"I did that," I replied.

"Then you can," she said, explaining that the bread and juice represents Jesus' death and through partaking in these elements, we are thanking Him for His sacrifice. Bowing my head, I quietly said, "Thank you, Jesus, for dying for me so that I can go to Heaven."

* * * * *

Angela Ruth (Goering) Fitzpatrick

How thankful we were as parents to know that Angela had come to Jesus as a little child, knowing that Jesus accepts little children as well as adults. Our little Angela has become a lovely woman who radiates Christ in her life and embodies the Lord's admonition:

Trust in the LORD, and do good; dwell in the land and befriend faithfulness. Delight yourself in the LORD, and he will give you the desires of your heart. Commit your way to the LORD; trust in him, and he will act. He will bring forth your righteousness as the light, and your justice as the noonday. Be still before the LORD and wait patiently for him. (Psalm 37:3-7)

June 9, 1983 ~ Tragic wedding dance

A telephone call came. "My neighbor has had a stroke. He's only in his forties." There was a pause, and then the voice on the line quietly requested, "Could you visit his wife?" We agreed to stop by their home.

Del invited James and me to come in. As she shared their story, our hearts went out to her. Her husband had suffered a stroke eight months earlier at their daughter's wedding. During the father-daughter dance, he had collapsed and been rushed to the hospital where he lay in a coma for some time. Later, he had been transferred to a nursing home.

Del worked during the day and spent the rest of the time caring for her husband. Life had become overwhelming. She had been doing her best but was exhausted. Del said that she prayed all the time and that God gave her the strength to cope. Curious, I asked if she had ever been born again. She said that she didn't know what I was talking about. Once again I turned to the Gospel of John, Chapter 3, and explained the beautiful story of Jesus' death on the Cross, so that His blood can be the atonement, or covering, for our sins. Reading Scripture, we saw that being *born again* was the term that Jesus used with Nicodemus to communicate what happens when we personally receive Christ's death as the sacrifice for our sin. We are born into the family of God, as taught throughout the Bible (John 1:12).

Del understood, and eagerly prayed. That day she transferred her sin to Christ and received His blood atonement. After her prayer she exclaimed, "I feel so light, as if a big weight has been lifted from my shoulders. Thank you so much for showing me how my sins can be forgiven."

God provided a blessing from a tragedy. As Del continues to love and minister to her husband, she still has heavy burdens. Her desire is to see her husband improve physically and come to know Jesus, too. Romans 8:28 is still true: *"And we know that for those who love God all things work together for good, for those who are called according to his purpose."*

* * * * *

July 4, 1983 ~ Better than fireworks

We stopped at my grandma's home in Lincoln, Nebraska, on our way to help James' father and brother harvest wheat in Kansas. Staying overnight, we joined a backyard Fourth of July celebration the next day with some of my cousins. Our family greatly enjoyed the visit.

Afterwards, one of my cousins and her husband lingered. We began talking about the Lord. I asked Diane if she and her husband would like to read some Scripture with us. When Eddie agreed, we sat down together on the couch. We talked about God's plan for getting to Heaven: we can know that we are born into the family of God (John 1:12, 13; 1 John 5:11-13). As evening turned to morning, Eddie and Diane decided that it was time to pray and receive Jesus Christ as Savior. They wanted to be born again into God's family. Holding hands, they prayed and received the best gift ever, God's gift of everlasting life.

Better than the Fourth of July fireworks, the conversation with Diane that evening was especially meaningful to me. Diane is the youngest daughter of my Aunt Mary who had gone to be with the Lord one month earlier. Aunt Mary must have been so happy, celebrating with the angels in Heaven and seeing her daughter make the decision that would unite them for eternity.

Knowing that we have an audience of God, the angels, and those who have gone on before should greatly encourage us to faithfully do our part for the Lord: *"Therefore, since we are surrounded by so great a cloud of witnesses, let us also lay aside every weight, and sin which clings so closely, and let us run with endurance the race that is set before us"* (Hebrews 12:1). Let us pray for one another that we may be faithful, as were those heroes of the faith.

* * * * *

August 7, 1983 ~ Making it personal

James and I visited a young wife and mother who had attended Bible-preaching churches for quite some time. It appeared that she was waiting for someone to talk personally with her about the state of her soul.

"No," she had not yet trusted Christ as her Savior, but "Yes," she was interested. With her husband in the living room and young son in the bedroom, she trusted Christ to save her soul from eternal separation from God. James and I were so happy that she accepted God's rich gift of salvation. God would do His work in her life: *"And we also thank God constantly for this, that when you received the word of God, which you heard from us, you accepted it not as the word of men but as what it really is, the word of God, which is at work in you believers"* (1 Thess. 2:13).

How sobering to realize that some need only a gentle nudge to come to Christ for salvation. May our steps and words be guided by God so that we receive a commendation of "well done" from our Heavenly Father (Matthew 25:23). God will help us meet the appointments He has scheduled when we ask.

* * * * *

August 1983 ~ Time preparing hearts

Traveling through a small town, we contacted Libby. James and I had met her several years earlier after her son's first surgery for brain cancer. Always friendly, she had spoken with us frequently during that time. Since then, her son had undergone a second surgery, and her husband had died suddenly.

Libby admitted that, at times, she struggled with understanding why there had been so much sorrow in her life. Assuring her that such a response is natural, we read together passages that reveal how much God loves us:

Walk in love, as Christ loved us and gave himself up for us, a fragrant offering and sacrifice to God. (Ephesians 5:2)

In all these things we are more than conquerors through him who loved us. For I am sure that neither death nor life, nor angels nor rulers, nor things present nor things to come, nor powers, nor height nor depth, nor anything else in all creation, will be able to separate us from the love of God in Christ Jesus our Lord. (Romans 8:38-39)

God wanted to give us all a blessed life. I asked Libby if she would like to receive Jesus as her Savior and have Him pay for her sins and give her a home in Heaven.

Quickly she answered, "Yes."

Libby prayed, and God met with her. James and I were so glad that God had prepared her heart since the last time we had talked. Having a new sister in the Lord and knowing that she could call on the Lord for daily strength and wisdom, we rejoiced. The Lord's promises to remove the death penalty for our sins: *"Repent therefore, and turn again, that your sins may be blotted out"* (Acts 3:19). He promises to give us the power to live God's plan for our lives; therein lies great blessings in this life and for the life to come. *"The Lord is my Shepherd; I shall not want"* (Psalm 23:1).

*   *   *   *   *

Gloria, James, Angela, Jessica, Victoria, ready to travel.

September 1983 ~ Clean rugs, clean heart

Three men stopped to demonstrate their rug cleaning service. They said they could make our office carpets look fresh. The main rug they suggested should be replaced; two other rugs they believed they could clean up nicely.

Two of the salesmen, we discovered, were born again Christians who had been praying that their partner would get saved. Their demonstration made me think: just as rugs get prematurely worn by sand and dirt, our lives need God's cleansing from sin. Thinking of God's promise, *"Purge me with hyssop, and I shall be clean; wash me, and I shall be whiter than snow"* (Psalm 51:7), I commented that our lives, like rugs, need cleaning. We all need to keep the "sand and dirt," or sin, from destroying our lives. Waiting to receive God's cleaning, people can become so soiled that their lives are ruined. Receiving God's powerful cleaning—the sooner, the better—has great benefits. A decision to receive God's cleaning service should not be delayed.

We made an appointment for them to come back to clean the two rugs, gave each a tract, and thanked them for the demonstration. Rug cleaning day came and the men cleaned the two rugs beautifully. After they had finished, I asked if they had time for us to show them how to know if they would go to Heaven when they died. They agreed. Noting that Gene seemed receptive to the Scripture, I asked if he would like to ask Jesus to be his Savior. Because of the fine testimony of the other two Christian partners and their witnessing, he desired the special relationship with God that he had seen in their lives.

Gene prayed a believer's prayer: "Jesus, thank you for dying on the Cross. I recognize that I am a sinner and need your blood payment applied to me personally in order for me to be reunited with you. I right now call upon the name of Jesus Christ to save me."

Far better than clean rugs is a clean life. After the cleansing of salvation, all Christians need daily cleansing. Teaching His disciples at the Last Supper, Jesus said, *"'Already you are clean because of the word that I have spoken to you,' Jesus Christ spoke to His disciples"* (John 15:3). But that evening, Jesus washed their feet, a daily washing. After being saved, Christians need daily cleansing (1 John 1:9).

We now had a new brother in Christ, his heart cleansed by the blood of Christ. It was worth much more to James and me than the cleaned rugs, which had been the motivation for another of God's appointments.

* * * * *

September 1983 ~ Timed just right

Gene trusted Christ in our office when he and his partners had cleaned our rugs; two months later, we felt compelled to visit his home and talk with his family. The cleaning van was in the driveway. Gene invited us in, and our girls went with his girls to play. During the conversation, his wife Sandy was interested in learning how she could be born again.

After I had explained Scripture, she trusted Christ as her Savior in their living room as her husband happily watched. Sandy recalled that her grandmother, sick and dying, had been terrified of death. But the night before she died, her grandmother said she had "trusted Christ," and her fear had disappeared.

"Until today, I could never understand what made that difference," Sandy remarked. "I have just done what my grandmother did. She was in her nineties, and I am only thirty-three."

As we left, Sandy told her twin six-year-old girls that she wanted to explain to them what Mommy had just done. Gene had wanted his wife to know Christ as her Savior. If we had come sooner or later, he would not have been home because, most days, he worked until 10:00 p.m. and sometimes until 3 o'clock in the morning. God knew the day and time for us to come. Praise the Lord for His guidance: *"The steps of a man are established by the LORD, when he delights in his way"* (Psalm 37:23).

* * * * *

September 14-21, 1983 ~ "I want to listen."

Two young men stopped at The Family Altar Broadcast Cattle Congress booth and listened carefully. "God loves us and wants us to come to Heaven," I said. "Not only that, He also tells us in the Bible how to get there."

As we read Scripture together, they understood that Christ had died for our sin on the Cross. If we individually choose to receive that payment for our sin, then His payment is applied to our personal account. Bowing their heads, first one and then the other prayed, admitting their need of salvation; they accepted Christ's blood as payment for their sin. When I asked their names, addresses, and ages so that we could contact them later for further encouragement, I discovered that they were fifteen-year-old fraternal twins. How unique, now they both have the same spiritual as well as physical birthday.

Gina and Marla, also fifteen-year-olds, stopped at our booth and trusted Jesus Christ as their Savior. Later, while I was visiting with someone else, two other girls came to the booth. They waited patiently until we were finished. Then I was free to ask if I could be of help to them.

"Yes," they responded, "our friends Gina and Marla told us to come over here and talk to you about what you told them."

I invited them into the booth. They listened eagerly. In spite of being in a public area with people passing by continuously, Libby and Julie bowed their heads and trusted Jesus to buy them back from sin. The Apostle Peter wrote, *"You were ransomed ..., not with perishable things such as silver or gold, but with the w precious blood of Christ, like that of a lamb without blemish or spot"* (1 Peter 1:18-19). How great that all four friends, within hours of each other, came to know the Lord.

Geneva Nell, another FAB booth worker, asked a young boy and Valerie, his mother, if they would like to see in the Bible how to know if they would go to Heaven. The young son was interested and asked to come into the booth, but his mother was reluctant.

"Let's go," Valerie insisted.

"But, I want to hear what she says," the boy pleaded, as he sat down in our booth.

A few minutes later, his mother again urged, "Come on, let's go."

"I want to hear the rest," the son requested.

Relenting, the mother sat next to her son and listened. After Geneva had finished her explanation, she asked Jacob if he wanted to receive Jesus as his Savior. He did.

Then looking at his mother, Geneva asked, "Would you like to pray and receive Jesus?"

"Yes," Valerie answered, "I believe I would."

Praise the Lord, a son not only trusted Christ, but was also used of God to bring his mother into God's family.

As we witness for the Lord, rather than becoming discouraged, let us ask God to give wisdom and boldness, even as Paul did, *"As it is my eager expectation and hope that I will not be at all ashamed, but that with full courage now as always Christ will be honored in my body, whether by life or by death"* (Philippians 1:20).

*   *   *   *   *

CHAPTER 9

1984

March 1984 ~ Wife in hiding

Seeking refuge from her husband, a Christian wife asked friends if she could stay with them. They graciously opened their home to her. Her husband contacted us, asking if we would tell her that he missed her.

We stopped to visit his wife and the family that had offered her refuge. The couple who had opened their home, Marlys and Dale, was a compassionate pair. As Maryls spoke, I could tell she seemed to be searching for something in her own spiritual life.

Expressing admiration for their concern and willingness to become involved in a complicated situation, I asked them if they had ever experienced being "born again?"

"No, not yet," Marlys replied.

"May I show you in the Scriptures where it tells how much God loves you and what He has done to make it possible for you to go to Heaven?"

"Okay," she agreed.

At the kitchen table, we read the Scriptures where Jesus explained to Nicodemus that the path to Heaven required all of us to be born again: *"Jesus answered him* [Nicodemus], *'Truly, truly, I say to you, unless one is born again he cannot see the kingdom of God'"* (John 3:3). Marlys and Dale listened with interest. When it was obvious that they understood, I invited them trust Christ. To say "Yes" to Jesus, thereby transferring their sin to Christ on the Cross and receiving the promised forgiveness of sin.

Marlys prayed first and after a short pause, Dale prayed too. Looking at each other, they tried to explain how they both felt, agreeing on the same descriptive words, "I feel so much lighter!" they exclaimed. "It is as if a great burden has been removed from my shoulders." They were experiencing Christ's promise, ***"For my yoke is easy, and my burden is light"*** (Matthew 11:30).

We rejoiced in their coming to know Christ as Lord and Savior and also prayed for God to work out the many details involved with their guest, the wife in a difficult marriage situation. How wonderful it was, we observed, that because of their willingness to protect a wife they themselves received the wonderful gift of everlasting life.

* * * * *

May 1984 ~ Spiritual twins

A lively, five-year-old sweetheart, Lori had visited our church and trusted Christ. We made a house call to meet her parents. Her mother kindly invited us in. When I asked if Darlene would like me to show her from the Bible where Jesus explained how a person gets to Heaven, she was interested. Just as we opened the Bible, there was a knock. Dawn and her children, friends from Grundy Center, had come to visit. Interested in the conversation, Dawn joined us.

The children played, coming in and out, interrupting for this and that while I explained the Scriptures, beginning with a favorite soul-winning text, John 3, where Jesus told Nicodemus that he must be born again in order to get to Heaven.

"We must have two birthdays—a physical birthday and a spiritual birthday," I explained.

When Darlene and Dawn understood their need to call upon Christ as their Savior, both bowed their heads and hearts, praying aloud, asking the Lord to save them from the dreaded disease of sin. Darlene remarked, "How interesting. A year from now I'll be only one year old in the family of God." She was experiencing the truth in Scripture,

"Therefore, if anyone is in Christ, he is a new creation. The old has passed away; behold, the new has come" (2 Corinthians 5:17).

These two, friends and mothers became spiritual twins, infants in God's family, excited about starting their new Christian lives. Setting forth to begin acquiring needed spiritual nourishment, *"Like newborn infants, long for the pure spiritual milk, that by it you may grow up into salvation"* (1 Peter 2:2).

* * * * *

May 23, 1984 ~ Testimony by daughter Victoria

We prayed that Victoria would trust Christ as her Savior and Lord at an early age. When James played with our girls, he emphasized, over and over, how much he loves them, but that Jesus loves them more. Victoria's two older sisters, Angela and Jessica, had also talked seriously with her about how important it is to trust Jesus.

One night after Christmas, Victoria was singing in her bed. I went to encourage her to go to sleep.

"Mommy, Jesus loves me," she stated with her arms wrapped around my neck. "And Jesus loves Angela, and Jesus loves Jessica, and Jesus loves Daddy, and Jesus loves you." she continued.

"Yes, Honey, He does," I assured her.

"I want to trust Jesus," she said simply.

At first, I was not certain what to do—dismiss her statement as unimportant, or what? "You want to trust Jesus?" I asked.

"YES." she agreed emphatically.

"Then pray, Honey, and ask Him to pay for your sins."

In her little, childish voice, Victoria prayed, "Jesus, I want you to pay for my sin and take care of me." She looked up, and smiling said, "Mommy, Jesus said, 'Yes.'"

"Go tell Daddy what you just did," I told her. Pattering feet made their way to Daddy.

"Daddy, I have trusted Jesus," she told James.

As much as she understood, she received in faith. Who is to say at what point a child is able to understand and trust Christ? Simple as

God's salvation is, we just need to take God at His Word. We should not make salvation harder than it is.

We had taught her the things of the Lord, and she believed us and exercised simple faith. Not only in our own lives, but in our household, we have seen God's promises hold true. Paul writes about his concern for believers and faith in God's power to keep them, *"And I am sure of this, that he who began a good work in you will bring it to completion at the day of Jesus Christ"* (Philippians 1:6). Based on Victoria's heart commitment, God has continued to work to bring her to a more mature understanding.

Victoria, however, remembers her time of salvation as coming a little later. She always points to a Sunday morning when she believes she came to know the Lord. Perhaps previous experiences were preparation, leading to the event. Sometimes a genuine understanding comes in stages. Those times are important, but we need to avoid telling children that they do not need to "do it now," because they have "done it before." We do not know at what point, in childlike faith, people actually connect with God for salvation. This respect for God's leading is especially important when dealing with children. We need to be patient, seeing how much they understand and assisting them in coming to God, who loves us.

Written by daughter Victoria, age fourteen

My name is Victoria Goering. I was reared in a Bible-believing home. My father was the pastor at Calvary Bible Church for eight years. I heard my father preach every Sunday morning, Sunday night, and Wednesday night.

One particular Sunday morning, my father laid the sermon down pretty hard. It hit its target. I was three years old at the time and was just realizing what it really meant to be a Christian. I guess I had always known. But since I was so young, I really couldn't be expected to understand. That day it hit me. My father had just finished a sermon on God and His love for us and was giving an altar call for anyone who wanted to go forward. I remember squirming in my seat for awhile, looking around to see if anyone was watching. Silently, I slid out of my seat and made my way to the front. My mother had seen me go forward, so she came up to join me. There, both of my parents sat down with me, asking if I wanted to be saved. I did.

My parents wanted to make sure that I understood that I was not just going through the actions. I explained why I wanted to be saved and how I could go about doing just that. Then my parents asked me if I wanted to pray. So I did. I was so relieved when that prayer was over; it was as if a weight had been lifted from my shoulders. I was a little kid and had been scared to death in this terrifying world. But after I accepted Christ, I had nothing to fear.

On January 27, 1985, I was baptized. I remember that day. The organist played the Gospel song *"In My Heart There Rings a Melody."* I was so happy. That night I went home singing that song; since then, it has been my favorite hymn. In 1995, when I was fourteen, I rededicated my life to Christ. I know I have a lot to work on in my Christian faith, but I hope that with the help of God, I can get things resolved so that I can live my life fully for His glory.

Victoria Joy (Goering) Jergenson

* * * * *

Since the age of fourteen, Victoria has reconfirmed her commitment to Christ and today has a strong personal walk with the Lord. She has first-hand confidence in the power of God to protect: *"No, in all these things we are more than conquerors through him who loved us. For I am sure that neither death nor life, nor angels nor rulers, nor things present nor things to come, nor powers, nor height nor depth, nor anything else in all creation, will be able to separate us from the love of God in Christ Jesus our Lord"* (Romans 8:37-39). Yes, she is trusting Jesus.

* * * * *

June 1984 ~ Lame will walk

Occasionally our whole family ministered at the nursing home. One Sunday afternoon, our three daughters—ages seven, five, and three—sang a special song and James preached.

Sitting in a wheelchair, Doug was particularly responsive. A young man, he laughed and visited with us after the program. When I asked what caused him to be in the nursing home being so young, he recounted a terrible car accident involving a semi-trailer truck.

"I was drinking and driving, and I am lucky to be alive." Pointing to multiple ugly scars on both legs, Doug explained that his life had been turned around so quickly: before the accident, he had been preparing to be a priest.

Opening the Bible, I shared with Doug how he could call upon the Lord for salvation from sin and receive the precious gift of everlasting life. Doug gladly prayed, asking Christ to save him and give him eternal life.

"Please, come get me for church," he pleaded; "I want to go to church." We assured Doug that James and I would make arrangements.

One day in Heaven, because he received Christ, Doug will walk again. The New Testament records this promise, *"If the Spirit of him who raised Jesus from the dead dwells in you, he who raised Christ Jesus from the dead will also give life to your mortal bodies through his Spirit who dwells in you"* (Romans 8:11). Believers look forward to deliverance from the sting of sin, mortality involving disabilities, pain, tears, sickness, old age, and death (Revelation 21:3, 4).

* * * * *

July 1984 ~ Blind will see

When a building in downtown Waterloo was to be demolished, the owner invited FAB to take anything we wanted out of the building. Having already removed everything the owners wanted, they said that in three days there would be only a hole in the ground.

James and I could hardly believe our eyes when we inspected the building. Many items that FAB certainly could use were still there "for the taking." We needed a truck to transport all that we could use for our office. Someone we knew brought a truck and extra hands to help. Finally, at midnight, we unloaded the truck and moved the items into the FAB office.

Young and muscular, Mick was a hard worker. We chatted as we worked. Our girls asked us about another worker, Rick. They were concerned that he drank beer and smoked.

"That's bad," Angela, Jessica, and Victoria loudly agreed.

"That's right. It's bad," Mick said. "I used to do those things too, but I stopped. Those habits do not make life happy." When I asked Mick if he knew if he was born again and ready for Heaven when he died, he responded, "No, I'm not." Since Mick seemed open to the Gospel, I gave him a tract.

A few moments later, Rick took me aside. "He'll never be able to read that tract—Mick is going blind. He's had a disease of the eyes from birth, and it's getting worse."

Our hearts went out to Mick. After we had finished the work, James asked if he could show Mick how God tells us we can get to Heaven.

"I'd like that," he quickly responded.

James explained to Mick about God's rich gift of eternal life, Mick prayed and received Christ as his Savior. He received the promise of eternal life in Heaven where his eyesight will be restored, and he will see the nail-scarred hands of his Savior. Paul encourages us all explaining, *"For we know that the whole creation has been groaning together in the pains of childbirth until now. And not only the creation, but we ourselves, who have the firstfruits of the Spirit, groan inwardly as we wait eagerly for adoption as sons, the redemption of our bodies"* (Romans 8:22, 23). God promises us new bodies in eternity.

*   *   *   *   *

Calvary Bible Church in Washburn, Iowa

September 1984 ~ Right place, right time

A friend and I visited a young girl who had been attending the Washburn church services. Greeted at the door by the little girl's mother and a visiting friend, we were invited to come in. Enjoying a conversation with them, I had explained how they could know the Lord Jesus Christ as personal Savior. Both ladies bowed their heads and prayed, receiving Christ. They were excited to know that they had a home in Heaven.

Since the friend was visiting from another location in Iowa, we mentioned the name of someone who could help her grow in Christ and take her to the church there. How fascinating it is to see the Lord bring people, at just the right time and the right place, to hear the good news of salvation. It is also fantastic to find believers everywhere, no matter where we go. We have discovered precious fellowship with part of the family of God. As new believers are interested in being faithful to Christ, they will need to ask God to help them be obedient to the leading of the Holy Spirit in their lives; then they will grow in Christ.

* * * * *

September 1984 ~ Tragic fire

Kathy regularly attended Calvary Bible Church in Washburn. She was a truly delightful young woman. One day, a terrible fire destroyed her home. Kathy's invalid mother, alone at home, had smelled smoke and quickly telephoned her nearest son. Rushing over immediately, they arrived too late. Kathy's mother did not survive.

Choking back tears, Kathy and her family sifted through the remains to salvage what they could and talked of plans to rebuild. When James and I drove past the home later, only charred ruins remained. We took dishes of food to Kathy's brothers' house with heartfelt sympathy for the family's loss.

After that tragedy, Kathy resided at the Harmony House Care Center, but she requested that we continue to pick her up for church. A number of Sundays after that, we dropped Kathy off after church at her sisters' home, planning to pick her up later for the evening church service. When we picked Kathy up that evening, her sister Jane called out to us, "I love you."

Taken by surprise, I asked, "What?"

She repeated, "I love you."

"We love you, too," I replied, with a smile.

Jane appreciated the love and help we had shown Kathy through the years. How often does someone tell you they love you like that? It warmed my heart and gave me a concern for Jane's soul. As far as I knew, she had never received the atoning blood of Christ to her personal account. When Kathy had requested prayer for Jane during her battle with cancer, we had prayed for her. The cancer had been removed, and she was healing fine; but having cancer can certainly prompt a person to think of what happens when this life is over.

Returning that week with a friend, I asked Jane if we could visit. She warmly invited us to come in. As Jane and her husband sat at their kitchen table, I shared from Scripture how God sent His Son to save us from the wages of sin and death. After a while, I felt led to ask Jane the question.

"Jane, would you like to pray right now and call upon the Lord to save you and give you a home in Heaven?"

"Yes," she said. Praying aloud, Jane did just that.

When I asked her husband, he responded, "No, Ma'am, not now."

As we left, we rejoiced for the opportunity to visit with this couple. Tragedy brought a victory. Our prayers continue that her husband will make that life-altering decision.

* * * * *

November 1984 ~ Deathbed vigil

When James's cousin Ernie and his wife, in Galva, Kansas, bought a new car, they donated their used car to the Broadcast. We desperately needed reliable transportation, but we just didn't have the money to purchase a newer car. God supplied our need. Their gift was beautiful—a white, 1983 Chevy Caprice diesel—and we were thrilled. Fetching the car meant a fun trip to Kansas for our family.

Arriving at their home, we took care of the legal paper work involved in transferring the car. Angela, Jessica, and Victoria stretched their legs, running around the farm, playing with their friendly dog.

During that visit, word came that one of James's distant cousins in the Wichita hospital was dying of cancer. Family members requested that we come. To the best of our knowledge, James's cousin, Jack, was unsaved; his loved ones hoped that Jack would receive Christ before dying. We made our way to Wichita.

Upon arriving at the hospital, we rushed to Jack's bedside where he lay in a semi-conscious state. Doctors believe that the last sensory ability to leave a person on their deathbed is the sense of hearing. After working in the Omaha hospital, I believe people unable to move or speak who are trapped inside a body unable to respond, may hear and understand what happens around them.

As Jack hung on to the last threads of life, I read aloud passages in the Gospel of John, Chapters 1 and 3, and carefully explained how a person can trust Christ as his Savior. Of course, he could not speak with us, but I assured him that Christ Jesus was on the inside with him, listening to his thoughts. All Jack needed to do was to tell Jesus that he recognized himself as a sinner, trust Jesus, and ask Him to pay for his sin, giving him the gift of everlasting life. Then I invited Jack to pray silently with me as I talked with God about his trusting Christ to be his Savior.

Carefully, I repeated the verses and prayer a number of times, hoping that he would be conscious enough to hear and understand. Marie, his wife, had shared with us that through the years, Jack had resisted anything Christian. But recently at home when she had the Christian radio station on, he had begun to listen to the programs rather than turn the dial.

Before leaving that hospital room, I asked Jack that if he had trusted Christ just now, if he was ready to die and go to Heaven, "Blink your right eye for me." Praise the Lord, Jack blinked his right eye! Marie took my hand and shared with me that it was at her brother's bedside, years before, that she herself had trusted Christ. Later, Marie told us that before we came, Jack had been struggling to stay alive, as if he wasn't ready to die. After we left, he relaxed. A day and a half later, he peacefully slipped into eternity.

Those praying for Jack's salvation felt their burden from the Holy Spirit lifted. Marie had the peace that she would see her husband again in eternity. We believe that Jack did indeed call upon Christ for salvation. We believe this situation was similar to Paul and Silas's telling the Philippian jailer, *"Believe in the Lord Jesus, and you will be saved, you and your household"* (Acts 16:31). What a precious promise.

* * * * *

November 1984 ~ High-speed crash

When Harmony Nursing Home invited local pastors to conduct Sunday afternoon services for their residents, on occasion, James volunteered to preach. One Sunday, as James prepared for the church

God's Appointment

service, I circled the area, stopping to visit people and invite them to attend the service. I also encouraged our three daughters to greet the people in the lounge where the service would be held. Since the mostly senior citizen residents enjoyed the children, we made it a point to come as a family.

While mingling, I noticed a young man in his mid-twenties sitting on a couch, assembling a difficult puzzle. I felt that it must be difficult for such a young person to live in the nursing home. Bob matched a number of pieces; he was obviously good at working difficult puzzles, and I told him so. Engaging him in a conversation, I asked what had brought him to Harmony House. What a story. He had been high on drugs, drunk, and speeding down a road when suddenly his car had swerved and hit a tree. The impact sent him and the car engine into the back seat. It was a miracle that he survived!

Bob's prognosis was grim. At the hospital, when he had finally awaken from a coma, his life was drastically changed. Eventually Bob left his bed for a wheelchair, and he was transferred to Harmony for the duration of a slow recovery.

"Bob, if you had died in the accident, what would have happened to you?" I asked.

"I don't know—" he replied, shaking his head, "—maybe Hell."

Compassionately I explained from the Bible how God has made it possible, through the work of Christ on the Cross, for all of us to get to Heaven.

It was time for the service to begin. Inviting Bob to come hear James preach, I promised to show him later, more passages from the Bible. Bob listened to the preaching. After the service, we talked and reviewed how he could simply trust the Lord Jesus as his Savior.

Bob rested his head on the back of the coach, looked up to the ceiling and beyond, and asked Christ to pay for his sins and be his Savior. Bob's decision was sincere. Learning that we provided transportation for some nursing home residents to attend our Sunday services, he was interested.

For a number of years, we picked up Bob and a few other residents, taking them to Calvary Bible Church for services. Bob's strength increased, yet he continued to struggle with addictive substances. Drinking was not difficult for him to give up because that substance was not available; cigarettes were harder. More than once, he left the church services to go outside and smoke. Finally, God gave him victory, and he stopped smoking.

Bob often shared his testimony. He would say, "I thank God for my accident. It changed the direction of my life from Hell to Heaven." After a public confession of his faith in Christ, Bob was baptized and remained faithful in attending church services.

Eventually, Bob obtained a job working as an orderly at the same nursing home. When I would come to the nursing home, Bob would take me to meet one or more patients with whom he worked. The patients responded well to him; he understood their situation and cared. Bob was concerned for friends and family that they would get saved, and he became a diligent soul winner himself.

We encouraged him to write out his testimony and helped him make a tract to pass out. This is his testimony as he told it.

"I THANK GOD FOR MY ACCIDENT"
Bob Spahn

Hello. My name is Bob Spahn. I want to tell you a true story about the effects of drugs and alcohol on my life. I was enjoying living the "good life," married to my attractive wife whom I loved very much. As a top auto mechanic with a good job, I was paid an excellent salary. In fact, I could easily support my rapidly growing alcohol and drug addiction.

One night I drove 75 mph on a mountain road following a fight with my wife, and under the influence of alcohol and drugs, I suddenly hit a tree. The impact sent the engine and me into the back seat. I am told my blood alcohol level was a .27, which is three hundredths of a point from killing a person. Had the impact been just six inches to the left of that tree, I would have careened off a steep cliff into eternity in Hell.

I was taken to a local hospital and quickly sent by helicopter to a large trauma center. Three weeks later, following brain surgery, a respirator, oxygen, and excellent medical care, I woke from the coma. After weeks in a wheelchair and learning to walk again, I was transferred to an outstanding head-injury rehabilitation hospital hundreds of miles from home. I remained there for months of intensive rehabilitation. The worry, grief, and fear I put my family through were beyond description.

As a result of that severe head injury, I experienced a major and permanent personality change. Then my wife left me. In retrospect, my head injury was the best thing that ever happened to me. I'd still be drinking and using drugs if—in fact, I would still be alive. I was far from God, and He had to knock some sense into me.

Pastor James Goering presented a chapel service at the health care center where I was getting further rehabilitation in 1986. I attended because I was bored and had nothing else to do. His wife, Gloria, came and showed me how to trust Jesus as my personal Savior. On that day, I was saved. Now I have confidence that I am one of God's children and will go to Heaven when I die. By God's grace, I am serving Him the best I can. God had a plan for my life and allowed me to live following that terrible accident. It was a blessing in disguise for me.

My advice for all is, do not wait to have an accident that could take your life before you get saved. Ask Him now to be your personal Savior. Just trust in Jesus to save you from all your sin. He died on the Cross and rose again to save you.

A couple of my favorite Bible verses are from the Gospel of John: *"But to all who did receive him, who believed in his name, he gave the right to become children of God"* (John 1:12). *"For God so loved the world, that he gave his only Son, that whoever believes in him should not perish but have eternal life"* (John 3:16).

* * * * *

Bob was promoted to glory December 5, 2010. His life had changed and he enjoyed giving testimony of God's saving grace in his life and helping others to find in Christ what he had found. Bob often vocalized through the years his appreciation for God using us to bring him to Christ. He referred to me as "My spiritual mom." Of those I have led to the Lord through the years, Bob has said the most often, "Thank you!" Bob reminds me of the story of the ten lepers in Luke 17:11-19. Jesus healed ten and one returned to say thank you. In Heaven I can imagine all those our lives have influenced for eternity will be grateful. I know I am looking forward to expressing my appreciation to those who were instrumental in my coming to know the Lord! Maybe it would be good for me to find ways to be grateful even now.

* * * * *

December 1984 ~ Testimony by daughter Jessica (Written by her later, at age 16)

My name is Jessica Anna Goering. I've been reared in a Bible-believing home my entire life. My father was my pastor for my first eight years, and he played a very significant role in my salvation experience.

I can still remember the euphoric, indescribable feeling that came over me during one Sunday church service when I was about five. My father was preaching a message on salvation, and even though I had heard him talk about his relationship with Christ numerous times before, it was as if all of a sudden, it made sense to me. When he said the closing prayer and gave the invitation, I knew that I didn't want to go to hell. I wanted to go to heaven and be with my friend Jesus. I think because of a mixture of intimidation and shyness, I didn't go forward that day. Instead, I prayed right there on my own in the pew.

Much has changed, but I am still excited to be counted as a child of God and am looking forward to a long life with Him. At age fourteen, I rededicated my life to Christ while attending Clear Lake Baptist Camp. I realize that I have a lot to work on in my spiritual walk, but I accept the challenge, and God in His strength will help me meet it.

Jessica Anna (Goering) Wood

* * * * *

Jessica has remained strong in her walk with the Lord and has claimed the promise that God will use our hurts to make us strong to help others. *"Blessed be the God and Father of our Lord Jesus*

Christ, the Father of mercies and God of all comfort, who comforts us in all our affliction, so that we may be able to comfort those who are in any affliction, with the comfort with which we ourselves are comforted by God. For as we share abundantly in Christ's sufferings, so through Christ we share abundantly in comfort too. If we are afflicted, it is for your comfort and salvation; and if we are comforted, it is for your comfort, which you experience when you patiently endure the same sufferings that we suffer. Our hope for you is unshaken, for we know that as you share in our sufferings, you will also share in our comfort" (2 Corinthians 1:1-5). She is a beautiful woman, both inside and out.

* * * * *

CHAPTER 10

1985-1986

January 1985 ~ Spiritual heart surgery

When a lady in our church had surgery, we decided to visit her in the hospital on the way home from the office. Suggesting that I go upstairs to Margaret's room, James waited downstairs with our three daughters—Angela, four; Jessica, two; and Victoria, one month.

Margaret was sleeping. I didn't want to wake her up, but I felt compelled to stay in the room and visit with her roommate. Between phone calls, nurses' visits, and other interruptions, Patricia and I became acquainted. She told me she was scheduled for gallbladder surgery the next day. Patricia also shared that she had recently begun attending a Bible study. When the medical activity in the room ceased for a while, I asked Patricia if she knew if she was a "born-again Christian."

"I am not sure," she replied. "I would like to be, but I don't know how."

"Would you mind if I showed you from the Bible how you could be born again?"

"Yes, I'd like that."

We read several Scriptures together, including Jesus' instruction in John 3, *"Unless one is born of water and the Spirit, he cannot enter the kingdom of God. That which is born of the flesh is flesh, and that which is born of the Spirit is spirit. Do not marvel that I said to you, 'You must be born again.'"* I could see that each verse registered its meaning on her heart. Since she was receptive to the work of the Holy Spirit, I asked her, "Would you like to pray right now and trust Jesus Christ to apply His shed blood to your account and give you everlasting life?"

"Yes," she replied, "I would." Bowing her head, Patricia prayed aloud, asking Jesus Christ to apply the blood He shed on the Cross to her sin, be her Savior and to give her everlasting life.

Before leaving I asked her, "Do you know for sure that you are going to Heaven when you die?"

"Yes, I do," was her answer.

"How do you know — because I told you so?"

"No, because the Bible says so," Patricia replied. "Thank you for talking to me."

Joining my family, we rejoiced in having a new sister in Christ. The next day, our pastor, Sarge Lusthoff, went to the hospital and led Patricia's husband to Christ. Just before Patricia left for home, we visited over the telephone; she mentioned that she was glad that God had brought our paths together there in the hospital. Another of those Divine appointments; *"The steps of a man are established by the LORD, when he delights in his way"* (Psalm 37:23).

* * * * *

January 1985 ~ Worth a second visit

A husband and wife had trusted Christ the previous week and had asked us to come back.

When we knocked at the trailer home, their teenage son opened the door and explained, "The folks aren't home right now, but they should be back any time — come on in and wait."

Their son, Gary, introduced us to Karen, his fiancée, who was visiting him. As we talked, I asked if Gary's parents had told them about their decision to trust Christ as their Savior.

"Yes," there had been discussion, and Gary had been impressed by changes in his parent's attitudes and lives that week.

Then I asked the young couple that all important question, "How about you, Gary and Karen, do you know for sure that you have trusted Christ as your Savior?"

Gary was certain that he had, but Karen was not. As I shared with her from Scripture, she listened carefully. Karen bowed her head and prayed, receiving Jesus as her Savior. When she had finished, Gary wanted to pray. Already born again, he was conscious of the fact that his life was not what it should be; he needed to get things right between him and the Lord. Christians can allow many things into their lives that are displeasing to God and need constant cleansing to get rid of sin. Just as after a bath, we still frequently need to wash our hands; in our spiritual lives, we need that daily cleansing, The Apostle John writes about keeping clean. *"If we say we have no sin, we deceive ourselves, and the truth is not in us. If we confess our sins, he is faithful and just to forgive us our sins and to cleanse us from all unrighteousness"* (1 John 1:8, 9). What a blessing to have such a faithful and merciful Heavenly Father.

When the parents came home, we visited with them, and asked Karen and Gary to share with them what they had just done. How pleased Gary's parents were that Gary and Karen had also made decisions for Christ.

* * * * *

April 1985 ~ Daughter of the King

A precious nine-year-old girl with short, blond hair, Shelly looked across our living room shyly. She and her older sister, with another neighbor girl, had stopped to see how I was feeling, having heard that I was sick.

When I had previously spoken with the two older girls about the Lord, they had trusted Christ as their Savior. The three had occasionally attended church with us, but I could not remember Shelly ever having made a decision for Christ.

Prayerfully looking at Shelly I inquired, "Have you asked Jesus to be your Savior yet, Shelly?

"Not yet," she replied.

"Do you want to now?" I continued.

"Yes," nodding her head, she added, "I would like that."

We all sat on the coach as I read verses from the Bible which explained that by accepting Jesus Christ as our Savior, God receives us as His sons and daughters. As so often, I read, *"But to all who did receive him, who believed in his name, he gave the right to become children of God"* (John 1:12). After I had answered Shelly's questions from Scripture, she bowed her head and trusted Jesus as her Savior. Praise the Lord that young people can be reached before their hearts become hardened.

* * * * *

May 27, 1985 ~ Broken dryer

It all began when I went outside to hang the wash on the clothesline. Since our dryer was not working, I had been rediscovering the "joy" of hanging up clothes outside. Adjacent to our back yard, a young man sat at a picnic table, apparently deep in thought. The Holy Spirit prompted me to talk with him about the Lord; nevertheless, I debated within myself, whether or not I should. Finally, after asking the Lord for guidance, I stepped over to the fence and spoke, "Hi. Do you think it's going to rain?"

"I don't know," he replied with a shy smile.

Then I asked if he went to church anywhere.

"Sometimes I do," he replied, "but not often."

"May I ask you a question?"

"Sure," he replied.

"Do you know for sure if you are going to Heaven?"

"Yeah, I guess so," he replied.

"How does a person get to Heaven?" I continued.

"By faith, I guess, and doing what's right," he replied. When I asked his name and age, he responded "Steve," and he was sixteen years old.

After introducing myself, I continued, "You know, once I was really wondering how to get to Heaven but didn't know whom to talk to or what to believe. I remember thinking, 'If only I could talk to Jesus, He would be able to tell me the right way.' Then I discovered a place in the Bible, the Gospel of John chapter 3, where a man named Nicodemus asked Jesus how to get to Heaven. Jesus clearly answered him. I thought, 'Wow. If I read how Jesus answered Nicodemus, I'll know how He'd answer me if I could talk with Him directly.'"

"Steve, would you mind if I go into my house to get a Bible and share with you how Jesus answered Nicodemus?"

"No, that would be fine with me, if you want to," was his response.

Returning, I put the Bible on the picnic table between us so that he could follow along with me. Opening to the passage where Jesus instructed Nicodemus on how to be born again, literally born from above (John 3), I began reading,

> *Jesus answered him, "Truly, truly, I say to you, unless one is born again he cannot see the kingdom of God."*
> *Nicodemus said to him, "How can a man be born when he is old? Can he enter a second time into his mother's womb and be born?"*
> *Jesus answered, "Truly, truly, I say to you, unless one is born of water and the Spirit, he cannot enter the kingdom of God. That which is born of the flesh is flesh, and that which is born of the Spirit is spirit. Do not marvel that I said to you, 'You must be born again."* (John 3:3-7).

Continuing in the same chapter, we read,

> *Whoever believes in him may have eternal life. For God so loved the world, that he gave his only Son, that whoever believes in him should not perish but have eternal life. For God did not send his Son into the world to condemn the world, but in order that the world might be saved through him. Whoever believes in him is not condemned, but whoever does not believe is condemned already, because he has not believed in the name of the only Son of God.* (John 3:15-18)

At the end of that chapter, Jesus again clearly explains that *"whoever believes in the Son has eternal life; whoever does not obey the Son shall not see life, but the wrath of God remains on him"* (John 3:36). Another favorite verse in the same Gospel of John, we read aloud, *"But to all who did receive him, who believed in his name, he gave the right to become children of God"* (John 1:12). What clear promises for all who believe. After sharing these Scriptures, I suggested that we have a word of prayer. Steve readily agreed.

Thanking God for the opportunity to talk together about how one can get to Heaven, I continued praying aloud, "Dear God, help Steve to talk to you just as I'm talking to you right now and call upon your Son Jesus Christ to apply the blood that He shed on the Cross to pay for sin to his sin. How about it, Steve, would you like to pray, going to the foot of the Cross and invite Christ into your life?"

Just then a couple of young girls walked past. Seeing the open Bible between us, they began to giggle and laugh.

"Does that bother you?" I asked him.

"No," he replied. Bowing his head, he prayed aloud, unabashedly receiving Christ.

"What are you talking about?" twelve-year-old LeAnn, and nine-year-old Sheri, inquired.

"About how to know if you're going to Heaven," Steve replied.

"We'd like to know, too." they said.

I shared with both of them what I had shared with Steve, they also prayed, receiving Christ as their Savior. I returned to my house.

A short time later, a knock at the door came—it was Sheri with her five-year-old brother, Bruce. He wanted to trust Jesus, too. Even later, Sheri wanted me to come out in the front yard where she and LeAnn were talking to eleven-year-old Angie and fourteen-year-old Rita.

"Hi," I said. "The girls and I have been talking about how to get to Heaven. Would you be interested in having me show you, in the Bible, how Jesus told Nicodemus how to get to Heaven?" I asked.

"Okay," they agreed and followed me inside. After listening, they both eagerly asked Jesus Christ to save them.

When James came home from the office and hospital visitation, we sat down for supper. There was a knock on the door. Four of the girls were back. They had questions, and one of them wanted to pray some more and have God forgive a sin she had committed since she had received Christ. Carefully showing her a Bible verse that shows us how to keep clean after we trust Christ, I explained that even if we've just had a bath, we may need to wash our hands often. Just as we pick up physical dirt in life, we also pick up spiritual dirt, anger, coveting, and disobedience. Near the end of the New Testament, John gives instructions on to how to confess and let God forgive and cleanse us from daily sin, *"If we confess our sins, he is faithful and just to forgive us our sins and to cleanse us from all unrighteousness"* (1 John 1:9).

Sheri went outside but soon returned to our door dragging nine-year-old Mike with her. "May Mike come in?" she called.

"Sure, if he wants to," I replied.

Because of the large number of kids in the house, I invited him and his sister Rita to come to a more private place, in our bedroom. Mike listened and prayed, asking Jesus to help him to be born again and have his sins paid for.

As we said "goodbye," I told the kids that they had a common second birthday. All of them had trusted Christ as their Savior May 27, 1985. According to the Bible, they were born into the family of God. They asked if we could get together when school was out for Bible teaching and devotions together at the park.

P.S. It didn't rain and my clothes dried.

*   *   *   *   *

June 1985 ~ Living in a church bus

Economy problems can change lifestyles. James and I noticed a white and blue bus lettered *Hillcrest Baptist Church* parked across from our house by the park. Home to a man, woman, and a child, the windows had been curtained. Neighborhood children told us that the people drove around at night, warming the bus until they ran low on gas.

One day I noticed the lady returning with clothes from the Laundromat. Since I had stayed home from the office that day to do some indoor painting, I was happy to invite her to join me for a glass of Kool-Aid. She gladly accepted. As we visited, our neighbor mentioned that someone had recently given her a Bible. She had read it all the way through, twice, and was almost through a third time. She was eager to understand more about the Word of God.

We studied together, reading the Gospel of John. I shared with her that favorite passage in John 3, how Jesus had taught Nicodemus about being born again,

> *Now there was a man of the Pharisees named Nicodemus, a ruler of the Jews. This man came to Jesus by night and said to him, "Rabbi, we know that you are a teacher come from God, for no one can do these signs that you do unless God is with him." Jesus answered him, "Truly, truly, I say to you, <u>unless one is born again he cannot see the kingdom of God.</u>" Nicodemus said to him, "How can a man be born when he is old? Can he enter a second time into his mother's womb and be born"* (John 3:1-4).

When I asked if she would like to get on her knees with me to pray and receive Christ, she did. Not many days later, the bus left. Where they went, we do not know. God has undeniably prepared tender hearts all around us, even in unlikely places. As for God, His appointments are precious, timely, and perfect.

* * * * *

September 21, 1985 ~ Cattle Congress interview

(The following is a transcript of an interview taken at the National Dairy Cattle Congress in Waterloo, Iowa.)

Interviewer: Good morning, Gloria. You are busy talking to people about Christ, and it looks as if you enjoy what you are doing.

God's Appointment

Gloria: Yes, I am enjoying the opportunity to visit with such a large number of people in a relatively short time about Christ.

Interviewer: How many people do you think will come to the fair and walk past your booth here?

Gloria: The newspaper says that they expect about 200,000 people will come for the nine-day fair. Not all of the people come by our booth, but probably a good percent of them do.

Interviewer: What are you trying to accomplish by having a booth at the fair?

Gloria: I am being obedient to the leading of the Lord in my life. I have a strong desire to help others come to know Jesus Christ as their Lord and Savior. After my husband James and I were married, we saw the potential for witnessing at fairs; for ten years now, we have been involved in setting up booths and going soul winning. We pray, all year, that God will draw individuals who will be open to the Gospel to come past our booth and that we will be diligent in speaking with them.

Interviewer: Do you come all nine days of the fair?

Gloria: No, with three daughters—ages three, five, and eight—I need to be home some of the time with them. Also, I work at the Family Altar Broadcast home office and am active in Calvary Bible Church which my husband pastors. But I am going to be here at the booth five days for about thirty hours.

Interviewer: Do you have a favorite day, or times, to be at the fair, and why?"

Gloria: "My favorite day at the fair is 9/20, as that is my spiritual birthday, the day I trusted Christ twenty-six years ago. It is especially meaningful to me to introduce people to Jesus as their Savior on that day.

Interviewer: Would you mind my asking how many decisions you had at the booth on your birthday this year?

Gloria: Thirty-three, mostly teenagers between the ages of thirteen and sixteen.

Interviewer: Praise the Lord. Do you think they were sincere?

Gloria: Only God knows for sure, but I personally believe most were. It takes courage to come into the booth, sit down, and have someone open a big Bible and talk with you for fifteen to twenty minutes or more, then bow your head in public and pray. All the time, of course, people are walking past, looking at you. Some stop and watch for a while.

Two young men, whom I especially respect for their courage, stood in the aisle in front of the booth, asking questions. Then, with people walking past them, they bowed their heads and called upon Christ as their Savior. Few people are willing to do that, but I shared with them that Christ died on a public Cross with people walking past, staring at Him. They were brothers, fourteen and twenty-two. They were pleased to discover that by receiving Christ as their Savior at the same time as they did, they were not just physical brothers, but spiritual "twin" brothers in Christ.

As time permits, after a decision for Christ is made, I encourage them to grow in their Christian life, counseling them to pray to God regularly for everything and anything, read their Bible daily—God's love book to them, pray about finding a good Bible-preaching church, get baptized to show publicly they have received Christ, and tell others how to get to Heaven. We also try to follow up, the best we can, by sending literature, praying, and personally following up whenever possible.

Interviewer: Is your husband supportive in this fair work?

Gloria: Very. He makes the arrangements for the booth, helps get it set up, and spends many hours at the booth himself. Of course, the financial burden also falls on him with the Broadcast. It costs to have a booth at the fair, tickets to get in, and parking. Additionally, it seems that the fair always comes at a financially difficult time for us. The summer months are usually financially tight; and by the time the necessary bills are paid, we find ourselves having to pray for extra funds for the fair outreach.

Interviewer: Do people always respond in a positive way to the booth and to you?

Gloria: No. And no matter how many trust Christ at the fair, the lasting impression on my heart is of the thousands that go by on their way to a Christless eternity. For every *one* open to listening, it seems as if I talk to *a hundred* who are not. Many who pass our booth with its Christian design, smirk; many deliberately ignore us; some are rude; and many refuse the tracts. Some deliberately take a tract and then in front of us, drop it to the floor or toss it into the trash at the end of the row. Some parents or friends prevent others from stopping to visit. One man who ran another booth walked past while I was talking to two teen-aged fellows, picked up a tract entitled *Death—What Then?* He laughed and loudly told the people in the booth next to ours that it was all a bunch of trash and nonsense. In spite of that, the two boys still bowed their heads and received Christ. The people in the next booth seemed friendlier afterwards, as if to say, "If he doesn't like you, we do."

To work at the fair, people need to be willing to be considered *"fools for Christ's sake,"* this is from Corinthians 4:10. They can not let negative responses bother them. Who knows, down the line, how those who scorn or ridicule now might be in the future? As Christ prayed on the Cross, **"Father, forgive them, for they know not what they do"** from Luke 23:34. Soon after the crucifixion, a soldier, in charge of one hundred soldiers, proclaimed, **"Truly this was the**

Son of God" in Matthew 27:54. We'll probably see that soldier in Heaven. People do change.

However, there are many supportive people at the fair. Christians stop to visit, glad to see a booth like this. An official from the fair stopped to say that he was thankful for our type of booth. Others working in various booths are also Christians; they smile when there are decisions and pray for our work in this booth. Some are 'almost persuaded,' not ready to make a decision or needing to give the decision more thought. Others would like to talk, but they have to keep up with friends or family or have time deadlines and can't visit further.

Interviewer: Thank you for sharing with me. I trust God will continue to bless your fair ministry in years to come.

* * * * *

December 1985 ~ Family's cry for help

We knocked on the door. No answer. The lady, who had called us earlier that day requesting counseling, evidently wasn't home. Half an hour later, still no answer. But an hour later when we knocked, Carol answered. She apologized. Although she vaguely remembered having heard a knock, she had fallen asleep and had been too tired to get up. Her husband was not home, but she was glad we had come.

Carol and her fifteen-year-old daughter, Sheila, invited us to sit with them around the kitchen table. Both expressed the need for help with family problems. After listening to them for quite a length of time, I urged them to see their problems from God's point of view. They were responding back and forth to each other; they needed to take a look at their relationship with God. When we are not in a right relationship with God, everything else is off kilter. Their pain could very well be a symptom and not their actual problem.

Many serious diseases start out without pain. Something is wrong, but we do not know what it is. The bad news is that we have a terminal disease. The good news is that there is a cure. Our terminal disease is sin. Sin damages relationships—our relationship with God, as well as with other people. We can suffer through the sin disease and pay the consequences, or we can avail ourselves of the cure provided by Jesus Christ when He died on the Cross. Seeing ourselves as God sees us as sinners is a real wake up call, God says, *"We have all become like one who is unclean, and all our righteous deeds are like a polluted garment. We all fade like a leaf, and our iniquities, like the wind, take us away"* (Isaiah 64:6).

That is not a very pretty picture. We want to justify our actions and claim our rights. Of all our relationships, it is important to get right with God and stay right with Him. Once we resolve our relationship problems with God, it affects our other relationships. Going to the heart of the matter—God has provided us a way to make peace with Him. It is through the sacrifice that Jesus Christ made for us. We all have the basic problem—we need Christ and His cleansing blood in our lives. His great love caused Him to leave Heaven and come to earth to make the payment for sin. Although we are unable to come up with the payment for our own sin, we can respond to His offer to give it to us as a free gift—all we have to do is receive it.

Carol said, "I understand more now than in all my years of church attendance." Both of their hearts were open to responding to Christ. They prayed, seeking a right relationship with God by receiving the blood payment Christ provided for their sin and receiving Him as their personal Savior. Jesus said, *"The Spirit of the Lord is upon me, because he has anointed me to proclaim good news to the poor. He has sent me to proclaim liberty to the captives and recovering of sight to the blind, to set at liberty those who are oppressed,"* (Luke 4:18). His instruction is *" to all who did receive him, who believed in his name, he gave the right to become children of God, who were born, not of blood nor of the will of the flesh nor of the will of man, but of God"* (John 1:12-13). We also prayed for her husband, Randy, to get saved and for God to help them with their problems.

The following week when we returned to the house, Randy was there alone. He told us that Carol and Sheila had excitedly shared their decision to trust Christ with him, and Randy wanted what his wife and daughter had discovered. James opened his Bible, and we shared with him how all have sinned and the wages of sin is death: *"For all have sinned, and come short of the glory of God"* (Romans 3:23); *"For the wages of sin is death, but the free gift of God is eternal life in Christ Jesus our Lord"* (Romans 6:23). The only alternative to the sting of death is "believing on the Lord Jesus Christ," thus appropriating His payment for sin.

Randy was clearly fighting in his mind a battle of pride—to admit that he was a sinner. Ask Christ to save him? But when James asked Randy if he understood what the Bible was saying, Randy responded, "Yes, I do."

That night, Randy prayed, receiving Christ as his Savior. Praise the Lord for this family getting things in the right perspective, God's point of view so that they could allow Him to help them.

* * * * *

March 1986 ~ Tears of deliverance

We had the opportunity of providing transportation for a number of mentally handicapped individuals to our church. We enjoyed their presence, and they responded easily to Christian love. One who especially touched our hearts was Gary.

One Sunday, during the service while seated in front of me, Gary eagerly listened as James preached. Gary nodded his head, often saying "Amen." At the end of the service, James asked those wanting to get right with God to raise their hands. Gary raised his hand and kept it raised; but at the invitation, he did not go forward— He was crying. The lady in front of him turned to comfort him.

But when he continued crying, I softly whispered, "Have you asked Jesus to be your Savior yet?"

"No," Gary answered, weeping.

"Would you like me to help you ask Jesus to forgive your sins?"

"Yes," he replied. Gary prayed, and then shared with James and the deacons that he had just received Jesus as his Savior. Jesus said we must come to him "as a little child." We are glad that the Gospel is for everyone.

* * * * *

May 1986 ~ Jesus thrills my heart

It was time for our three girls who were playing across the street at the park, to come home. But seeing that they were engrossed in a conversation with other children, I waited a while before calling them for supper.

When Angela, nine years old, did come in, she asked, "Mom, can you sit on the couch with me for a minute? I want to tell you something." Her face was aglow. "You know what I was doing when you called?"

"No—what?"

"I had just been talking with Shelly and Erin. They asked me all kinds of questions about God and Heaven, "I was telling them what I knew. When Shelly said that she was not sure she was going to Heaven, I told her she should ask Jesus to forgive her sin. Then she could go to Heaven. So Shelly did pray."

As I looked at this little soul winner, my mother's heart was thrilled. Angela was discovering the greatest joy a person can experience—leading others to a saving knowledge of Christ.

* * * * *

June 1986 ~ Life-changes, in an instant

Tall, athletic, and good looking—Jeff had shared a tragic motorcycle ride with his friend. They had been drinking and missed a curve. Jeff had plowed the side of the road with his head without a helmet. He received brain damage; his friend's back had been severely broken.

Three years later, in a church service at a local health care center, Jeff listened as James presented Christ. Following my husband's message, I talked with Jeff about whether he had ever received Jesus Christ as his Lord and Savior.

"No," was his response.

"Would you like to?" I asked.

"Yes, I would," he answered. Bowing his head, Jeff asked Christ that afternoon to pay for his sins and be his Savior. According to Scripture, that afternoon Jeff became a son of the King. From then on, Jeff regularly came to our church services. He rejoiced in knowing Christ. Today, Jeff walks slowly with a cane; although doctors had told him he would never talk again, he is able to talk quite well.

* * * * *

Family Altar Broadcast ministry experienced a major blessing in June by purchasing the building at 108 and 110 E. 4th St., downtown Waterloo. The structure definitely needed considerable fixing up, but it provided lots of needed space.

* * * * *

July 4, 1986 ~ Firecracker convert

Dave had been attending our church. He trusted Christ and asked if we would talk with his wife about the Lord. His wife's' name was the same as mine, Gloria. Pressures of time, particularly our working on the FAB's monthly mailing, prevented our going right away, but we added Gloria's name to the mailing list.

As we tried to generate mailing labels, the computer would stop every time at Gloria's name and wouldn't continue past it. We worked and worked, trying to finish the mailing list, but the computer continued stopping at Gloria's name. Each time it did, it reminded me of Dave's request, and I sent up a prayer for her salvation. By the time we finally had things working correctly and the mailing finished, we not only knew that God wanted us to visit Gloria, but there had been a lot of prayer made on her behalf.

Carrying a sack of groceries as a gift for her and the family, we knocked at her door. To our surprise, we met a very angry woman. Gloria evidently was looking for an excuse to "haul off and hit somebody," and we were good candidates. She did, however, invite us in. After a little while, God softened her heart, and Gloria trusted Christ that day, the Fourth of July. We became good friends, and I called her our firecracker convert. Gloria grew in the Lord, was baptized and attended our church until she moved out of state. She wrote her testimony which is shared below.

(What a blessing it was to see how God worked in Gloria's life.)

Gloria D. & her three sons

Testimony by Gloria D.

I thank God that He saved me when He did, or I might not be living today. On drugs and alcohol, I didn't care what happened to me. One day, I took an overdose of drugs. I didn't know what had happened until I woke up in the hospital, but I was thankful to be alive.

While I was drinking, I was pregnant with a son. Doctors told me that he had a little brain damage because of my drinking. I kept drinking, not caring what happened until one day my older son left home because he couldn't stand my making his life miserable. He said he never wanted to see me again.

Then Pastor Goering and his wife came to see me. I really didn't want to see them, but thank God, they cared enough to come. We visited awhile; then they asked me if I were to die tonight, would I go to Heaven? I knew I was headed in a different direction by the way I was living. I had hurt one son and another had left home. When they told me the plan of salvation, th I accepted Christ as my Savior that day. I thank God that they cared enough to come. But most of all, I thank God that He delivered me from my drugs and alcoholism and forgave all my sin.

Later, I told my sons what happened. They have both forgiven me and now, at the time of this writing, I have my three sons back home again. I love the Lord with all my heart.

Gloria D.

*   *   *   *   *

A son, Josiah, was born and now we were a family of six.

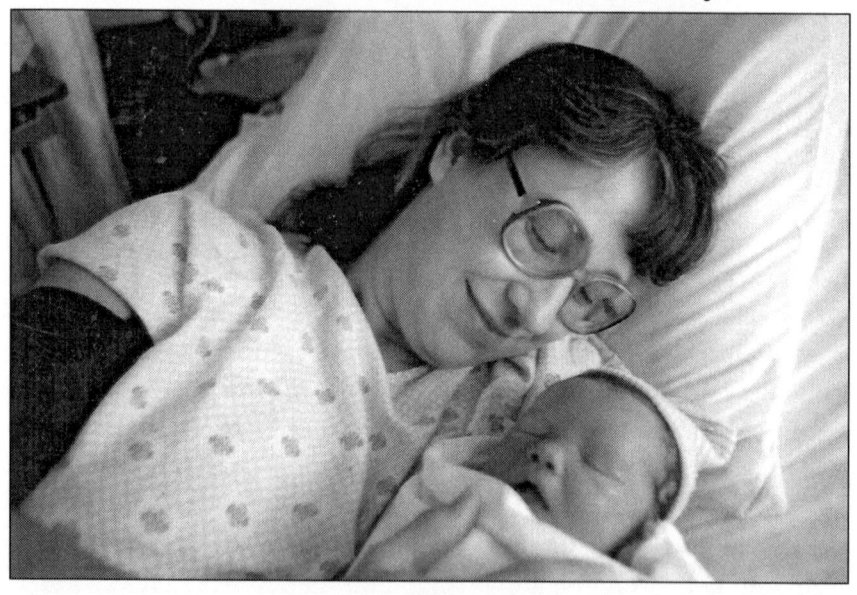

On August 20, 1986, Josiah James Goering was born. We were now a family of six, three girls and a boy. James had always felt that God had promised him a son. The son had arrived and

although James had had to wait, he was forty five years old, we were glad it wasn't as long as Abraham had to wait for his son.

*   *   *   *   *

December 26, 1986 ~ Copier problems, again

Fairly often at FAB, we had trouble with the copy machine. God provided a trained, independent man from Cedar Rapids to service the machine; his price was reasonable, and his work was good. Tall, slim, red-headed—Mike was a godsend, but he did not claim Christ as his Lord. I was burdened for him and began praying that he would come to know Christ.

Again and again, Mike came to our rescue. One day while he worked, Mike shared with us that he was in the process of getting a divorce. Certainly we were concerned for him, aware of the pain involved in such a situation.

Then just before Christmas, our copier went on the blink again. The day after Christmas, Mike was there to fix it. As he worked, I asked how things were going.

"No wonder people don't like to talk about divorce!" Mike exclaimed. "It's a terrible thing."

Pain was easy to see on his countenance, "Difficult times often make us more serious about God," I gently commented. "Sometimes those difficulties help people to begin wondering if they have a right relationship with Him, and if they're on their way to Heaven."

"I am trying to do my best, but I don't know for sure if I am on my way to Heaven," he stated.

"Well, talking about getting to Heaven can be awkward because so many people say different things. It is hard to know just who is right." Continuing, I explained, "We only have one life to live, and we do not want to miss being able to go to Heaven—we certainly would not like the other place. There is one person though that I would trust to tell me how to get to Heaven—and that is Jesus. In the Bible, John, chapter 3, Jesus explains to Nicodemus how to get to Heaven. If we could talk with Jesus Christ face to face, He would tell us the same facts He told Nicodemus."

As we read additional Scriptures, Mike listened attentively. There, in our office, with activity all around, Mike bowed his head and prayed, accepting the blood of Christ as payment for his sin. When Mike left, he observed, "This was my Christmas celebration here with you. I always enjoy coming and talking with you both."

Praise the Lord for copier problems and for God's sending Mike. Our prayer is for Mike's family to get saved as well.

* * * * *

CHAPTER 11

1987-1989

February 1987 ~ Hell is worse than jail!

When James and I were expecting our first child, we were on a very limited income. I prayed earnestly that God would enable us to feed and clothe the family He was giving us. Mysteriously, people began dropping off clothing and items at FAB with instructions to help ourselves to anything we could use and pass the rest on to others. Through the years, we made items available to those locally in need, participated in mission projects, and sent truck loads to other countries during special Good Samaritan projects as well as disasters. With our large building, we had lots of space to collect, organize, and distribute clothing and other donations. As a result of the abundance that God gave, FAB established a mission in downtown Waterloo.

One day a man came in asking permission to look through the clothing. He found a number of items for his personal use. As I talked with Bill, I learned that he could not read, but that he was looking for a job. He also needed a different place to live since his current apartment was crawling with cockroaches. A friend of his, to solve their financial difficulties, had suggested that they rob a business, but Bill had refused, responding, "No way. I am not going to rob and be dishonest. It isn't worth it."

God's Appointment

Having already served time in jail, Bill didn't ever want to go there again. The day after their conversation, his friend was arrested for attempted robbery. Bill was glad that he had not been involved.

Agreeing with him wholeheartedly, I remarked, "You know, Bill, Hell is a lot worse than jail. Jail is only a small taste of what Hell would be like."

When I asked him how he would explain to someone else how a person could get to Heaven, he replied, "No way could I tell someone because I don't know how myself."

Opening the Bible, I showed him how Jesus explained to Nicodemus how to get to Heaven. Bill listened carefully. Understanding that he himself needed to receive forgiveness for sin and call upon Jesus Christ to be his Lord and Savior, Bill bowed his head in prayer and got things squared around with God. That day he personally received the blood of Christ applied to his sin.

Work with the FAB Mission in helping others with their basic needs provided opportunities to meet people, and we saw souls trust Christ. ***"For whosoever shall give you a cup of water to drink in my name, because ye belong to Christ, verily I say unto you, he shall not lose his reward"*** (Matthew 9:41). God blesses when we care about the needs of others.

* * * * *

While standing in line at the grocery store, I felt discouraged. Candy bars were displayed so temptingly before me. Complaining to God in my heart, I whispered, "Lord, I love chocolate candy bars. And it seems as if like all my life, I've had to watch pennies so closely that I don't feel right about buying one. I'd like to be able to have a candy bar once in a while."

Months after that, I stood looking at cases of candy bars that now belonged to us. FAB had rented a space to an advertising fellow who had walked out, owing back rent and utilities. He abandoned not only his furniture and office equipment, but also 7,000 chocolate candy bars.

To dispose of the candy bars and to pay the outstanding bills, we decided that I should take our children around selling candy bars.

After all, who can resist buying candy bars from cute little kids? This turn of events was an overflowing answer to my prayer about wanting a candy bar once in a while. By a loving God who even hears our discouraged prayers, the children earned money for each bar they sold. They practiced their math skills, keeping track of their earnings. The owed amount was repaid and any damaged candy bars were for us to enjoy.

* * * * *

May 1987 ~ Little trouble-maker

If there ever was a little neighborhood trouble-maker, Jason qualified. In spite of his ways and bad language, my heart went out to him. To be so "worldly-wise" and "hard" was a shame for a seven-year-old. He often threw rocks at our girls, calling them bad names as they played outside. I prayed for Jason to get saved and sought opportunities to sow seeds of kindness and love. When opportunities allowed, I quoted appropriate Scriptures.

Jason surprised us one day. He brought a friend, and knocking on our door, asked a direct question, "Can you tell us how to get to Heaven?"

Of course, I invited them in. Since my father was visiting, I asked Dad to talk with the boys. Carefully, he explained how Christ made it possible to get to Heaven. After praying and trusting Christ, they both left.

A little later, Jason returned with another friend. They both listened as my husband James explained about receiving Christ as their personal Savior. That friend also trusted Christ. Later that day, Jason returned with a teenager and requested that I talk to her. She trusted Christ, too. Then later yet, he brought another teenager. That boy also made a profession of salvation. Jason was certainly becoming grounded in the plan of salvation as often as he heard it that day.

Jason not only had become a Christian himself, but also a missionary. After that, as far as I was aware, Jason no longer was a neighborhood problem, and it became much easier for my girls to play safely outside. In the New Testament, Luke writes that, *"the*

Lord added to their number day by day those who were being saved" (Acts 2:47). God looks past the outward exterior and sees the heart of people.

* * * * *

Years have passed. Occasionally, I see Jason, a responsible, hard worker, and now a father himself, as he faithfully picks up his son at the same school that my grandchildren attend. Jason always gives me a warm smile.

* * * * *

August 1987 ~ "Jungle Jim"

When heavy file cabinets in the FAB office needed to be moved, I prayed for God to provide muscles. Not long after that, several young men came by the office; two I knew, the third I had never met. Jim stood in his army uniform and nervously fingered his hat. Beneath his short-cropped red hair beamed a broad smile. Across his right arm in big letters, he sported the tattoo "Jungle Jim."

"Could you fellows give me a hand, moving these cabinets?" I asked.

They graciously consented. It was a hot day, but they quickly carried the file cabinets upstairs; I deeply appreciated their willingness to do that heavy job in the summer heat. After we had finished, I felt compelled to ask Jim if he could visit with me for a while about getting to Heaven.

"Sure," he replied. "I'd like to know about that."

As I read Jim Scripture verses about receiving Jesus and believing on His name, he listened carefully.

"I don't think I could trust Christ as my Savior right now," Jim said sadly. "I'm in the army training to murder, and I don't think God will accept me."

"Are you a murderer or a defender?" I inquired. "There is a difference. God expects us to defend ourselves as a nation. In the Bible, God speaks extensively about armies and soldiers. In the

New Testament, being a soldier and a Christian was compatible. In fact, Christians are commanded to be good soldiers for Christ; one example is Paul writing: *'Share in suffering as a good soldier of Christ Jesus. No soldier gets entangled in civilian pursuits, since his aim is to please the one who enlisted him'* (2 Timothy 2:3, 4). Cornelius was a Roman centurion and a respected Christian. Clearly, the Bible is not opposed to the sacred responsibility of defending a nation."

"Are you interested in being a soldier for Jesus Christ and to call upon Him to be your Lord and Savior?" Jim indicated that he would indeed like to do just that. "Would you be embarrassed to pray right now and receive Christ as your Savior?"

"No, I don't embarrass easily," Jim seriously responded. He bowed his head and prayed, trusting Christ and receiving the blood atonement for his sin. Afterwards, "Jungle Jim" sat quietly for a minute and then said, "I sure feel lighter, as if I just lost twenty pounds. All the problems that seemed so big do not seem so bad now." My prayer is that Jim will be a good soldier for Jesus Christ.

* * * * *

September 12, 1987 ~ Newspaper boy

The paper boy came to our downtown office to collect. Working late that evening, we were surprised to hear a knock at the downstairs' back door. As James wrote the check for the newspapers, I explained to twelve-year-old Mark that we had just returned from the Nebraska State Fair where we had been telling people how they could know that they were going to Heaven when they die.

Desiring to make it personal, I asked him, "Mark, do you know if you are going to Heaven when you die?"

"No," he said, smiling self-consciously.

"You'd like to know, wouldn't you?"

"Yes," he firmly replied.

"If you have a couple of minutes, I'll show you from the Bible."

"Sure," he responded.

After I had explained God's simple plan from the Bible, Mark paused a moment, then asked, "Is this what you did at the fair?"

"Yes, it is."

"It sounds like fun," he said. Mark prayed, asking forgiveness for his sin. As he was leaving, Mark told James, "Tonight I prayed and trusted Christ as my Savior."

"Are you glad you stopped?" James asked.

"I sure am." Mark answered emphatically.

* * * * *

October 1987 ~ Bingo

Having trusted Christ, two young men in our church youth group, concerned about their parents, wanted us to visit their home. One evening, James and I did just that. Their father, Jim, had seen a change in the boys' lives and was interested in understanding what had made the difference; their mother had come with the boys to our church a few times. As James and I talked with Jim, we could tell that he understood the problem of original, as well as personal sin and the need to receive the blood of Jesus Christ to pay for his sin. When we asked if he was ready to receive Christ as his Savior, he was, and he did. Looking up after praying, Jim challenged his wife to trust Christ with him.

That evening his wife said she was not ready yet to trust Christ. Explaining that she was "really into playing bingo" and had just won a lot of money, she was afraid that God would ask her to stop playing bingo. I tried to explain to her that playing bingo would not keep her out of Heaven. But since we are all sinners, each of us does need to confess that fact to God in repentance and accept the blood payment that Jesus Christ made on our behalf to be applied to our sin. Her response that evening was still, "No." We continue praying for that mother to make a decision. When people choose something of this world instead of being willing to follow Christ, it is sad. Even Christ at times met with reluctance, ***"When the young man heard this he went away sorrowful, for he had great posses-***

sions" (Matthew 19:22). How dangerous to allow anything to stand between us and making a positive decision for eternity.

* * * * *

June 1988 ~ Eager learner

Ryan and his family moved next door. When warm weather arrived, the children began playing outside and became acquainted with Ryan. At first, we were concerned about his foul language, but after I spoke to him about it, I could tell that he was trying to be more careful.

Our eleven-year-old daughter, Angela, often witnessed to him about the Lord and invited Ryan to come to church with us. The first time he came, he excitedly got up at five o'clock that morning to figure out what to wear. At our door early, he was ready, waiting to go to church with us.

Intelligent, with lots of questions, Ryan quickly understood spiritual concepts. One Sunday I taught a lesson about a boy who asked his father what would happen when the Rapture (a future event talked about in the Bible, when Jesus comes and takes those on earth who have accepted Him as their Savior to Heaven) took place to those who had not yet trusted Christ as Savior and were not ready. The lesson was to challenge the students to make sure that they had Jesus Christ as their Savior and would not be left behind.

As the students prepared to leave, I asked them individually if they knew for certain that they would not be left behind at the rapture. Each said, "Yes," except Ryan. Even before I asked, he volunteered, "I don't know that I am." Inviting Ryan to stay after class, I showed him from the Bible how he could be ready and then asked if he wanted to go to the Cross and receive Christ's blood payment for his sin.

"How do you get to the Cross?" he asked his bright eyes intensely sincere.

"That is easy; we simply get on our knees and pray to God, He takes us to the Cross." We knelt together, and Ryan trusted Christ as his Savior. As we sat quietly afterwards, he exclaimed, "I sure feel different."

* * * * *

Ryan and his mother moved from the neighborhood. Years later, during a garage sale at my parent's home, a tall, red-headed, bearded young man walked up and asked, "Do you remember me?" It was Ryan. Still single, he was driving trucks and had an apartment not far from my folks. Recognizing me, Ryan had stopped to say, "Hello." In the course of our conversation, I asked if he remembered trusting Christ as his Savior. With a broad smile, he responded, "I sure do."

* * * * *

August 1988 ~ Not too late

We happened to stop by the home of an older couple, also believers, at the same time as their friends, Katherine and Howard, were visiting. Our son, almost two, was entertaining both couples with his playful activities. After awhile, James read a portion from Scripture and led in prayer. Curious about their spiritual condition, I asked Katherine if she had ever trusted Christ as her Savior.

"I don't know," she replied.

"It is good to make sure, and it is not hard to do," I stated. "There is no need to live in doubt. Just tell the Lord that, if you have not before, you are now trusting Christ to pay for your sin. That way you can know that He is your Savior for eternity."

"Go ahead," her husband prompted her, "you should."

"Okay, then," she decided. Moving so that Katherine could read with me, I opened the Bible to a number of passages. After I had explained how a person becomes a born-again Christian, Katherine prayed, receiving Christ as her Savior.

"Thank you for praying with me," she said, looking up and smiling.

Howard had watched and listened so I asked him if he had been born again yet. He answered. "No, not yet."

"Would you also like to pray and receive Christ as your Savior now?" I asked.

"No, I'm not ready," was his reply.

When I explained how important it is to make that decision soon, he responded, "I know, but I'm not ready yet."

"Do you know how to pray, if you want to later?" I asked.

Then I simply reviewed God's wonderful gift of salvation one more time with him to make certain that he understood how to accept that gift when he was ready. As we left, Howard assured us that he would not wait until it was too late to make his decision for Christ.

* * * * *

August 1988 ~ Looking for a hand-out

A heavy-set man stopped at the FAB Mission seeking items for his sizeable family. He was accustomed to living off welfare and whatever else he could find. We helped him where we could. Maynard kept returning, pressing us to meet his needs, suggesting in fact, that it would be our fault if his children went hungry. I felt he was trying to manipulate us by laying a guilt trip on us. Resisting him, I challenged him to be the man God intended him to be so that He could bless him and his family. Then he would not have to depend on the charity of others. At first, he responded in self defense; his testimony of what happened later worked out to be a blessing.

Testimony, as written by Maynard

One day I walked into the Family Altar Broadcast's Mission to get some free clothes. Since my family and I were on welfare, I liked to get anything freely offered, even though I didn't think they would have any clothes large enough to fit me. Gloria Goering had me look around. Although I didn't find anything that day, I was impressed with the overall atmosphere. I was not treated as a *welfare person*, but as a *person*. I wanted to come back again. I had met people I wanted to be around more.

God's Appointment

For years, I had asked God to show me people who were solid Christians, who really knew God and the Bible, who could show me the way, someone I could hang onto. Here were some good, Godly, mainstream Christians, and I wanted to get the spiritual relationship with God that they had.

For about one and a half years, I kept coming back. I would explain my doctrinal view to James and Gloria and her parents, the Vermaases. They would listen and then show me what the Bible had to say about each point. After seeing what the Bible had to say, I could see flaws in my thinking. Most of my Bible knowledge had a "twist" to it which they exposed. They often said that they were not perfect, but that the God they served was. They allowed me to search things through and accept things at my own pace. They never let me trick them with religious double talk.

The Goering's and Vermaases knew what they believed and were not just talking religion. They would ask me if I knew whether or not I was saved. To this, I would answer "Yes," because I thought I was. I had attended other churches and had tried many different solutions to salvation. However, I had never directly asked Jesus to be my Savior and had never really fit into a church. One question Gloria constantly asked me was, "If I died today, did I know if I would go to Heaven or not?" That question I could not answer. I wanted to go to Heaven, but I didn't know how. From carefully reading the Bible, I came to realize that there was only one way to Heaven, and there was a way to know if I had met God's qualifications.

Many times James and Gloria, and Martin and Bernice Vermaas helped me and my family with food, clothing, transportation, money, and love. One day I had a real confrontation with Gloria. I had approached her once again to help my family. Gloria insisted that I needed to stop leaning on them or welfare or anyone else, and I needed to learn to lean on God directly. She told me that the reason I needed help was that I was not following God's plan and purpose in my life, and that God was against me until I would face up to putting my life in line. She explained that their desire was to help me spiritually so that God would help me in the other areas.

I said things that I should not have said and left in anger. But God spoke to my heart. Gloria was right, and I needed to go back and apologize. I did apologize. At that point, in August 1988, I started questioning whether or not I was saved. We are instructed, *"Beloved, do not believe every spirit, but test the spirits to see whether they are from God, for many false prophets have gone out into the world"* (1 John 4:1). At that time, there was a lot of discussion about the possibility of Christ's coming soon. I realized that it was foolish to put off getting right with God. I started talking with my wife about being saved. There was a real battle with demonic spirits that did not want me to get saved, and I feared for my life and the life of my family. We knew it was time to run to Jesus. I had been told that in order to be saved, all I had to do was repent of my sins and ask Jesus to be my Savior. I had nowhere else to go at that point. I felt that this was my last chance to get it right. My wife and I repented, accepting Jesus as our Savior. Soon after that, we were baptized and began attending and became members of Calvary Bible Church.

My wife and I desire to be witnesses for the Lord. As Martin Luther King said, "I'm free at last. Thank God, I'm free at last."

* * * * *

August 1988 ~ Not by good works

Hope regularly listened to our Family Altar Broadcast radio program on KNWS. She also corresponded occasionally, interested in growing in the things of the Lord. Each time she wrote, she requested prayer for Linda, her adult daughter. We took all the prayer requests we received before the throne of God during our staff prayer time. Hope feared that Linda did not know the Lord. On more than one occasion, James and I went to their home to visit. Linda was always polite, but firm. She was convinced that she could not successfully live a Christian life and would not be able to keep her salvation, should she try.

Of course, we prayerfully continued to explain from the Bible that people cannot earn their way to Heaven; only faith in the finished work of Christ on the Cross secures Heaven. *"For by grace you have been saved through faith. And this is not your own doing;*

it is the gift of God, not a result of works, so that no one may boast" (Ephesians 2:8-9). After a person is redeemed by the blood of Christ, only His power enables us to live the Christian life, as the Apostle Paul also desired, *"That I may know him and the power of his resurrection, and may share his sufferings, becoming like him in his death"* (Philippians 3:10).

One night, as Linda sat talking with me, she finally decided to trust Christ as her personal Savior. From then on, what a thrill it was for this mother and her daughter to sit in church services each week and worship the Lord together. Hope has since gone on home to Heaven; Linda faithfully attends church services and is especially interested in missions. The following is her testimony.

Linda Miller

Testimony, as written by Linda

I went to the Lord for salvation in August, 1988, and was baptized at Calvary Bible Church in Washburn on September 4, 1988. My mother had told me that Jesus would be returning to the world very soon. She showed me a copy she had of the book, *Why the*

Rapture Could Be in 1988. After reading what this book had to say about the things to come on earth during the Tribulation, I made the decision to get myself ready to meet the Lord when He comes.

* * * * *

There was real enthusiasm about the possibility of the Rapture taking place in 1988. Although the Rapture did not take place that year, the signs that were being considered then are as true now. It is still wise to be ready today.

Gloria in the 1988 Soul-Winning Booth

September 1988 ~ Daring to stand alone

FAB staffed a soul-winning booth for nine days during the National Dairy Cattle Congress in Waterloo, Iowa. Reportedly, over 222,000 people attended the fair. Martin and Bernice Vermaas, Amal and Carol Bejjani, Maynard, Ida Ann, and James and I took turns working at the booth, passing out thousands of tracts, trusting that God's Word would not return void, *"So shall my word be that goes out from my mouth; it shall not return to me empty, but it shall accomplish that which I purpose, and shall succeed in the thing for which I sent it."* (Isaiah 55:11).

We saw people reading the literature; others put the literature away to read later. We asked many the question, "How does a person get to Heaven"—and received many different answers. Some people were open when I showed them that Jesus had answered that very question. His answer is recorded for all to read in the Gospel of John, chapter three. Of those who sat down and listened to an explanation of God's plan of salvation for twenty to thirty minutes, over eighty prayed, receiving Christ as their Savior. Many others listened, but wanted to think about it further. We pray that they yet will make a decision for Christ.

**

As I started talking to two teens, one became interested and came into the booth against the pleas of her companion who wanted to keep going. As I shared Scripture with her, her friend impatiently paced back and forth saying, "Let's go." But the teenager insisted that she wanted to hear the story of Nicodemus and Jesus' answer to his question. Finally, I asked if she was ready to pray and receive the blood payment for her sin.

She said, "Yes."

Then I asked, "What is your name?"

"Kathy," she replied.

So I began, "Dear Lord, help Kathy right now to ask your Son to be her Savior and Lord." Then looking up at her, I suggested that Kathy talk to Jesus and tell Him that she wanted Him to apply His blood payment to her sin. Kathy warmly responded and received Christ. When we were finished, she left with her still disapproving friend. She was willing to stand alone.

**

A sixty-three year old Catholic lady stopped at our booth and shared some of her life's hardships. As true of many, she needed a listening ear. When I shared with her about God's "Heaven Instructions," she gladly received Christ as her Savior and friend.

**

A U.S. Army sergeant and one of his recruits stopped at our booth. After hearing how Jesus had instructed Nicodemus about being born again, literally born from above (John 3), the sergeant said that he wanted to think about it for a little while before making a decision. When I asked the recruit, he was ready to pray and invite Christ to be his Lord and Savior.

**

Praise the Lord for every one of those precious decisions.

*   *   *   *   *

April 1989 ~ Paralyzed

A Christian orderly at a nursing home, Bob called to make an appointment for James and me to talk to Rick, one of the patients. Bob's testimony was recorded earlier, **November 1984 ~ High-speed crash.** When we entered Rick's room, we found a handsome young fellow lying in bed, completely paralyzed and unable to speak. Rick had tried to commit suicide by hanging himself; the rope had cut off oxygen to his body but had not taken his life.

Now, he was trapped in a body, day after day, year after year, and the doctors said that he would never move.

Diligently, Bob took care of him, and Rick communicated by blinking "yes" or "no," using a code they had developed to blink letters of the alphabet. Bob often witnessed to Rick.

In order for Rick to see me, I moved to the side of the bed and then greeted him. "Hello, Rick," I said, "my name is Gloria. Bob invited my husband and me here today to visit with you. So, you're trapped inside a body that doesn't work? I understand that you can hear and understand me, even though you cannot respond? "

"We can't help you, but Jesus Christ can come and be with you. You do not have to be alone; He understands your thoughts so that you do not even need to be able to speak to be able to communicate with Him." Immediately, two intense brown eyes became riveted on my face. Rick didn't move a muscle outwardly, but I had his full attention.

I continued, "Once I knew a young boy named Leonard who had smashed his legs terribly. He was in such pain that the morphine helped for only about an hour. Then he would cry for help until he could receive another shot for pain. I shared with Leonard how pain is easier if there is someone to share it with and told him that he could invite Jesus to come into his life, forgive his sin, and be his Lord and Savior. Then he would not be alone. Leonard did just that. The loneliness, the helpless edge of pain left him, and he was able to handle the physical pain better.

"The greatest verse from the Bible—I would like to share with you. I will say it two times—first, as it is in the Bible; the second time, I am going to put your name in it." ***"For God so loved the world– Rick–that he gave his only Son, that whoever –Rick–believes in him should not perish but have eternal life"*** (John 3:16). "God loves you, Rick, and He cares about your situation. He can help. He can come right inside with you, and you can talk to Him with your thoughts." Then I carefully explained why he needed to call upon Jesus and just how he could do it.

"If you would like Jesus Christ to forgive your sin and be your Lord and Savior, you can pray along with me, with your thoughts. He will hear you," I explained. Then I repeated a prayer several times to make certain that Rick would be able to pray with me if he so desired. Afterwards, I wondered if Rick had received Christ. His eyes had been intensely focused on me the entire time. Then he began to struggle to speak, making gurgling noises. He wanted me to know something.

As I looked deep into his eyes, he blinked, "Yes."

"I know what you are saying, Rick. You trusted Christ, didn't you?"

His eyes clearly expressed, "Thank you."

Though still trapped inside his body, he had Christ. He now would need the Word of God to be "pumped" into him as spiritual sustenance so that he could grow in the Lord. Bob made arrangements for Bible audio cassettes to be played in the room while he worked with Rick. One day in Heaven, Rick will talk and walk again, rejoicing in his salvation. As God has promised that He, ***"will transform our lowly body to be like his glorious body, by the power that enables him even to subject all things to himself"*** (Philippians 3:21).

* * * * *

May 14, 1989 ~ Freedom from Satan

The following account was written by a woman in our church. I remember telling my children after this incident that Yvonne had trusted Christ. Although I had thought she was a Christian, all four of my children affirmed that they were aware that she was not a born-again Christian, in spite of the fact that she, at times, had been their Sunday school teacher.

Testimony, as written by Yvonne

When I was ten, we lived two hundred miles from Grandpa and Grandma. Grandpa was dying of cancer, and my parents knew that he wasn't going to live much longer. One day the telephone rang. It was Grandma saying that we should come right away. Mom packed our things. When we arrived, Grandpa was sleeping. We had supper, and then waited. It was dark when Grandpa woke up screaming to his youngest son, "Don, get me out of the fire. I'm burning," and then he was gone. This experience has been in my memory ever since.

For more than thirty years, I thought I was saved after making a profession for Christ at the age of twenty. But I was wrong. I married my husband Bill on February 21, 1959 thinking I had been born again. I was baptized with my husband sometime in 1959, joined the church, brought two boys into the world, taught a Sunday school class, and even did some witnessing— all while I was unsaved. I learned Scripture verses and did all the right "Christian" things. To the outside, I looked like a Christian; but inside, my heart was a different story. I had evil thoughts, I hated my mother, but I went to church every Sunday.

Also, I was a lonely person and started to have "company." My company talked to me, became my "friends," and began to control me. They used such names as my "Conscience," "Personality," "Other-self," but in reality they were demons. They were in my life for more years than I can remember, but they didn't start to talk to me until the late 1960s. The day finally came that I saw them for what they really were—demons.

The main demon decided to cause trouble. He had me type two letters: one to my pastor; another to a young lady in our church. He had me sign another person's name to the letters. Apparently God gave wisdom to Pastor James's wife about who had written the letters. She and Pastor James brought the letters to our house and showed them to me. Gloria said that she knew I had written the letters. When I insisted that I didn't, Gloria said, "Either you wrote the letters, and you know you did; or you wrote the letters, and you don't know you did—either way we have a problem." After they left, my husband found the typewriter upstairs. After matching the pattern of print, he called Gloria to tell her that he was 99.9% sure that the letters had been written on the typewriter in our house.

I cut the cord of the typewriter and got rid of it to avert further suspicion. But at that time, I began to suspect that this "friend" was really my enemy, a demon. I called Gloria and confessed that I must have written the letters as I recognized the way the "e" and the "a" were smeared in the typed letters, just like the typewriter in my home. As I talked to Gloria on the phone, another voice came out of my mouth and began talking to her. She sang the song, "There is power in the blood," and said, "Yvonne is my friend and I will talk to her, but not to you," and hung up. That was the beginning of the worst seven-day battle of my life.

The next day, I went to the Family Altar Broadcast office to talk with Pastor and Mrs. Goering. I realized that I was not saved and again, made an attempted profession of salvation; but it was not real. The next day I returned to the office, but the demon was in control; I talked to the secretary telling her multiple lies, including that I wasn't married to my husband.

Saturday, May 13, was the big day for me. I was bothered all day with demons. I had tried to trust Jesus three times, but I still felt as if I was on my way to Hell. I didn't want to go to Hell but wanted Jesus to be my Savior. I was at the church performing my job of cleaning in preparation for the Sunday services. I called Gloria and told her that I was scared and needed help. She told me to stay there; she would contact others and come. She contacted the pastor, Mr. and Mrs. Vermaas, the head deacon, Maynard, and my husband, asking them to meet at the church. I was shaking like a leaf and very frightened.

The group arrived at the church around 9:30 p.m. and immediately went with me into the auditorium. Questions were asked; the demons answered. I knew I had done a great wrong against my husband. Gloria suggested that I go into a back room with my husband and talk with him. My husband and I talked privately, and I confessed to him a terrible wrong I had done. I was eaten up with guilt. My husband forgave me. With the guilt gone, my husband thought everything was all right with me, but Gloria and her mother Bernice were convinced that there was more that needed to be done.

My husband sat with me near the pulpit. The demons were asked to identify themselves. They resisted, but finally, one by one, their names were revealed; five times I was thrown to the floor when they left. After I was clean, I was able to truly trust Jesus, and I also asked the Holy Spirit to fill me. Before, when I had tried to be saved, the demons had prevented me; but this time, they were gone, and I was free to trust Christ. I will always remember Sunday, May 14, 1989, at 1:00 a.m. as the day I was set free from the prison house of Satan.

* * * * *

Yvonne was re-baptized and has grown in the Lord. We have a strong enemy, but we have a stronger Savior. We are told, ***"Submit yourselves therefore to God. Resist the devil, and he will flee from you"*** (James 4:7).

* * * * *

August 6, 1989 ~ Visiting New Brunswick

We took a family trip to the east coast, up into New Brunswick to visit missionary friends Ward and Sara Jane Harris. James and I had the privilege to help them with visitation in the area seeking to help their mission church grow. Afterwards, we received this letter from them.

Dear Brother James and family,

I especially wanted to write you a note, as tonight we baptized Matthew. He is the young boy Gloria dealt with the Sunday you were here, and he confessed Christ that day. He came forward a week ago tonight to surrender to be baptized. When I dealt with him concerning his salvation, he told me that he received Christ the day Gloria had spoken with him. He remembered the date and understood what he had done. Also, when he met with the deacons, he gave the same testimony. Thought you would be interested in knowing the part you had in leading this young boy to Christ.

Yours for the Proclamation of the Gospel,
Ward and Sara Jane Harris

* * * * *

Gloria and Clint Lloyd

September 1989 ~ Hand-delivered from Oregon

One day, while we were preparing artwork for the FAB booth in my parents' home, they had company come from Oregon, eighty-two year old Clint and his wife, old friends of the family. Watching us lay out pictures and lettering for a *Walk through the Bible Panorama*, Clint's questions and interest made me think that he would be open to the Gospel. Although we were in a rush to finish our project, it seemed a shame to go to all the trouble and expense of reaching people for Christ at the fair, yet miss an opportunity to visit with someone whom God had brought all the way from Oregon.

Following the prompting of the Holy Spirit, I asked Clint if he knew for sure that he was going to Heaven when he died. His answer indicated that he did not have confidence in his salvation, although he certainly would like to. We talked about how God has made provision for our salvation through the work of Jesus Christ on the Cross. When I asked if he was ready to go to Christ for salvation, he nodded vigorously, "Let's go to it." Hallelujah, he did pray and trust Christ as his Savior. Later that evening, he and his wife went with us to Wednesday night church service. Before they left the next morning, Clint bought a set of cassettes to help him read through the Bible. He wanted to grow in the knowledge of the Bible, even as we are all instructed, ***"Do your best to present yourself to God as one approved, a worker who has no need to be ashamed, rightly handling the word of truth"*** (2 Timothy 2:15).

* * * * *

September 1989 ~ Religion, not the answer

At the Cattle Congress fair, we met several teens who told us that they had trusted Christ through a local youth ministry, Teens for Christ, led by Roger and Lisa Sejje. Other teenagers, though, walked past our booth still needing the saving mercies of our Lord and Savior. One was eighteen-year-old Chad. When he and a friend came by our booth, we handed them a tract and asked, "Do you know if you're going to Heaven when you die?"

Chad answered, "No, I don't think I do."

His friend said, "Religion is on its way out. It's not needed any more."

I agreed with him that *religion* is not the answer, "What I'm interested in is a *personal relationship* with Jesus Christ, not religion." Chad's friend still didn't seem interested, but Chad's curiosity was piqued. We invited Chad to sit in our booth and learn more about a personal relationship with Christ.

"He died on the Cross in order to make the blood sacrifice necessary for our reconciliation with God, I explained." God's message of love made sense to Chad, and he understood. After a short while, I asked Chad if he was ready to ask Christ to apply the blood atonement to his personal sin.

He responded, "Yes, I am ready and want to do just that." He bowed his heart to God in prayer, asking Christ to pay for his sins and to be his Lord and Savior. Interestingly, the entire time Chad and I talked, the friend with him was deep in conversation with another of our workers. When the friend saw that Chad was finished, the two left together. Our nine-year-old daughter, Jessica, was at the booth helping at that time.

"Mommy," she said. "I could tell that guy was really serious and really meant it when he prayed." Her comment was an encouragement.

Another young couple passed our booth. Susan (20) and Jeff (22) were asked the question, "Are you going to Heaven when you die?"

They replied, "I hope so."

"Seriously, we do not want to go to Hell," I responded, "In fact, the Bible tells us about a man who came to Jesus one night, asking Him how he could be sure of getting to Heaven. Jesus told him. May I show you Jesus' answer, recorded in the Bible?" They both came into the booth and eventually prayed aloud, receiving Christ. Afterwards, I pointed out that now they shared the same spiritual birthday. They thought that was "pretty neat."

Sometimes Christians came by our booth and responded to our question with a smile, willing to share with us how they had come to know the Lord. We always enjoyed hearing the testimonies of brothers and sisters in Christ. It lifted our spirits and refreshed our determination to keep spreading the Good News.

* * * * *

James felt that it was time to conclude his time as pastor at Calvary Bible church. The church called Pastor Rik Reuter to lead the church. Rik's wife is my sister, Sue. It was a joy to have their family living in the area. We felt led of the Lord to join the church at Walnut Ridge Baptist in Waterloo, Iowa.

CHAPTER 12

1990-1994

April 1990 ~ Testimony by son, Josiah

Josiah, at age nineteen, wrote this report for a college class assignment.

I remember praying the sinner's prayer when I was almost four, with my sister Victoria's help, on the couch in our living room. I had just heard a sermon from Pastor Greg Curtis at our church about how to be saved. Even at that young age, I felt the need to trust Christ as my Savior. At the age of seven, I decided to pray again and reconfirm my salvation to make sure. I rededicated my life at the age of twelve at the Clear Lake Baptist Camp and committed myself to full-time Christian ministry.

The Bible clearly states that we can know that we are Christians, *"I write these things to you who believe in the name of the Son of God that you may know that you have eternal life"* (1 John 5:13). I believe in Jesus Christ and have trusted Him as my Savior and have asked for His forgiveness, which is as much as I can do in order to reserve my spot in heaven. I have faith that I am saved and on my way to heaven when I die. Works can only earn me jewels in heaven; they cannot be my ticket there. The Word of God, to me, is the greatest tool that we possess here on earth. It is filled with wisdom and answers for all of life. The Word of God is infallible. To me, the greatest aspect of the Word is that it gives us a way to know God and his plan for our life. Prayer is another power tool that was given to us by God. Prayer in my life has picked up drastically with all the decisions that are ahead of me. I don't know exactly where I am going with my life, but I do know that God is going with me. I am currently a student at Moody Bible Institute in Chicago, Illinois, preparing for the ministry as a youth pastor.

* * * * *

Josiah James Goering

Josiah has become a man of God, searching Scripture and choosing to invest his life in discipling others in Christ. After graduating from Moody, he is working as a youth pastor with middle school students in a church near Chicago. He is seeking to do his part in fulfilling the Great Commission, ***"Go therefore and make disciples of all nations, baptizing them in the name of the Father and of the Son and of the Holy Spirit, teaching them to observe all that I have commanded you. And behold, I am with you always, to the end of the age"*** (Matthew 28:19, 20).

* * * * *

May 10, 1990 ~ Road trip

A young lady in her twenties, Mary was a friend of my younger sister Carol. Mary had roomed for a while in my parents' home and worked at the local Christian bookstore. Coming from an unsaved family background, Mary was deeply concerned for her parents' salvation; but Mary's parents had resented her changed religious convictions. On more than one occasion, Mary asked us to pray specifically for her father, seriously ill with cancer and slipping toward a Christless eternity. Mary's distress touched my heart.

That spring, my parents were interested in going to the tulip festival in Pella, Iowa. My dad has a strong Dutch background and heritage. Mary's parents lived in a small town along that route. I asked Mary for her parents' address, praying specifically for God's direction in the situation. Stopping in her hometown while my parents and our children waited in the van, James and I knocked on the door of Mary's childhood home. Mary's mother opened the door, and we introduced ourselves to her as friends of Mary traveling to the Pella festival. We had just wanted to stop and visit with her and her husband. First, I told her what a wonderful daughter they had; in fact, my folks felt that she was like a daughter to them. Additionally, we wanted to express concern about her husband's condition, and asked how he was doing. She invited us to her husband's bedroom where he was confined to bed.

It was obvious that he was indeed, sick to the point of death. Still, he was happy to have company, friends of his daughter. We visited. When I asked how he was doing, he said that he knew he wouldn't be long on this earth. I mentioned that facing death brings an increased awareness of God and eternity.

"Yes," he admitted. He had been seriously considering eternity.

"Would you be interested in a prayer of renewal?" I asked.

"What do you mean by a prayer of renewal?"

"That is a prayer, affirming our love for God and the work of Jesus for us, so that we can go to Heaven."

"I'd like that," Mary's father responded. Opening my Bible, I shared a number of salvation verses with them, explaining how

Jesus had died on the Cross to make the payment for our sin so that we can have everlasting life.

"Would you like to pray right now?" I asked. "Tell Jesus how you love him, thanking Him for dying on the Cross for your sin, and trusting Him to apply His blood payment for sin to your account." He shook his head affirmatively and did just that.

When I asked Mary's mother if she, too, would like to pray, she declined. Soon it was time to leave. We assured them that we would be praying for them as they walked through the valley of the shadow of death. Then we joined our family, still waiting in the van, and finished the trip. When we next talked with Mary, she was thrilled. Mary was confident that after her father's death, she would see him again—in Heaven.

* * * * *

June 1990 ~ Appointments with the teacher

As part of Vacation Bible School (VBS) at Calvary Bible Church, I taught the third and fourth grade class, with six students. Toward the end of the week, I told the children that I would like to talk with each one of them individually about whether or not they understood how a person gets to Heaven. They needed to know that all we need to do is to receive Christ's payment for our sin. They all shook their heads, affirming their desire to speak with me.

Dustin was the last to leave the classroom. I took the opportunity to approach him first. When I asked if he was ready for "our appointment," he said, with a wide smile, "Yeah." Dustin did pray that day, receiving Christ as his Savior.

As he was leaving, in came another member of the class, Angela. She wanted to be next. She too, trusted Christ as Savior. Following her, Jodi was waiting to talk; and after Jodi, came James. The next day during class, the four children shared their testimonies. When I remarked how great it was that four of them now had the same spiritual birthday, Derek said that he, too, wanted to trust Christ. Later that morning, he did. The enthusiasm must have spread, because one of the boys' younger brothers also wanted to trust Christ. The children in my classroom made the decision of a lifetime. It thrilled my heart to know that our class would be united in Heaven.

* * * * *

September 1990 ~ Celebrating in style

September 20, 1959, is my spiritual birthday because I trusted Jesus Christ as my personal Lord and Savior on that date. That day I made the most important decision I have made in my life, and it was a lasting decision. One reason I enjoy the fair ministry so much, especially the National Cattle Congress in Waterloo, is because the work at the fair gives me an opportunity to lead others to Christ on the actual date of my birthday. Know of a better way to celebrate? Let me share some of the testimonies of those who made professions accepting Christ this year.

Sixteen-year-old Eric, from out of town, paused at our booth. When I asked if he knew for certain if he were going to Heaven when he died, he said that he "hoped so."

Earnestly, I explained that a man had asked Jesus how he could be sure of getting to Heaven; Jesus' answer is recorded in the Bible. A large family Bible on the front display table lay opened to the Gospel of John, chapter 3. We read together the historical account, and Eric could see how Jesus would answer us if we could visit with Him, face-to-face.

While Eric and I stood at the front of the booth studying Jesus' command to be born again, people walked noisily past. Eric asked questions and listened attentively to what I was saying. Finally, when I asked Eric if he would like personally to go to the Cross asking Jesus Christ to apply the blood payment that He had made for sin to his account right then, Eric said, "Yes."

We prayed, and Eric trusted Christ. Afterwards, I told him how much I respected his willingness to pray in such a public place. That takes courage.

*

Amber and Celena were sisters, eleven and twelve years old. They came into our booth to learn how to be "born again." They had been going to church, but had not yet made a personal decision for Christ. That day, praying together in the booth, they became sisters in the Lord, sharing the same spiritual birthday.

*

Billy and Josh, eleven and twelve years old, also stopped and received Christ at the booth. Billy said he did not have a Bible of his own to read. We had a number of Bibles to give away to those needing one. Taking a Bible, I wrote his name and that day's date in the front. He was really happy to receive a Bible for his very own use. An altar boy at his Catholic church, he was noticeably grateful. Much later, I saw them walk past our booth again. Billy held up his Bible with a big smile to let me know that he still had it.

*

A thirteen-year-old Mormon, Steve and his friend stopped. When I asked them if they knew if they were on their way to Heaven or not, Steve's friend talked as if he was a Christian already. He listened as I shared the Gospel with Steve. Eventually, Steve bowed his head and prayed right there, in the busy aisle, right in front of his friend.

*

Molly, a fourteen-year-old, stopped with one of her friends who claimed to be a Christian, but she did not want to linger at our booth. Molly wanted to hear more. Earnestly, I urged her friend, as a Christian, to encourage Molly to take the time to listen. We talked and Molly eventually prayed there in the aisle, in front of her impatient friend and the crowd, receiving Christ as her Savior.

*

A fourteen-year-old, Travis also came into the booth with a friend. They both listened. But when I invited them to pray and receive Christ as their Savior, his friend got up quickly and left. However, not caring what his friend thought, Travis prayed aloud, receiving Christ. I told him that I admired him for his willingness to stay.

* * * * *

The Mayor welcomes the opening of Christian Family Video.

February 7, 1991 ~ Videos for rent

Many Christians have used VHS and DVD players to help monitor their family television. Convinced of a real need for good Christian videos and caring about what people were watching, I started a Christian/Family Video rental store in our downtown Waterloo building. Desiring to encourage and strengthen Christians, as well as provide tools for reaching others for Christ, I believed that there was an open door for the Gospel through video, especially since it was through Gospel Video that I personally had trusted Christ.

One day, a tall, slender, quiet young man in his middle twenties entered the store. Edward wanted to rent a video tape. He commented, "I don't understand religious things very much, but I saw a program on television about Christ's death on the Cross. Although I didn't know what was going on, it really touched my heart."

Edward allowed me to read John 3 with him and explain what Jesus told Nicodemus about being born again. The simplicity of God's provision of salvation was new to Edward. He had never had someone explain the Good News to him before, but he understood.

"How wonderful that is!" he exclaimed. We talked of the source of sin through Adam and how spiritual death came upon all men at that time. We are born physically alive, but spiritually dead until we come to the Cross and receive our payment for sin through Christ's precious blood. Then we are born again into the family of God. Finally, I asked Edward if he was ready to receive Christ.

"I don't feel quite ready yet," was his response.

We talked a while longer. I could tell that he wanted to make the decision to trust Christ, but that he was fearful of the unknown. Sharing with him my own testimony of salvation years earlier: the fear I had felt and, at the same time, the deep desire to have this salvation of God. I asked Edward if it would be all right with him if I were to pray, talking to God right then.

He answered, "Yes."

As I prayed, thanking God for bringing Edward to our store and the opportunity to visit with him, I also asked God to remove from him the fear and hindrances keeping him from making this decision.

Pausing, I asked once more, "Edward, are you ready now to pray and tell Jesus Christ that you want Him to be your very own Lord and Savior, applying the blood payment made on the Cross to your sins?"

"Yes," Edward replied, "I am ready. I want to do that now." He prayed a beautiful and meaningful prayer.

We sat quietly for a while, Edward deep in thought. Finally, pressing his hand to his chest, he shook his head wonderingly, "I just feel so different inside with a peace I have never experienced before. It is wonderful. I just feel like being alone with God for a while." As Edward left, I felt that God had brought this sensitive young man to our office in answer to my prayers.

* * * * *

March 10, 1992 ~ "Come to Lincoln."

When my brother Steve trimmed a tree in his front yard, one of the limbs fell and hit him, knocking him off his ladder. He fell about eighteen feet, hurt his right shoulder, and broke his ribs in ten places, but he managed to drive to the Veteran's Hospital for treatment. Dismissed after three days, he was in no condition to be alone. Our dad went to Lincoln, Nebraska and brought him back to Waterloo to recover. At the same time, my mother had foot surgery on both of her feet. Steve and Mom recovered together at my parents' home. The two "invalids" helped each other, and we were able to spend precious times together.

Steve had been telling us for years that he didn't need God's help in his life; he would work things out by himself. Now he was surrendering his life to God. He recognized that it was God's hand that had protected him from greater injury, and he knew that he wasn't going to be able to work out problems in his life by himself. He asked for our prayers. Our hearts were thrilled at this new attitude.

When Steve was twelve, he had been saved at the Nebraska church camp; he knew that God had now forgiven him for his years of rebellion. How precious it was to talk with my brother freely about the things of the Lord again.

"Pray for my ex-wife to get saved," Steve entreated me, "even if things don't work out for us together, she needs salvation." Then I shared with him my last conversation with his second wife. In August, when I had been in Nebraska for my niece's wedding, I had visited with Linda one morning before she went to work. Over a cup of coffee, I had shared from John 3, Jesus' explanation to Nicodemus how a person gets to Heaven. She had listened carefully. When I asked if she had ever done what Christ was talking about, had she been born again, she had answered, "No, I've never done that." Following with another question, I asked, "Would you like to do it right now?"

She had replied that she wasn't ready, at that time, to consider such a decision. I simply promised that I would be praying for her. After that, my heart had often been burdened for her and her daughter's salvation but had wondered with the divorce if I would ever have another chance to talk with them.

When it was time for Steve to return to Nebraska, he asked a favor, "Gloria, come back to Lincoln with me and try to talk to Linda about salvation again." As a result, I joined Dad and Steve on his return trip. We had a heartwarming time of Christian fellowship as we drove and prayed for God to work in Linda's life. I wanted so much to help Steve and to see Linda make the most important decision of her life, but wondered how could I approach her now that they were divorced? Would she still be open to talking with me? I prayed that God would open her heart and open the door for me to talk with her. When we arrived, Dad called to give Linda a report on Steve's condition and asked if I could get together with her. Linda invited me to come over the next evening.

As we sat together in her house, I asked if we could continue our last discussion about how to get to Heaven. She answered, "Yes." We sat with an open Bible on her kitchen table. Linda confided, "You know, Gloria, I was disappointed that you didn't make it back for your grandma's reunion. I wanted to talk with you again. I hoped we'd have a chance sometime. I'm ready now to trust Christ." Praise the Lord, her heart indeed was prepared. After I shared Scripture with her, she trusted Jesus Christ to pay for her sins and give her everlasting life, then she would be His, and He would be hers, forever.

After Linda's prayer, Holly, her seventeen-year-old daughter, came into the kitchen. Linda told Holly what she had just done. I asked Holly if I could share the same Scripture with her that I had just shared with her mother. Holly sat next to her mom and listened attentively.

"Would you also like to trust Christ," I finally asked.

"Yes," she said. Praise the Lord, both mother and daughter share the same spiritual birthday. Steve was thrilled that Linda and Holly had trusted Christ. It is up to the Lord now, what He will do in their lives.

* * * * *

October 10, 1992 ~ At John's store

Just before closing time, I decided to leave our office and take a walk. Strolling toward the river, I passed the corner store and saw John, working inside. We had hired John, years earlier, to add a garage to our house; he had also installed the entrance glass doors to our office building. Recently, he and his wife had rented the building down from our office and set up a specialty store. Their glass door had been broken by vandals the night before, and the cold air made it necessary to wear a coat inside. John had boarded up the door temporarily and ordered new glass; he was minding the store until closing time.

As we visited, John said that someone had recently told him that they wished that he would get killed. Looking at him with sympathy, knowing that such a statement was bound to sting, I asked him what would happen to him if that were to occur.

He laughed and said, "I knew you'd ask me that."

Smiling, I replied, "And I knew you wanted me to ask you. Seriously though, John, would you make it to Heaven?"

"I don't know," he replied. "I hope so, but I'm not sure." As we talked further, it was obvious that he was open to the Gospel.

"John, my Bible is out in the car. Would you like me to get it and show you from Scripture how God tells us we can get to Heaven?"

"Yeah, I'd appreciate that." he replied. Quickly, I retrieved my Bible.

As we studied the third chapter of the Gospel of John and then John 1:12 together, his wife called several times to let him know that supper was ready. He explained to her that he was visiting with Mrs. Goering and would be a little late. He didn't act as if he wanted to rush away; he had questions he really wanted to have answered. After an hour and a half, I asked John if he would like to bow in prayer and receive Jesus Christ as his Savior.

"Yes, he said, "I understand it better now than I ever have. I think I'm ready." He prayed a simple, humble prayer of salvation. Looking up, John smiled, "Gloria, your coming here tonight tells me that God hears and cares about me. Just this morning, on the way to work, I looked up to Heaven and asked God if He was even there or if He ever heard me or even cared. Your coming tonight, I think, is His answer."

The Lord moved strongly on my heart about ministering again with college students. After marriage and four children, I had a strong desire to work again, on a voluntary basis, with Campus Bible Fellowship, ministering with international students at UNI in Cedar Falls. My challenge was transportation. To have the freedom to travel back and forth from Waterloo, I would have to have a car. Ruby Witt, a lady in our church had a 1970 Oldsmobile for sale for $700, and she was willing to trust me for the payments which in time were paid in full.

* * * * *

March 1993 ~ Students from around the world

From around the world, students come to "Christian" America to attend our universities. What a tragedy for them to return home without understanding what "Christianity" really is.

Chin Ling, a beautiful Chinese girl, was excited about having a Bible study once a week so that she could better understand Christianity and improve her English skills. Seeking answers to many questions, she shared that when she met me, she knew in her heart that she could trust me and that I would be able to help her know what decisions she needed to make. Meeting at the campus library, we used a study room to discover the God of the Bible. It was all new to her that there was a God with character and personality that knew her, loved her, and wanted her to become acquainted with Him.

*

Emmanuel left his home in Rwanda two years previous by walking fifty miles in one night with a flashlight and his Bible; he wanted to go to college. Now his country was in a blood bath, and he was pretty certain that his whole family has been murdered along with thousands of his friends and neighbors. He appreciated being able to talk to someone—to express his feelings, his grief and be encouraged in the Word of God. Like Emmanuel said, "It's hard to explain to my countrymen why God has allowed this terrible suffering!"

*

Chikako had visited a church in Japan five years ago, now here in America; she wanted to find out more about Christianity. We began with **"In the beginning God"** (Genesis 1:1). We studied together the foundations of who the God of the Bible is, how He made all things, how sin entered and God's provision for that sin. It was all new to her, but she quickly grasped the concepts. Asking if she wanted to open her heart's door to Jesus and allow Him to come into her life and apply His blood payment to her sin, she said that she wasn't ready yet. I can respect her decision knowing that God will continue working in her life for salvation. Her mother, back in Japan, has cancer and Chikako went home in May. It is uncertain if she will be able to return to America, but like I explained to her, reaching God from Japan is just a heart's cry away—the same distance as from here in America.

* * * * *

April 1993 ~ Hope, not lost!

One day, after talking with students on the University of Northern Iowa campus, I walked down the hill toward the Campus Bible Fellowship Campus house. As a young man passed me, I commented, "It's a beautiful day, isn't it?" He slowed down, and we walked together, visiting about this and that. Emir had come to America from Bosnia. His English was very good. We stood, talking in front of the men's high-rise dormitory for almost three hours. He shared how in the war in Bosnia and in imminent danger, he had despaired of his life and prayed to the God of Heaven, "If You get me out of this alive, I'll seek You." Within days, he had been airlifted to America and enrolled at UNI as a student.

"God heard your prayer." I commented.

"Yes, and I will keep my promise to seek Him."

"Emir, I believe that is the reason our paths have crossed today: God wants you to get to know Him."

God's Appointment

Thus began a friendship that lasted for years. Emir studied long hours at the library. About once a week, I would meet him there, and we would find a quiet place to talk. He had many questions. I explained what Christianity was, how I personally had come to know the Lord Jesus Christ as my Lord and Savior, and the impact that decision had made on my life. We talked about sin, how we need to acknowledge our inherited, as well as our individual sin because those sins keep us from a personal relationship with God. We talked about how Christ had deliberately left Heaven and died on the Cross to pay for that sin, and the need for all mankind, including Emir, to have that payment applied to their personal account. Occasionally I would take another student or sometimes my son, Josiah, would accompany me.

It was hard for him, as a Muslim, to think of Jesus Christ as God, and the Bible as God's Word to mankind. Our conversations lasted for hours. Always polite and interested, Emir struggled with faith in something that he could not see. He would believe in the deity of Jesus, "if," and "only if," Jesus Christ would show himself to Emir in a personal way. Also, he felt restrained by his love for his mother and other family members who would not understand if he converted to Christianity. I challenged him that since he had promised to seek God when he found the answer, God would enable him to help his mother and others find God. If there is only one way to Heaven, as Jesus claimed, then his mother and family needed to know how to get there as well as him. He would have to find the answers first and then help others.

Emir had other concerns. He needed financial support to continue his studies. I was able to help him find some jobs. One such job was for a local church and involved an Easter production. Amazingly, they needed the script translated into the Bosnian language for the growing local Bosnian community. Emir also needed to find off-campus housing. A Christian family, whom I knew, lived near campus. The family opened their home to him. There Emir experienced firsthand, the day-to-day testimony of a Christian family.

* * * * *

Emir lived with the Schmidt's for a couple of years before transferring to another college where he finished his doctorate in microbiology. After he graduated from UNI, Linda heard from him and she gave me his telephone number so that I could visit with him. Eleven years after Emir and I met, he enthusiastically told me of his new faith in Christ and how wonderful God had been to him. He thanked me for the role I had in his life, teaching him spiritual truths. Presently attending church, he was ready to follow the Lord in believer's baptism. He had met a Christian girl and was getting married that summer. Great things were happening for Emir.

* * * * *

May 1993 ~ Twins with different birthdays

One Sunday morning, Jean stopped me in our church hallway to ask if I would visit a friend with her that she felt would be open to the Gospel. "Certainly, I'd be glad to go with her." We prayed, asking God to bring her friend to Christ and His salvation.

While we talked and prayed, Jean's nine-year-old daughter, Stephanie, stood patiently next to her mother. Months before, Stephanie had been deathly sick; her appendix had ruptured and she faced the possibility of not recovering. God had graciously intervened. I asked how she was feeling. She said she was, "Doing fine."

After church, Jean came up to me again with Stephanie beside her. "Gloria, Stephanie says that she wants to trust Jesus as her Savior this morning. Would you help her?"

The three of us sat in the now empty auditorium, my Bible open, as so often, to the Book of John. I showed her how Jesus invites us to believe on him and become a child of God. Deeply moved, Stephanie prayed words that must have been sweet to the Heavenly Father's ear. Her mother and I rejoiced together.

That next Wednesday evening, after the regular adult prayer service which also happened to be the conclusion of our AWANA program for the year, I saw Stephanie and her twin sister in the hallway. Stephanie was all smiles. I asked Stacey, her twin, if Stephanie had shared with her what she had done Sunday morning.

"Yes."

Then I asked, "Have you trusted Christ yet?"

"No, not yet."

"One of these days, you should, it is important. I would be glad to help you."

"I'm ready now." Stacey stated.

Hardly believing my ears, I asked, "You would like to trust Christ tonight?"

"Yes, I am ready—I would like to do it tonight."

Going to a quiet spot, we talked, sharing Scripture about how to ask Christ to be our Lord and Savior. Stacey sweetly prayed in a similar fashion as had her sister.

How wonderful that both she and her sister had trusted Christ. Physically, as twins, they have the same birthday; but spiritually, they have their very own spiritual birthdays—just days apart. Praise the Lord for His opportunities.

* * * * *

September 1993 ~ No coincidence

A voice over a speaker at the National Dairy Cattle Congress blared, "Gloria. Could you stop by the booth later?" I turned and looked. It was Jay.

There in the middle of demonstrating the Health Craft Cookware, Jay was cooking delicious, healthy meals for an audience of interested fair-goers and taking orders for the quality kitchen products.

"Okay." I responded. Later, between demonstrations, I returned to visit.

"I've been hoping to see you this year. I missed you last year. Remember what happened two years ago? You led me to Christ," Jay reminisced.

"Yes, I remember."

Two years earlier, I had met Jay and listened to his presentations and stayed to visit with him and others in his booth. Each day of the fair, I spent time talking with him. Before the fair was over, Jay had decided to trust Christ as his Savior.

The year before, I just didn't have the strength to handle the schedule. Fibromyalgia had kicked in; I was hardly able to walk. This year, we had been unable to have our FAB soul-winning booth, but the Farmers for Christ booth had called, asking if I could help them at their booth. Claiming strength from the Lord, I had come and already enjoyed the opportunity of leading a number of individuals to Christ. Taking a short break from the booth, I was walking down the aisle when I had heard Jay over the speaker phone. This reunion with Jay was no coincidence, I was certain.

Jay eagerly shared what had transpired in his life over the last two years. He had indeed grown in the Lord, studying his Bible, and actively witnessing to others about their need to be born again. When I offered him tracts from my purse, he eagerly accepted all that I had with me. He wanted to use them to share with coworkers and others. His boss had suggested that they cancel the National Dairy Cattle Congress in Waterloo to concentrate on larger fairs because of business growth. Jay had insisted that Waterloo was important to him; he wanted to keep coming back because the Waterloo event was the place of his spiritual birth and meaningful to him.

Having moved his family from Florida to Missouri, Jay wanted me to have his new address. Then we shared a time of prayer for his wife and children, requesting that God would also bring them to know Christ as their Savior. Praise the Lord for that opportunity to see someone who had come to know Christ; who was still excited about his decision two years later.

*   *   *   *   *

1993 the Goerings

May 19, 1994 ~ Vietnam vet

A young woman whom I had counseled six years earlier, stopped at our downtown office. She was accompanied by a friend in need. Rebecca had lost her identification card; without it, she couldn't get help or a job. She also needed a copy of her birth certificate from Colorado. Rebecca was living on the street, collecting cans for money in order to survive.

So that Rebecca could get her ID, I wrote out a check and sent a letter to the court house in her home town, requesting that it be mailed to me to give to her. Rebecca returned often, checking to see if the letter had arrived; in the process we became friends. One day she was accompanied by her boy friend, Danny. To help Rebecca keep warm at night, I gave her a sleeping bag; she had bread, so I gave her a jar of peanut butter. Rebecca liked to stop in for prayer and a visit, but she was running out of options. Additionally, she was drinking heavily. Danny stopped to ask for my telephone phone number so that he could forward it to Rebecca's mother in Wisconsin as her mother wanted to talk with me. Danny was worried about Rebecca, afraid that she wasn't going to be alive much longer if she didn't receive help. Both he and her mother thought that she needed rehabilitation for "drying out." We talked about how to help Rebecca.

Danny shared much of his own life story with me. He had spent two terms in Vietnam and was unable to handle the memories and guilt. We talked about God and about the Bible.

God's Appointment

When he left, Danny turned at the door and said, "I just want to see Rebecca helped, but there is no hope for me."

"Danny, there is too hope for you." I insisted.

A few days later, Danny and another fellow brought Rebecca to my office. They were all drunk. Danny was almost dragging Rebecca.

"You listen to this woman, Rebecca. She knows what she is talking about—she can help you."

Danny and Bill physically made Rebecca sit and listen. We talked. But when Rebecca haughtily suggested that she would get down on her knees and pray, I told her "No," she didn't need to mock God. When she was really ready to let God have control of her life, she could, but not in mockery.

Then I showed Danny a picture of Jesus, asking if Danny would be able to look at that picture and ask Jesus to forgive him.

Danny humbly said, "I can't look at His eyes."

When the three left, I felt spiritually drained. I wanted so much to help them, but didn't have the power to keep them from walking right into Hell. Oh, I prayed for the power of the Holy Spirit to use my words and my life to help bring them to Jesus Christ.

Rebecca's mother and I did talk by telephone. Eventually, Rebecca was picked up, put in jail, and then the hospital. There, I visited her. She was practically climbing the walls. Thanking me, she said that until she had come to Waterloo, she had never found a friend who cared for her as I did. She wanted to change and had trusted Jesus Christ as her Savior; but she knew that changing her life would be hard. Drinking alcohol seriously since she was seven, she didn't know what life was like sober. She looked forward to getting help at the short-term treatment center in Mt. Pleasant for a month. Then she hoped to come back to Waterloo.

In my earnest prayers for him that week, God laid on my heart a passage that could be the key to reach Danny. On May 21, Danny stopped to see if I had heard from Rebecca yet. He was lonesome and felt like talking. I shared the passage about the woman who had been a great sinner who had washed Jesus' feet with her tears and dried them with her hair. Jesus said about her, *"Her sins, which are many, are forgiven—for she loved much. But he who is forgiven little, loves little. And he said to her, 'Your sins are forgiven.' . . . 'Your faith has saved you; go in peace'"* (Luke 7:36-50). Danny's heart melted. He bowed his head and talked to the One who loved him "much," He who could forgive his sin and change his life.

Smiling, he said, "I like that. Now I have a purpose for life."

My prayer is that Danny will be a good soldier for Christ. Shortly afterwards, Danny left Waterloo. I have not heard from him or Rebecca since. It will be interesting to get together in eternity and find out what happened in their lives.

* * * * *

CHAPTER 13

1995-1999

The Rapture sign

August 1995 ~ Rabbits and everlasting life

The Waterloo YMCA director invited me to relocate the Christian Video Store to their facility, as he felt it would be a good addition to their program. Additionally, with considerably more traffic passing the video store, there would be many opportunities to interact with people. During the summer especially, young people come for all-day activities. I decided to take him up on his offer and moved.

Ed had parked his pick-up truck in front of our building, and then it wouldn't start. I was cleaning the almost empty space, having moved my Christian Video Rental Store to the Family YMCA location. Lending Ed some tools, we visited while he tried one thing after another to get his truck started.

We talked about the 4'x8' wooden sign, still in the window, that my mother and I had painted, a visualization of what may very well happen at the Rapture. It depicted cemetery graves opening, the resurrected dead in Christ rising to Heaven, driverless cars and planes suddenly without pilots, crashing and a Scripture verse encouraging people to seek the Lord. Finding a way to transport the large sign was a challenge. Mentioning that I thought the Lord's coming could be soon, he informed me that he had always thought that he would go through the tribulation.

"I hope not." I responded, "But, if you do, you should know what to expect." Giving him the video tape *The Years of the Beast,* a movie about a man who was left behind at the Rapture and experienced the tribulation, I encouraged him to investigate how to avoid living through the tribulation. Not long after that, Ed and his girlfriend Debbie, kindly stopped at the office with their truck, picked up the rapture sign, and delivered it to the YMCA for me.

At the time, I had been looking for a cage for my white rabbit and was considering buying one from Ed. Meantime, one morning I had put my rabbit outside in the front yard for some fresh air and sunshine. After going back into the house, I heard a commotion and my daughter screaming. Running back outside, I saw neighborhood dogs which had come into our yard, wrestle the door of the borrowed cage open and took off with Homer. Following the dogs as they dragged Homer into the park across the street, I managed to take him away from the dogs. He died in my arms. When Ed called, asking if I still was interested in the cage, I told him about Homer and said I did not need the cage any more.

About a week later, Ed called, asking if I could stop at his house after work. He had seen a dwarf rabbit advertised in the Sunday paper and had purchased it for me. My nine-year-old son Josiah and

I stopped at their house on our way home the next day. Debbie was there and gave me the rabbit—he was adorable. I thanked her, saying how very nice it was of them to give me a rabbit to replace Homer, as well as a cage.

Asking Debbie if she had watched the video I had given them, she replied, "Yes, several times."

"Would you like to talk about it?"

We talked for almost two hours. Josiah patiently petted the rabbit, praying for God to lead in our conversation. Debbie told me about a bad experience in February when she had "actually felt as if Satan were taking her to Hell." She had been scared, but after talking to a number of people and being ridiculed, she had decided to stop talking about it. Fear still gripped her. There was no way that Debbie wanted ever to go to that place, but no one understood her nor had any answers for her.

Of course, I told her that I believed in Heaven and in Hell, and agreed with her. I also certainly didn't want to go to Hell. Then we talked about Jesus' defeat of Satan, His work to rescue souls; I explained that we are able to get to Heaven by being born again, literally born from above (John 3) into God's family. By the power of Christ and His resurrection, Hell has no hold on our souls if we have His blood protection. After answering numerous questions, I asked Debbie if she would like to pray and ask Jesus to pay for her sin, come into her life, and give her everlasting life.

She answered, "Yes, I would indeed like to." As she prayed aloud, her telephone began to ring and ring. She ignored it, not wanting to be interrupted as she talked with God. The telephone stopped for a while then started ringing again. Eventually, when she was finished, she answered the phone. After hanging up, she turned to me and joyfully stated that now she understood the wonderful gift of a home in Heaven. She marveled at the peace and joy she felt. All fear of being Hell-bound was gone.

Days later, I passed Debbie at her place of work. She waved boldly and smiled. Both Debbie and Ed kept busy, showing *The Years of the Beast* video to their family and friends.

* * * * *

August 4, 1995 ~ YMCA

Ten-year-old Shelby came regularly to swim at the YMCA. Afterwards, she would come in and look through the videos displayed in the store and ask lots of questions. Shelby especially enjoyed watching me edit and put together programs for Public Access Television on my Amiga computer. We talked about God and Heaven, how to get there, and a lot of things. One day, I sensed that her questions were more serious.

When I asked if she wanted to trust Jesus Christ to be her personal Savior, she answered, "Yes, I'd like to do that." Right there in the video store, she trusted Christ. It was delightful to have her stop by after that. She always volunteered to assist in filing video cards or help with any other current project.

* * * * *

December 5, 1995 ~ High school volunteer

A local high school counselor asked me if I would participate in a program which allowed students to work in local businesses for a few hours a week for experience. The students gained practical experience and also earned school credit for their work. I agreed to have a student come. During the first semester, Lonnie came three hours a week, to help in any way he could. At the time, I was designing lettering and art work for the Christian Video Rental store window in the YMCA. Lonnie helped prepare and assemble the window design, among other tasks.

We visited as we worked. After high school, he wanted to be a truck driver. Naturally, we also talked about my concern that people consider the claims of Christ in their lives. Before his time with me ended, Lonnie told me that he had received the Lord Jesus as his own Savior.

The next semester, a second student from the high school came. In appreciation for his help, I allowed him to take a video home for free and when he returned it, he could take another one. It was disappointing to me that he selected non Christian titles. I was hoping he would become curious about being a Christian. One day, the subject of policemen came up. I told him I had a true-life movie about policemen. When he went home that day, I handed the video *Heaven's Heroes* to him, encouraging him to view it.

In that movie, a Christian policeman who had been witnessing to his unsaved partner gave his life to save his partner in a shootout. The policeman couldn't understand how his partner could deliberately give his life for him. But the Christian police officer knew that he was ready to face eternity; his partner was not. In trying to understand, the surviving policeman came to realize that someone else had also given His life for him, Jesus Christ. He becomes a Christian; then he too, as was his Christian partner, was ready to face eternity.

The next time the student came to work and returned the video, I asked what he thought of the movie. He said that it had deeply touched his heart and asked me a lot of questions. Before he left for home, he asked me if I would pray with him and help him to receive Jesus Christ as His Lord and Savior which I was happy to help him execute.

* * * * *

December 1995 ~ Baby bunnies

Having one dwarf rabbit, I ended up buying a second one. Why not raise bunnies as a hobby? I enjoyed the cute, furry babies. Sometimes I would bring them to the video store in a cage with a "For Sale" sign. Walking by, kids would come in, pet, and even hold the baby bunnies. One girl stopped more than once. She picked out one of the bunnies and received permission from her parents to buy it. While getting acquainted with the bunny there in the store, Debbie also came to know Jesus as her personal Savior. Animals can be a natural attraction for making contacts for Jesus.

* * * * *

January 17, 1996 ~ Brown mouse

After the rabbits in my video store were all sold, I decided to raise pet mice to sell. Krystal came in to look; then she chose the one that she wanted. In and out of the store she came to visit her mouse until her parents gave her permission to bring it home. I enjoyed talking with her about pet mice, yes, but even more, about how God loves us and wants to make sure that we know how to get to Heaven. Krystal trusted Christ as her Savior there in the video store. And soon after that, in God's perfect timing, was able to take her mouse home.

* * * * *

June 1996 ~ Cousin Mike

Aunt Mary's son, Mike, was in a Lincoln, Nebraska, hospital with a brain tumor; we stopped to visit. At the time, I was trying to learn how to use a computer, and it was "driving me crazy." Interestingly, Mike had a computer with which he was quite competent. As we talked, he tried to explain to me the basics.

Mike also shared some of his experiences in the Marines. Since Mike hadn't liked his mother's telling him to get up in the morning and having to do things for her, after high school, he decided to join the Marines. He thought they were going to kill him. They told him to get up a lot earlier than his mom had, and they didn't ask him to do things—they ordered him. He could laugh now about that "mistake."

When I asked Mike if he knew for sure that if he were to die, he would be in Heaven with his mother, he answered, "I don't know for sure."

"Would you like me to share with you from the Bible how you can know?"

"Yes, with this brain tumor, things do not look very good for me. I would like to know how to get to Heaven," he said soberly.

After I had shared several passages of Scripture with him sitting in his hospital bed, Mike made certain that his ticket to Heaven was secured. Mike's condition improved for a while, but not very long after that visit, Mike joined his mother in Heaven.

* * * * *

September 1996 ~ "Farmers for Christ" booth

Fatigue, muscle and joint pain, difficulty concentrating and making decisions—all symptoms of fibromyalgia—threatened to change my life. Some days I made my way from the living room to the kitchen on my knees, unable to stand or walk; shopping became impossible without a wheelchair. One day while I was doing dishes, Josiah came up behind me and gave me a gentle hug.

"That hurts, Honey," I softly protested.

"Mom, that *can't* hurt you," Josiah responded in disbelief.

"You don't understand."

That year again, because of my health, we were unable to have our booth at the National Dairy Cattle Congress. I was excited when The Farmers for Christ couple again called, asking me to help them with their booth for one day, September 20. God provided strength, and gave me the opportunity to lead Michelle (20), Jessica (12), Heather (16), Rose (16), Tracy (17), Eddie (13), and Jennifer (13), to Christ. Praise the Lord.

* * * * *

August 18, 1997 ~ Missing Mother

Nick came often to the video store at the YMCA. He was half Cherokee Indian. Quite concerned about family problems, he asked for prayer for his mother who had left the family and not returned; he missed her very much. Jesus' promise, **"I will never leave you nor forsake you"** (Hebrews 13:5), greatly comforted his heart, and Nick trusted Jesus Christ as his Savior.

* * * * *

Not wanting to surrender my lifestyle to fibromyalgia, I prayed earnestly for God to show me what to do. I knew He could heal, He could reveal what I should do, or He could use my weakness. A customer at the video store told me about USANA, a high quality nutritional product. Skeptical, I hesitated to give it a try, but the Lord seemed to speak to my heart. If I was praying for help, I should be willing to accept help. I decided that if God was trying to answer my prayer in this way, I should at least be open to trying the vitamins. I honestly gave the product a chance. Praise the Lord, after a period of time, I remember walking out of church feeling as if a fog had lifted from my mind and the sun was shining again. Not long after that, I could enjoy walking again. As long as I continued regularly with the USANA vitamins, I did better; slacking off, the symptoms would gradually return.

* * * * *

September 13, 1997 ~ Understanding Scripture

Age eleven, James came into the video store and visited with me.
"What do you do in here?" he asked with youthful curiosity.
"Whatever needs to be done."
Picking up a packet of cards with Scripture verses printed on them, he began reading. He looked puzzled.
"Do you understand what you are reading? I asked.
"No."
"Would you like to understand them?"
"Yes."
The Scripture cards quoted verses about God's love for us and how God loved us enough to provide a way for us to be united with Him, including John 3:16. After explaining the Scriptures one by one to him, James wanted to trust Christ as his Savior. As James left the store, he gave me a warm hug and a sincere, "Thank you."

* * * * *

Others found Jesus Christ in the video store. It was a good place to meet young people. Eventually, the YMCA needed the space. I closed the Christian Family Video store, realizing that the video ministry would soon require changing from VHS tapes to DVDs. And although the store had been a great ministry, it had not supported itself. Not enough people had availed themselves of the family and Christian videos, and I could not continue to shoulder the financial burden.

* * * * *

Our home in Waterloo.

October 1997 ~ Amiga computer parts

In 1988, Elaine Jaquith had asked me to help produce a program she wanted to do for Public Access Television, *Telling It Like It Is*. Since I had never done anything along that line, it was a challenge; we learned together. The Lord confirmed the open door, and it provided an avenue of expressing my faith on local television. Since God had used the visual of a movie to reach my heart for Christ, I knew that television could be a valuable method of presenting the Gospel. I bought a SVHS camera, editing units, and an Amiga computer. I was tempted a number of times to toss the equipment out the window, only to discover it was me, not the equipment that was messing up. Anyway, after I learned how to use the equipment, it worked rather well allowing me to design video programs and create screens, including the introduction and ending of programs.

As time went on, the Amiga computer was no longer available and parts were hard to find. When my monitor went out, I was in a bad situation. Calling around, I was directed to a dealer in Washburn who had owned an Amiga shop and still had some parts. He delivered a used monitor and helped me hook up the equipment. I explained him that I was using the Amiga to do a weekly program for Public Access TV.

When I mentioned the conversation Jesus had in the Bible about how to get to Heaven, he was interested in knowing more. The whole idea of Jesus talking about the subject was fascinating to him. After I had shared with him about trusting Christ as his Lord and Savior, he wanted to make the decision to accept Christ, and he did, right there in our basement.

Often our problems are God's way of maneuvering us into position to help others learn about Christ. This was another God's Appointment.

* * * * *

Downtown Waterloo made plans to change Fourth Street, a reshuffling of businesses made it advisable for us to sell the Family Altar Broadcast building. With the use of computers, we no longer needed the obsolete bulky machinery that required so much space. Additionally, we had discontinued the Mission and fully distributed all the clothing. The building was too big for us and too costly to maintain. We moved the Family Altar Broadcast ministry into our home.

December 1999 ~ Honorary Grandma

The neighbor kids who lived just behind us—Lisa, Patty, Kim, John, and Bret—often came to visit and play with our children. They asked if they could call me, "Grandma." Honored, I said, "Yes."

After that, most of the neighborhood children called me "Grandma." In December of 1999; sitting on the couch in our living room, Lisa and Patty prayed and received Christ as their Savior. After that, they enjoyed going to church with us.

CHAPTER 14

2000-2004

✳

December 2000 ~ Christmas gift for Jesus

Our neighbor girls, Lisa and Patty, wanted to invite three friends of theirs who were brothers to come along with us to church. We picked up twins James and John and their younger brother, twelve-year-old Shane. It was the Sunday evening service, December 3, at Walnut Ridge Baptist Church. That night, Pastor Van Heukelum's sermon was about *James and John,* part of a series on the Disciples of Christ. The twins were excited that their names were in the Bible. On the way home, we talked about the sermon. I explained that the pastor was talking about friends of Jesus who were His "disciples" and were with Him while He was here on earth. I shared how Jesus calls us "friends," if we love Him, according to the Gospel of John, chapter 15. Also, in the Old Testament part of the Bible, Moses is called "a friend of God." It would be wonderful if God were to call them friends, I suggested. They thought that would be great.

We continued to talk for about an hour. When I asked if they would like to trust Christ to forgive their sins and give them everlasting life, they were interested but not ready yet. James and John's fourteenth birthdays were coming up the following Tuesday; they wanted to wait and have their spiritual birthdays on their physical birthday. The next Wednesday, they came to AWANA, a tremendous youth program at our church, "**A**pproved **W**orkmen **A**re **N**ot **A**shamed," as taken from 2 Timothy 2:15.

On the way home, I asked if they had trusted Christ. They responded, "No." Then I asked if they were ready to receive Jesus as their Lord and Savior. James was ready, even though his brother was not. James prayed right there in the car, receiving Christ as his Savior.

Saturday, December 9, we planned to move the supplies we had been storing for the Family Altar Broadcast from the downtown building into our garage. All three brothers—James, John and Shane helped us; their combined muscles accomplished the task. For lunch, we fed the boys pizza. As we were eating, I asked John if he thought he was ready yet to trust Christ. Praise the Lord—he replied, "Yes."

Several times after that, I would ask Shane if he felt ready to make the same decision his brothers had made. He always replied, "No."

On December 14, the neighbor girls participated in a dress rehearsal for the Living Christmas Tree Choir. The three boys came along to watch. Shane came up to me and asked if I would come out into the hallway and talk with him. He said he was ready and wanted to trust Christ, "Now." Shane and I read the Gospel of John chapter 3, where Jesus said, *"But to all who did receive him, who believed in his name, he gave the right to become children of God"* (John 1:12). God promises to give power to become "sons of God" to those who believe. Shane bowed and prayed, trusting Christ as his Savior. All three boys freely shared with others there at the church how they had trusted Christ as their Savior.

* * * * *

These decisions for the Lord came during the Christmas season. Each year as I decorate my home, I like to wrap a small box and lay it in my nativity scene next to the Christ child. In that box, I mentally place my gift to Christ for His birthday present that year. This year, I had asked the Lord what He wanted for a birthday present. The opportunity He gave me to touch these boys' lives, I believe, was what He had in mind for His Christmas gift.

* * * * *

March 10, 2001 ~ The next step

"I'm getting married, and I'd like you to meet her," Don called to tell James. A lonely bachelor, Don frequently called our home needing transportation or interesting reading materials.

James and I did stop to visit Yvonne and Don at her apartment. A pleasant lady, Yvonne nevertheless had suffered a difficult life. Both expressed concern about their habit of smoking cigarettes; they asked us to pray with them. Married previously, Yvonne had raised her family alone. Those children were now grown with families of their own, Yvonne enjoyed Don's companionship. They were planning a June wedding.

When Yvonne mentioned that she was Lutheran, James noted that I had once been a Lutheran and suggested that I share with her my testimony. So I explained, "I used to be a Lutheran, as a teenager. And I've come to learn, as Martin Luther taught, that we should depend not in the church or our own good works, but rather, in salvation by faith in Christ: As Martin Luther quoted from the Bible, *"For by grace you have been saved through faith. And this is not your own doing; it is the gift of God, not a result of works, so that no one may boast"* (Ephesians 2:8, 9). As well as, *"For in it the righteousness of God is revealed from faith for faith, as it is written, "The righteous shall live by faith"* (Romans 1:17). What really changed my life was finding that personal relationship by faith with Jesus Christ."

Yvonne asked, "You mean being baptized?"

"Not necessarily." Explaining that Jesus told us in the Bible how to get to Heaven, I asked if I could show her what He said.

"Yes," she replied. She took her Bible and sat down beside me. Then we read together the passages in John, chapter three. I explained about being born again and the difference between believing "about" and "in" or "on" Jesus. Then we continued, *"For God so loved the world, that he gave his only Son, that whoever believes in him should not perish but have eternal life"* (John 3:16); and *"Whoever believes in him is not condemned, but whoever does not believe is condemned already, because he has not believed in the name of the only Son of God"* (John 3:18). That chapter concludes with the passage, *"Whoever believes in the Son has eternal life; whoever does not obey the Son shall not see life, but the wrath of God remains on him"* (John 3:36). Then we turned to another favorite passage in the same book of John, *"But to all who did receive him, who believed in his name, he gave the right to become children of God"* (John 1:12).

"Was this something you've done before?" I inquired.

"No," she replied.

"Would you like to pray right now and ask Jesus to forgive your sin personally and give you the everlasting life He offers?"

"Yes, I would."

Don broke in saying, "I'd like to receive Jesus, too." First Yvonne and then Don prayed aloud, inviting Christ to be their Savior.

As we left, we offered Don a ride home. In the car, he wanted to know what we thought of Yvonne. We assured him that we thought Yvonne was, "Very nice—but it's up to you to know if you are in love and if you're ready to give up bachelorhood for marriage."

* * * * *

Don and Yvonne did not get married. Yvonne suffered a stroke. One side of her body became paralyzed, requiring her to be cared for in a nursing home, but they continued being friends, and Don seeks to visit her as often as he can.

* * * * *

June 2001 ~ "Cattle Congress Lady"

Rhonda Moore was interviewing two guests at the Public Access Television Studio, Jill and Marcus, for her *Words of Life* program. The past year, Jill and Marcus had worked with a ministry that sponsored groups of musically talented Christian young people, sharing their Christian testimony and values in public schools all over the United States. Since I was doing the filming and producing the program for her, I was introduced to the guest speakers. Rhonda mentioned that I enjoyed talking to people about Christ and that, among other things, had staffed a soul-winning booth at the Cattle Congress.

Jill asked a few questions and then exclaimed, "You're the Cattle Congress lady. You led my best friend and another girlfriend to the Lord there. My friends were telling me that a lady at the Cattle Congress had talked to them about having two birthdays, one physical and one spiritual, by being born into God's family. They both trusted Christ as their Savior there that day."

"Have they grown in the Lord?" I inquired.

"Oh, yes," she enthusiastically affirmed. Jill gave me a warm hug and kiss on the cheek saying, "Thank you for leading my friends to the Lord."

My heart leapt for joy. How encouraging it was to hear her testimony. I would have never guessed that I had acquired an alias, "The Cattle Congress Lady."

* * * * *

July 10, 2001 ~ Little charmer

A pastor and his wife from India spoke at our church. During that visit, they took time for me to videotape their personal testimonies of salvation. Editing the tape at home, I added an introduction, pictures, and a conclusion—compiling a program to air on *Interesting People,* a local Public Access TV show I had started producing in 1999. I wanted to give the couple a copy of the program before they left to use in showing churches their ministry. The tape would be able to travel further then they could.

My fourteen-month-old granddaughter and I went to the bus depot to deliver a gift copy of the tape. Arriving at the bus depot before the Indian couple, little Ashley, with big blue eyes and strawberry blonde hair, was not shy and immediately set about winning friends.

With a number of tracts in my purse, I thought I would see what would happen if I gave her a tract for each of the two men she had charmed. Ashley waddled up to each of them, slightly crumbling the tract and putting it in her mouth before giving it to them. Both men smiled broadly and said, "Thank you," then proceeded to read the tract from cover to cover. Ashley thought this task was great fun. I handed her another tract to distribute at will. She gave it to a lady who placed the tract Ashley gave her on top of her suitcase without reading it. I had to keep Ashley from taking it back. Not a single person rejected the tract from her hands. Before we had finished visiting with our Indian friends, Ashley had shared about fifteen tracts

When I told her mother about Ashley's actions, Angela cuddled her little daughter and commented, "Maybe when you get to Heaven, Honey, you'll find that someone is there because of you."

* * * * *

July 25, 2001 ~ Practice pays off

At the Cedar River Bible Conference in Cedar Falls, Iowa, my sister Sue and her husband Rik were in charge of the children's Bible program. Our son, Josiah, age fifteen, helped on Wednesday night. When the invitation was given, a number of children came forward for salvation. Josiah helped his Aunt Sue with the kids, but didn't feel comfortable speaking with any of the children on his own. He listened intently to his aunt's explanation of God's plan of salvation. After the service, Sue asked Josiah if he would practice leading someone to the Lord during the next days so that He would be able to help her that Thursday evening.

The next night, Josiah, Bible in hand, took five children and explained to them how to trust Christ as their personal Savior, and then prayed with them. On the way home, he shared, of the five he had talked with, two had previously made decisions, one was too young and didn't really understand, but he felt that the other two had trusted Christ that night. This experience was invaluable for Josiah's spiritual growth, even though that evening wasn't Josiah's first soul-winning experience. Years earlier, he had led Chris, a neighbor friend to Christ. As with any other skill, however, practice is important. And this skill brings great reward.

* * * * *

September 8, 2001 ~ Visiting Dorothy

Dorothy helped us for years at the Family Altar Broadcast office. She would read our monthly newsletters, proofreading for grammar and spelling errors and other secretarial duties. Now at age ninety-six, she lived in Parkview Nursing Home. She had become confused and hardly recognized anyone except me. Never married, she was alone and had asked me, as a friend, to help her. Eventually, she couldn't remember even how to tell time; she still remembered her relationship with Christ and was happy.

Her roommate, Carol, age fifty-four and afflicted with multiple sclerosis, was confined to a wheelchair. One day, while visiting Dorothy, I talked with Carol about God and how people can be certain that they have done what God requires in order to get to Heaven.

When I invited Carol to put her faith in Jesus, she responded, "I can't." When I asked why not, she replied, "God could never forgive me—I can't forgive myself." No matter what I said, I could not get her past that point.

Invited as guest speaker for an AWANA group of girls, I told them about Carol and asked them to pray for her. The AWANA leader and three of the girls made beautiful cards for me to give Carol. Their friendly letters assured Carol of God's willingness to forgive. I carried the cards in my purse.

On Thursday, September 8, I visited Dorothy again. Carol had been moved to a different room; but when she saw me, Carol requested that I come in and see her new room. She also had a new roommate, Sharon. Sharon had undergone surgery to remove a tumor on the back of her neck leaving her paralyzed. Slowly she was regaining the use of her hands, but she had not yet regained any use of her legs.

When I gave Carol the cards, she was deeply touched. Wiping tears from her eyes, she responded, "Yes," when I asked her if she would like to trust Jesus Christ to forgive her sins and receive Him as her Savior. As I knelt on the floor beside her, she trusted Christ.

Since Sharon was right there and saw and heard what we were doing, I asked her if she had ever received Jesus. She said she wasn't sure.

"Would you like to make sure?" I asked.

"Yes."

Both Sharon and Carol received Christ as their Savior that afternoon. They both can look forward to having a new body in Heaven.

*   *   *   *   *

March 6, 2002 ~ Inaudible voice

The neighbor kids wanted their friend, twelve-year-old Mandy, to come with them to our church's AWANA program. Mandy's mother, having had surgery to remove a brain tumor, was undergoing weekly chemo treatments. One evening, on the way to AWANA, I asked about how her mother was doing. Shouldering responsibilities way beyond her years because of her mother's illness, Mandy was mature for her age and of necessity, was seriously facing the reality of death in her family.

After AWANA, while driving the children home, I asked Mandy if she had given much thought to the subject of how to get to Heaven. She said that she had thought about it but didn't know what to do.

"Mandy," I explained, "a person can be born into God's family just by receiving Jesus as their Lord and Savior—just by believing on Him. We just need to ask Him to forgive our sin; He gives us everlasting life. "

Coincidentally, Mandy was the last young person to be delivered home. Arriving at her house, we sat parked in her drive-way talking. The street light made it possible for us to read the Bible verses. One of the verses we looked at was, *"But to all who did receive him, who believed in his name, he gave the right to become children of God,"* (John 1:12); Also the warning, *"Whoever believes in the Son has eternal life; whoever does not obey the Son shall not see life, but the wrath of God remains on him"* (John 3:36).

Mandy's eyes glistened brightly; the words *eternal life* intrigued her. She sat thinking seriously about our conversation. Obviously,

Jesus was speaking to her heart; she was not ready to get out of the car. I asked her if she'd like to talk to Jesus; she replied that she would like that. Praying aloud, she called upon Jesus Christ to forgive her sin and give her eternal life.

Then I asked Mandy if she thought Jesus had said, "Yes," to her request and kept His promise in the Bible. Did God claim her now as His daughter, or had He said, "No?"

"I didn't hear His voice," she said, "but I feel here," pointing to her chest, "as if He did."

"God doesn't have to talk to us with a big, strong voice," I explained. "The Bible is the book God wrote to us. When He promises to do something, He keeps His promise. What did John 1:12 and John 3:36 say?" We reread the verses.

Afterwards Mandy confidently replied, "God says He did, so I know He did." I promised to give her a Bible for her own use so that she could read for herself about God and the things He wants us to know.

* * * * *

May 2002 ~ Happy Birthday

When I became a Christian, I determined to follow the Biblical instructions that warn against being "unequally yoked" in marriage with a non-Christian. I refused to expose myself to the temptation, recognizing that it is easier to control emotions before they come into play rather than afterwards. I did not even date an unsaved person. Should I ever marry, I absolutely wanted to marry a Christian who knew and loved the Lord.

My daughters, however, did not have the same conviction. When they dated, I was always concerned that the boys be born-again Christians. If they weren't, I considered God had brought them into our lives for a reason and prayed earnestly that they would make a genuine decision for Christ.

Victoria dated a nice, young man named Ben. But, he was not a Christian; I prayed for God to open up an opportunity for me to visit with him. One day I mentioned to him that sometime I would like to share with him how Jesus explained in the Bible how a person can get to Heaven.

"Why not now?" he asked.

Sitting together in the living room with an open Bible, I pointed to the verses where Jesus told Nicodemus that in order to get to Heaven an individual must be born again. We have a physical birth, but we need to also be born spiritually. By simply receiving the blood payment of Christ on the Cross to their personal account, one can experience a second birthday and be born into the family of God. Ben listened and seemed interested. Not feeling like there was a need to hurry, I went through a thorough explanation of the Gospel message.

"Have you ever received Christ in the past?" I inquired.

"No, I never have," he replied.

"You need to then. Would you like to now?"

"No, I'm not ready right now."

"Just saying the words does not help; a person has to mean it." I told him if he was not ready to make the decision, he should wait. "Perhaps the timing is not right for you now, but keep in mind, that not to make a decision for Christ is, in reality, a decision against Christ. Is it all right with you Ben, if I pray asking God to work in your heart toward that end?" I asked.

"Sure," he responded. We prayed together and I asked God to work in Ben's heart to the point that he would indeed call upon Jesus Christ to be his Lord and Savior.

As Ben left our home I requested, "Do me a favor, when you do get around to making a decision, let me know so I can rejoice with you."

Ben promised. A few days later the telephone rang. It was Ben. "Today is my birthday."

"Oh, I didn't know it was your birthday—Happy Birthday."

"No, not that birthday, the other birthday" Ben said. "This morning about one o'clock, I trusted Jesus Christ."

"Ben, that is great." I rejoiced. God had indeed continued working in his heart until Ben was ready.

*   *   *   *   *

Victoria and Ben did not ultimately marry, but God used him to be a blessing in our lives. Also, I believe God brought him into our lives for a time so that he could come to know Christ. In 2004, Victoria married a fine Christian young man named Andrew.

Becoming careless in using the nutritional vitamins which had been so helpful to me, I experienced a return of the fibromyalgia symptoms. Sherry, a former CBF co-worker, suggested that I try Reliv. The nutritional drink was very helpful; again, the symptoms faded as I used the product.

* * * * *

April 21, 2003 ~ Thank you, Jesus

Angela, my eldest daughter and her husband, Michael, needed a new roof on their house. Michael's brother Tim was an experienced roofer; he came from Wisconsin to help with the job. Tim also brought his girlfriend, Jenny, to meet the family. Jenny was with me as I "Grandma sat" my three grandchildren as the men worked. As we talked, the conversation turned easily toward God and the Bible. She was obviously spiritually searching.

"Would you like me to get the Bible out and show you how a person can reach God?"

"Yes," Jenny replied.

Turning to the Gospel of John, chapter one, beginning with the first verse, we read together, *"In the beginning was the Word, and the Word was with God, and the Word was God. He was in the beginning with God. All things were made through him, and without him was not anything made that was made. In him was life, and the life was the light of men."* She was excited to learn that the *"Word"* in those verses is Jesus; He is the *"Light"* that came but was not received. I continued reading, *"But to all who did receive him, who believed in his name, he gave the right to become children of God"* (John 1:1-4, 12). The three children played around us, as we talked.

When Angela came home from work, the children were glad to see their mother. As usual, we exchanged the news of the day, and I prepared to go home. Jenny went outside to the back patio—I joined her.

"Since we were in the middle of a thought when we were interrupted, would you like to finish talking out here before I leave?"

"I'd like that," she answered.

"Receiving Jesus," I continued, "is like saying 'yes' in a wedding ceremony. It begins a relationship designed to be beautiful that should strengthen with time. Not only do we become the *'bride of Christ'* when we receive Jesus as our Lord and Savior, but God the Father receives us as His child." Then opening the Bible to John 3:3, we read that all mortals need two birthdays, one physical and one spiritual. The physical birth comes when we are born as a baby. Our spiritual birth comes after God's Spirit brings us to understand that we need to have Jesus pay for our sins, and we decide to receive Jesus. In turn, God receives us. Then when God calls us His daughter or son—we are part of His family.

"It has been my experience that before a spiritual birth there are often periods of time when we are conscious of God and have the desire to go toward Him, but we haven't yet been born into His family spiritually." Turning to Jenny, I asked, "Where do you think you are in your spiritual journey? Have you been born again, or are you still, so to speak, developing in the womb?"

"I think I'm in the womb," she said emphatically.

I was surprised, but pleased to hear her diagnose her own spiritual condition. "If you are in the process of developing and growing, then you can be born again any time you want, even right now."

"I would like that, but I've never prayed with anyone else," she quietly spoke.

Putting my arm around her shoulders, I encouraged her, "It's a good experience. I'll pray with you. 'Dear Jesus, Jenny and I have been talking about you. She would like to trust you and have you apply the blood you shed on the Cross to her personal sin. I know that you will hear her prayer.' Looking up at Jenny, I urged her to just tell Jesus what she wanted Him to do. Jenny prayed, receiving Jesus Christ.

"Thank you, Jesus!" she exclaimed.

"Did He hear you?" I asked.

"Yes, I know He did," she replied. We wrote down the date of her new birthday. Then she asked if I could find a Bible for her; I promised her I would, and the next day I did.

"I will have questions for you when I see you again," she promised. Eagerly, I awaited the chance to talk with her again.

* * * * *

June 2003 ~ Adam fixes my tire

"Gloria, guess what?" the teenager next door called out as I came outside.

"What?"

Holding his right arm high in the air that was encased in a solid, white cast, Adam answered, "I broke my wrist Monday while riding my bike."

"I'm sorry!" I exclaimed. We talked a while. He told me of his summer plans; Adam hoped to get the car running that his dad had given him.

As we talked, I looked over at my 1986 Oldsmobile station wagon parked in our driveway. Pointing to the front left tire, definitely still flat, I laughed, "I'm going to have to get my car fixed too."

"I saw that," Adam observed. "I'll fix it for you."

"Not with a broken arm."

"Sure, it won't take that long" he insisted.

"I'll pay you for doing it," I offered, smiling.

"No," he said. "I'm fine—you don't need to pay me. I want to do this for you."

Adam got his tools and started working on the tire. James came outside, and the three of us worked together. Getting that old tire off was harder than we had anticipated. Doing most of the work, Adam doggedly persevered, trying hard not to get his clothes too dirty. As he worked, we reminisced about some of the things we had done together in the past. Curious as to how he would answer, I asked, "Where do you consider yourself to be spiritually? Do you know for sure you are on your way to Heaven when you die?"

"I know I'm on my way to Heaven—don't you remember when I trusted Christ during Vacation Bible School?" he answered.

Yes, I remembered. He had made a decision for Christ one summer when we had VBS at the First Baptist Church in Jesup, Iowa. He came along with other young people we brought to the services. But it was refreshing to hear him recall that moment. He went on to tell me that he fairly regularly attended church. It sounded as if he was really growing in the Lord.

Finally all finished, Adam collected his tools and prepared to leave on an errand with his mom. When I again offered to pay him for his help, he insisted, "No, I wanted to do this for you." This kindness was his way of thanking me for caring, and helping him to come to know the Lord.

* * * * *

July 23, 2003 ~ Phone call from Brandon

Brandon was interested in our teenage neighbor Lisa and came around the neighborhood often. When they officially became boyfriend and girlfriend, they asked me to take pictures of them. I videoed them, then captured pictures off the tape for them onto a CD.

One day, Brandon stopped at our house by himself. I had been praying for an opportunity to visit with him regarding spiritual matters. Lisa thought that he was possibly already a Christian. But as Brandon and I talked, it became clear that not only did he not know the Lord, but he seemingly had no comprehension of spiritual truths.

Several weeks later, Lisa asked if we would be willing to also pick up Brandon for church. After that, we regularly took Brandon to AWANA Club on Wednesday nights.

One evening after AWANA, while the others played in the gym, I asked Brandon if he had been considering trusting Jesus as his own personal Savior. He looked down and said, "No, I've been busy with other things and haven't given it much thought."

"You seriously should," I urged.

The next evening, I received a telephone call from Lisa. Brandon had asked her how to trust Christ as his Savior; she had responded,

"I'll ask Grandma (the honorary title given me by the neighborhood children) and call you back." Lisa had previously trusted Christ and knew how, but she needed help explaining it to Brandon. We went over the Bible verses on the telephone. She then explained the simple plan of salvation to him; Brandon said that he would talk with God that night.

The next time I saw Brandon, I asked if he had yet trusted Jesus Christ as his personal Savior.

"Yes, I did," he quickly assured me.

Brandon also followed the Lord in believer's baptism. The Apostle Paul explains the meaning of baptism in the letter to the saints in Rome,

Do you not know that all of us who have been baptized into Christ Jesus were baptized into his death? We were buried therefore with him by baptism into death, in order that, just as Christ was raised from the dead by the glory of the Father, we too might walk in newness of life. For if we have been united with him in a death like his, we shall certainly be united with him in a resurrection like his. (Romans 6:3-5)

Baptism is to follow a personal decision to trust Christ. It identifies us with Him and is commanded in the Great Commission. Obedience to Christ in this matter is important for our growing in Christ, but it is not necessary for salvation itself.

* * * * *

May 2004 ~ Missing Grandma

The doorbell rang. Twelve-year-old Brooke, her bicycle parked in our front yard, wanted to visit with me. Brooke's mother, Billie Jo, had grown up in a home one block behind us and had often played with our children. When Billie was about twelve, the Lord gave me the opportunity to lead her to Christ. Now she had her own family, and Angela had babysat Chris, Brad, and Brooke when Billie Jo worked. We loved them and took them everywhere with us, including church, Vacation Bible School, and lots of family activities. Chris, the oldest, made a decision for Christ while in our van, talking with our son Josiah who was a year older than he. Brooke, on the other hand, had never seemed ready to make a decision for Christ.

After her mother had passed away, Billie Jo and the children moved to North Carolina. We kept in touch some through those years, and then they moved back to Iowa and made contact with us again. On one occasion, Brooke went along with me to my daughter's house to help me babysit my three granddaughters. She was good with children and a big help. Later, she came to our house to visit. As we sat on the couch, I asked if she had given any thought about how to get to Heaven.

"No, not really."

When I commented that she was twelve years old, old enough to be thinking about God and how to be sure she was going to Heaven when she died, she nodded, but she was not open to the subject. At an earlier visit, I had shown Brooke and her mother pictures in my album book of the kid's younger days and had said I'd make copies of the pictures for them. This time, Brooke asked, "Have you made copies of the pictures yet?"

"Not yet. But if your mother will let you go with me to Wal-Mart, we could go now and get them copied."

She rode home on her bike to get permission and returned quickly. We had fun running a few errands and getting the pictures copied. Brooke talked about her grandma—she was certain that Grandma Shirley was in Heaven. Heading back home, I asked, "Brooke, do you know how to get to Heaven so that you can be with your grandmother?"

She shook her head, "No, but I suppose I would have to be a good person to get to Heaven."

Assuring her that "being as good as we can be doesn't work," I explained briefly, "No one can ever be good enough—we still need our sins to be paid for by Jesus' blood." Then I paused, "Brooke, when you are ready, I would be glad to show you how you can get to Heaven." She nodded in agreement.

When we arrived home, it was dark. Her bike, still in our yard, needed to be taken to her grandpa's house. I thought it unwise for Brooke to ride home alone.

"Why don't you come into the house," I suggested. "I'll show you how to trust Jesus as your Savior, if you are ready. Then we can walk your bike together to your home."

"I would like that," she answered.

Sitting on the couch, we read passages in the Gospel of John, chapters 3 and 1 which included John 3:3, *"Jesus answered him,*[Nicodemus] *'Truly, truly, I say to you, unless one is born again he cannot see the kingdom of God'"* (John 3:3). After our discussion, I could tell Brooke understood her spiritual condition, so I asked her, "Would you like to pray and talk to God?"

Brooke prayed, expressing in her own words her need of salvation and asked Jesus Christ to pay for her sin. Afterwards, I encouraged Brooke to share with James and Josiah what she had just done. They were pleased. Finally we walked back to her grandpa's house. As I turned to leave, she followed me a few steps on foot, put her arms around me, gave me a heartfelt hug, and said "I love you."

Returning Brooke's hug, I assured her, "I love you, too, Brooke."

* * * * *

July 16, 2004 ~ Car trouble

My son wanted me to listen to the strange noise his car was making. We lifted the hood—the water in the radiator was boiling. Leaving the engine to cool, I called Joel our mechanic. He said that we should fill the reservoir with water, if it was low, and bring the car in Thursday or Friday; he was swamped right then. Thursday came, and although there had been no further problems with the car, I still drove to the shop to see if Joel could check it out.

Joel was not there, but his sixty-two-year-old brother, Jerry from Dunkerton, pulled into the driveway right beside me. We began a conversation, and he suggested, "It may be a thermostat problem."

Jerry was using an oxygen tank; he explained that his lungs had been diseased from smoking for many years. Their family was facing other problems as well—his son had cancer, and his grandson was quite sick.

Softly I observed, "Jerry, eventually we all die. I will, you will—do you know where you will go? Will it be Heaven or Hell?" When Jerry paused for a moment, I added, "Everything I hear about Hell makes me not want to go there."

Jerry said that a friend had described his near-death encounter as a peaceful atmosphere, a place which he had not wanted to leave. Then I told Jerry that I had been quite excited to find in the Bible, an occasion when a man asked Jesus just how a person gets to Heaven. "Would you mind if I shared it with you?" He told me he didn't mind if I shared that with him. Reaching through the open window of my car, I pulled out the Bible and opened it to John 3. As I shared, I could see that Jerry was not only following what I read, but wanted to know that he was on the way to Heaven.

When, finally I asked Jerry if he wanted to ask Jesus to be his Savior and Lord, his reply was, "Yes." After he had prayed, Jerry was interested in having more information to read. Since I had run out of tracts in my car, I told him I'd go home to get some and come right back. He was still there when I returned and eagerly accepted the literature. Time was up. I had to leave. Strangely, the car didn't have that particular problem again. It made me think that the car problem was simply God maneuvering me into position to talk with Jerry.

* * * * *

CHAPTER 15

2005-2006

February 27, 2005 ~ Right there, ready!

Bob Spahn was excited as he telephoned to tell us of the great weekend he had. Twenty-one years before, as a patient in the nursing home in 1984, Bob had trusted Christ as his Savior. A diligent witness for Christ, he was now working at the very nursing home where we had first met. Bob had a way with patients; he understood what it was like to be helpless, at the mercy of others for even basic needs. On Saturday, he had led six patients to the Lord; then another on Sunday. He wanted to share the news with me so that we could rejoice together.

He described it as "a hard-core day—see what you started." he gushed. "They were like I was when you talked with me, and I was there and ready."

How wonderful when those we lead to the Lord, in turn, lead others to Christ. It is almost like being a spiritual grandparent.

* * * * *

May 23, 2005 ~ Letter to Bradley

This letter was written by our daughter Jessica to her son Bradley. Hi, Honey. Tomorrow, you are turning five. I can't believe it. You are such a joy—I am proud to be your mom.

This past year, you have grown to be the best big brother I have ever seen. You play so well with Caleb. If he is playing with something he's not supposed to, you get him away and come get Mom. You're the best helper I could wish for.

You really LOVE animals, all animals, except dogs, that is. You have learned to read most three-letter words, you can add up into the teens, and you know subtraction, too. You pick up things extremely quickly and retain most information you hear. Almost everyone thinks you are an animal expert. Your favorite species are snakes. You can't get enough of snakes. You love to go snake hunting at the Air Force Base Lake, even picked up a pretty big garter snake by the tail. For your fifth birthday, we gave you a corn snake for a present, and you really loved it.

The most wonderful thing you did this year was to pray the salvation prayer again. You prayed at age three, but later mentioned that you didn't sin, so we were not sure how much you understood. You wanted you to pray again and you did so on January 1, 2005. I really feel you understood that you are a sinner and Christ died for you. How exciting. I'm sure the angels rejoiced, as we did.

Your dad and I are very proud of you. You are well-mannered and obedient, most of the time. You have a gentle spirit and a fascinating personality. The most difficult thing for you right now is missing your daddy, as he is in Iraq serving our country. We are very proud of him. You tell me that you are a "Daddy's boy" and you miss him very much. You sleep with "Daddy Bear" (a bear dressed in fatigues) and, of course, you still love your "blankie."

You made me a better person by coming into my life five years ago. Thank you so much for making me the luckiest Mommy on the planet. I love you with all my heart.

Love,
Mommy

* * * * *

September 15-18, 2005 ~ Cattle Congress

This year, the church where James and I are members sponsored a booth at the National Dairy Cattle Congress. Friday, Saturday, and Sunday, I spent about twenty hours at the booth talking with people about their salvation. My prayer was that God would bring people searching for the Lord past the booth, and I would be diligent to speak to them. We had numerous witnessing conversations, and in addition, distributed lots of tracts and literature.

During the fair, God gave me the privilege to pray with twenty-two individuals as they called on the Lord Jesus Christ to come into their heart and life and apply the blood that He shed on the Cross for sin to their personal account.

* *

Every story is unique. Two boys were with their Grandparents. The grandparents waited patiently for their two grandsons, encouraging the boys to listen. After the boys had received Jesus' blood payment for their sins, I visited with the grandparents; they requested prayer for the rest of their family to come to the saving knowledge of Christ.

* *

Crystal, 24, Heather, 29, Kirsten, 10, and Kirsten's mother stopped at the booth. Heather was Kirsten's godmother. At first, their mother was not interested in talking, but she did listen as I talked with Heather and Kirsten. Later, she talked at length with me, but did not, at that time, make a decision. Both Heather and her goddaughter, however, chose to celebrate the same spiritual birthday.

* *

A high school freshman, Zach, and his two brothers, Ryan and Cody, trusted Christ as Savior. A couple of hours after the three boys left, Ryan and Cody came back with their brother, London, 14. The two brothers excitedly announced that London wanted to do what they had just done. Listening as they stood with him, London also became born again—four brothers with the same spiritual birthday.

* *

Colin, 19, read smoothly the Bible verses I shared with him. His grandfather had died recently, and presently there was considerable turmoil in his family. After he had trusted Christ as his Savior, he asked me to pray for his sister, mom, and aunt.

* *

Cecil, 34, and his friend stopped to talk. Cecil trusted Christ, but his friend indicated that he wasn't ready yet. When I asked Cecil's friend if he thought he might be ready soon, he shrugged his shoulders, saying he would think about it and maybe do it later.

Putting my hand on his arm I said, "I hope it is before you die."

"Then it would be too late," he said.

"You are right. I want to see you in Heaven. Be sure you get it done, the sooner the better." Cecil nodded in agreement. I suggested that maybe he could help his friend later by reading together the tract I had given both of them.

* *

Lucas, 12, said he had prayed at home for God's help last week, but he didn't think God had heard him. Talking with him further, I explained that we are separated from God by sin; we need to go through Jesus Christ and the finished work of the Cross for us to be reconnected to God. Lucas prayed again, this time receiving Christ as his Savior. He stood for the longest time, obviously experiencing a rush of deep emotion. I gave him a Bible with his new spiritual birth date written in it and a video for him to share with his family. As he started to walk away, he turned and said a warm, "Thank you."

* *

Luke and Ashley, both 16, boyfriend and girlfriend, also came by our booth. They indicated that they were not sure how to get to Heaven. I showed from the Bible how Jesus answered the question of how one gets to Heaven. They were interested, understood, and prayed, receiving Christ as their Savior.

* *

My daughter Angela and her three daughters stopped at the booth to visit for a moment. They had come to see the fair. Since my oldest granddaughter is named Ashley, I introduced her to a girl also named Ashley, a seventeen-year-old farm girl, still in the booth. She had prayed a prayer asking God to save her, as had her friends Melissa, Daniel, and Dana.

* *

Our desire is that each person who trusted Christ will follow the Lord's example and be baptized and join a Bible-believing church for fellowship and further instruction. Leading people to Christ is the first step in the Christian life. But soul winners are also instructed to help new believers to grow in the Lord, *"Go therefore and make disciples of all nations, baptizing them in the name of the Father and of the Son and of the Holy Spirit, teaching them to observe all that I have commanded you. And behold, I am with you always, to the end of the age"* (Matthew 28:19, 20). This would include their learning to read Scripture, pray, get baptized, go to church, and share with others about Christ.

* * * * *

December 13, 2005 ~ "Rebel"

Tall, beautiful Vanessa was my guest on the *"Interesting People"* TV program that airs on Public Access Television. Her published book shares insights about how God was faithful to her as a single Mom, rearing three children. As a strong Christian woman, Vanessa was burdened for her stepfather at Allen hospital, sick with cancer. Since Vanessa asked if I would visit with him about the Lord, we went to visit him after we had taped the interview.

Her stepfather, "Rebel," had worked at John Deere, where it had been said of him that he could "work circles around others." Rebel had been there for Vanessa and her siblings, but his strength was gone; he was facing death's door. After visiting a few moments, I took his massive hand, looked straight at him, and told him that I had come to talk with him about how to get to Heaven.

As I talked, Rebel never took his eyes off mine. He often said just one word, "Unha." I did not understand what he was saying but lifted my Bible up to enable him to read along. Even though he wasn't wearing his glasses, he could know the words that I was reading as being from God's Word. Finally, I asked if he wanted to pray, trusting Jesus Christ to pay for his sins.

"Unha," he replied.

Running my hand gently along his jaw, then across his lips, I urged him, "Rebel, you need to talk to God yourself and tell Him what you want him to do for you."

"Unha."

"Rebel, say 'Jesus,'" I requested.

At first he couldn't. Then after a pause, he said, "Jesus."

Marveling that he had finally said a word, I continued, "Tell Jesus you are in trouble, Rebel."

He did.

"Tell Jesus you want Him to pay for your sins with His blood."

He did.

We paused. "Rebel," I asked, "what just happened?"

"I got Jesus in my life," he stated. His hand pressed mine, and he said, "Thank you."

As we prepared to leave the hospital room together, I asked Vanessa if she had peace that her stepfather had received Christ as his Savior and was now on his way to Heaven.

"Yes," she replied, wiping tears from her eyes. Vanessa's mother, a Christian, had joined us in the room while we were talking. Taking her hand, I asked if she was comfortable that her husband had honestly received the Lord. She smiled and nodded.

As we left the hospital, Vanessa marveled at his decision. "You had laid the foundation," I said, "and praise the Lord, Rebel was ready."

Later, we received this Christmas card from Vanessa.

Gloria,

    I wish I could make you know the appreciation that my mother and I feel toward you for the comfort and peace you brought to my father on his deathbed. It is official that he is now terminal. My mother and I talked for a couple of days after your visit about the remarkable change in my dad's demeanor and attitude.

    I pray God richly bless you for your unselfish behavior. My daughter, Hannah, has not met you; but as we shared with her about your act, she sends her warm sentiments also.

Vanessa

* * * * *

January 2, 2006 ~ Child of the King

Five-year-old Ashley wanted me to lie down with her when I put her and her two sisters in bed for the night. I agreed to stay with her for a few minutes.

"Grandma, guess what? Mommy prayed with me, and I trusted Jesus last night. Now I will live in Heaven with you!" she exclaimed.

Surprised, but thrilled, I told her how happy I was. I was pleased that she had told me. Still, Ashley had a few questions about Jesus, including if it had hurt Jesus when He died, paying for our sins. I answered her questions as honestly and simply as I could.

"Will you pray with me tonight and say the words for me so that I can say them again," she requested.

"Sure," I agreed, and then we talked to Jesus together.

Later, I mentioned to Angela what Ashley had told me regarding her "prayer with Mommy." Angela recalled that bedtime preparations had led to questions, and Ashley had a lot of them. Then Angela had asked Ashley if she knew how to get to Heaven; Ashley seemed to understand that Jesus was the way.

"Would you like to pray to Jesus and have Him pay for your sins so that you can go to Heaven?" Angela had asked. Ashley was ready.

Before that decision, Ashley had been struggling with bad dreams. Since then, Ashley had prayed for God to keep her from having bad dreams; apparently the nightmares ceased. Ashley had also been asking God to help her pay better attention during school, and she started receiving much improved reports.

For a long time, I had been praying that Ashley would come to know Jesus as her Savior at a young age. It thrilled me that my granddaughter, as a child of the King, also knows *"the steadfast love of the LORD* [which]*is from everlasting to everlasting on those who fear him, and his righteousness to children's children, to those who keep his covenant and remember to do his commandments"* (Psalms 103:17-18). I know that God will be faithful in her life as He has been in mine. It is a double joy to know that my daughter was able to lead her own daughter to Christ.

* * * * *

September 2, 2006 ~ Needing battery cables

There was a knock and a request for help. A truck driver, Miguel, working for a company down the street, had just returned from Texas. After parking the company truck, he discovered that his own car wouldn't start, leaving him unable to get home. He stopped at our house to ask if he could borrow our battery cables.

When we lent him the cables, he said, "God bless you." Shortly thereafter, he returned; success, his car had started. Accompanying him this time was his beautiful Mexican fiancée, Juanita.

I remarked that I had appreciated his earlier statement, "God bless you."

"Yes, I'm a Christian," he said. "I think we should be acknowledging God every day of our lives."

As we talked, Miguel translated the conversation for his fiancée since Juanita spoke only Spanish. We told them that one of our daughters, currently living in Germany, was learning German.

"I'm learning English," Juanita shyly stated.

Miguel asked if we would pray with him, asking God to help him collect wages from the truck company. It was Labor Day weekend, and they were closed. We formed a circle, James and I, Miguel and Juanita. We prayed for them to be able to collect his wages so that they would be able to get home. Still holding her hand, I asked Juanita if she knew how to get to Heaven.

"No, not really," she said. "That is why I was drawn to Miguel. I could see he loved Jesus, and I wanted to find out more."

Then I shared with Juanita how Jesus came down from Heaven to die on the Cross to pay for our sin so that we could live in Heaven. As we talked, I could see she was figuring out how to establish her own personal relationship with God. I told her how I had trusted Jesus Christ on September 20, 1959; it had been a valuable and lasting decision. Then I asked if she would like to receive Jesus.

"Yes, I would," she replied. Acknowledging that she was a sinner, Juanita prayed, asking Jesus to apply the blood He shed on the Cross to her sin. Tears rolled down her cheeks, leaving a trail of black mascara.

"What did Jesus say, 'Yes' or 'No'?"

"He said, 'Yes.'"

"How long will it last?" I continued.

"For the rest of my life," Juanita responded as she tightly squeezed my hands. Then she put her arms around me, and said, "Thank you." We watched Miguel and Juanita as they walked back down our road to their truck, arm in arm, rejoicing.

Reflecting on a thought recorded on the front pages of my Bible, I smiled, "Anyone can count the seeds in an apple, but only God knows how many apples there are in a seed." Only God knows the fruit that will come from planting the seed of the Gospel in Juanita's heart.

* * * * *

September 14-16, 2006 ~ On assignment

Age thirty-seven, Sarah was stationed in the sewing machine booth next to the Walnut Ridge Baptist Church National Dairy Cattle Congress booth. She had watched the activity at our booth and seemed curious. When I asked her if we could talk together when she had some free time, Sarah agreed. Later that afternoon, about three o'clock, I took my Bible into her booth, asking if that would be a convenient time.

We read together in the Bible Jesus' answer to the question of how one gets to Heaven. Sarah explained that in college she had become religious, but what I was sharing made it clear to her what Jesus was actually teaching. I asked if Sarah would be willing to recommit her life in prayer. She said she would. We prayed. Sarah asked Jesus to come into her life; she asked Jesus to apply the blood He shed on the Cross for sin to her account so that she would be His forever.

Afterwards, I asked her what had just happened. She answered that she had asked God to apply Christ's blood to her sin. We continued to visit, off and on, throughout the day.

The next day, Sarah was waiting in the aisle for me when I came to the booth. She wanted to know if I knew of any Bible study opportunities that spring when she would have extra time, since her church didn't have many Bible studies. When I told Sarah about *The Stranger on the Road to Emmaus* by John R. Cross (published by GoodSeed International) Bible study that we were using at our church, she was excited and wanted to come.

* *

Cody and Ryan stopped, smiling and friendly. When I asked if they knew if they were going to Heaven when they died, they replied, "Yes."

I asked, "How do you know?"

"The blood of Jesus has paid for our sins." They explained that during the fair the previous year, they had spoken with me and decided to trust Christ. (See 9-15-18, 2005 Cattle Congress).

"Did you receive my Valentine card in February?" I had mailed a card to all who had made decisions last year.

They answered, "Yes," and thanked me for the chocolate candy piece that I had taped to the heart.

* *

When I first saw Pat coming, I almost didn't try to get her attention because she appeared unreceptive to the claims of Christ, surprisingly, however, Pat did stop. She shared serious burdens with us. There is a song I have heard that gives real comfort,

> *"God is too wise to be mistaken,*
> *and God is too good to be unkind,*
> *when you can't understand His hand*
> *— trust His heart."*

Pat received Christ and I promised I would pray for her niece Emily, twenty-eight, who had just suffered a second serious stroke. As we watched people pass our booth, it would have been easy to pre-judge that some would not be open to the good news of Christ's salvation by their looks or attitude. I tried to fight that assumption.

* *

God's Appointment

Cullen, age twelve, shyly stood by the pillar at the side of our booth, waiting for his mother. I spoke with him for quite a while. Finally, when he seemed to understand Jesus' instruction that a person must be born again, literally born from above (John 3), I asked if he wanted to pray and receive the blood of Jesus to pay for his sin.

He replied, "Yes."

As we started to pray, his mother came. Standing next to him, she folded her hands and waited for him to finish his prayer. When we were finished, I asked Cullen what had just happened.

"I got the blood to pay for my sins."

Then I asked, "How long does that forgiveness last?"

His mother spoke up— "Until you sin again. Then you have to again confess your sins to God for forgiveness. Some people believe it lasts forever, but our church doesn't."

At her response, I quickly turned to the little letter, I John which includes a wonderful promise to God's children. Then I tried to explain, "I believe that here the Bible teaches that, yes, we have to confess our sins to be cleansed daily. *"If we confess our sins, he is faithful and just to forgive us our sins, and to cleanse us from all unrighteousness"* (1 John 1:9). But being born again is a one-time commitment that lasts forever, as clearly stated, *"For God so loved the world, that he gave his only begotten Son, that whosoever believeth in him should not perish, but have everlasting life"* (John 3:16). The mother wasn't listening; her mind was made up. Grabbing her son, she quickly walked away. As she disappeared, the Scripture's warning that if individuals were able to lose their salvation, then they would not be able to again get saved, was in my mind:

> *For it is impossible, in the case of those who have once been enlightened, who have tasted the heavenly gift, and have shared in the Holy Spirit, and have tasted the goodness of the word of God and the powers of the age to come, and then have fallen away, to restore them again to repentance, since they are crucifying once again the Son of God to their own harm and holding him up to contempt.* (Hebrews 6:4-6).

The blood atonement is a one-time experience that cannot be put away and then picked up again because of our being fickle.

* *

A mother and her three sons were at the fair together. Mathias, 11, reached our booth first. When his mother and two brothers arrived, we had already started talking. They listened while Mathias prayed, receiving Christ. After his prayer, I asked him what just happened. As he tried to verbalize his new-found faith, his mom put her hand on his shoulder and informed me they had their own religion; he had already been baptized. She was ready to go. His brother Michael tarried behind. I asked him if he wanted to pray too, since he had attentively listened to what was said and seemed to be concerned. He said, "Yes," and he did. Then his mom called, and he left. Now there were two brothers who were also brothers in Christ. A precious promise which can be claimed is *"Believe on the Lord Jesus Christ and you shall be saved and your household"* (Acts 16:31). May these two brothers be just the beginning of other family members coming to know Christ.

* *

Fifteen-year-old Zach, his mother, and older brother and sister Ashley, stopped at our booth. Though they had already trusted Christ at a different booth at the fair, they asked me to go over the explanation again with them. We read quickly together from the account in Genesis chapters 1-3 of sin separating man from God, *"Of the tree of the knowledge of good and evil you shall not eat, for in the day that you eat of it you shall surely die."* (Genesis 2:17). and God's instruction concerning the sacrifice of a lamb as a covering for sin, (Leviticus 16:30) how He had sent Jesus Christ as the Lamb that would pay for sin and make it possible for Him and man to be reunited. *"Behold, the Lamb of God, who takes away the sin of the world"* (John 1:29). *"Consequently, he is able to save to the uttermost those who draw near to God through him, since he always lives to make intercession for them"* (Hebrews 7:25).

Then we turned to the New Testament where John the Baptist identified Jesus as that "Lamb of God" (John 1:29). It was by the blood of Jesus Christ that sin was dealt with (Hebrews 9:22, 28). Both Zach and Ashley said they appreciated hearing the details again, only from a different prospective and claimed that they better understood their earlier decision.

* *

Jessica, twenty and friend Trisha with a younger girl, Charlie, stopped to visit. Jessica and Trisha trusted Christ. They agreed to read the tract with Charlie later that night and help her to trust Christ if she wished.

* *

Ruth, fifty-five, and her daughter, seventeen-year-old Katharine, thought maybe they had trusted Christ at an earlier opportunity, but they were not sure. When I asked if they would like to confirm their salvation, making certain that they, indeed, were born again, they both prayed. If they hadn't before, they were now receiving Jesus Christ as their Savior. Afterwards, mother and daughter seemed confident for the first time that they did just experience new birth in Christ. As described in Scripture, *"Therefore, if anyone is in Christ, he is a new creation. The old has passed away; behold, the new has come"* (2 Corinthians 5:17).

As someone wisely commented, "Peace with God comes before the peace of God."

* *

That week at the fair there were a number of other witnessing conversations; additionally, many accepted tracts and literature distributed for God to use in lives. Let us not be shy in sharing our faith with others; the Psalms frequently encourage us to *"Let the redeemed of the LORD say so"* (Psalm 107:2). God is the Lord of the Harvest, not us—we only need to be available to help Him.

* * * * *

December 13, 2006 ~ "Home last, please?"

Our car was packed full with children on the ride home from AWANA, our church youth program held on Wednesday nights. Everyone wanted to be dropped off last. Meanwhile, I was silently praying; one of the AWANA leaders had told me that another one of "my kids" made a decision for Christ that evening, but he didn't know the name. Since I thought it might have been Rylea, I was burdened to talk privately with her. I made the loop so that she and her brother, Rider, were last.

"Rylea, do you understand how important it is to trust the Lord Jesus as your Lord and Savior," I quietly asked. She nodded.

"Have you asked the Lord yet to be your Savior?" I prodded.

"Not yet," she confided, "but I'm thinking strongly about it."

"Would you like me to show you how?" I asked.

"No," she said, "I want to do it tonight in my room, alone." We talked a little longer; then the two young people went into their house for the evening.

I prayed, "Lord, be with Rylea tonight and help her come to the foot of the Cross."

The next evening, Rylea and some of the other kids came over to my house. For refreshment, we peeled and ate some apples. Then I asked Rylea if she had spoken with God about getting saved.

"Yes, I did," she replied.

After asking if she had any questions, I shared some Scripture with her, one of which was *"But as many as received him, to them gave he power to become the sons of God, even to them that believe on his name: Which were born, not of blood, nor of the will of the flesh, nor of the will of man, but of God"* (John 1:12-13). Then I encouraged Rylea to write her name and the date she had trusted Christ in the front of the new Bible that had recently been given to her.

* * * * *

December 2006 ~ Teamwork

This is the story of how a boy I couldn't take to AWANA trusted Christ as his Savior.

I care about the kids in my neighborhood—it is a mission field. The children have responded by giving me the honorary title, "Grandma." On Wednesday evenings, during the school year, I take kids to the children's program called "AWANA," an acrostic meaning Approved Workmen Are Not Ashamed, based on the Scripture, *"Do your best to present yourself to God as one approved, a worker who has no need to be ashamed, rightly handling the word of truth"* (2 Timothy 2:15).

The AWANA clubs are found throughout the United States, as well as other countries. The youth program puts strong emphasis on Scripture memorization and Biblical instruction, as well as games and activity times. Walnut Ridge Baptist Church has sponsored the program for many years. This year my station wagon, again, overflowed with kids. It is difficult for me to say, "No," when they want a ride to a place where I know they will hear the Gospel. Thirteen of us regularly rode together, and I needed help with transportation.

James picked up three of our grand children. An AWANA leader offered to transport three former neighborhood children home that had moved, yet still wanted to come. A friend, Phyllis Mortensen, offered to come to my house and help provide transportation for some of the others.

One of the boys wanted his friend Enrique, who lives a couple of miles from us, to come with us. Without any space in the car, I had to say, "No, we had better not." But later, with Phyllis's help, I was happy to say his friend could come; there would be room. The second time Enrique came to AWANA, Dan Payne, one of the leaders, told me that Enrique had indicated interest in knowing more about the Gospel. At first, Enrique had had difficulty understanding, but then he grasped the Bible truths and had prayed a heartfelt confession of sin and desire for Christ to be his Savior.

God is doing a work in him. As many of us do, Enrique may appear as a gem in the rough. It will be interesting to see what God will do through him. It is important to reach children for Christ.

* * * * *

CHAPTER 16

2007

❋

January 4, 2007 ~ Touch of love

Stopping at Danielle and Sharin's home, I let them know we had missed their coming with us to AWANA the previous Wednesday. Their mother answered the door. Warmly, she expressed appreciation for my involvement with her girls. Then she identified herself as one of the kids who, years ago, had come into our home and received Christ as her Savior. She went on, "It meant so much to me that I received that touch of love you gave me. I often reminisce of the times in your home, how we would sing songs and talk, learning about God and His love. Jason, my brother, and I still talk about it. Now twenty years later," she added, " living again in the same neighborhood, knowing that you are still here, and knowing your love is still there, means so much to me. I am greatly comforted, as a mother, to have my daughters experiencing your love as I did."

    The love she felt through me, I reflected, was the love of Christ that I could give, only because HE had first given to me to pass it on. Even as the Bible explains, *"Beloved, let us love one another, for love is from God, and whoever loves has been born of God and knows God. Beloved, if God so loved us, we also ought to love one another."* (1John 4:7, 11).

* * * * *

January 26, 2007 ~ "Lady who takes us to church"

The telephone rang. On the other line was a young boy's voice, "Are you taking us to AWANA tonight?" Nine-year-old Ryder and his sister, Rylea, hadn't been able to go the week before, and they had missed going. In the background, I could hear their dad asking Ryder who he was talking to.

"The lady who takes us to church."

"Okay," the father kindly responded.

Before it was time to leave for AWANA, another neighbor knocked, wanting to know if she could wait inside until time to go. Danielle wanted to practice the verses in her AWANA book; besides, she needed a place to escape from Ryder and the snowballs he was throwing.

As we started reviewing the verses for class that night, Ryder knocked on the door; he wanted to come in. While we practiced a couple of verses; he sat on the couch. I explained the meaning of Scripture. We talked about the reason Jesus left Heaven and came down to die on the Cross: He came to pay for our sins. Then I asked Ryder if he understood how people can invite Jesus Christ into their lives and have their sins paid for so that they may have everlasting life. He understood which surprised me because in every prior conversation, he hadn't seemed to grasp spiritual truths.

Then my friend Phyllis arrived to help with transportation. Once again, more children wanted to go to church than would fit into my station wagon. The girls went in her van, and Ryder went with me to pick up the rest of the kids going to AWANA. Alone in the car with me, Ryder mentioned that it was very nice of me to take kids to church. He thought God was probably happy with me for doing it. Smiling, I told him what a joy it was to help others learn about Jesus so that they could find out how to get to Heaven. "It will be fun for us to be in Heaven together!" I exclaimed.

That evening, during AWANA, someone stole a candy bar from Rylea's purse. Two kids described the culprit, but the boy they thought had taken it, had left already. I was burdened to talk with the accused boy. Two days later, I went to his home and talked with him. He convincingly said he didn't do it. On the way home, I stopped at Ryder's house since he was one of the kids that had named the supposed culprit. Asking him to sit with me in the car for a minute, I inquired if he had seen the boy take the candy bar, or if it only seemed as if he had. Apparently, he had not actually seen the boy take the candy bar, but he had seen him snooping around the area.

Then I asked Ryder if he had trusted Jesus as his Savior yet.

"Not yet, I'm not ready," he repeated. He had some questions like, "How can you know if someone is a Christian?" He thought that his grandmother was a Christian, but did not think his father was.

"What should I do to get my father into Heaven?"

"You need to have the blood that Jesus shed on the Cross applied to your sins first, and then you can pray for your father and talk to him and help him know how," I replied. Suddenly, he put his hands over his face and began to sob. After a moment, I asked gently, "Ryder, do you want to talk to Jesus right now and ask him to pay for your sins?"

"Yes," he responded. Then he bowed his head and prayed.

As he left the car, I promised to pray with him for his father to trust Christ.

*   *   *   *   *

February 11, 2007 ~ Public access TV

Recording four half-hour segments for airing on television, James and I were in the public access studio. I was working in the back, switching the camera views. Ed, the production coordinator was working nearby, and we visited back and forth. Ed shared that he had been reared in a home where they didn't attend church often. When he went to college and met his wife, to be married he had converted to Catholicism so that they could worship together. At that moment, I wished I had one of my tracts to give him to read but

God's Appointment

did not have any in my purse. Determining to give him one later, I began earnestly praying for Ed.

On February 7, 2007, I had scheduled the studio for an *Interesting People* program interview. After the guest had left, I had DVDs to drop off, as well as others that I needed to pick up from Ed. I was hoping for an opportunity to go into more detail about how a person can reach God. Ed was on his lunch break and was comfortable taking time to visit. Explaining how excited I was to discover the written conversation Jesus Christ had about the subject of how to get to Heaven, I asked if he would be interested in seeing that passage in the Bible.

"Yes," he was interested.

Standing at the doorway to his office, we talked for close to a half hour. During that time, the office was unusually quiet. A lady from WRBC came to deliver their DVD for airing; I paused as Ed helped her. When she left, I asked if he was interested in resuming the discussion where we had left off.

"Yes," he wanted to.

I continued. "In our spiritual life journey, Jesus indicates that we are either 'pre-birth,' 'at-birth,' or 'post-birth.' We are either leading up to, in the process of, or already have been born again, literally born from above (John 3). For example, physically, a child develops to the point of birth in the womb. Before spiritual birth, movements toward God and our responses to Him are designed to bring us to spiritual birth. At spiritual birth, we are actually born into the family of God. At that time, God declares us no longer separated from him by sin, but born again. Our first birth is physical; the second is spiritual. Finally, I asked him if he were to place himself on a life line, where did he think he stood spiritually?

With a startled jerk, he said, "I'm before birth."

Surprised that it was so clear to him, I responded, "Then you need to go to the next stage and be born spiritually. How would you go about such a life-affirming move?"

"Well, I'd be alone and I would—" He stalled, unsure how to continue.

"When you are ready, you simply need to talk to Jesus, letting Him know that you want Him to apply the blood that He shed on the

Cross for sin to your account, personally. For example, let's say a rich man came to Waterloo, Iowa and deposited millions of dollars in the Veridian bank. He then announced that individuals wishing a million dollars could go to the bank, sign for it, and claim it. Whose fault would it be for the people who didn't go to the bank and then complained that they didn't get any money?"

"I see," Ed said.

"May I put your name on my prayer list so that God will help you get to the point of birth?" I asked.

"That would be fine."

"Do me a favor, Ed."

"What's that?

"When you do cross over, would you let me know so that I can rejoice with you?"

"Sure."

To help him, I gave him my tract with the verses we had discussed so that he could read and ponder over it. On February 9, I saw Ed again and reminded him that I was praying for him. Apologetically, he told me he had been busy and hadn't read the tract yet, but it was on his desk. He planned to read it over the weekend. On Tuesday, the thirteenth, James and I again used the studio, trying to work ahead in preparation for an upcoming trip to Germany. As we worked, I told Ed I was still praying for him.

"Oh, by the way, on Feb. 11, I did it!" he excitedly announced. He explained that on Sunday, he had been in his Catholic church. The priest had said that it should be more important to emphasize God in our lives than being excited about events such as the Super Bowl. As the congregation knelt on the prayer stools, Ed thought to himself, "I'm ready." He told Jesus that he was ready to ask Him to apply the bloodshed on the Cross for sins to his personal account. Ed was all aglow as he shared with me. I asked him if he would mind sharing his testimony with James; and Ed did, with enthusiasm. It looks as if we'll be together in Heaven.

* * * * *

March 2, 2007 ~ Trying to wait

I felt burdened to ask Leon about his doing an interview on Public Access TV. Previously, I had interviewed him as a political candidate. A man of integrity, unafraid of doing what he thought was right, I respected him. Leon freely honored God in his public speech, but I wasn't certain that he had ever received Christ as his personal Savior. Wrestling with God about calling him, I nevertheless soon recognized that God was sending the burden, and I'd better obey.

The next morning, I telephoned Leon. Thankfully, he was open to doing the interview. Then I asked if we could get together to discuss his ideas for the interview. He said he would come to our house about 7:00 p.m. My heart leapt, realizing how rare it was for a man of his position and stature to respond so quickly.

That evening, we visited about the interview. Eventually, I asked if he would be open to my sharing from the Bible how Jesus explained the path to Heaven; we leisurely went through John 3 about being born again, including how to experience a spiritual rebirth. Leon emphasized how impressed he had been after hearing the televised testimony by Tony Dungy, the Indianapolis Colts' winning coach of the 2007 Super Bowl game. Tony had said that, to him, being a winning black coach for the first time in history wasn't as important as being a Christian coach, who had proved that winning could be done in a Christian manner.

After further conversation, I asked the important question, "Where do you see yourself, Leon, in your spiritual journey—before birth, at birth or after birth?"

After a moment of reflection, he said, "Before birth."

"If that is what God is telling your heart," I responded, "then that means you need to progress to the birth stage. Do you understand how to make that step when you are ready?" We talked a bit more. He wanted to clean up his life first before he was ready to make the commitment.

When I asked if I could put him on my prayer list, asking God's help for him to make that step of being born again, he said, "Sure."

"Do me a favor, though," I requested, "please let me know when you make that decision so that I can rejoice with you." He promised that he would. Later, at the Public Access Studio, we recorded the hour-long interview. As Leon left the studio, I reminded him that I was praying for him.

Smiling, he said, "I know. I have your telephone number handy to call you." Promising to give him a copy of the interview and the times of its airing, I left prayerfully.

On Friday, March 2, school was canceled because of the severe ice and snow. Angela stopped by with the grandkids on her way to Wal-Mart. I went with her to get some groceries but forgot to take my cell phone. Later, when I returned home, James said that Leon had stopped to pick up the DVD with his interview. Since James had been unable to find it, I should call Leon. So I called Leon, apologizing for missing him and said that I'd be home the rest of the evening. He said he'd stop by in a little while.

Soon there was a knock. It was Leon. Standing in our living room, Leon told me how thoroughly James had looked for the DVD. Then, James had tried calling me three times on the cell phone to ask where the DVD was. Each time James had dialed my number, music began playing in the kitchen. Finally, they discovered the cell phone I'd left behind and had a good laugh.

"Actually, I'm glad I forgot the cell phone," I chuckled. "After all, I wanted to be here when you stopped to pick up the DVD because I'm concerned that you are postponing making the 'born again' step. I wanted to talk with you."

Sheepishly, he nodded, "Sunday, I'm planning to be in a church in Cedar Rapids. I'll do it then. I am one of the speakers in the program that will be my benchmark of turning. I've determined that I will join my mother and father in Heaven. They are my 'heart' and 'soul,' and I miss them so much since their deaths last year. It's what I know they would want me to do."

Looking seriously into Leon's eyes, I asked, "Can the three of us have prayer right now, Leon?"

Holding hands, Leon, James, and I formed a prayer circle. Talking to God, I prayed, "Father, Leon is here now. You had me forget my cell phone so that we could talk again, and he may be put-

God's Appointment

ting off what he knows he should do. Help him consider right now talking to you and becoming your child, born from above." Looking up at Leon, I spoke seriously, "Leon, why don't you tell Jesus what you want to say to him. Are you ready, or do you want to take a rain check?"

"I'm ready now," Leon replied.

"Then why not go ahead?" That evening Leon told Jesus he recognized that he was a sinner and in need of His help, and he was ready and asking for Him to apply His blood payment now to his sin.

He paused, and I asked, "Then what do you say?" Puzzled, he shook his head. "Thank you." I said.

"Yes, Jesus, thank you," he replied.

Pointing in the Bible to the wonderful promise to all who believe, ***"But to all who did receive him, believed in his name, he gave the right to become children of God"*** (John 1:12), I continued, "What does God call you now?"

"A son," Leon said with excitement.

"As of when?"

"Right now," he answered.

"For how long?"

"Never ending," he replied.

Again pointing to the Bible the Source of our faith, I could not help but smile, "That's not just what Gloria says; it is what God says. And what He says, you can take to the bank." I asked Leon how he felt now, having made the decision to trust in Christ.

He answered, "I feel a lot lighter than when I came." With hands pointing to both shoulders, he indicated, "My shoulders were burdened—I've been really down. I'm a stubborn man. God knew I needed a push."

"—Or rather, a gentle tug."

"Yes, a tug," Leon agreed smiling. Handing him a tract with his new birthday written on it touched him. He marveled, "My spiritual birthday is one day after my physical birthday; March first was my physical birthday."

We all hugged. "Now, you're my brother in Christ."

God's Appointment

"Yes," he affirmed with a nod. Leon shared how he had felt compelled, "On the way over here, I was talking long distance to my sister on the cell phone, and she asked where I was going on such a day of ice and snow and dangerous driving conditions. 'I have to pick up a tape,' I told her. I knew I needed to come today."

We laughed at the way God had arranged for me to forget the cell phone so that we had to talk face to face. Our steps had been arranged by God. The conversation finishing I said, "Leon, everyone else has to do what you just did to get past the gate of Heaven. Anytime you would like me to talk to somebody you know about Christ, just feel free to bring them by. I'd be happy to talk with them."

He replied, "I'll do that, thanks." He returned to his car and, waving, drove off. Later, in April of 2008, I called Leon for permission to use the summary of our conversation in this book, not wanting to embarrass him.

"Nothing embarrasses me," he stated, and I read this account to him over the telephone.

"It's perfect." he said. Leon told me that he had indeed gone to the Cedar Rapids church where he and a number of other political candidates were to speak. He had also gone forward in the church to make it public that he had trusted Christ as his Savior, and he was not ashamed.

"I believe that the crossing of our paths was a 'God thing,'" I said.

"Yes, a 'God thing.' Even I can get weighted down and over-burdened."

When I asked how he was doing, he said he was terribly busy on the road, traveling. The previous night, he had arrived home after midnight and needed to be back on the road again by ten that morning. But he emphasized that his priorities in life had been rearranged and were God, family, and country—in that order. With his active fighting of illegal drugs, he acknowledged that his life was in jeopardy, but he claimed ,"God takes care of babies and fools—and I ain't no baby."

* * * * *

March 6, 2007 ~ Two birthday gifts

There was a knock at the door. It was Danielle, checking to make sure we were giving rides to AWANA Club the next day. Additionally, she wanted to show me her new, five-month-old Beagle puppy named Shiloh. The puppy was friendly, curious, and wanted to explore our home. It took Danielle a lot of wrestling to keep Shiloh under control. As she monitored the puppy's antics, she announced that the little Beagle was an early birthday gift from her grandmother.

"My tenth birthday is coming up on April 26." Congratulating Danielle, I told her that I had two birthdays.

"How can that be?" she asked.

"I have one birthday into my parent's family, and one birthday into God's family. Don't you think that sounds like fun?" Danielle agreed. "Jesus told Nicodemus in the Bible that in order to get to Heaven, we need to have two birthdays. I showed her the following passage about being born again, literally born from above (John 3):

Jesus answered him, "Truly, truly, I say to you, unless one is <u>born again</u> he cannot see the kingdom of God." Jesus answered, "Truly, truly, I say to you, unless one is born of water and the Spirit, he cannot enter the kingdom of God. That which is born of the flesh is <u>flesh</u>, and that which is born of the Spirit is <u>spirit</u>. Do not marvel that I said to you, 'You must be <u>born again</u>.'" (John 3:3, 5-7).

Then Danielle asked, "When did you get your second birthday and how?"

I explained that when I was fifteen, I asked Jesus Christ to apply the blood He had shed on the Cross to pay for sin to my personal account. The reason why we need to have our sin paid for goes way back to Adam and Eve in the Garden. They had a wonderful relationship with God until they ate of the fruit of the one tree God had told them not to eat. Then they were separated from God until He had covered their sin. God promised one day to send a perfect Lamb whose blood would not only cover sin, but would pay for it, in full.

God's Appointment

He fulfilled that promise through the death and resurrection of His one and only Son."

And this is the testimony that God gave us eternal life, and this life is in his Son. Whoever has the Son has life; whoever does not have the Son of God does not have life. I write these things to you who believe in the name of the Son of God that you may know that you have eternal life. (1 John 5:11-13)

"Danielle, would you like to ask Jesus to pay for your sins so that you can be born into God's family?" I asked.

"Yes, I would, that means I will be in Heaven with my baby brother, right?" she wondered. Three years previously, her newborn brother had not survived open heart surgery. To realize that she could see him again was a precious promise indeed. While Danielle talked with Jesus, I held the puppy who was trying hard to wash my face. Danielle asked Jesus to pay for her sins and make her His daughter.

After Danielle had prayed, we read, **"But to all who did receive him, who believed in his name, he gave the right to become children of God"** (John 1:12).

"If God calls you a 'child of His' because you received Jesus and believed on Him, then what are you?" I quizzed.

"A daughter."

"Not because I said so, but because God says so in the Bible," I affirmed. Soon the two headed home. Danielle turned to wave goodbye—a happier, changed little girl. The next evening, Danielle arrived at the door for a ride to AWANA Club at the same time two of the other girls did. I could hear her announcing to both of them that she now had two birthdays. Praise the Lord!

* * * * *

March 9, 2007 ~ Missed appointment, God's appointment

A guest was scheduled to tape a TV program with me from ten until noon. The Public Access TV apprentice, Lakisha, volunteered to do the tape switching for me since she needed experience in doing studio work. We set up the studio—cameras were in focus, lights adjusted, mikes hooked up—and waited for the guest to arrive. Lakisha and I visited at the desk while we waited. Among other things, Lakisha talked with excitement about a friend's potential visit that coming weekend.

Assuming Lakisha was a Christian, I asked if she was comfortable explaining to others how to get to Heaven, thinking she might have an opportunity to talk with her friend about the subject.

"Not really," she said. "Show me how you do it."

I said I'd be glad to practice with her. I reviewed the verses and illustrations I usually use. I emphasized the importance of maintaining good eye contact with the individual, pointing out that the other person should read the actual verses out loud. Finally, I asked her, "Would you describe your position on the spiritual time-line of your life as being before birth, at birth, or after birth?"

She thought a moment and to my surprise said, "At birth. I've never done t hat yet, and I would like to." Practice became the real thing. As I took her hand, she went to the Cross, asking Jesus to apply the blood He had shed for sin to her personal account.

She marveled, "Had your guest come today, I might have missed out on my second birthday."

Then I shared with her that I'm really deeply concerned that there are many people like us. I, too, had thought that I was a Christian before I had personally asked Jesus Christ to pay for my sin, and I became born again, literally born from above (John 3). A lot of people, although Christ paid for *all sin*, haven't been to the spiritual bank yet to get their personal check cashed.

Finally, I called the home of Rik, my scheduled guest. His wife Sue answered the phone. It turned out that the missed appointment was my fault. The guest had called the night before and left a message to cancel the appointment, but I hadn't checked the messages.

Lakisha shared with Sue that the scheduling problem had worked out just fine because the Lord had had other plans.

As Lakisha left, she told me that she had been feeling depressed recently; she had married at the young age of nineteen and had just received her divorce papers that day. Then she added that, although her problems hadn't disappeared, she now had a new outlook on life. She commented, "Now, I'm feeling way up."

Lakisha can take her problems to the Lord just like I learned I can, *"God is our refuge and strength, a very present help in trouble. Therefore we will not fear though the earth gives way, though the mountains be moved into the heart of the sea, though its waters roar and foam, though the mountains tremble at its swelling."* (Psalms 46:1-3).

* * * * *

March 14, 2007 ~ Sandra in Germany

James and I arrived in Germany to spend some time with our daughter Jessica and her family. Her husband was stationed at the Ramstein Air Force Base. Jessica was scheduled to have surgery, and I wanted to be there to help her. Going with her to check into the hospital room, we met Angela and Sandra, Jessica's roommates, both of whom were being released that day. Both were military wives who spoke English. After the initial visiting, I mentioned that my husband and I had just come from the United States the day before to help Jessica.

Looking at Sandra, I mentioned, "One thing I enjoy is sharing with others how Jesus explains in the Bible the way for people to get to Heaven." I believe people enjoy talking about a subject when they feel comfortable with the person with whom they are talking and do not feel pressured.

I asked Sandra, "Would you be interested if I shared from the Bible?"

"Yes," she nodded.

Taking my Bible out, I read a number of verses with Sandra. When I paused with my finger pointing, she read the words "<u>eternal life" (John 3:15), "in" and "on" (John 3:16, 36, John 1:12), "receive" (John 1:12), and "power to become a son (daughter) of God" (John 1:12). All these pointed to the promise of God to give eternal life to those who believed in and on Jesus Christ as Lord and Savior and received His free gift of salvation, becoming a son or daughter of God.

When the doctors arrived to check on their patients and to mark Jessica for surgery, I left the room returning after the doctors left. Both ladies had been told that they could check out and they happily dressed and packed. After Sandra was ready and waiting for her husband to arrive, I asked if she'd like to pick up where we had left off.

"Yes, I would," she responded.

"Sandra, I believe you understand what Jesus said about being prepared for eternity. Would you choose to admit to God that you know you are a sinner in need of His help? Believe in, rather than about Him by receiving the free gift of salvation offered to you, and to all who call upon His name? Are you ready to do that right now?"

"You don't have to be in a church to talk to God, do you?" Sandra asked. "Some people say you can't talk to God unless you're in a church or by a Cross; I think you can talk to God anywhere, but I'm not sure."

With confidence, I replied, "You're right, Sandra," the Bible says that God is every-where, and we can talk to Him wherever and whenever we want. That is what the Bible consistently urges believers to do. Men and women anywhere and anytime can have audience with The Almighty God, as the Bible says,

Where shall I go from your Spirit? Or where shall I flee from your presence? If I ascend to heaven, you are there! If I make my bed in Sheol, you are there! If I take the wings of the morning and dwell in the uttermost parts of the sea, even there your hand shall lead me, and your right hand shall hold me. (Psalms 139:7-12). Also, *"Let your reasonableness be known to everyone. The Lord is at hand; do not be anxious about anything, but in everything by prayer and supplication with thanksgiving let your requests be made known to God"* (

Philippians 4: 5, 6). *"Pray without ceasing"* (1Thessalonians 5:17).

Holding her hand in mine, we went to God in prayer. Sandra told Jesus that she wanted to ask Him to pay for her sin with His blood so that she could go to Heaven. Angela had followed our conversation, so I asked if she was interested in also becoming born again. Smiling she said, "I did that when I was seventeen years old."

Sandra was very pleased to have talked to God and gained assurance that she was going to Heaven. She said she appreciated having our conversation and thought her husband Gregory had personally accepted Christ when he was younger. Though her family had not been interested in spiritual things when she was younger, she had been curious. She had met Gregory in Germany and later they married. After two miscarriages, they had two girls, a ten-year-old and a fourteen-month-old.

Finally, the husbands arrived to take the ladies home, and we said, "Goodbye." Several times, while in Germany, we saw Sandra at the Doctor's office, as both she and Jessica had checkups following surgery; we had a nice time of visiting.

* * * * *

May 26, 2007 ~ Graduation open house

Billie Jo invited us to her oldest son's open house as he was graduating from high school. My girls had babysat for Billie's three children when they were babies, and we had kept in contact through the years. When we arrived at the park, Chris's younger brother, sixteen-year-old Brad, joyfully ran and gave my husband and me a hug. He had warm memories of being in our home. We visited, gave graduate Chris a gift, and shared the picnic lunch with them.

Another lady at the open house introduced herself and her husband to us, "Remember me from Washburn?" She had come to the Washburn church when James was the pastor there. She had moved, then married, and was presently quite active in a local church. As we talked, Brad listened. Turning to Brad I asked, "Do you remember coming to the Washburn church when you were younger?"

"Yes."

"Do you remember trusting Christ as your personal Savior?" He remembered some things and had learned some verses, but he didn't understand what I was talking about. I asked if I could share some things from the Bible with him. As we sat at the picnic table, I took out my Bible, and we talked. Brad prayed, asking Jesus Christ if He would apply His blood payment to his sin so that he might have everlasting life.

* * * * *

May 28, 2007 ~ "Got Jesus?"

My friend Beverly was moving and had a Memorial Day garage sale in her backyard. Stopping to look around, I picked out some miscellaneous items to purchase. As we visited, a young lady and her mother also stopped for the sale. The mother looked around while the young lady waited patiently by their car. She was wearing a tee shirt with the words on it, "Got Jesus?" Going over to the car, I complimented her on her shirt.

"It looks as if you have Jesus," I commented.

She smiled and nodded, "Yes."

Then I continued, "May I ask you a question? How does one go about getting Jesus?"

"By reading the Bible and going to church," she sweetly replied. Her name was Joanna. Probably in her middle twenties, she attended the Hispanic Catholic Church and was the mother of four little ones.

Pulling out the New Testament from my purse, I asked Joanna if I could share some things with her from the Bible, specifically about Jesus' explanation on how a person gets to Heaven. We talked about being born again and the need for sin to be paid for by the blood of Jesus Christ. As a baby has life during a woman's pregnancy, it moves, and its purpose is to be born—where did she think that she was in her spiritual journey? Was her seeking God in the before birth, at birth, or after birth stage? Had she gone to Jesus and asked Him to apply His blood to her life and her sin personally?

Joanna said, "No," she hadn't done that.

"Would you like to?"

She nodded, "Yes."

Holding her hand, I prayed, first thanking God for the opportunity for the two of us to talk about that important subject. Then Joanna prayed, trusting Jesus Christ as her Savior.

"What do you think just happened?" I asked.

"I believed on Jesus, not just about Him."

Then I asked, "Would you mind telling Beverly what you just did?"

Joanna smiled and told Beverly, "I got Jesus in my life, for real!"

* * * * *

June 1, 2007 ~ Anna from the Ukraine

When a friend held an open house for their youngest daughter, James and I went to congratulate Kim and celebrate her high school graduation. There were a lot of people gathered and visiting. Anna, 17, was there from the Ukraine as an exchange student; her host family was related to Kim's mother. Sitting next to each other at the table, enjoying the tasty treats prepared, I asked Anna what differences she had noticed between her home and America.

"The schools are very different, and the foods much more varied in America," she replied. Then I asked her if she was acquainted with Jesus there in the Ukraine.

"Yes," she said. But she didn't get to go to church very often, as her father worked long hours.

"People here in America are often considered Christians," I explained, "and it is confusing to people who come here from other countries, especially when they see the television programs, read the newspapers, or see and hear things here that do not seem very Christian. Anna confirmed that she had found such a situation confusing.

"It may help you," I offered, "if I explained that there are two different kinds of Christians—coat Christians, who put on or take off their Christianity like a coat whenever it is convenient; and heart Christians, who are Christians of the heart indeed." I asked Anna, "Would you be interested if I were to share with you from my Bible how Jesus explains how to become a heart Christian?" Anna said she would be interested.

Going out to the back porch, we talked together about how to be born again, literally born from above (John 3). Finally, I asked, "Are you interested in trusting Jesus to apply the blood He shed on the Cross for sin to your personal account right now?"

"I am not sure how to pray in English," she replied.

"That is okay," I replied. "God understands your language. Go ahead and tell Him what you want Him to do." She prayed, most likely in Russian. I didn't understand a word, but God did. I asked her what she had told God, and she told me.

"Then what just happened?" I asked.

"I have become a daughter of God and have everlasting life!" she excitedly responded. "Thank you," she said, smiling. I gave her a tract with the verses we had talked about so that she could read the verses again.

As we stood, the rain that had been threatening cut loose—it poured. I walked to the car, getting soaked, but telling the Lord, "Thank you for holding off the rain until we were finished."

* * * * *

June 6, 2007 ~ VBS at Washburn

Calvary Bible Church had Vacation Bible School was Monday through Thursday this year. Since neighbor kids wanted to go, between my folks and me, we gave rides to ten young people. On Wednesday evening, after Pastor Rik Reuter had presented a Bible lesson, he asked for hands of those not sure if they were on their way to Heaven. Hands were raised. He instructed those who wanted to make sure that they were going to Heaven to go to the back of the room with Gloria. Four girls, about ten-years-old, followed me downstairs to a quiet room.

Sitting in a circle on the floor, first I asked the girl on my left if she wanted to talk to Jesus. I emphasized that she needed to ask Him to come into her life, acknowledging that she was in trouble and needed Jesus' blood to be applied to her sin. Katlin prayed out loud, expressing her desire to have Jesus pay for her sin. After Katlin, Sharin wanted to pray also. The other two girls were not quite ready to make a decision. I asked Katlin and Sharin to go ahead back upstairs to rejoin the group, but suggested the other two girls wait behind a moment.

"I do not want you to feel that you have to pray if you are not ready because talking with God has to be something you really want to do. It's not just the words you say but what your heart says."

"I do want to pray," Hayley said.

"Are you sure" I asked.

"Yes," she replied.

"Okay, go ahead and tell Jesus what you want Him to do in your life."

She did.

The fourth girl still wasn't ready yet. I told her that it was fine for her to think about talking to God for a while, but it was important for her to do it soon. We rejoined the rest of the group.

* * * * *

July 4, 2007 ~ Fun in the "Son"

Jerry Dykes asked me to participate in the Music in the Park that he and a group of musicians have each year, including a program of music, an Elvis impersonator, food, and other activities. They wanted me to mix with the people in line who would be waiting to get twisty balloons and face painting.

* *

In line were many parents with their children waiting to order an attractive balloon. Accompanying a younger boy in line were Choy, 23, and Mike, 15. When I asked if they knew for sure if they were

God's Appointment

going to Heaven when they died, they replied, "No," they were not sure. When I asked if I could show them how Jesus answered that question in the Bible, "Yes," they were interested. Sharing, as so often, from John 3 and 1 about being born again, I concluded by asking them if they were open to praying and trusting Jesus Christ to apply the blood that He shed on the Cross for sin to their account. They both wanted to and first Choy prayed, then Mike.

* *

Later, I visited with Christina and Jeremy, a couple in line with their young sons. Christina prayed first, and then Jeremy prayed quietly.

* *

Two friends Alyssa and Alexis, both eleven, were in line. They listened and prayed.

* *

Later, I noticed Mitch, sixteen, standing by a tree, watching the kids go round and round on the playground equipment. When I asked if he knew for sure if he had a reservation for Heaven, Mitch said he didn't know. He was concerned, though, because he had read in the Bible about Hell and thought "it would be a bad place to end up." After Mitch had prayed, calling on Jesus Christ to apply His blood payment to his sin, he said he would love to have a Bible of his very own. He asked where I went to church; he would like to get a ride with someone to church. His only transportation was his bicycle. Later, I gave his name to someone who could help get him a Bible and offer him a ride to church.

* *

A mother of three, Heather, age twenty-five, was at the end of the line, waiting patiently for a couple of extra twisty balloon flowers. She wanted to put the balloons on her grandparents' graves to get a picture at the gravesite with the flowers. She listened and then prayed, trusting Christ to pay for her sins.

* *

Eight people prayed with me for salvation that day; others took literature, some said, "Maybe another time, but not now."

* * * * *

Gloria Goering at the WRBC Booth 2007

September 14, 2007~ Church booth at Cattle Congress

Here are a few recollections of opportunities on September 13-15, 2007, at the National Dairy Cattle Congress in Waterloo, Iowa.

* *

Haley and Lily, both thirteen, were volunteers. They carefully pushed an elderly lady in a wheel-chair. That lady, who attended a Salvation Army church, encouraged the girls to stop and listen. Both girls did indeed pray and receive Christ. One might ask-who performed the greater good? The girls who assisted the handicapped lady, or the lady encouraging the girls to be born again?

* *

Melissa, thirty, had experienced a hard life. She believed that there had to be something, somewhere worth living for. As we visited, she studied the verses in the Bible I shared with her. She was relieved to find that it was Christ she was looking for, and she received Him as her Lord and Savior.

* *

Cori, fifteen, stopped with a friend her age. Her friend listened, but clearly was not interested. After Cori trusted Christ, I talked with her friend. She said that although she was not interested right then, she might be later. Offering her the same "Heaven" tract that I had given Cori, I suggested that they might study it together. Cori could possibly help her do what she had just done. The friend nodded earnestly in agreement.

* *

An adult nervously hovered over Danielle, Chile, and Christiana—two were aged eleven, and the other twelve. The three girls really wanted to find out what Jesus had said about going to Heaven. Understanding Jesus' instruction, the girls wanted to be born again, literally born from above (John 3). After the three girls had prayed, the adult companion was ready to go. No way was she going to let them give their names and addresses. The girls were elated as they left together.

* *

A Grandmother brought Santiago to our booth. She patiently and prayerfully waited while we talked with him. Encouraging Santiago, eleven, she clearly wanted him to find Christ as Savior, and he did. Although the grandmother had been unable to explain the message of salvation to her grandson, she found someone who could.

* *

Thomas, fourteen, stopped at our booth with his sister to find out what I meant about knowing if one is going to Heaven. The sister was already a Christian, having listened attentive-ly. Thomas also wanted to receive Christ and be born again, and he did. Their mother finally caught up with her children and wanted to keep moving; they had to leave, but the Lord had delayed her arrival at our booth until after his prayer.

* *

Tamara, twelve, trusted Christ. She was highly energetic, talkative, and friendly. Her hair was in tight braids with colored beads on each end. She was going to a hairstyling booth to have her braids sprayed red. I invited her to come back and show me her new hairdo. I was just finishing a conversation with another girl when she came back. Tamara happily picked up the pink and blue optical illusion tracts on our table and shared it with the other girl, who had just trusted the Lord. Having already shown the illusion tracts to her brother and father, she planned to show them yet to other friends. Tamara had a happy smile as she lingered at the booth seeking to spend time with us.

* *

Brandon, eleven, was intensely interested as he followed my explanation. When his older brother arrived, he also listened, on and off, to the conversation, sharing with a worker at the booth that he was already a Christian. Brandon prayed to receive Christ, and the two walked away together—brothers, both physically and spiritually.

* *

Brody, thirteen, trusted Christ. He left and came back a little later, bringing a friend who wanted to get saved too. Now, they will be friends together, for eternity.

* *

Boyfriend and girlfriend, both nineteen, stopped together. After they had received Christ, they expressed interest in coming to church.

* *

Praise the Lord, a total of 43 trusted Christ at our booth, but others burdened our hearts. One husband and wife with two children came and paused; the husband was very interested. He listened intently to the entire plan of salvation. His wife, uninterested, continued on down the aisle. Just as the husband was ready to pray to receive Christ, the wife frantically came running, imploring him for help. Their son was missing, and she needed his help to find him. His eyes yearned to stay, but he had to leave. I encouraged him to come back if he could, but he didn't. My prayer is that perhaps by reading the literature given him, or another avenue, he finishes what he started.

* *

A middle-aged lady stopped—her father was on his deathbed. The certainty of death had frightened her, making her concerned about where she would go for eternity. She had come with a couple who were in a hurry, so she couldn't stop right then but said that she would try to get back if she could. I waited until the doors were locked that night, but she never made it back. The work is God's. We prayed and sowed the seeds.

* *

Besides the opportunity of winning souls was the joy of training and encouraging others who helped at the booth to go beyond planting seeds and watering. As God leads, let us seek the opportunities to bring people to Christ.

* * * * *

CHAPTER 17

2008-2010

❋

February 6, 2008 ~ AWANA Club time

Every Wednesday afternoon, the telephone rang. John wanted to know if I was going to pick up Bret, his brother, and him for AWANA Club. John a teenager and Bret in fifth grade were accustomed to us picking them up for years. If I am not able to come, John is very disappointed. Both of his older sisters trusted Christ as their Savior in our home when they lived right behind us. One evening as I visited in their home, his father trusted Christ. We've interacted often. And even after they moved, we still picked up the boys for AWANA. John told me that he trusted Christ as his Savior one night at AWANA, and I could tell he had grown in the Lord. His younger brother, Bret remembers trusting Christ "the very first time you talked to me about it."

As we drove to AWANA, Bret and I were talking about a musical group who claimed to be Christian, but the words to their songs were "very poor." I told him that many people claim to be Christians, and many actually think they are. In fact, I thought I was before trusting Christ as my personal Savior. Then I pointed out that it doesn't matter what we think, but it does matter what God says. When we get to the gates of Heaven after we die, we will have to have the blood of Jesus Christ applied to our sin personally, or we can't get in. He reflected for a minute and then said, "There are no illegal aliens in Heaven, then, are there?"

"You're right," I said. I had never thought about it that way before. "Although there will be people from every nation and language there, no one can enter Heaven illegally." I enjoy the fresh insights from young people.

* * * * *

April 16, 2008 ~ Silver coins

A friend introduced Leonard to my husband. On a number of occasions, the three of them got together for coffee or meals and visited. James was concerned that Leonard was un-saved, and hoped that there would be an opportunity to witness to him.

Having collected a few coins through the years, James was curious about their value. Leonard, an avid collector, said he would come over someday to take a look and maybe buy some coins from James. Shortly before Leonard was to come, James's other friend Don had come to our house to teach us a little about coin collecting- how to clean and shine coins up before showing them to perspective buyers. Leonard was to come to our house Tuesday morn-ing.

The collection was all laid out for viewing on the kitchen table, but I was unable to be home with James that morning. Something came up and Leonard didn't make it. It crossed my mind that maybe God was working it out so that I would be home when he did come. Wednesday he called about coming over to see the coins.

He arrived, a charming person, who knew how to establish rapport, using many compliments. As Leonard, James, and I visited over the coins, Leonard told us he had sold his business for a million dollars and retired, and he shared interesting tales of his many travels to various places.

"Where would you like to go to retire?" I asked. He said his choice, and I mentioned that I was anticipating retiring in Heaven.

Leonard made the comment that he expected "to go to Hell." Startled, I responded, "I hope not. Everything I've heard about Hell makes it a place I wouldn't ever want to go." He laughed. After the coins were sorted and priced, I brought my Bible and tract to the table. At the end of our coin conversation, I asked permission to share with him how a person can make a reservation for a trip to Heaven. Leonard graciously listened as I explained being born again, literally born from above (John 3), as Jesus had shared with Nicodemus.

Time passed, and Leonard had an appointment to keep. Still, I asked if he would be interested in praying with James and me before he had to leave.

He answered, "Yes."

The three of us stood, making a circle of prayer. I prayed, thanking the Lord for the opportunity of meeting Leonard and remarked before God that Leonard had said he thought he was headed to Hell. Then I asked God to open Leonard's understanding and show him how he could make a reservation for heaven.

"How about it, Leonard, would you be interested in praying, telling God that you know you are a sinner and that you need the blood of Jesus Christ to be applied to your personal sin and that right now you want to ask Him to be your Lord and Savior?"

"Yes, I would," was his answer; then he prayed, doing just that. As Leonard left, I said that I looked forward to seeing him in heaven, where gold coins probably are not needed, as we will be walking on streets of gold—what a place. *"And the twelve gates were twelve pearls, each of the gates made of a single pearl, and the street of the city was pure gold, transparent as glass"* (Revelations 21:21). That day, Leonard changed from thinking that he was going to Hell, to believing in Jesus and His bloodshed on the Cross for us. He was born again into God's family and was appreciative of what Christ had done for him.

* * * * *

June 24, 2008 ~ Spiritual and physical birth

Victoria, our youngest daughter, was expecting her second child any time. Jessica and I went to Minnesota to help her. Our rushed trip up North turned out to be slightly premature, so to fill some waiting time, we all went shopping. Bradley and Caleb, Jessica's two boys, were along for the ride, as well as Christian, Victoria's firstborn.

Christian had fallen asleep so the boys and I waited in the van for the mothers to return from the last store. Four-year-old, Caleb was full of questions. He shared with me how far he could count and other things he had learned in church and in the home. His thoughts focused on the nature of God and His Son, including the reason why Jesus had come from Heaven to die for our sins.

When the sisters returned to the van, Caleb indicated that he wanted to talk seriously with his mother. He wanted to trust Jesus so that he could have his sins forgiven. As we drove, Jessica prayed with Caleb and with the "faith of a child," my precious grandson called upon the name of the Lord Jesus to save him. How important children are to the Savior: *"Jesus called them to him, saying, 'Let the children come to me, and do not hinder them, for to such belongs the kingdom of God. Truly, I say to you, whoever does not receive the kingdom of God like a child shall not enter it'"* (Luke 18:16, 17).

Since that time, Caleb has often expressed that he now knows Jesus as his Savior. He relates to the time when his "mommy" helped him in the van to trust Christ. What a fond memory for our family.

* * * * *

July 3, 2008 ~ Jumping on the bed

While their parents were at work, my three granddaughters were at our house. Previously, I had allowed the girls to jump on the spare bedroom bed. But this time I spent time explaining that they must not jump on it any more, fearing that the bed could break. They agreed and began playing while I went to wash the dishes. After a little while, I decided to check on them. There they were all three gleefully jumping to their best heights on the box springs with the mattress tossed to the side.

Having deliberately done what they had been instructed not to do, I scolded them saying I was disappointed; I felt that I could not trust them. Additionally I explained, "Deliberate disobedience is sin. You owe both me and God an apology," I firmly explained. Two of the girls immediately apologized; but six-year-old Hayley was sobbing uncontrollably. The two other girls were asked to leave the room and shut the door so that I could speak with Hayley alone.

"Hayley, Grandma loves you very much. But you know that Jesus loves you the most, don't you?" She nodded her head. "I still love you, even though you disobeyed me," I reassured her, as I took her in my arms. "But sin is a terrible thing. Sin is the reason Jesus had to leave Heaven and come down here to die on the Cross to pay its penalty. We were in trouble, and Jesus was the only one who could help us. We have all sinned. I am a sinner too and need to have Jesus pay for my sin. Jesus will pay for your sin if you ask Him. Would you like to ask Jesus to pay for your sins so you can live with Him in Heaven?"

"Yes."

"Then tell Jesus what you would like Him to do." We had talked about this in the past, and she had had many questions, yet she had never been ready before to make this decision.

In a whisper, she told Jesus, "I want You to pay for my sins so that I can live with You in Heaven." Her tears dried up, and she smiled.

She gave me a warm "Thank you," and a hug, and then asked, "Grandma, may I sing a song to Jesus?"

"Yes, I'm sure He would like that." Such a sweet song came from her heart. I can only imagine that music brought tears to Jesus' eyes—I know it did mine.

* * * * *

November 15, 2008 ~ Writing on the wall

Walking past the couch in my living room, I noticed writing on the wall. One of my granddaughters had been busy, but which one? The next time the girls visited, they created get-well cards for their Great Grandmother who was in the hospital. Comparing their writings with the words on the wall, I could easily determine the culprit. But when I asked the girls who had done the work, all three pleaded innocence. Madison, 6, stated, "It was Hayley." But Hayley age 7, denied it.

That night, "Grandma-sitting" at my daughters' home, I tucked each into their bed for the night. As I tucked the youngest in bed, I knelt next to her and told her I knew she had written on my wall and that I was very disappointed not only that she had done it, but had lied about it, even accusing her sister of doing it. Madison dissolved into tears and apologized. I assured her of my love, but also my sadness at her lying. Before more could be said, her mom and dad returned. Before leaving, I told Angela about the writing on the wall and the situation with Madison passing the blame.

At home that night, as I lay in bed, I worried about Madison's condition. Her tears told me she was aware of her sin and felt badly about what had happened. Possibly it was time for Madison to trust Christ as her Savior. In the morning, I called my daughter, asking if it would be possible for Madison to come clean the wall. I offered to come pick her up and then bring her home afterward. Madison did clean the entire wall, and I complimented her for doing such a fine job. Continuing with the image of cleaning, I asked her, "Now that the wall is clean, do you know how to get sin cleaned off?"

Shrugging her shoulders, she shook her head, "No."

"Well, the problem that we all have with sin is the reason Jesus had to leave Heaven and come down here to die to pay for sin. We can't get rid of sin, but Jesus can. Madison, you are old enough now to trust Jesus to pay for your sin. Would you like to do that today?"

"Yes," she murmured.

"Now?" I asked.

"No, at home," she replied. Then we returned to her home. Together in the kitchen, I told Angela about our conversation. Angela leaned down and asked Madison if she wanted to trust Jesus now; she quietly answered, "Yes." As I stood by, Angela led Madison to the Lord. My heart was thrilled.

* * * * *

Kathy Vermaas

December 19, 2008 ~ No longer a pagan

    Kathy had grown up Catholic Irish in Southern California. Very inquisitive, she had studied many different belief systems, among others, Mormonism, Buddhism, Jehovah Witness, North American Indian, and Wicca. Intrigued by the wisdom of the old ways, she became a Druid priestess and for years was a spiritual leader in Sacramento, California. Having a following of hundreds, she performed many weddings, funerals, children's dedications and pagan festivals. When her sister in Nebraska became ill, Kathy came to the Mid-West to help. She and my brother Steve met, and in December of 2004 they married.

    Both had experienced turbulent times in their lives, had previously been married and had adult children with their own families. How in the world did Steve from Lincoln, Nebraska and Kathy from Sacramento, California, with such different backgrounds come together? Steve, after a time of spiritual rebellion, had become a devout Christian; she was a practicing pagan, yet, they obviously were in love.

    Deeply concerned that Kathy would be a negative effect on Steve, we as his family went to earnest prayer. Understandably

Kathy was apprehensive as to how Steve's "very" Christian family would receive her, but since Steve loved her, we did too. More than once we had friendly discussions about how Jesus says people get to Heaven. The ideas of Jesus being "The Son of God," that He was the only way to Heaven, and the Bible being the "Word of God" were difficult for her to believe.

Kathy noticed a change in her health. Sadly, the dynamic Kathy who loved kayaking, biking, karate, and many other activities, was diagnosed with fourth stage cancer. Surgery was performed, and the surgeon said it was as if someone had thrown a handful of sand into her, each particle of sand being cancerous. He removed as much as he could and hoped he had gotten it all.

Waking up from surgery, she was in so much pain, she was sure she probably would not live through the night. She fitfully slept and dreamt that she was in a car with Steve, going the wrong way on a mountain road. The car went over the edge falling towards a deadly crash. A song that she had heard on the radio earlier played in her mind. The soloist sang about going through a difficult situation and crying, "Jesus take the wheel." Kathy grabbed that phrase and made it her own cry for help and urgently cried out, "Jesus take the wheel!" She surrendered her life to the Lord Jesus Christ and no longer clung to being the one in control. Suddenly, in her dream, she found herself upright in the car, and they were turned around traveling in the right direction. From that moment, Dec. 19, 2008, Kathy knew Jesus had made a difference in her life, and she was born again.

Miraculously Kathy fought cancer to live. She said in an interview for Public Access Television, "I'm at peace now. Before I was content, but now I am fulfilled! I'm no longer afraid to die. I would be sad to die because of the pain for my family, but I am at peace. Should I die, remember where I am, and that I'll be waiting for you to join me in Heaven. Celebrate my life when I am gone. I thank God that He gave His Son to die on the cross to forgive and pay for my sins; for our sins, and if you want to be forgiven, just ask Him because He will be there for you too." [Copies of that interview are available on DVD].

Kathy made a public declaration of her new relationship with Jesus Christ by believers baptism in Lincoln, Nebraska at Scott and

Melody's (Steve's daughter and son-in-law) church. Kathy gave a vibrant testimony to everyone she came into contact and implored family, friends, and all who would listen, to "take that extra one step towards Christ!" Her life was changed forever.

Steve was a constant source of strength, care and support for Kathy. She marveled at her husband's willingness to be there for her in all the trials they had to walk through together. God used Kathy to encourage Steve to attend church regularly and to actively live out his Christianity. I asked her during the TV interview, "Are you now a pagan?"

She firmly answered, "No, I'm a born again Christian!"

Following a time of victory over the cancer, it returned. On November 3, 2010, Kathy left this mortal life and entered into the presence of her Lord and Savior. I can only imagine the joy she experienced as she discovered the reality of the promise of God, *"Death is swallowed up in victory. O death, where is your victory? O death, where is your sting? The sting of death is sin, and the power of sin is the law. But thanks be to God, who gives us the victory through our Lord Jesus Christ"* (I Corinthians 15:55-56).

* * * * *

January 7, 2009 ~ Eternal Life Insurance

As my sixty-fifth birthday neared, it was time to make a decision about Medicare supplements. A one o'clock appointment with an agent would explain the different plans and answer any questions.

Larry was well-informed and experienced. I made my decision and enrolled in the same plan that he had selected for himself when he turns sixty-five. "I do have another question," I broached as the conference ended. "I would like to ask you a question somewhat related. Have you ever heard of Eternal Life Insurance?"

Larry thoughtfully shook his head. "No"; he hadn't.

"You so kindly have taken the time to explain the benefits of Medicare coverage with a supplement, which may last twenty or thirty years, or more. Coverage for the next three hundred years or three thousand years—or what we call 'eternity,' a far longer

God's Appointment

time-span than a few years, would be even more important and is available."

He agreed about the wisdom of having eternity insurance and asked, "Just how does one go about it?"

"Well, an official in Bible times, a man named Nicodemus asked Jesus how a person can get to Heaven; Jesus answered him. His answer is recorded for us to read."

Larry asked me to show to him the passage. For the next hour, we read Scripture in John chapters 3 and 1. He was concerned about just how one believed "*in*" and "*on*," rather than just "about." We read carefully the following passages:

For God so loved the world, that he gave his only Son, that whoever believes in him should not perish but have eternal life (John 3:16); *Whoever believes in him is not condemned, but whoever does not believe is condemned already, because he has not believed in the name of the only Son of God* (John 3:18); *Whoever believes in the Son has eternal life; whoever does not obey the Son shall not see life, but the wrath of God remains on him* (John 3:3); and finally, *But to all who did receive him, who believed in his name, he gave the right to become children of God* (John 1:12).

When we ask God, "believing in His name," we do become a child of God.

"Just as with the Medicare supplement, knowing about the medical plan wasn't enough; I had to put my signature on the line and become enrolled. Knowing about God isn't enough, we have to personally make a commitment. Instead of my signature, I need Jesus Christ's blood signature to enroll me into the Family of God." Seeing the light of understanding reflected across Larry's face, I asked him, "Where do you feel you are in your spiritual life journey? Do you consider yourself in the before birth, at birth or after birth stage?"

Larry paused, "Earlier, I would have said after birth, but now I think I am at birth," he answered with a hint of bewilderment.

"In that case, let's pray," I suggested. First I prayed, then Larry. After he had finished, he exclaimed, "I did it."

Desiring to hear Larry express his new found faith, I inquired, "What just happened here?"

He blinked back tears and swallowed hard, "I just received the blood coverage for my sin; I now have Eternal Life." Since my husband had been in and out of the room as we had talked, I asked Larry to tell James what he had just done, and he did. It is wise to have insurance, but it is far wiser to have eternal life assurance.

* * * * *

January 28, 2009 ~ Need a vacuum cleaner?

There was a knock at the door. Two young men introduced themselves and asked if they could clean a rug for me as part of a Kirby vacuum cleaner demonstration. Leaving to pick up grandchildren from school, I was in a hurry. Could they come back in an hour? An hour later, Jason and Ryan were back. My granddaughters popped corn and then served it to the fellows. James came with some groceries. Shaking hands, they asked him his occupation. When James replied, "Retired minister," Jason commented that he had started going to church recently.

As they unpacked their vacuum cleaner, I asked him, "Since you're going to church, are you familiar with the term being "born again?"

"Actually, I'm just getting started searching—I'm reading the Bible some," he responded.

At that point, Ryan explained, "Jason is concerned, especially since his father died recently. We talk about a lot of things."

Looking at the two, I explained how wonderful it is that Jesus was asked about how to get to Heaven and that His answer is recorded in the Bible. Since both expressed interest in just what it was that Jesus had said, I got out a couple of Bibles, and we began an hour of discovering together the truth of new life in Christ.

"Just where would you place yourself on a timeline of your spiritual journey—before birth, at birth or after birth?" I asked.

"At birth" Jason quickly volunteered.

God's Appointment

His friend stammered, "Probably at birth. I always thought that since God created us all that I was going to Heaven, but now I wonder?"

As we talked, Jason observed, "This all makes so much sense. I've never before had it explained to me."

Finally, I asked, "Would it be all right if I prayed right now?"

"Sure," they both agreed.

I prayed, "Thank you Heavenly Father, for bringing these two men to our home and allowing us to talk together about this subject. Help them right now to talk to you and receive your forgiveness for their sin through Jesus' blood. I know if they were to ask you, you would say, 'Yes.'"

Turning to Jason, I asked, "Would you like to call upon the Lord and believe 'in' and 'on' Jesus and receive His blood payment for your sin?"

"Yes, I would," he replied. He prayed aloud for Jesus to apply the blood that He had shed on the Cross for sin to his personal account.

When I asked Ryan where he was he said, "Frankly, I'm not ready yet to make that kind of commitment. There are things in my life that I know are wrong, and I'm not ready to give them up yet."

Complimenting him on his honesty, I agreed with him that just mouthing the words wouldn't work; he needed to wait until he was ready. I told both that I would be praying for them if that was all right. They both said that they would appreciate it if I would.

"Ryan, would you do me a favor? When you are ready and have talked to the Lord about this, please give me a call, so I can rejoice with you."

"Sure," he eagerly replied.

Turning to Jason, I asked, "What just happened here?"

"I became 'born again.'" he offered.

Giving the young men literature, I invited them to get back with me if they had any questions or if I could be of any help to them.

As we talked, I realized I had a problem. Since it was Wednesday evening, children were arriving at the door waiting for their ride to AWANA at our church. I needed to stop to pick up others. It was time for me to leave, and we hadn't had the demonstration yet. I apologized. They both generously assured me that what they had received in our discussion was more valuable than their demonstration pay. When they asked if they could return the next evening to shampoo my rug, give their demonstration, and have further discussion, I assured them that would be fine; they had an open invitation, any time, to contact me.

* * * * *

March 19, 2009 ~ Spring break

It was spring break with no AWANA at church. Jasmine and Corey, brother and sister who were aged nine and eight, had been going with me on Wednesday nights. They came to my door, bored. They played on the piano requesting, "Would you teach us how to play?"

Not knowing very much myself, I simply showed them middle "C", how to recognize which key was which and how to finger the piano. After that, over a bowl of cereal, we talked about what they were learning in AWANA. They shared their view of Bible stories. Then we talked about how Jesus came from Heaven to pay for sin and that, thankfully, we can ask Him to pay for our sin so that we can go to Heaven. I challenged Jasmine and Corey to consider trusting Christ as their Savior.

The next day they were back. Jasmine announced that she had talked to Jesus last night. When I asked what she had talked to Him about she responded, "I knew I was a sinner and needed God's help so that I wouldn't have to go to Hell. I asked if He would pay for my sins so that I could go to Heaven."

"What did He say?"

"Yes!"

"Last night I talked to Jesus, too," Corey quietly shared.

"What did you want Him to do?"

"I imagined I was at the Cross, and I asked Him to pay for my sin so that I won't have to go to Hell."

The faith of children is precious, just as Jesus acknowledged, ***"Let the little children come to me and do not hinder them, for to such belongs the kingdom of heaven"*** (Matthew 19:14).

* * * * *

June 2009 ~ Twenty years later

Duane was a super nice guy and really good at fixing cars. He was married to the granddaughter of one of the ladies in our Washburn church. In the late eighties, when we had mechanical problems with our '83 Chevy car and '77 Ford van, Duane would fix them. As he worked on the vehicles we often talked to him about the Lord. He was very honest and open with us that he was not yet a Christian. When asked if he would consider becoming a Christian, he would smile and say sincerely, "I can't; I'm not ready."

It became obvious to us as time passed that there were a lot of "little" problems requiring Duane's help. It was almost as though God was deliberately making opportunities for us to witness to him. Even Duane and his wife talked about our unusual problems that brought us again and again to talk with him. July 7th about midnight, we talked again with Duane as we picked up our car. We stressed the importance of his settling his salvation soon. He still wasn't ready.

"I hope you don't sleep tonight until you get it settled with God," I said, "call us tomorrow and let us know it is settled." Duane smiled and laughed as he went into his house, "I probably won't sleep tonight," he remarked, "I'll give you a call if I do." We were heavily burdened for him to trust Christ as his personal Savior.

Duane had given us a pet rabbit and when we had to leave town for any amount of time, he would take care of it for us. "If you postpone salvation, and the Rapture takes place, will you take care of the rabbit—there's no need for her to be left alone with no one to take care of her."

"Yea, I'll do that," he self consciously promised. Duane, as often as we talked with him, still wasn't ready.

When we concluded our ministry at Calvary Bible Church, our contact with Duane stopped. Through the years, his name would come to mind to pray for his salvation.

Twenty years later, curious as to how he was doing, I stopped to see if he still worked at the same place he used to. Yes, he was there. Visiting for a minute with him, I asked how he was doing—had he

God's Appointment

ever gotten around to trusting Christ as his Savior? Smiling, Duane assured me that yes he had. In fact, he had gotten baptized and was a member of a church. God had indeed continued to draw him to Himself.

* * * * *

June 15, 2010 ~ The last breath

Billie had come to our home with her fiancé. Thirty years before, she was one of the kids in our neighborhood. She was twelve years old when we first became acquainted. Now in her forties and deeply distressed, she wanted me to help her find peace with God. She told me she had become angry with God because of her mother's agonizing death. Mike her husband? had been diagnosed with 4th stage cancer, and she was once again facing the death of a loved one.

When Mike was in the hospital, I visited them often. Billie was reading the Bible I had given her and was hoping to start going with me to church. Mike continued to be uninterested in considering God in his life. Mike was released for awhile, and Billie attempted to care for him in their home. Later, I received a tearful plea on my answering machine, "Gloria please come to the hospital; I need you." Mike had been taken by ambulance to the hospital. This time they transferred him to Hospice; he would not be going home.

Finding them, I attempted to comfort Billie. She prayed with me and finally was able to surrender to Gods' will and trusted Christ. I asked Billie if it would be okay for me to pray with Mike. He had tried so valiantly to hang onto life, but now all he had strength to do was labored breathing. Sitting down next to him, I took his hand in both of mine and said, "Mike, its Gloria, you remember me." I am going to talk to you in case you are able to hear even though you cannot speak to us. Medical personal tell us that the last thing for a person to lose is their hearing. You love Billie and have tried hard to stay alive to be there for her, you knew she was not ready to be left alone. But it is okay, you are going to have to leave. Billie has made her reservation for Heaven; she loves you and wants you to be there with her. I hope you can hear my voice. Even though you can't move or speak, you can with your thoughts still talk to God. He will hear you."

I explained that when the thief that was being crucified on the cross next to Christ called upon Him, Jesus said, *"Truly, I say to you, today you will be with me in Paradise."* (Luke 23:42-44). The thief was saved by calling upon Jesus—he did not have time to do anything before he died. (Ephesians 2:8, 9) Works are not the root of our salvation but rather receiving the gift of God.

"Right now, in your thoughts, call upon Jesus and accept Him as your Savior. Mike, it's not too late as long as you have life." Slowly and distinctly I quoted, *"For God so loved the world, that he gave his only Son, that whoever believes in him should not perish but have eternal life"* (John 3:16). I stated, "Mike that means you as well as Billie and me." Then quoting

> *Yea, though I walk through the valley of the shadow of death,* (Mike, you're in that valley now) *I will fear no evil; for thou art with me; thy rod and thy staff they comfort me.* (The valley doesn't last forever; you'll soon be on the other side of it. It is important that you call upon Jesus to be your Savior right now while you still have breath!) *Thou preparest a table before me in the presence of mine enemies: thou anointest my head with oil; my cup runneth over. Surely goodness and mercy shall follow me all the days of my life: and I will dwell in the house of the LORD forever.* (Psalm 23:4-6) KJV

Considering the possibility of his being able to hear me, yet maybe going in and out of consciousness, I continued to hold his hand-massaging it gently for forty-five minutes repeating the account of the thief on the cross, how to trust Christ and shared Psalm 23.

Finally, I felt a release in my spirit and for some reason I told him we would look for him when we came to Heaven. He should meet us at the eastern gate. When I made that statement, Mike took one final breath, and he was gone. Turning to Billie, I asked her what she thought had just happened. We both felt it was as if he wasn't afraid anymore; he stopped struggling to hold on. Relaxing-ceasing his struggle to stay alive was his ways of letting us know, "I have found it, thank you, now I can go." God gives peace in death to those who are His!

Will Mike be in Heaven? I can't say for certain, but instructing him to meet us at the eastern gate was not normal for me, why did the Holy Spirit have me say those words? Both Billie and I had peace in our spirit that he will be there. God is faithful to give opportunities to choose Christ even up to the last breath; He had arranged the situation for me to talk with him one more time.

* * * * *

8-4-2010 ~ A Slow Day

My hair was getting bushy and needed to get cut, so I went to the local Wal-Mart hair salon. The hairdresser commented that she was experiencing a slow day and was glad to have me walk-in for a shampoo and trim. As Randi worked on my hair, we visited. I shared that I was from out of town.

"Where are you from?" she inquired.

"The middle of Iowa."

"What brings you here to New Mexico?"

"I brought two of my grandsons to visit their father in the Air Force. I will be driving them back to Iowa for school."

"I have two sons," she shared, "thirteen and seven years old. Is your son-in-law a bad person?"

"Not at all." I assured her. "He did have a lot of problems, but recently he trusted Christ as his Savior and now is really living for the Lord." As Randi continued snipping my hair, I asked her if she was familiar with the concept of a person trusting Christ.

"Not really," she responded. "When I was younger, I went alone to a church near my home and really enjoyed going. I've never met anyone though whose life changed. The people I know who have problems don't seem to ever change."

The Bible tells us that, although people on their own can't change, God changes people. In fact He specializes in those thought impossible. *"Therefore, if anyone is in Christ, he is a new cre-*

ation. The old has passed away; behold, the new has come" (2 Corinthians 5:17).

"In my background," I shared, "I was deeply religious, thinking that because Jesus Christ died on the Cross for a payment for sin that it was automatically distributed to everyone. I felt that I was a Christian. I didn't realize that one had to personally receive the blood payment that Jesus offers to make it theirs. I was excited that in the Bible, Jesus had a conversation with a man named Nicodemus. Jesus explained to him how one gets to Heaven and what He said is recorded for us to read. We must be "born again" to get to Heaven. September 20, 1959 I prayed knowing I was a sinner in trouble and needing help. I asked Jesus Christ who came from Heaven to pay for sin, if He would apply His payment to my sin. He did, and it changed my life!"

My hair was finished, and still no one had entered the shop. Feeling comfortable to talk further, I pulled some tracts out of my purse to give to her that she readily accepted. Then I took my little New Testament out and turned to John chapter 3. Verse-by-verse she followed my finger and read the words aloud.

"'Born again' means baptism?"

"Actually the water in verse 3:5 is referring to the physical birth. *'Jesus answered, "Truly, truly, I say to you, unless one is born of water and the Spirit, he cannot enter the kingdom of God.'* Remember when you carried your sons, the water broke just before they were born?"

"Yes."

"That is what it is referring to, the water and the spirit and in the next verse it repeats saying physical and spiritual birth. *"That which is born of the flesh is flesh, and that which is born of the Spirit is spirit."* We have to have two births; obviously one physically and one becoming born into God's family. Death is separation. Ever since Adam and Eve sinned in the Garden, we have been separated from God and need to be born into His family."

Randi was quick to understand and when I asked her if she would like to pray now and invite Jesus Christ to be her Lord and Savior to pay for her sin, she said, "Yes, I would." She indeed prayed right there.

"What just happened?" I asked.

"I received Jesus Christ, and God now calls me a daughter," she replied referring to John 1:12 which we had discussed. *"But to all who did receive him, who believed in his name, he gave the right to become children of God."* Smiling, she confirmed her joy in knowing that since receiving Jesus, now God called her His daughter. She now had the everlasting life He promised in John 3:36. *"Whoever believes in the Son has eternal life; whoever does not obey the Son shall not see life, but the wrath of God remains on him."*

I told her I had been going to the First Baptist Church in town and was very impressed; she might enjoy attending there. Randi gave me her name and phone number and indicated she would like to visit the church and learn more.

"Now that you know how to get to Heaven, don't go alone. Talk with your sons and take them with you!"

"Absolutely!" she replied.

* * * * *

9-13-2010 ~ Our mechanic

Our daughter's car needed an oil change and a check up. She was working long hours, so I traded vehicles with her so that she could drive my van while I took hers in to be serviced. Joel had been our mechanic for many years and was a friend as well. He always did a great job, and we could trust him to be honest and fair. An added blessing is that his shop was close to where we live.

A new set of sparkplugs was ordered to be delivered, and Joel changed the oil. He removed the bad plugs, replaced the gas filter and did a number of other miscellaneous things to the car. He also did auto work for my folks and mentioned that he had read a tract mom had given him. The parts had not yet arrived, so there was time to visit as he worked. I asked Joel when it was that he had become a Christian. He responded sharing that he had been brought up Catholic. When he got married—he married an angel and joined the Presbyterian Church.

God's Appointment

Agreeing with him that he was indeed blessed with a wonderful wife, I shared that I had been born again September 20, 1959. Since he was unfamiliar with the term "born again," I explained, "Usually a person knows their physical birth date. They should also know their spiritual birth date. I thought maybe he had made a commitment earlier in life and just hadn't recorded the date and therefore was vague on the matter.

"When we become a Christian, it is establishing a relationship much like marriage," I continued. When I ask someone if they are married, they usually say "yes" or "no." If I ask them when they were married, they normally know the date of their wedding. If they are vague or say they have "always been married," I think something is strange. Since you are vague about the time of your spiritual birth, I suggest that it would be wise for you to consider confirming your relationship with God. This would give you confidence that you are covered in regards to spending eternity in Heaven or Hell."

Using the Bible application on my cell phone, I shared with him the 21 verses in John chapter 3 of Jesus' conversation with Nicodemus about being born again. By Joel's comments and questions, it was clear he understood Jesus' instructions.

The spark plugs still had not been delivered. "While we are waiting, would you like to pray right here, now, and confirm your reservation for Heaven? Believing 'in' and 'on' Jesus Christ instead of just 'about' him? Ask Him to apply His Blood payment to your personal account because you genuinely want to?"

"Yes I would," Joel replied. We bowed our hearts together, and Joel called upon Jesus Christ to be his Savior and to apply His blood payment to his sin. "I feel great! Thank you for talking with me about this. It is so easy-yet so vitally important. No wonder the parts are so unusually late coming, God wanted us to talk about this!"

The parts finally came and Joel finished his work. He backed the car out of the garage. As I started to pull away, he said with a wide smile, "September 13, 2010; my Birthday!"

With a laugh I said, "Yes, happy Birth day, Joel!"

A friend stopped by to visit. I shared how God had blessed with an opportunity to introduce someone to the Lord that morning. The next afternoon, Carol called me on the phone excitedly sharing that a

God's Appointment

lady had come to have her do some sewing. She thought that maybe she could be bold enough to ask her if she knew for sure if she was going to Heaven. The lady didn't know, and Carol explained to her how she could know. The lady had trusted Christ! Joel's testimony was bringing fruit for others to get saved!

* * * * *

11-8-2010 ~ Something good from cancer?

The question was asked at Kathy's funeral, "Can any good come out of cancer?" Cancer had brought Kathy face-to-face with death, and she had called upon Jesus Christ for her salvation. Miraculously, God gave her two years of life following her near death experience. Kathy gave a clear and frequent testimony of her coming to know Jesus as her Savior and going from spiritual death into everlasting life.

Saturday was the funeral. On Sunday, one of Kathy's granddaughters wanted to go with us to Heartland Bible Church in Lincoln, Nebraska. Kayla was obviously searching for spiritual answers to questions. Before she had to fly home on Monday, the opportunity presented itself for me to visit with her. Kayla was a high school senior from California, the daughter of Kathy's son Rob. She told me that she had had difficulty getting along with Kathy before, but after her coming to Christ, Kayla saw a real difference in her life. They had strongly bonded. I asked her if I could talk with her and share what I had shared with her Grandma Kathy. My niece Amanda had become friends with Kayla, and I asked her to come to the room with us. Amanda was very helpful, praying and sharing about her own decision to trust Christ at an earlier age. Kayla understood the instructions Jesus gave to Nicodemus in the Scriptures, yet she was not sure she was ready to make a personal decision.

My brother Steve, her grandpa, came into the room. Sharing with him what we were discussing, I told him that Kayla was not ready right now to make a decision. Maybe he would be able to follow up with her at a later time? Steve looked her in the eye and explained to her how important it was for her to just let go and let

God. Reconsidering, she decided to pray and make her commitment. As we joined people in the other room, Kayla told my mother about the decision she had just made.

One good thing that came from cancer was that Kayla obtained a ticket to Heaven, and one day she will be able to join Kathy and praise Jesus Christ for His work on the Cross that enabled those that believed in Him to have everlasting life.

Arriving back in California, Kayla sent this message to us on Facebook. "Dear Vermaas family, I'd like to say to all of you that I'm so glad to have met you guys. Thank you for making me feel so welcome into your family and opening your hearts, especially to Grandma. You opened my eyes even more to help me take one more step in the right direction for my life and I'd like to thank you all for that as well. I hope you guys stay in touch and hopefully I'll come back soon and spend more time together."

* * * * *

12-23-2010 ~ A Chinese lunch

Billie, her daughter, and her daughter's best friend wanted to do some Christmas shopping and invited me to join them. Billie had trusted Christ earlier in the year. She had brought her daughter Brooke to my home to talk with me at which time she also trusted Christ. Her twenty-year-old son Brad had recently believed in Jesus.

Before shopping, we stopped for lunch at East China. Sitting around the table together the conversation between us turned to spiritual matters. Katie, the friend, was very open and she wanted to talk with me further. The other two went on ahead and started shopping, we promised to join them later. I explained to Katie the Biblical concept of being born again. Understanding her need she wanted to trust Jesus Christ as her Savior right there at the table. She prayed a sincere prayer and did just that.

As we joined the mother and daughter as they were shopping, Katie shared with them her good news. Now Brooke & Katie were more than best friends they were also sisters in Christ, and can look forward to spending eternity together. It is wonderful how one person can lead to another, and then to another coming to Christ. Only the Lord knows where it will go to next! Just like in the New Testament, **"And believers were increasingly added to the Lord, multitudes of both men and women"** (Acts 5:14).

* * * * *

The Bridge Builder
(by an unknown author)

This is a poem that has warmed my heart. It has been said, "We build too many walls and not enough bridges."

An old man going a lone highway
Came at the evening cold and gray
To a chasm vast and deep and wide;
The old man crossed in the twilight dim;
The sullen stream had no fears for him
But he turned when safe on the other side
And built a bridge to span the tide.
"Old man," said a fellow pilgrim near
"You are wasting your time with building here.
You never again will pass this way
Your journey will end with the closing day;
You have crossed the chasm deep and wide;
Why build you this bridge at eventide?"
The builder lifted his old gray head
"Good friend in the way that I've come," he said,
There followeth after me today
A youth whose feet must pass this way,
This stream that has been as naught to me
To the fair-haired youth might a pitfall be.
He too, must cross in the twilight dim:
Good friend, I am building the bridge for him."

People that you have never met have painstakingly built bridges for you. May you go the distance in your life's journey towards Home.

The principals for obtaining access to God and Heaven are the same regardless of the time frame that you are in. If you have been left behind, refuse the mark (Revelation 13:16-17; 14:9, 11; 15:2; 16:2; 19:20; 20:4) and call on Jesus Christ as your personal Savior and become "born again." Yes, many will be saved during those terrible seven years, but it will be a very difficult time to live through. (Revelation 7:14) We'll look forward to meeting you later!

~~~~~~~~~~~~~~~~~~~~~~~~

* * * * *

The coming "Rapture" by artist Charles Anderson

The Future

Paul described an event called the "Rapture." Should it have taken place since the writing of this book; realize you have been prayed for. I know that I will honestly be able to say, "Wish you were here!" *"Then we who are alive, who are left, will be caught up together with them in the clouds to meet the Lord in the air, and so we will always be with the Lord"* (1 Thessalonians 4:16-17). Do not worry—the door to Heaven is not shut. God tells us He will raise up 144,000 individuals who will go around the world preaching and will connect people with Himself (Revelation 7:1-17). Because of God's promises in the Bible, I, along with others, have been concerned; knowing there would be searching hearts after we are gone. Tools have been left behind to help you! God cares, and we care—it is not too late!

The same principals for obtaining access to God and Heaven are the same regardless of your time frame. If you have been left behind, refuse the mark (Revelation 13:16-17; 14:9, 11; 15:2; 16:2; 19:20; 20:4) and call on Jesus Christ as your personal Savior and become "born again." Many will be saved during those terrible seven years, but it will be a very difficult time in which to live. (Revelation 7:14) We'll look forward to meeting you later!

* * * * *

The Book of Acts, in the Bible, is thrilling to read, showing how the Gospel spread around the world from one heart to the next. In a sense, God's work in lives today is a continuation of the Book of Acts as it crosses over the generations of time. In eternity, it will be interesting to see the rest of the story revealed. *"And they said, 'Believe in the Lord Jesus, and you will be saved, you and your household'"* (Acts 16:31).

The work that God has begun in bringing people to Himself He has promised to continue until the last person that will be reached makes their decision. He promised, *"I am sure of this, that he who*

began a good work in you will bring it to completion at the day of Jesus Christ" (Philippians 1:6).

* * * * *

Many have asked me to share tips and observations that I have learned through my years of soul winning. In the following section, I have sought to put into writing some thoughts. I pray that they may be of help. The following chapters are designed to share practical tips with those who are looking for their God given appointments!

CHAPTER 18

Tips for Soul-Winning 1-7

"Everyone who calls on the name of the Lord will be saved."
(Romans 10:13).

What Is Soul-Winning? It is simply being obedient to the Lords' command to share the good news of salvation with others. It is working in unison with the Holy Spirit and the body of Christ to help people come to a saving knowledge of Christ. Jesus asked some to leave their home and go to distant lands to be witnesses, (Matthew 29:19, 20; Matthew 4:19; Mark 1:17; Luke 5:10) while He told others to go home and proclaim Christ to family, friends and neighbors (Mark 5:19). It is a fact, however, that if we can not witness for Christ where we are, changing our location does not help. Wherever we are—that is where we are to give witness. People are watching our lives. If God's will is for someone to minister to a particular land or people group, He is perfectly capable of making that known. Soul winning is something that God does through us. If He does not do it, we can not do it in our own strength!

Soul winning is cultivating relationships that may be made up of just a few minutes or many years. It is a variety of opportunities which may involve onetime only contacts with someone, multiple contacts over a period of time, friendship evangelism, as well as a life time of acquaintances. Consider that sharing the Gospel involves laying a necessary foundation. One concept builds on another until there is understanding of the basics: we are a sinner estranged from God, Jesus Christ died to pay for sin, and we must receive Christ's payment for sin personally. It is step-by-step that the Gospel is shared and comprehended. We may see someone take all the steps and actually see them come to Christ, while at other times we may only be involved in building one or two steps and the Holy Spirit will continue to work in lives towards the completion.

It is vital not to separate soul winning from discipleship. Our instructions are to make disciples. *"Go therefore and make disciples of all nations, baptizing them in the name of the Father and of the Son and of the Holy Spirit, teaching them to observe all that I have commanded you. And behold, I am with you always, to the end of the age"* (Matthew 28:19, 20). A wise individual said, "The goal of our lives is to walk with God and to help others walk with God." But remember, it is the Holy Spirit that seals, indwells and makes individuals into disciples. Often God uses many people over a lifetime to influence Christian growth in individuals' lives. This is the body of Christ and local churches' purpose.

Hopefully the reading of actual accounts of people coming to know the Lord will encourage others to be aware of opportunities that they have to share Jesus Christ! Soul winning is basically preparing for that opportunity, looking for it, and doing it as God leads.

Personal Preparations

1. Focus on eternity.

In setting goals and making decisions, we need to prioritize what we want to accomplish with our lives. Do we want to focus on achieving wealth, fame, pleasure, or influencing people for Christ? We can have the overall goal of reaching others for Heaven regardless of what our actual occupation in life may be. Some may be full time Christian workers, but all should be full-time Christians. Eternity will last much longer than the brief years of this life, so let us wisely invest in tomorrow. Remember everything we accumulate here on earth will be left behind. Only what is done for Christ and invested for eternity will last. We are instructed, *"But seek first the kingdom of God and his righteousness, and all these things will be added to you"* (Matthew 6:33).

Life is preparation for Eternity. Puzzle lovers know that it is important to have a picture of the finished product, otherwise it is hard to make sense of the loose pieces and where they are to be placed. God is working in our lives unique pictures. The results of the finished products are reflected in the Bible for us to visualize. Each piece, each situation, needs to be examined to see how and where it fits. *"If any of you lacks wisdom, let him ask God, who gives generously to all without reproach, and it will be given him"* (James 1:5).

2. Be willing to try.

When witnessing, I have probably made every mistake possible. As a young Christian, I remember crying into my pillow night after night, asking the Lord to help me express the plan of salvation clearly so people could understand what I was trying to share with them. I still make mistakes. The problem isn't in making mistakes, but rather not trying. How did I learn to tell others about Christ. The answer is—through tears! God's promise is, *"He who goes out weeping, bearing the seed for sowing, shall come home with shouts of joy, bringing his sheaves with him"* (Psalm 126:6). Someone aptly stated, "God doesn't call the qualified, He qualifies the called."

Maybe you have tried leading people to Christ and were not successful—try again. A beautiful example of keeping on until you succeed is watching how children learn to walk. When my children were learning to walk, I would stand them up against something solid, then move a short distance away, stretch out my arms and call them to come to me. With their eyes fastened on me, not looking at their feet or the floor, they would come one step at a time. Such a look of pure joy was on their face with each successful step. Each time they fell, we started over. They were proud of themselves, and I was proud of their willingness to take the steps to come to me. Soon, following my voice, they were walking and it wasn't long before they were off and running.

To be successful as a soul winner, we need to keep our eyes on Christ and follow His voice. Every time we fail, try again. Anyone one who has learned how to walk, ride a bicycle, roller skate, play basketball, football, soft ball, golf, bowl, cook, sew, or drive, has had to keep trying. Success doesn't necessarily come with the first attempt. If we as human parents can patiently teach our children, even so much more, Our Heavenly Father can teach us how to grow in faith, even in the area of soul winning.

3. Study the Bible.

Witnessing creates a desire to understand the Bible, not only for our own sake, but also so that we can explain it to someone else. It is true that people have been led to the Lord with only one Bible verse. For instance, John 3:16 is a fantastic verse, capturing the Gospel message, *"For God so loved the world, that he gave his only Son, that whoever believes in him should not perish but have eternal life."* But we should grow in our knowledge of God's Word beyond just using one verse. The *whole Bible* is a living, exciting book, and God's plan of salvation for mankind is woven throughout its pages. We are not all the same; one size does not fit all. God will use different Scriptures and approaches to reach different people. A skilled mechanic is not satisfied with only one screw driver in his tool box but keeps adding other tools. Effective soul winners constantly will add Scriptures and illustrations to their base of knowledge.

We will also discover that the things that God shares with us in our daily devotions are often used by Him in witnessing opportunities that He gives to us. The more we absorb the Bible, the more we can draw upon its concepts and illustrations when we talk with people. The Word of God is to flow through us into the lives of those with whom we come into contact (Romans 1:16; 10:13-17).

Do not put off soul winning until you have read the whole Bible; start with where you are. Reading the entire Bible would, however, be a worthwhile project. More than once I have been asked if I have read the Bible all the way through. Thankfully, I can say, "Yes, many times." Actually, it is not difficult to read the Bible through in a given year. If one reads a portion of Scripture morning and evening, enough to turn a page each time, it can happen. We need to realize that the Bible is the power source which the Holy Spirit uses for winning souls. Paul wrote to Timothy, a young man, encouraging him to be diligent in his study of the Word, *"Do your best to present yourself to God as one approved, a worker who has no need to be ashamed, rightly handling the word of truth"* (2 Timothy 2:15).

4. Have a Bible handy.

It is important to have a Bible handy so that we are ready when an opportunity comes. I have often had frustration dreams in which I was trying to lead someone to Christ, and I could not locate a Bible to use. It is an impossible situation if we are not able to connect the individual with the source of the power which allows the Holy Spirit to minister to their heart. When we open the Bible and have others read along with us, they recognize that the words are what God says. Such a situation holds infinitely more weight than simply sharing our opinion! Seldom will individuals make a decision for Christ without the actual use of verses from the Bible. This is one of the reasons, through the years, that it has been a goal to provide different language groups around the world with Scripture translated into their heart language.

An open Bible unleashes God's powerful witness. As we explain the Scriptures, it gives confidence that what we are sharing is based on God's Holy Word. The Holy Spirit is able to do more with an open Bible than with just our verbal assertions. We need God's power; His Book, the Bible, along with His Holy Spirit is the key to that power.

In my purse, I try to carry at least a New Testament with a readable print size so that I can point to the verses and individuals can read the verse along with me. I also keep a full-sized Bible in my car and one easily accessible by my front door in my house. Those who are technology efficient can use a Bible application on their cell phone, however even then it is wise to have an actual Bible with you in case your battery doesn't last long enough. Having a variety of tracts available to use is also helpful. Knowing that God is still actively working in people's lives to draw them to Himself, we can volunteer to be available for Him to send them our way if He would so desire. Having a Bible handy indicates we are prepared for Him to send people our direction.

Our battle is spiritual and the victory is God's! The power of God's Word is illustrated in Scripture by the image of a living sword: *"For the word of God is living and active, sharper than any two-edged sword, piercing to the division of soul and of spirit, of joints and marrow, and discerning the thoughts and intentions of the heart"* (Hebrews 4:12).

5. Be the third party.

The soul winner is the third party in the peacemaking situation, together with the individual with whom the Gospel is being shared, and the Holy Spirit. To use an illustration, consider the fact that plugging in an iron to the wall socket takes three things: the object-the iron, the source-the electricity, and the third party-the one who brings the two together. As individuals come to Christ, we are witness to a miracle in the making. Paul explains, *"if anyone is in Christ, he is a new creation. The old has passed away; behold, the new has come. All this is from God, who through Christ reconciled us to himself and gave us the ministry of reconciliation"* (2 Corinthians 5:17, 18). Only God can arrange a successful soul-winning encounter.

Remember the conversation with others should not be considered a contest or intellectual debate, but simply the reconciling people with God. "Be ye fishers of men; you catch 'em - He'll clean 'em," is a cute saying, but actually we are powerless to do either; it takes Christ in us to see either task accomplished.

We do not get points for how many people we lead to Christ. Rather God rewards us for our obedience to Him in speaking with them. The obedience is our responsibility; the fruit of that obedience is the Holy Spirit's job. My reward is not dependant on the outcome of the witnessing attempt, only in the obedience in attempting the contact and following it to its rightful conclusion. Sometimes the result is planting seeds or watering. Sadly, it may be used of God to give proof that God provided an opportunity for salvation and that it was their decision to reject. For soul winners, it does not matter if the person made a decision or not, only that they faithfully communicated the message God wanted them to share. The result that comes from our witness is God's part.

How encouraging it is to know that even when our encounter with an individual is over, though we may be limited by time and location, the Holy Spirit can and will continue working in their lives according to His perfect purpose! He brought them to us, and He is able to arrange the next step for them with or without our help. Our contact with people is time limited, but the Holy Spirit can continue working in lives after we are no longer in the picture. He can be with them over their entire life span, *"And I am sure of this, that he who began a good work in you will bring it to completion at the day of Jesus Christ"* (Philippians 1:6).

6. Practice.

Practice sessions in soul winning can be helpful. Know which verses to use, the context, the location, as well as which words to emphasize. Be familiar with the passages well enough to be able to read the words upside down or from the side, while showing them to someone. Practice with someone else, if possible, taking turns role-playing. Additionally, choose illustrations valuable in helping individuals understand Biblical truths. The better we know God's Word and what we want to share, the easier it is to share God's truths with others. Also, make a practice of inviting individuals to make a decision, including the prayer of acceptance, thus conditioning yourself to follow through and not stop short of the goal.

All of us gravitate to and seek out people who know what they are doing—dentists, doctors, mechanics and so on. We want our lives and our possessions in experienced hands. The unsaved, too, respect and listen more readily when they sense confidence in what is being shared. Let us consider Paul's advice, **"do your best to present yourself to God as one approved, a worker who has no need to be ashamed, rightly handling the word of truth"** (2 Timothy 2:15).

7. Be in prayer.

God usually leads someone to pray specifically for individuals before they can be reached for Christ. When God lays a heavy burden on a heart to pray for someone's salvation, it indicates the Holy Spirit's intention to work. Having a strong compulsion to pray for someone is different from praying through a prayer list. Sometimes the call for special prayer is so strong that all the individual can do is find a quiet place to weep and plead until the burden lifts. *"Likewise the Spirit helps us in our weakness. For we do not know what to pray for as we ought, but the Spirit himself intercedes for us with groanings too deep for words"* (Romans 8:26). This is true in the lives of individuals as well as nations. Christ prayed for us, *"I am praying for them. I am not praying for the world but for those whom you have given me, for they are yours"* (John 17:9). This prayer time is also a heart preparation that makes us more sensitive to opportunities as they present themselves.

As God works in people's heart for salvation, He will match them with people who are available to witness. When we pray specifically that God will bring people across our path, He is capable of doing just that. God wants to use us! His desire is to bring others to Himself just as God did with us and many others throughout the years. There are many people today with whom God is dealing. Let us ask for His leading because God is seeking to save. *"For God so loved the world, that he gave his only Son, that whoever believes in him should not perish but have eternal life"* (John 3:16).

CHAPTER 19

Tips for Soul-Winning 8-25

Personal Attitudes

8. See the need

World population according to the encyclopedia Wikipedia is now estimated to be around 6,908,688,000. There is a deep hunger in the human heart for God and there are many different religions. People are asking, "Where is God?" and "Does He care?" Approximately 2,000,000,000 identify themselves as Christian. What percent of those are born again Christians? Only God knows, but my guess would be a small number. Recent research states that there are now 195 million non-churched people in America, making America one of the top four largest unchurched nations in the world. Essentially, what was a churched Christian American culture has become an unchurched post-Christian culture. Many people in America are not anti-church; they simply view the church as irrelevant. Being churched does not make a person a Christian, but it is a barometer we can use to determine the need. America was at one time, the greatest resource for missionaries being sent to other areas of the world. Now other countries are seeing the need to send missionaries to America!*

An illustration helps put this into perspective. A young boy was standing on the beach among what looked like millions of starfish washed ashore by the tide. The boy picked up one stranded starfish after another and flung it back into the sea. An onlooker remarked that it was hopeless for him to make a difference; there were too many, the starfish were going to die. "It makes a difference to this one," the boy replied as he picked up yet another and threw it back into the life giving water. We may not be able to make a dent in the need, but we can make a difference to the individuals we can help. Pray for God to raise up laborers and be willing to do your part! Jesus' challenges us, *"Do you not say, 'There are yet four months, then comes the harvest?' Look, I tell you, lift up your eyes, and see that the fields are white for harvest"* (John 4:35).

*(Earley,Dave.July 2006. *The Desperate Need For New Churches*, p.1, www.liberty.edu/media/1162/cmt/churchplanting/The%20Des perate%20Need%20for%20New%20Churches%202%20page.pdf). In order to find the entire article, do a search on the LU home page for the title.

9. Visualize Hell.

If we know we should be involved in soul winning, but are not motivated, visualizing people-a mother, daughter or neighbor in Hell would change us, maybe even help us to turn off the television and agonize with God for souls. Not wanting to believe in such a terrible place does not change the fact that it exists. Jesus spoke more often of Hell than Heaven. If we believe the Bible, that there is a literal Hell, then we should have an attitude of urgency in reaching people for Christ. It is a real place, and real people go there. Jesus shared this account.

> *There was a rich man who was clothed in purple and fine linen and who feasted sumptuously every day. And at his gate was laid a poor man named Lazarus, covered with sores, who desired to be fed with what fell from the rich man's table. Moreover, even the dogs came and licked his sores. The poor man died and was carried by the angels to Abraham's side. The rich man also died and was buried, and in Hades, being in torment, he lifted*

up his eyes and saw Abraham far off and Lazarus at his side. And he called out, 'Father Abraham, have mercy on me, and send Lazarus to dip the end of his finger in water and cool my tongue, for I am in anguish in this flame.' But Abraham said, 'Child, remember that you in your lifetime received your good things, and Lazarus in like manner bad things; but now he is comforted here, and you are in anguish. And besides all this, between us and you a great chasm has been fixed, in order that those who would pass from here to you may not be able, and none may cross from there to us." ("Luke 16:19-26).

God gives us protection from Satan by giving us instructions to be defensive in our actions. (Ephesians 6:13-18) He also gives us marching orders to be on the offensive. We can actually march right up to the gates of Hell and rescue souls. Jesus said, **"I will build my church, and the gates of hell shall not prevail against it"** (Matthew 16:18). The gates of Hell can not stand against the power of the Gospel.

In Genesis 18 God told Abraham of His plan to destroy Sodom and Gomorrah. Concerned for his nephew, Lot and his family, Abraham agonized with God. He asked Him to spare the city if there were 50 righteous souls in it. Then, worried that there might not be 50 he asked for 40, then 30, then 20, but surly he thought—there would be 10. Abraham showed us how to agonize for souls—we can do it too.

10. Volunteer for harvesting.

Most Christians sit back and wait for someone else to reach unsaved people for Christ. Sadly, only a small percent of Christians have actually led someone else to Christ. Some think that soul winning should be left to "professionals" such as pastors and missionaries. God is the Professional; we are only His assistants. God's command to win souls is to every Christian! It is not an optional task. He is looking for laborers to join Him in HIS harvest field; we can be willing laborers! Each one of us have our own circle of influence, you have contact with people that I do not.

A challenge in my own life has been the parable written about a large group of orange pickers. The orange pickers went into an orange grove and gathered around a single tree, chose an official orange picker, and sent him up the ladder with a flourish to pick a few oranges. They then rejoiced in the harvest and returned home, leaving the rest of the oranges unpicked on that tree, and other trees as far as the eye could see. The oranges fell to the ground overripe. What a missed harvest—if only everyone in the group could simply have joined in the work and spent more time at it, there would have been a better harvest. There needs to be more orange pickers and less content just to watch. Someone has said, "We too easily become keepers of the aquarium instead of fishers of men." How true!

Each of us has our own circle of influence. A friend, Kirsten Cundiff, shared with me a song she learned in Denmark: *"You bring the one next to you, and I'll bring the one next to me. In all kinds of weather, we'll all work together to bring them, win them, one by one."* We all have a plot of ground. May we stand before the Lord of the harvest one day hearing, "Well done thou good and faithful servant." Jesus spoke about the harvest of men's souls needing laborers, **"The harvest is plentiful, but the laborers are few. Therefore pray earnestly to the Lord of the harvest to send out laborers into his harvest"** (Luke 10:2; Matthew 28:19-20).

11. Be confident in Christ.

When the Lord asked me to consider working with college students, I thought, "Me?" I had preconceived ideas of what it would take; I did not feel intelligent, cool, or fashionable enough to relate to college students. The Lord would have to do it *through* me and *in spite* of me. I claimed the promise, **"He who calls you is faithful; he will surely do it"** (1 Thessalonians 5:24). Students ended up being interested in seeing someone that was real in their walk with the Lord, and God was indeed visibly faithful in my life. Only eternity will reveal the extent of fruit from those years.

Many feel unable to witness. That is good—God enjoys choosing those unable in themselves to do His work. This way, He gets the glory! If a person has a natural ability, it is easy to rely on that rather than to depend on Him. God often asks us to serve Him, not in areas of our strengths, but in areas of weakness. That way we do not get the credit—He does! God is in the constant process of stretching us and getting us to grow in our walk of faith. Feeling inadequate to lead others to Christ is a good sign because then we are dependent on God. He uses ordinary people to do extraordinary things. All we can humanly do is be an instrument, used by God, to bring someone to Christ. All we can do is make ourselves available to serve. Our confidence is not in ourselves but in Christ! *"My grace is sufficient for you, for my power is made perfect in weakness. Therefore I will boast all the more gladly of my weaknesses, so that the power of Christ may rest upon me"* (2 Corinthians 12:9).

12. Avoid "class" consciousness.

When we are insecure, we can be easily intimidated by people whom we consider "above us." Our perception of the world, others, and ourselves may make us class conscious. Perhaps we feel more at ease talking to a poor individual rather than a bank president, a grocery clerk rather than a Congressman. In reality, who could be in a higher class than being a daughter or son of God? The Gospel of John says, *"But to all who did receive him, who believed in his name, he gave the right to become children of God"* (John 1:12). Who has a better status than that? We do not have to feel inferior! A study of who we are "in Christ" is amazing.

When we know that God loves us as much as anyone else, we should have the confidence to talk to anyone, regardless of age, status, or any other differences. The Psalmist, who as a shepherd boy killed a lion and a bear, was confident in God's strength as he went out and killed Goliath. We can ask God for that confidence! Later, as king of Israel, David wrote:

> *I praise you, for I am fearfully and wonderfully made. Wonderful are your works; my soul knows it very well. My frame was not hidden from you, when I was being made in secret, intricately woven in the depths of the earth. Your eyes saw my unformed substance; in your book were written, every*

one of them, the days that were formed for me, when as yet there was none of them. How precious to me are your thoughts, O God! How vast is the sum of them! If I would count them, they are more than the sand. I awake, and I am still with you. (Psalm 139:14-18)

Being class conscious can work both ways. We also must not allow an attitude of superiority dictate to whom we will witness. We are not more valuable than anyone else. My being blessed is not because of my parentage, race, talents, monetary value, or appearance, but that, "God loves me." He also loves other people as much as He loves me, and He wants me to let them know of His love. Paul warns, *"I say to everyone among you not to think of himself more highly than he ought to think"* (Romans 12:3).

13. Be involved.

Many Christians seclude themselves and avoid going beyond their comfort zone. Being surrounded only by Christians while working on campus as a student in Bible College, I experienced spiritual frustration. There was no opportunity to witness, and I felt compelled to catch a public bus to ride around town to distribute tracts, pray for people going about their daily activities, and talk with individuals about Christ. After all, one has to be around the unsaved in order to win them to Christ.

The Holy Spirit can lead us in ways to associate with people such as joining a club, taking sightseeing tours, going to a park, giving lessons, receiving instruction in something we enjoy, becoming better acquainted with neighbors, befriending neighborhood children, taking a dog to obedience school, or volunteering to help in worthwhile activities. There are opportunities all around us! Jesus uses a parable to tell us, *"And the master said to the servant, 'Go out to the highways and hedges and compel people to come in, that my house may be filled'"* (Luke 14:23).

14. Lift up Christ.

An ex-druid priestess gave this testimony, "Before, I was content, but now, in Christ, I am fulfilled." It is all about a wonderful, personal relationship. There is a saying, "We were called to be witnesses, not lawyers or judges." The personal testimonies that we have, give us opportunities to effectively share the good news of salvation. We do not need to be shy talking about our precious Lord; God has commanded us to represent Him to people. The more people get to know about Christ, the more the Holy Spirit will be able to draw them to Him. Our mission is to lift up Christ. The Word of God does not say that Scripture verses, proof texts, and arguments should be lifted up, that they will draw all men to Christ. Instead, it says, ***"And I, when I am lifted up from the earth, will draw all people to myself"*** (John 12:32).

15. Attract others with joy.

A young bride-to-be usually has a favorite topic of conversation which is all about the most wonderful man in the world and their wedding plans. There is a glow on the bride's face as she talks about her fiancé, and she seeks to be near her groom as much as possible! We are referred to as the **"*Bride of Christ*,"** (Revelation 21:9). When we are in love with the precious Lord Jesus Christ, our thoughts and conversation should easily turn to Him. Moses, when he was in the presence of God, came down from the mountaintop with a glowing face, so much so that he had to put on a veil (Exodus 34:35). So too, there should be a glow to our countenance that says we've been with Him.

A joyful countenance will attract more than a sad face. Why should people want what we have if we are sad, discouraged and negative all the time? Searching hearts are attracted to joy and peace. They are drawn to those who have such a spirit and can be pointed to Christ who is the source. Ask God for the joy of the Lord that others will see and desire.

16. Notice people.

If we do not *seriously* see some people, if they are just part of the scenery, we will fail to realize daily opportunities to witness. Ask God to open our eyes to those who are not always noticed—sales people, delivery people, mailmen, hair stylists, and people walking. It is easy to be caught up in our own thoughts, so concerned about our own situation that we are oblivious to people around us. When we notice people, we are able to make eye contact with them. A polite smile communicates a pleasant and friendly attitude. When we have a smile and, perhaps, a warm word, we are recognizing their existence and affirming their worth. Friendliness and common courtesy open up opportunities to communicate with people.

When we choose to smile, it keeps our mind focused, allowing us to be more socially aware of others. It is true that there are certain areas of the world that are more prone to friendly expression between people than others. Still, regardless where we are, when we are friendly, we are in a positive rather than a negative mood and treat others in a more encouraging way. Some people in life experience being avoided or go unnoticed, and they seem to react the most warmly to friendliness. When a person is acknowledged by someone else, it uplifts their spirit. When we respect others, we will find that they in turn will be more inclined to respect us. The Bible counsels, *"A man that hath friends must show himself friendly"* (Proverbs 18:24) (KJV).

Sadly, friendliness can be misunderstood. Some people wonder, "Who are you, and why are you talking to me?" Individuals recognize, but do not necessarily understand, the joy and love of God. That does not mean that we have to avoid being friendly. We do not have to let other people's attitudes affect our own. We can be wise and use common sense at the same time, knowing that we live in a sinful, cursed world. Being alert, we will be more likely to discover God's appointments for us.

17. Learn to love.

Developing a love for people is vital. After all, God loves them, and He asks us to allow Him to love them through us. We cannot manufacture enough love within ourselves to love people to Christ—only He can. We may be surprised how many people are isolated and will respond in a positive manner to someone who genuinely cares. Jesus was asked, "Which is the most important commandment?" He answered,

> *The most important is, 'Hear, O Israel: The Lord our God, the Lord is one. And you shall love the Lord your God with all your heart and with all your soul and with all your mind and with all your strength. The second is this: You shall love your neighbor as yourself. There is no other commandment greater than these.* (Mark 12:29-31)

In the subjects of our love, what order of priority should we have? I'll share with you a conversation I had with my little love bug. It was just before Christmas, my daughter Victoria was seven years old, and she was all curled up on my lap. She posed a question again, "Do you love me Mommy?"
"Yes."
"How much?"
"Lots."
"Do you love Daddy?"
"Yes."
"Who do you love the most—me or Daddy?"
"I love you both, only different."
"Yes, but who do you love the most?"
"I guess Daddy, but I love you very, very much too."
There was a pause for a moment and then with a happy satisfied smile she said, "Good choice."
It is difficult to explain to a seven-year-old the difference between a woman's love for her mate and for her children. It is true, a mothers' love is very strong—God designed it that way. When a child is born, you train them in eating, dressing, potty training,

schooling, etc. You begin preparing for the day he or she will leave and to live on their own. A mate is one you join together with to walk together for life. A child is secure and happy in knowing Mommy loves Daddy.

Just as my love for Victoria was less—it was okay because there was enough love to share. When we love God—the very most, above anyone else—it is good. Our love for Him makes it possible to love others more! What we have leftover to share with others is more than we would have if we didn't love Him the most! Loving God first, our mate second, our children and family next is beautiful and attractive. It draws others to you and to God. They know what is leftover for them is more than it would be otherwise. When it comes to Love, the more we give, the more we have.

The familiar love chapter in I Corinthians 13:13, lists the following virtues: ***"So now faith, hope, and love abide, these three; but the greatest of these is love."*** We can prayerfully seek all three as we serve God who so loved the whole world that He gave His Son (John 3:16) as a love sacrifice for the ransom of souls. We can ask God to help us love other people!

18. Avoid prejudging.

It is easy to jump to the conclusion that certain individuals are not open to the Gospel. We have a tendency to pre-judge people which must be resisted. God specializes in reaching persons we consider to be unlikely. The outside of the "package" does not reveal or indicate what is on the inside. We are in the wrong if we allow the way a person dresses, the length of their hair, nationality, financial status, attitude, or the cleanliness of their person to influence us. At the same time, we can think someone will be open to the Gospel, and they are not.

Since we cannot tell how people will respond, it is wise to try to approach everyone we can. In Heaven we will meet people we would have considered unlikely to be there. And on the other hand, we will miss people we thought surely would be there, and they are not. Only God knows *"the secrets of the heart"* (Psalm 44:21).

19. Let God be in control.

Some people try to give God orders as if He was supposed to jump at their command. A woman often called me on the telephone- asking me to pray that it would not rain. It always irritated me, and I tried to explain, "I don't do weather." It is dangerous to assume that we know what is best enough to determine whether it should rain or not. What if the crops in the field need moisture, should I ask God to keep it from raining so that she can go on a picnic? God is all-knowing; I am not. It would be better to ask God to work out details in a manner that would be according to His will. Let God be the one that is in control, *"Teach me to do your will, for you are my God…I am your servant"* (Psalm 143:10-12).

The Bible does tell us that we can move mountains when we pray. Our God can indeed literally move mountains, but at the same time does He have to? A mother, traveling by train with a young child, knowing it would be scared of the approaching long dark tunnel, prayed that God would move the mountain. A traveling companion scoffed at her prayer. Shortly before they entered the tunnel, the child fell asleep in her arms, and awoke contently on the other side of the mountain. Did God answer her prayer and move the mountain? He did resolve the problem which was what the mother actually wanted. God is not limited to answering the words of our lips but is able to meet the cry of our hearts.

He is also in the process of working in people's lives. Where people are spiritually at any given time, may not necessarily be indicative of where they will be in the future. We cannot, ultimately, change people or correct them—but the Holy Spirit can! If He does not do it, then genuine change will not happen. What things we would seek to change in people's lives may not be the areas that God considers priorities. He knows each individual better than even they know themselves. King David observed, *"O LORD, you have searched me and known me. You know when I sit down and when I rise up; you discern my thoughts from afar"* (Psalm 139:1, 2). Listening to people's prayers gives insight into their concept of God. How scary it would be to live in a world that we had to control. When we recognize how big and powerful and all knowing God is, it is easy to trust Him. We can relax and let God be God. He may choose to use us in the process of working in peoples' lives. *"Therefore, if anyone is in Christ, the new creation has come: The old has gone, the new is here"* (2 Corinthians 5:17).

20. Overcome shyness.

God wants us to learn to be bold, and He is able to teach us to be confident in Him. After all, if we allow the Holy Spirit to do His work through us, He is not shy. Truthfully, it does not matter if we are naturally shy or not; we can trust God to make us what we need to be. God considers boldness an asset to be sought after. People who know me now cannot believe that I once was naturally shy. I was, but now I am not. My precious mother used to be terribly shy, but through the years, I have seen a transformation in her life. Her love for the Lord and her genuine concern for people's souls give her the boldness to sing beautifully in public without musical accompaniment and speak freely to an audience.

Be careful however, being bold is not the same as being brass, obnoxious, arrogant or presumptuous. Paul specifically requested prayer in his own life, *"that words may be given to me in opening my mouth boldly to proclaim the mystery of the gospel, for which I am an ambassador in chains, that I may declare it boldly, as I ought to speak"* (Ephesians 6:19).

21. Be obedient.

We need to live in obedience to the Holy Spirit's leading in our life. If something does not come easy, it is tempting to give up. Soul winning is important, and we need to keep working on it. Simon Peter and his partners were finished with fishing when Jesus asked to use his boat as a platform from which to preach. When Jesus was finished teaching, He told Peter to go out again to fish.

Peter was a professional fisherman, and he had been trying all night to catch fish in his own strength and wisdom without results. Experienced fishermen in that area fished by net in the shallow water at night, not in the deep during the day. Simon Peter responded,

"Master, we toiled all the night and took nothing! But at your word I will let down the nets" (Luke 5:5). He obeyed and ended up with full nets. Peter did not catch all the fish in Lake Gennesaret—just the ones God had prepared for him. Jesus instructed him where and when to fish, and afterwards said, *"Follow me, and I will make you fishers of men"* (Matthew 4:19). God wants us to be fishers of men, and He can direct us to the individuals He wants us to speak to.

Not everyone will get saved. There are people that no one will lead to Christ. Even Jesus, during His earthly ministry, talked with people who did not receive salvation. He said, *"For the gate is narrow and the way is hard that leads to life, and those who find it are few"* (Matthew 7:14). *"But when he (Rich Ruler) heard these things, he became very sad, for he was extremely rich. Jesus, seeing that he had become sad, said, 'How difficult it is for those who have wealth to enter the kingdom of God!'"* (Luke 18:23, 24).

The secret in soul winning is trust and obedience. God trained the Israelites during the forty years of wandering in the desert to follow the cloud by day and pillar of fire by night. When the Ark of the Covenant moved, the people followed. When the Holy Spirit moves us, we need to obey. One of these days we will stand before the Lord and give answer to Him, not as to how many souls we've led to the Lord, but rather if we were obedient to speak to those He wanted us to speak. Based on whether we did or did not will bring the words, "Well done good and faithful servant." Or, "Why didn't you obey?" We should not try to play games with God, but rather be obedient. Do not try to use God; let Him use you!

The words that describe my feelings when soul winning are compelled, burdened, or concerned. That compulsion on my heart requires action; I am released by God when it is lifted.

22. Purify your lives.

We are all imperfect and God is continuing to deal with us in various areas of our lives. About the time we successfully have victory in something, God points out another area that needs our attention. Each true Christian knows what spot God is currently putting His finger on in their life. I know what area God is concentrating on

God's Appointment

in my life right now. We are a work in progress. There is a saying, "Please be patient, God is not finished with me yet." This is true about all of us.

There is a difference between struggling to be obedient in areas, and being rebellious. If we are in rebellion in an area of our life and are choosing to live in sin, God will not as effectively be able to use us in soul-winning. David invited God to *"Search me, Oh God, and know my heart! Try me and know my thoughts! And see if there be any grievous way in me, and lead me in the way everlasting"* (Psalms 139:23, 24).

When we hear an inner voice compelling us to do something, it is from one of three sources, either from our own thoughts, satanic, or the Holy Spirit. We are instructed to determine the source. *"Beloved, do not believe every spirit, but test the spirits to see whether they are from God, for many false prophets have gone out into the world"* (1 John 4:1). Identifying the source simplifies the dilemma as to how to respond. If it is of God, we want to be positive in our reaction. If it is of self we need to evaluate it carefully. If it is from Satan we should be negative in our response.

Jesus, when He lived here on this earth, sought the leading of the Holy Spirit, prayed, fasted and studied the Scriptures. We certainly need to do these things as well. In soul winning, the Holy Spirit will lead us as to whom to approach and what to say. It's not just going out on a hunt, but rather following His leading.

Marvelously, God is able to use people regardless of their spiritual condition. Even unsaved people have been used to show others how to get saved. Dr. Maurice Rawlings, a heart surgeon, tells in his book *To Hell and Back* how one of his patients died in his medical office and he administered CPR. The patient franticly described himself as having been in Hell, and he did not want to go back. He pled with Dr. Rawlings to do something so that he would not, if his heart were to stop again, go back to Hell. Dr. Rawlings shared with him a verse his mother had taught him as a young boy. (John 3:16) The man trusted Christ, even though Dr. Rawlings, at that point in his life, was not himself a believer!

A believer that is walking with the Lord will find that their life reflects Jesus Christ. I consider a clear conscious to be one of my most valuable possessions.

23. Let problems position us.

Problems are often God's way of maneuvering us into position to talk with someone about Christ. The copier, computer or car breaks down—and we need to have contact with someone. Rather than becoming discouraged when things go wrong like a flat tire or a leak in the roof, look for someone God might be bringing across your path. Recognizing those frustrating inconveniences as part of God's plan helps us to ask God how He wants to use the situation for His glory. His words are true, *"The steps of a man are established by the LORD, when he delights in his way"* (Psalm 37:23).

24. Recycle the Gospel.

The first time we hear a truth, illustration or story, we can enjoy it. But, after we have heard it a few times, what could our reaction be? Instead of it being a turn-off for us, we could consider how to use the material in our interaction with others. Rather than becoming bored, we can pay special attention to details so that we can use it to share with someone else. There is a big difference between having heard something and being able to effectively repeat it. The attitude, "I already know this," or "I've heard this before," should be avoided.

25. Avoid "missionary" dating

Dating unsaved individuals for the purpose of reaching them for the Lord is not wise. My advice, "Don't do it!" One of Satan's most effective methods of trapping Christians is getting them into a vulnerable relationship in which they can easily fall in love with and then marry an unbeliever. Why play with fire? Beware of having spiritual pride—thinking you are strong enough and will not make a mistake. The Bible warns believers sternly, *"Do not be unequally yoked with unbelievers. For what partnership has righteousness*

with lawlessness? Or what fellowship has light with darkness" (2 Corinthians 6:14). How can a believer pray together for God's will, for God's power, with an unbeliever? In contrast, God's promises are precious, ***"for where two or three are gathered in my name, there am I among them"*** (Matthew 18:19, 20). This promise basically referring to a church situation is also true in a marriage.

History is full of examples of individuals making a profession of salvation, but after marriage, the partners discover, too late, that their mate's conversion was not real. Too many times I have been in a heart-throbbing conversation with an individual who failed to guard their heart. Because emotions are not easily controlled, preventive measures work best!

Even between two Christians, there can be an unequal relationship. A Christian should consider the life goals and values of the other Christian before beginning to date. Prayerfully consider each date to prevent tremendous grief. If changes are needed in lives, those changes should be evident before couples become seriously involved rather than hoping for changes to take place later. Changes made in lives, even though well-intentioned and honest, are not usually lasting when done to please someone else. What is done through Christ truly lasts!

CHAPTER 20

Tips for Soul-Winning 26-41

Approaches

26. Reach children.

"The world's most fruitful mission field is not a particular place. It is not a particular country. It's a certain kind of people—its children. If children are old enough to know that they have sinned, they are old enough to know that they need a Savior," wrote George Eager, Founder and Director of *The Mail Box Club*.

"A survey of Christian leaders revealed that 86% were saved before reaching the age of 15, 10% between the ages of 15 and 30, and only 4% were saved after the age of 30," according to the *Handbook of Children's Evangelism* by Lionel Hunt.

"When a child is saved, not only is a soul saved, but a life as well," stated D.L. Moody.

"A child of five, if properly instructed, can as readily believe and be regenerated as anyone," observed Charles Spurgeon the renowned preacher of preachers.

Isaac Watts was saved at the age of 9, Jonathan Edwards at 7, Matthew Henry at 11, Jim Elliot at 6, and Corrie Ten Boom at the age of 5. "Faith comes easily to children— internationally, the effects of the work of Christ's redemption in the lives of children have been tremendous, as stated in *Good News for Little People's* training manual.

Jesus stated concerning a child,

> ***Truly, I say to you, unless you turn and become like children, you will never enter the kingdom of heaven. Whoever humbles himself like this child is the greatest in the kingdom of heaven. Whoever receives one such child in my name receives me, but whoever causes one of these little ones who believe in me to sin, it would be better for him to have a great millstone fastened around his neck and to be drowned in the depth of the sea.*** (Matthew 18:3-6)

My brother Tim believes that he trusted Christ at the age of four, the first day that he understood he was a sinner. He believes that, although it is a great testimony to be saved <u>out of</u> a life of sin, it is a greater testimony to be saved <u>from</u> a life of sin. To be healed of scars is one thing, to avoid scars is another! Tim is an evangelist traveling with his wife and daughter with *Good News for Little People,* and sees many saved every year. My sister Carol, a missionary working with her husband and two children, claims she was also saved at age four. Our daughter Victoria identifies her time of salvation to be a Sunday morning at the age of four.

Many raised in a Christian atmosphere feel as if they have always believed. It seems just a natural flow for them to believe and receive!

> ***Whoever believes in him is not condemned, but whoever does not believe is condemned already, because he has not believed in the name of the only Son of God. Whoever <u>believes in</u> the Son has eternal life; whoever does not obey the Son shall not see life, but the wrath of God remains on him.*** (John 3:18, 36)

It may be that children have to be taught <u>*not to believe*</u> for them to have problems trusting Christ. Every child has not only a sin nature inherited from Adam, but also a God-given consciousness, and the ability to observe nature.

*For what can be known about God is <u>**plain to them**</u>, because God has shown it to them. For his invisible attributes, namely, his eternal power and divine nature, have been clearly perceived, ever since the creation of the world, in the things that have been made. So they are without excuse.* (Romans 1:19, 20)

The "age of accountability" is the time in a child's life they become aware of their own sin. Before that awareness, a child is not able to believe or not believe. Since the blood of Christ was shed for all sin, I believe that His payment covered children in the womb and young children not yet able to believe or not believe. The Bible does clearly state that the children of even one believing parent is considered **"Holy"** or **"set apart."** (1 Corinthians 7:14) Yet, in time, they still need to make their own decision. The age of accountability seems to be flexible; some children understand spiritual matters much earlier than others. And naturally, those who are exposed to the concepts early in life understand it sooner than those that are not exposed.

When dealing with children, we need to see just how much they understand. There are steps of awareness needed for a genuine understanding of believing and receiving. When children are taught foundational Biblical concepts early, it is natural for them in simple faith to believe the message of salvation. Anyone of any age needs to comprehend basic salvation truths: (1) We are accountable to God; (2) We all have done things wrong, sinned, and we need God's help; (3) God requires a blood payment; (4) Jesus came from Heaven to help us and paid for our sin with HIS blood; (5) He died; but after three days was alive, never to die again, Jesus Christ now lives in Heaven; and (6) We each must choose to receive Christ's payment for sin.

One of the problems faced by those who deal with children is that they sometimes respond many times to their need for salvation. Telling children that they do not need to trust Christ again because they have done it at an earlier time is unwise. We do not know at what point a child's faith makes the actual connection with God for salvation. An earlier experience may have been a step of partial understanding. Take time to answer their questions, maybe this time will be their actual point of becoming "born again." It is important to explain to children the difference between becoming a Christian and confessing sin as a Christian. *"If we confess our sins, he is faithful and just to forgive us our sins and to cleanse us from all unrighteousness,"* (I John 1:9). Children can understand the need to wash their hands more frequently than they need to take a full bath. So too with salvation, our original sin, and sin up to that point are under the blood, at the point of salvation. But day by day we sin, and those sins need to be confessed regularly to keep spiritually clean.

Avoid keeping children from genuinely trusting Christ. At the same time be careful to not give children a premature assurance of salvation. Do not hesitate to deal with children; say with Jesus, *"Let the children come to me; do not hinder them, for to such belongs the kingdom of God"* (Mark 10:14).

27. Avoid defensive reaction.

Rather than genuinely listening, in a confrontational situation, people are normally thinking about what they are going to say or do next. If we avoid condemnation or ridicule in our interaction with people, we can avoid putting them on the defensive. If individuals perceive that they are not being attacked and that they are not being pushed, then they are more likely to listen and consider what is being said.

When comfortable in an exchange of ideas, most people are curious about how to get to Heaven. Many are likely to consider what we say when we are friendly and relaxed, rather than "pushy." By respecting people and treating them with kindness, we reflect Christ-likeness. That attitude can help to create a positive witnessing situation.

It is said that the best way to tell if a twenty dollar bill is Counterfeit or genuine is by studying the real thing. The best way to introduce people to our precious Lord and Savior is by presenting Him as He truly is. We do not have to attack peoples' perceptions or wrong concepts. They will make those comparisons as they evaluate the real thing. If they are seeking truth, the Holy Spirit will confirm it to their spirit. *"Ask, and it will be given to you; seek, and you will find; knock, and it will be opened to you"* (Matthew 7:7).

28. Find receptive people.

More people are interested in knowing how to get to Heaven, and are open to hearing the Good News than we might think. Some hesitate to discuss the claims of Christ because they are afraid they might be pushed into something for which they think they are unprepared. Others may not know how to initiate the conversation or feel uncomfortable talking about such a personal subject. But if a situation presents itself in which they are comfortable, they often are willing to listen.

A newspaper reported the plight of a family, trapped by floodwaters, stranded on the roof of their house. They were thirsty. Ironically, surrounded by water, they had nothing to drink—the water was polluted! Even though people may be surrounded by a flood of religion, they need the pure truth of the Gospel in an understandable way. People need the water of life that Jesus referred to, when He spoke to the Samaritan woman at the well, *"whoever drinks of the water that I will give him will never be thirsty again. The water that I will give him will become in him a spring of water welling up to eternal life. The woman said to him, 'Sir, give me this water'"* (John 4:7-29).

The Gospel message is readily available here in America, and there should be no excuse for anyone not to have heard a clear explanation of God's provision for eternity. But the reality is, there is so much pollution that people are fearful of the truth. Few really do see and understand the simple Gospel.

Our challenge is to relate to people so that they will listen and consider the claims of Christ. When the Word of God is planted in hearts, it produces its own fruit of conviction and faith. As people get a glimpse of our wonderful Lord and Savior, they will be more apt to receive Him into their lives. If we as Christians are available and alert, certainly God will arrange a meeting with seeking hearts.

29. Use the buddy system.

Philip was transported to the desert alone to speak with the eunuch in the chariot, (Acts 8:26-39). In everyday contacts, we need to take advantage of opportunities as they come, whether solo or with a partner. Teamwork is important. In the military and many sports, the use of the buddy system is practiced. This consists of two individuals teaming together. Jesus often sent His disciples out in two's. (Mark 6:7)

When we do work with another soul winner, it is important to be in agreement, personally and theologically. When doing witnessing as a team, it is not the time for discussion or expression of different opinions. One individual should do the main conversation; the other partner needs to avoid interrupting or adding to what is being said unless asked. It is easy to disrupt the direction in which the soul winner is trying to lead the conversation. The role of the colleague should include praying for the Lord to lead the partner, to open the understanding of those with whom they are talking, try to keep away interruptions, and be a witness helping to provide protection against possible false accusations. Without a companion as a witness, it is possible to be wrongly accused of improper behavior.

It is especially rewarding to work with others that desire to learn how to win souls to Christ. They in turn, gain encouragement and instruction from participating with a more experienced worker. Becoming a soul winner comes by actually doing, as well as by observation. Watching those that one trained lead someone to the Lord is as great as, or greater than, doing it ourselves. Training others simply multiplies ones influence for the Gospel. Recognize the fact that God can work through the trainee as well as the trainer.

30. Exercise caution in mixed company.

Should men deal only with men, and women with women? Not necessarily, but it is important to use common sense. Concern naturally arises when witnessing to a person of the opposite sex. The key is to follow the leading of the Holy Spirit which is always within the bounds of God's Word.

God's Appointment

In a perfect world, we wouldn't have to be cautious; but the time of innocence in the Garden of Eden did not last long! Be aware that when a woman and man are conversing—improper thoughts and intents can present themselves. If a woman witnesses to a man, or *vice versa*, another person should be present, or else it should always be in a public place. It would never be wise to be alone in private with a member of the opposite sex.

Even if nothing is wrong, the appearance of wrong can be damaging. Remember the story of Joseph being wrongly accused by Potiphar's Wife (Genesis 39:11-20). The same situation can happen to a soul-winner entering someone's home alone, or their allowing someone into their home when they are alone. Be careful also of being alone in a car with someone. Beware of Satan: he is wily, smart, and also a liar. Sadly, one can be accused of wrong doing even when there was none. Satan actively seeks to destroy a soul winner's testimony. Peter warns believers passionately, **"Be sober-minded; be watchful. Your adversary the devil prowls around like a roaring lion, seeking someone to devour"** (1 Peter 5:8). We are in a spiritual war and we need to be alert.

If the Lord opens an opportunity and the situation is proper, then yes, go ahead and speak for Christ.

31. Be one-on-one.

Presenting the Gospel to one individual at a time is preferable. Many times, in a group, there will be one who will not want to make a decision and will make it difficult for the others to do so, even if they wanted to. If it is not feasible to just speak with a single individual, it is important to treat each one in the group as an individual as much as possible, making eye contact, using names, and asking questions.

When dealing with more than one at the conclusion of the decision time, it is wise to choose the person that seems most under conviction to make the commitment to pray first. If the first one you ask says he or she does not want to receive Christ at that time, more than likely, the others will also choose to wait, though not always. Do allow each one the opportunity to respond. Often, I give them a choice saying something along these lines; "That's fine if you are not ready yet. But remember, this decision is important and you should make it as soon as possible." Looking at the next person, I then ask directly, "How about you? Are you ready now to trust Christ?" Allowing each individual to personally respond one at a time rather than in a group prayer helps avoid "copy-cat" decisions.

32. Use fair booths.

Any activity that involves a large group of people can be an excellent opportunity for witnessing, such as The Olympics, various sports activities, and bazaars. I have personally experienced soul-winning at fairs. Each summer, tens of thousands of people attend fairs all over the country. Picture with me the fun and excitement of going to a fair: entertainment, games, food, cotton candy—so much to see and do. Jesus went where the people were and let them know that He cared about them. The goal is to find an opportunity to present Christ to individuals among the thousands of people, as well as encourage Christians to grow in their spiritual lives.

At our first fair, during the summer of 1975, we saw over 50 souls profess to trust Christ as their personal Savior: In 1976, over 100; in 1977, over 150; in 1978, over 260; in 1979, over 250; and in 1980, again over 250 decisions. We continued the fair soul-winning ministry through the years, and were involved in over twenty- two fairs at five different locations.

Also, the Gospel was shared with many who were not ready at the time to make a decision that hopefully will yet. We pray that the seed planted will be watered and that the Holy Spirit will eventually bring about a harvest in other lives touched as well. Tens of thousands of pieces of literature were put into peoples' hands to be read later. There is a Biblical principal we can claim, *"Whoever sows sparingly will also reap sparingly, and whoever sows bountifully will also reap bountifully"* (2 Corinthians 9:6). If we prayerfully sow the Gospel, He will take care of the harvest!

Suggestions for soul winning in a crowded, noisy atmosphere

Ten feet wide by ten feet deep, most fair booths provide a very small space from which to gain the public's attention and engage them in conversation. How can an individual make contact with people in order to visit with them about trusting Christ during such a short window of opportunity? **Pray earnestly in preparation** before the fair for God to both prepare and guide the people He wants to be contacted. Realizing that it is not possible to reach everyone that comes past the booth, **prayerfully seek God's direction as to who to attempt to contact**. Talking to the wrong person could result in being busy and missing the right person.

Attempt to make eye contact with people as they approach the booth. It is reasonable to assume when people resist making eye contact, that they are not open at that time. If people make eye contact, but seek to avoid you, again they probably are not open. If they make eye contact, it gives the chance to see if there can be a connection for conversation.

When they are in front of the booth **have a warm genuine smile**. **Pose a question**, possibly inquire, "May I ask you a question?" Some people will pause. Then **ask if they know for sure that they are going to Heaven when they die**. Most are surprised by such a question and express different reactions. At this point again, it may be discernable who is being led by God to the booth. Many say, "I don't know," or "I hope so." You can **remark**, "I sure don't like the other place and prefer Heaven to Hell!"

Then, **in an animated voice, explain that a man asked Jesus how to get to Heaven**. Jesus answered him, and His answer is recorded in the Bible for us to read. **"May I show you how Jesus answered that question?"** Many times, people are curious about what Jesus said and allow one to share from the Gospel of John, chapter 3, what Jesus had to say. Not necessarily interested in what others may think, people respect and trust HIM to give a valid answer. Being able to read His answer in the Bible is the next best thing to being face-to-face with Jesus, so take individuals straight to the Bible, showing them Jesus' answer to the eternal question.

God's Appointment

As is fairly obvious, it is important to **have an open Bible**, and **point to the verses as they are read**. You can often **ask the individuals to read parts of the verses themselves** instead of just reading the passages to them. This interaction helps keep their attention. If we just read to them, their attention strays more quickly. **Use their name** and **keep eye contact** as much as possible. In this way, they are connected to the Source of Power who brings both understanding and conviction.

If they actually stay for the entire **explanation of how Jesus instructs us to be born again,** we can assume that they have been led to the booth by the Holy Spirit and that He is desiring to use the opportunity to plant Gospel seed, to water seed previously planted, or maybe they are ready for Harvest. If it is apparent that they understand what is said, **ask them if they would mind if you pray**. People at that point would usually hesitate praying themselves, but they do not care if you want to pray. Having already asked their first name, pray, thanking God for the opportunity to visit with the individual(s) about such a serious subject. State that you believe God's promise that if they were to right now trust Jesus Christ to apply the blood He shed on the Cross for sin to their personal account; He would. Pausing, **invite them to pray**, talking to Jesus just like you just did, telling Him that they would indeed like to trust Him and are right now asking Him to pay for their sin and be their Lord and Savior. Praise the Lord, many do choose to accept Christ!

We can gauge how much they understand and desire to call upon the Lord for His salvation if they pray out loud. Many times they state, "What do I say?" By summarizing what was previously discussed, we can suggest that they just, "talk to Jesus and let Him know that you realize you are a sinner and that you are in trouble. You recognize that He left Heaven to come down here to pay for sin so people can receive His payment and request that He apply the blood that He shed on the Cross for sin to their personal sin, their account. If you ask Him to, He says He will!"

If they understand, they should be able to say the prayer in their own words. If they are shy and want to pray silently, let them. After they pray, simply **inquire what is it that they asked God to do**. By hearing their prayer or by their explaining what they asked God, you can tell if they understood. If they pray, "Now I lay me down to sleep," or some other prayer that skirts the issue, let them know that God enjoys hearing their prayer, but they still need to get to the point of receiving the blood payment for sin applied to their sin. Go to prayer again, adding this aspect to their previous prayer. Understand that they were not saved by their prayer—but by their "believing." *"Believe in the Lord Jesus, and you will be saved,"* (Acts 16:31). Their prayer is basically so that we can tell how to help them if needed. If at any point they pull away, they are in God's hands—they are not ready.

If they pause, listen, understand, and pray out loud in a busy, public, crowded fair, we can respect them. Chances are that they mean their confession of trusting Jesus and that God had prepared their heart and directed their steps.

33. Watch for Home deliveries.

Sometimes we do not even have to leave home to find people to talk to about the Lord—God can bring them to our door and into our homes. Two young men, representing a life insurance company, came to our home to explain Medicare and health insurance supplements. Dan and Peter covered the four areas—medical, long term care, life insurance, and retirement income. As they were ending their presentation, I observed that they had mentioned four areas of insurance, but wondered if they had ever heard of Eternal Life Assurance. They both shook their heads; "No," they had not heard of it. But they were curious, and I shared with them that God actually was in the insurance business, through the work of His Son Jesus Christ. In fact, He had made a provision for people to be covered for Heaven. The conversation was interesting.

Finally, as they were leaving, I asked where they felt they were in their spiritual life journey in the relationship to being "born again." Did they consider themselves in light of John's illustration of being "born again" to be *before the point of birth, at birth,* or *after birth?* Both identified themselves to be at the *before birth* stage. James and I had prayer with them, asking God to bring them both to the point of appropriating the blood payment of Christ on the Cross to their personal account. When I asked them if it was alright if I prayed for them to eventually make the decision to receive Christ, thus becoming born again, they gladly said, "Yes." Then I asked if they would let me know after they had made that decision so that we could rejoice with them, they promised. God had designed for our paths to cross for those three hours, and His work in their lives did not end when they walked out our front door. His work will be complete in His own time.

At a later date, another almost identical situation occurred with another insurance man. In his middle thirties, Randy talked about making changes in his life. When I asked him if he was familiar with the term "being born again," he said "No." Very open, however, he wanted to see what Jesus' answer was. When Randy understood, he prayed, receiving Christ as his Savior. As Randy left our home, he warmly remarked, "In all the years of helping other people, I've never received something that helped me personally like this. Thank you!"

34. Talk to telemarketers.

Telemarketers often call—let's consider talking to them! The telephone seems to ring all the time about this or that product. "Annoying" has often described these interruptions, but the callers are guests in our home. Although we may not be interested in their product or service, we could visit with them about *something,* if they have time. I've discovered that such a call can become a witnessing opportunity. If they call us, why not see if the Lord will use it for His glory? Some people respond unpleasantly to telemarketers and just hang up on them. It may be refreshing for telemarketers to talk with someone who treats them as a person of value.

One telemarketer called to talk several times about investing opportunities. One day, I complimented Josh on being an exceptional salesman. Then I commented that the economy seemed to be in a time of transition; it was interesting to speculate about the future. Then I asked if he had given any thought to investments for eternity.

The concept was new to him, and he wondered what I meant. Explaining that we can invest in things eternal but in order to benefit, we have to make sure we get to Heaven to collect. Then I went on to share that Jesus, in John 3, told Nicodemus how a person gets to Heaven by being born again.

Josh responded that his grandmother was in Heaven and that her favorite verse had been John 3:16. Slowly and deliberately, I recited the verse and then stated, "I'm sure she would like you to join her in Heaven when the time comes." Asking Josh's permission, I prayed over the phone. I thanked God for the conversation and asked Him to work in Josh's heart so that he would be born again and able to join his grandmother.

Taken aback by the turn of the conversation, Josh's voice became soft and warm; "You have given me a lot to think about. I appreciate it."

Josh called occasionally after that. Each time he called, after listening to what he had to say, I reminded him that I was praying for him to make a decision to trust Christ and asked how he was doing. He assured me that he was giving salvation "a lot of thought," but he was not quite there yet. He asked me to send him a tract to the company address, with a note on the envelope, "Attention: Josh."

It will be interesting in Heaven to see who might be there!

35. Look for points of connection.

God is interested in people coming to know Jesus as their Savior more than we are. Being aware of God's deep divine love for people puts things into perspective. Our responsibility is to be observant and cooperate with God. Daily activities often provide opportunities for one to engage others in conversation. Ordinary discussions can turn into witnessing opportunities. A point of contact, or lead-in, is a bridge or bond that helps us relate to others, hopefully getting past a self-defensive barrier that people may have. Putting out a feeler, one can see if there is an opening for sowing seed, watering, or harvesting a soul for eternity. God provides points of entry to open conversations, keys to make contact that allow us to present the claims of Christ. When a conversation takes a spiritual turn, we can see how far it can go. Clearly sometimes there is no interest in spiritual truths; other times, there is openness and one can proceed to a conclusion.

Soul winners should keep in mind that only God can work in a person's heart and life for salvation. No human power can bring anyone to Christ. The challenge is to discover the reason God has brought individuals across our path. Jesus said, *"I told you that no one can come to me unless it is granted him by the Father"* (John 6:65).

In summation, soul winning is not about what we can do but what God is already in the process of doing, and we cooperate with Him in that process!

Sample Experiences of Points of Contact

(1) Physical <u>Health</u>

Stopping to sample a health food on display in a grocery store, I listened as the dietician explained the importance of diet, exercise, and the right lifestyle. After I had asked a number of health-related questions, the Holy Spirit provided a lead-in.

"We've been talking about <u>physical health</u> and how important it is. Could I ask you another question? How can we be <u>spiritually healthy</u>?"

The dietician shared things about his personal life and then paused. Continuing, I commented, "I become excited when I find, in the Bible, a man talking to Jesus, asking him how a person gets to Heaven.

(2) Extended <u>Car Warranty</u>

Patrick called again for the fourth time to try to persuade me to purchase an <u>extended car warranty</u>. He said that the automobile would qualify for the program if I signed up immediately and paid the first amount. Thanking him, I said that I really was not interested. How could I not be open to such a wonderful deal, he challenged.

"I'm not sure I'll need to use the car for much longer," I explained.

"Why's that?"

"The way things are going; I'm expecting to go on a trip to Heaven soon and <u>won't be taking the car</u>."

"What?" he asked obviously surprised.

As I explained, his voice turned thoughtful and soft. I told him of the conversation Jesus had with Nicodemus.

(3) **<u>Life Insurance</u>**

Again, a sales person telephoned and persuaded my husband to make an appointment for someone to explain Medicare and various supplemental programs; James commented, "It's probably life insurance." He was right. Two men came and shared information about how to be financially responsible. They said that <u>life insurance</u> was the answer to the unknown future.

When I asked the older gentleman if he had ever heard of <u>Eternal Life Insurance</u>, he shook his head, puzzled and answered, no, he had not. "Eternal Life Insurance provides assurance that a person is going to Heaven when they die. It is wise to be prepared for events now, but it is even more important to be prepared for eternity. We all know eternity in Heaven would be great, but how do we get there? I do not want to go to the other place, Hell!" Both men were semi-curious so I continued telling them about how Jesus' answer to that question is recorded in the Bible.

(4) Qualifying For A Place In Heaven

Curious about taking out a bank loan that would have our house as collateral; I stopped at the bank to talk with a loan officer. She explained that <u>qualifying</u> for their equity loan depended on the assessed value of our home and the terms we would choose for the loan. I thanked her for the information. Before leaving, I asked her how she would suggest an individual could <u>qualify</u> for going to Heaven when they die.

"I do not know how one could get qualified for entrance to Heaven," she replied. Since there was no one waiting for consultation, we had a nice visit.

(5) Hospital Nurse

A nurse came to my husband's hospital room to read his charts and take his vitals. James had passed out one Sunday morning while preaching and was taken to the hospital for tests. She was friendly as she went about her duties. We exchanged small talk. I remarked that her working in the hospital probably made her <u>aware that death can be just around the corner</u> for anyone, adding, "I'm sure glad that this is not all there is to life."

"Yes!" she agreed. She had seen much that made her conscious of mortality.

Mentioning how Jesus gave instructions in the Bible that show us how to get to Heaven, I wwwsaid, "I think <u>everyone should be ready to face eternity</u> and know how to get to Heaven."

She was open, but busy. Gathering her equipment, she had to leave to go to her next patient. As she left James' room, I gave her my Heaven tract and told her I'd love to visit with her again sometime.

(6) Purified Water Test

A salesman for <u>purified water</u> called, wanting to test our water. "Our water tastes fine. I responded. "We are not interested in having it tested," But, I asked, "Do you know of a <u>source for 'living water</u>?'" He had not heard about "living water." I shared with him that Jesus had offered "living water" to a woman at the well, Jesus answered her, *"If you knew the gift of God, and who it is that is saying to you, 'Give me a drink,' you would have asked him, and he would have given you living water"* (John 4:10). The salesman was curious about what Christ meant. I shared with him the conversation Jesus had with Nicodemus about our need to be "born again."

(7) What Did You Think Of The Movie?

The *Passion of Christ* movie was showing in theaters. James and I viewed the moving film depicting Christ's work on the Cross, showing how He provided salvation to all who will believe on Him. On following days as the film was still showing, I took the opportunity to go outside the theater about the time the movie ended, just to watch the faces of people as they left. It was easy to detect concern on faces of some of the people. Going up to different individuals, I asked them <u>what they thought of the movie</u>. This query led to interesting conversations about the reason Christ died on that Cross.

(8) Are You A Parent / Grandparent?

Children can unlock hearts! People are usually thrilled to talk about their children or grandchildren. When we ask individuals <u>how many children they have</u>, they usually eventually respond with the same question to us. If they do, we can say something like, "<u>Children say the cutest things</u> sometimes," which can often lead into a spiritual conversation. I've often shared this account, "One evening, my four-year-old granddaughter asked, 'Is God real, since we can't see Him?'"

I asked, "Is your Grandpa Dale was real?"
She replied, "Yes."
"But he lives in Wisconsin. Can you see him right now?"
"No," she answered.
"God is real and lives in Heaven; we will see him one of these days," I assured her. This can lead to an open door for further conversation.

* * *

Remember, as we seek to witness, expect the Holy Spirit to provide the right opening and then follow through. He is the chief fisherman and He can help us use almost anything to attract, or bait people's interest. After initial conversational contacts, we can ask the Holy Spirit to direct us to a key thought, allowing a smooth lead into a spiritual topic. If there is any interest, be ready to follow through! If it is God's opening, the connection will flow naturally. This is the way Jesus often communicated with people during his ministry on earth.

Jesus made points of contacts in everyday situations. He told the woman at the well, **"Whoever drinks of the water that I will give** *him will never be thirsty again. The water that I will give him will become in him a spring of water welling up to eternal life"* (John 4:14). Another time, Jesus asked, *"Who touched my garments"* (Mark 5:30, 34). A young man called Jesus "Good Master." Jesus asked, *"Why do you ask me about what is good? There is only one who is good"* (Matthew 19:17). Jesus continued the conversation, pointing him to his need for God's claim on his life. What if <u>we</u> used key questions, as Jesus did, at the grocery store, work place, sports events and other places that we go?

36. Practice role playing.

Anyone involved in sports knows the importance of practice. No one just goes out and plays games without practicing. The more practice, the better the game. Just as a coach prepares potential game plans, one can practice potential contact approaches.

At a fast-food restaurant, I stood in line behind two young men. I wondered, "If I were to try to approach them, how could I go about it?" One way could be to say, "Hi! We have a son about your age, middle twenties, I miss him. Would you mind if we sat with you and visited while we eat?"

If I see a young lady in a wheelchair, using my personal experiences, I could say, "Hi. My daughter was in a motorcycle accident a while back. She could have been terribly injured; it really scared me. May I ask what caused you to be in a wheel chair?"

We may not end up following through with possibilities, but it would not hurt to send up a prayer for the individual(s) that sparked your role play. Pray that God would touch their lives some way, somehow, even if you were not able to speak to them. God would be honored and glorified!

37. Remember the experience.

Sometimes people who have trusted Christ at an early age do not necessarily remember the actual date and time. Still, they should remember the general experience and know that they have accepted Christ as their Savior.

Those brought up with a religious background or exposed to the concepts of salvation from their youth may feel that they have always been saved. According to the Bible, no one has ever "always been saved!" If individuals make this claim, they do not understand how salvation is acquired. Everyone should seriously consider just where they stand with God!

The Bible uses marriage as an example of our relationship with Christ, *"Come, I will show you the Bride, the wife of the Lamb"* (Revelation 21:9). Dating someone and being married to that person are two different stages. In the spiritual realm, people may have a dating relationship with Christ without being "married" to Him. Dating might lead up to marriage, but it is not in itself marriage. There is a point of commitment that must take place between the man and woman in order for there to be a marriage. So, too, it is with Christ. Christ has made that commitment already towards us, *"By this we know love, that he laid down his life for us"* (I John 3:16); also, *"We love because he first loved us"* (1 John 4:19). Dying on the Cross was His love commitment to each of us, and His invitation is extended. But we must respond individually and say, "Yes," and actually receive Him as our Lord and Savior. At that point, we literally become His Bride; we have given our consent, and He is our Savior.

While dating James, I met and grew to respect his father. When we stood before the preacher and said, "I do" we were pronounced husband and wife. Afterwards his father called me his "daughter." How did I become a daughter of the father? By accepting the son. When I accepted the son, his father received me. The Gospels explain that when we receive Jesus Christ, the Heavenly Father receives us. He calls us a son or daughter at that time, and according to the Bible, we are indeed accepted into God's family. *"But to all who did receive him, who believed in his name, he gave the right to become children of God"* (John 1:12).

It is easy to let the comment, "I've always been saved" pass, but it is important to let people know that it is not a good answer. To let them continue thinking they have "always been," may be enabling them to spend a Christless eternity in Hell. Using Scripture to challenge their statement may bring doubt to their minds, perhaps allowing someone, even at a later time, to show them from the Bible that they need to consider coming to a point when they are born again, literally born from above (John 3). Jesus says in John 3:3, *"unless one is born again he cannot see the kingdom of God."* If Jesus says that act of believing and receiving is necessary, then it is necessary!

38. Know their standing.

Often, when people are unsure as to whether or not they are a born again Christian, they are not. The marriage analogy can be helpful. If one were to ask someone if they were married, how would they answer? If they are truly married, their immediate response would be, "Yes!" They should also remember the time and place when they made their marriage vows. If they say, "I think I'm married," "hope so," "maybe," or "might be," they probably are not married.

Paul instructs us to, *"examine yourselves, to see whether you are in the faith. Test yourselves. Or do you not realize this about yourselves, that Jesus Christ is in you?—unless indeed you fail to meet the test"* (2 Corinthians 13:5). Knowing our standing with God is the foundation for being able to go forward in Christian growth. People simply can't grow in the Lord until after they are spiritually born. Near the end of the New Testament, John writes,

> *And this is the testimony that God gave us eternal life, and this life is in his Son. Whoever has the Son has life; whoever does not have the Son of God does not have life. I write these things to you who believe in the name of the Son of God that you may know that you have eternal life.* (1 John 5:11-13) What a promise, what a source of comfort and strength!

Another useful analogy is the taking of an airplane trip. It is wise to verify reservations before departure. When there are concerns about whether or not a person has a reservation for Heaven, we can suggest that they confirm their reservation so that they can rest in the comfort of His assurance. There is no need to live in doubt on such an important subject! If there is doubt, then all they need to do is talk to God and make certain, letting Him know that they thought this was taken care of before, but if it is not, right now they are calling upon Jesus Christ to apply the blood He shed on the Cross for sin to their personal sin and to be their Lord and Savior. *"I write these things to you who believe in the name of the Son of God that you may know that you have eternal life"* (1 John 5:13). God wants us to know! The verse above assures us that we can know our reservation is in order.

Sometimes believers lack assurance of their salvation. One of the causes for this can be confusion because of sin in their life. All believers will sin, and although the sins need to be addressed, they do not need to be saved all over again. The new Christian should receive instruction on how to confess sin and receive forgiveness. In the physical realm, even when we have had a bath, we still need to wash our hands often. So too in the spiritual realm, we get soiled by daily sin and need to keep our hands clean. The promise in 1 John states, *"The blood of Jesus his Son cleanses us from all sin. If we say we have no sin, we deceive ourselves, and the truth is not in us. If we confess our sins, he is faithful and just to forgive us our sins and to cleanse us from all unrighteousness. If we say we have not sinned, we make him a liar, and his word is not in us"* (1 John 1:7-10).

Maybe they have been taught that salvation can be lost. Some do not realize that when the Scriptures say *everlasting* or *eternal life*, those words mean "without end." (John 3:16 and many other verses) Additionally, when Jesus says we must be "born born again, literally born from above (John 3), he is referring to being born physically and spiritually—twice. *"That which is born of the flesh is flesh and that which is born of the Spirit is spirit"* (John 3:6).

Just as Paul wrote, *"I ask you also, true companion, help these women, who have labored side by side with me in the gospel together with Clement and the rest of my fellow workers, whose names are in the book of life."* (Philippians 4:3). Our names are written in The Book of Life! Wonderful peace flows from the knowledge that being "born from above" is a position we can achieve!

39. Be patient with multiple decisions.

If people say that they have been "saved many times," they do not understand what "saved" means. Jesus said in John 3:3 that *"unless one is born **again** he cannot see the kingdom of God."* He did not say again and again and again and again and again. Being born again is being born a second time, once physically and once spiritually. There are some who keep asking God to save them over and over again, but if they are sincere, once is sufficient. However, if a connection was not actually made with God at the time of salvation, then another point of contact would be necessary.

Whenever someone is confused and concerned about their standing with God, they need to be sensitively dealt with. My heart aches when someone seeks spiritual help and is told, "You've already done that; you do not need to do it again." It is true we need to be saved only once, but sometimes an individual has prayed for salvation without proper understanding or heart attitude. In that case, they may need to do it this time for real!

After hearing a clear explanation of <u>what</u> salvation is and <u>how</u> it is obtained, individuals should know if they truly have been born from above. The Holy Spirit will confirm in their heart their condition. No one should tell someone else, if they are or are not saved. Individuals should know in their own heart where they stand with God. If they have already accepted Christ, they do not have to repeat that transaction. However, if there is any doubt, then they should pray something like this, "If I haven't before, I am now, Lord Jesus, trusting you to pay for my sin and give me your *everlasting life!*" Why live with doubt? With eternity in Heaven or Hell at stake, it is more than foolish to presume when it is so easy to make certain!

It is wise to explain that those who have been born again into God's family also need to confess sins on a daily basis. *"If we confess our sins, he is faithful and just to forgive us our sins and to cleanse us from all unrighteousness"* (1 John 1:9). When individuals show interest in becoming a Christian, I believe even if they do not fully understand, God has promised that the Holy Spirit will continue to work in their hearts until they come to an understanding or proper heart attitude, *"And I am sure of this, that he who began a good work in you will bring it to completion at the day of Jesus Christ"* (Philippians 1:6). It is important not to leave individuals one step short of Heaven; do not dismiss someone's distress of soul! If they are concerned, there is a reason; their problem needs to be resolved.

40. Discern between religious and "born again."

Judas Iscariot was one of the original twelve disciples called by Jesus Christ. He was with Jesus for three and a half years. He heard and saw everything, participated in healings, and saw the miracles that Jesus did. The other disciples had no idea that Judas was not a true believer—even up to the Last Supper and Judas's leading the Roman soldiers to arrest Jesus. But Jesus knew. If Jesus and the twelve disciples had an unsaved man in their midst, imagine the possibility of having the same situation in our churches.

I have met pastors who have told me that they were saved after they had been in the pastorate for years. Likewise deacons and Sunday school teachers have given testimony of being saved at a later date. It has been theorized that the average church, after the Rapture of the true body of Christ, will experience business as usual. Not only is our world filled with unsaved people, so are our churches!

People can be religious without being born again, literally born from above (John 3). This was my case for years. Being religious is not the same thing as being a Christian! Jesus sternly warns us: *"On that day many will say to me, 'Lord, Lord, did we not prophesy in your name, and cast out demons in your name, and do many mighty works in your name?' And then will I declare to them, 'I never knew you; depart from me, you workers of lawlessness'"* (Matthew 7:22, 23).

Often, when religious people take instruction on how to lead souls to Christ, they realize that believing "in" and "on" Christ is something they have not yet done themselves, and at that time they make their personal decision for Christ. I was deeply religious before discovering that although Christ died for everyone, believing that truth does not automatically make them a Christian, nor does acting like a Christian make a person a Christian.

Yes, I thought I loved God and Jesus. Yes, I went to church, was baptized, took communion, read the Bible, prayed. I believed Christ died for all and thought that was enough. However, though He did die for all, we must all, individually, at one point appropriate that blood payment to our personal account. We must receive it, and we must be "born again." It has been said that eighteen inches separates many from Heaven—the distance from the head to the heart. Knowledge must be acted on! If someone is standing on a train track and believes a train is coming, they get off the track. If they remain on the track, their belief is not producing the necessary action to save them. We are already in trouble and are under condemnation, we need to be rescued,

> *For God did not send his Son into the world to condemn the world, but in order that the world might be saved through him. Whoever believes in him is not condemned, but whoever does not believe is condemned already. Whoever does not obey the Son shall not see life, but the wrath of God remains on him.* (John 3:17, 18, 36)

A passive confidence in a loving God does not rescue us! It's not that we fall into judgment with God, we are born into it. There is nothing we need to do to get into trouble, we already are and need to get out. The Bible is very stern on that matter, *"For all have sinned, and fall short of the glory of God"* (Romans 3:23). *"Wherefore, as by one man sin entered into the world, and death by sin; and so death passed upon all men, for that all have sinned:* [for that: or, in whom] *Adam sinned and death came upon all"* (Romans 5:12). *"As it is written: None is righteous, no, not one; no one understands; no one seeks for God. All have turned aside; together they have become worthless; no one does good, not even one"* (Romans 3:10-12).

Many sermons are preached in which everything that is said is great—but one part is left out, the part about how one actually receives God's atonement for sin. This is a very necessary step!

It was not until I was shown how a person becomes a Christian that I actually received God's forgiveness of sin and according to the Bible, was declared by God to be a part of His family! Some amusing examples illustrating this are: "going through a garage does not make one a car," or "going to McDonald's does not make one a big Mac," True also, "going to a church does not make an individual a Christian." I cannot remember a time when I did not love God, but I was not saved until the age of fifteen. Because of that background, I am deeply concerned that religious people should make certain that they have personally asked Christ to be their Savior.

Although we should not assume people are Christians, I have met, as you probably have, people whose spirits give testimony to our spirits that they are indeed genuinely believers. Some people just have that glow, that joy, that love for the Lord that cannot be mistaken. However, the majority who call themselves Christians, we just have to take their word for it because there is no outward proof. The short book of 1st John deals at length with what our lives should be like if we are truly born again Christians. If those things are not present in one's life, then one should be seriously challenged to mean business with God and make sure the foundation is properly laid.

International students are often confused about America being a "Christian" nation on one hand, yet they witness the dark ugly side of life in America that is a contradiction. I simply explain that there are two different kinds of Christians: "coat Christians" and "heart Christians." Some people wear their Christianity like a coat, taking it off and on, for convenience. Heart Christians are different; Christ is in their heart and He is there, regardless of circumstances. They are what they say they are. Just this simple illustration makes them smile and assure me that "yes" they have met both kinds and now understand the difference.

Nicodemus was a very religious person, but had not previously understood the necessity for a new birth through the work of Jesus Christ that perfect Lamb of God who shed His blood on the Cross. Jesus explained to him what had been God's plan through the ages, ever since God provided Adam and Eve with a coat from the lamb. Another verse in the same chapter repeats the necessity

God's Appointment

for us to "believe" and "receive," *"Truly, truly, I say to you, unless one is born again he cannot see the kingdom of God"* (John 3:3). *"Whoever believes in the Son has eternal life; whoever does not obey the Son shall not see life, but the wrath of God remains on him"* (John 3:36). History tells us that Nicodemus did become born again and was one of two who stood for Jesus at His trial before the Sanhedrin.

In the womb, my children had life. They moved, kicked, and responded to stimuli, but they were not yet born. Their development in the womb brought them to the point of birth. So, too, the Holy Spirit works for a period of time in our lives to bring us to the point of birth into God's family! Being deeply religious is not salvation, but it can lead up to that point. I often have asked people where they think they are in their spiritual journey: Are they still in the womb before birth, in the channel at birth, or have already been born? Many times, after reading how Jesus described being born again in John 3, religious individuals recognize that they are actually "before birth" and not yet saved!

According to the Scriptures, both Old and New, by our works we can never be good enough to earn Heaven. *"For by grace you have been saved through faith. And this is not your own doing; it is the gift of God, not a result of works, so that no one may boast. For we are his workmanship, created in Christ Jesus for good works, which God prepared beforehand, that we should walk in them"* (Ephesians 2:8-10). We all—even religious people, need to open our heart to the redemptive work of Christ on the Cross and be born again, literally born from above (John 3).

Can we identify unsaved individuals? Asking people if they know for sure that they are going to Heaven when they die, or asking them how they would describe what is necessary in order to be a Christian, may provide a clue. An almost infallible guide is finding out what individuals think they have to do to become a Christian. Their answer will often make it clear just where they stand with God. A true 'born again' believer knows that he/she did not become a Christian by living a good life or doing good works.

We may ask this question: "In your opinion, what would you say a person has to do to get to Heaven?" People answer that question in many different ways. Rather than disagreeing with an answer which may be scripturally unsound, we can respond by saying, "Yes, that is important in our society—but what does a person have to do to become a Christian?" Then we can offer to take a few minutes to show them Jesus' explanation. Sometimes after sharing their own opinion, people are interested in listening to what the Scriptures do say; we can then show them from the Bible God's requirements!

41. Hear explanations.

Sometimes when conversing with people, I ask them how they would tell someone else how to get to Heaven. Their explanation provides a glimpse into their own position with Christ. Without putting down their answer, we can remark that many people often have not given much thought to the question and do not know how to give an answer. Asking them if they would be interested in how you answer the question, tweaks their curiosity and they are interested in what the Bible does say. They want to listen to your explanation and understand the truth.

Any time we avoid putting people into the situation of trying to defend their own position, it gives them freedom to consider Biblical instructions. Encountering Christians who have a good answer to the question, "How does one get to Heaven," is an encouragement to us. It also strengthens the one that gave the testimony. We are encouraged to verbalize our faith, *"If you confess with your mouth that Jesus is Lord and believe in your heart that God raised him from the dead, you will be saved"* (Romans 10:9).

42. Reach people in cults.

Invariably you will encounter people who are involved in a cult. If we believe in God, we must also believe Gods' warning that there is an enemy. *"Be sober-minded; be watchful. Your adversary the devil prowls around like a roaring lion, seeking someone to devour"* (1 Peter 5:8). When lions hunt, they normally seek out the stragglers, the young and weak. A herd of buffalos in times of danger form a circle around their young and sick. They face the source of danger as a unit. Predators do not risk such a situation but rather seek to separate their prey from a group. A good reason to be an active member of a healthy church is to give or receive protection.

There are so many cults. To try to address each one would take too much space. There are tools available to help you understand the basic doctrines of various groups and religions. We do not need to "reinvent the wheel." Marvelous testimonies abound of those who have been saved and delivered from cults and various religions. It happens frequently! I do want to encourage you not to be afraid to talk to people who are trapped in a cult or religion. If God brings your paths to cross, I believe it is for the purpose to plant seeds of doubt in their heart and mind and a curiosity as to what is real truth. Remember Jesus said, *"Truly, truly, I say to you, we speak of what we know, and bear witness to what we have seen, but you do not receive our testimony"* (John 3:11). The Holy Spirit can use you to begin a work or continue in a work of deliverance.

You may find that people of different religions and cults are not comfortable around you. You do not have to do or say a thing. The Holy Spirit within you does not agree with their spirit. There will be a clash between the two spirits without a word being spoken by you. I think demonic spirits are like cockroaches. They love to hide in the darkness and scatter when you turn on the light.

The devil is not against religion—he likes to use it to gain power for his own purpose. He is full of tricks and has a large variety of tools at his disposal. Various ticks work successfully with different people. His goal is to lay a foundation of truth but to deviate in the area of connecting with God for Salvation. All he has to do is take the truth and twist it. Missing the mark of salvation by an inch or a mile is still missing the mark. A religious cult member can be as unsaved as an atheist or a devil worshiper. The Bible instructs us to *"Beware of false prophets, who come to you in sheep's clothing but inwardly are ravenous wolves"* (Matthew 7:15). It also informs us, *"But false prophets also arose among the people, just as there will be false teachers among you, who will secretly bring in destructive heresies... And many will follow their sensuality, and because of them the way of truth will be blasphemed. And in their greed they will exploit you with false words..."* (2 Peter 2:1-3).

Recognizing the strategy of a cult to entwine one in various subjects is important to avoid the rehearsal of their packaged sell and consider up-front the basics. One of the most obvious heresies is what they believe concerning the Trinity of God: the Father, the Son, and the Holy Spirit. Be careful of feeling prideful and using your own human reasoning. Humbly assert relevant Scriptures. Normally witnessing to cult members consists of planting seeds for the Holy Spirit to nurture. Doubt in what they have been instructed to believe has to come before they can accept truth.

Years ago, I interviewed Fred & Elaine Reiter. They were born again Christians, went to Bible school, and pastored a church for six years. Becoming disillusioned, they left the ministry. While spiritually wounded, they were embraced by a Cultic Church for years. God eventually opened their eyes and the Reiters escaped but suffered heart break, hurt, wasted years, and family separation. They stated that they should have known better, but they did not; they were hurting and the group was initially loving and caring towards them.

Aside from the groups that are normally recognized to be cults, most of us are unaware of the fact that churches can be cultic. It is said that there are around 8,000 to 10,000 abusive Cultic Churches in America. There are a large number of different cults, so it is wise to be aware of common characteristics.

Cults:

- Mix truth with error. They seek to gain trust with truth then later introduce their false doctrines
- Use verses out of context. They seek to build with bits of Scriptures taken from here and there to justify their beliefs.
- Use deception. They feel lying is justified to achieve a desired end result.
- Use fear, guilt and threats. They believe being a member of their group is the only way to Heaven.
- Foster rigidity-authoritarian and dictatorial structure. They claim they are helping one to be obedient to the Lord but in reality, it is obedience to the leader.

- Seek to control and manipulate. They do not want individuals to think or feel for themselves.
- Discourage questions
- Make leaving painful
- Control peoples' minds

The best way to recognize if something is a counterfeit is to be well acquainted with the genuine. Know what you believe so that your foundation is not only unshakable but capable of reaching out to others to rescue them.

Witnessing to family members and friends that are caught in a cult takes unconditional love, patience, and lots of prayer. Bind the spirit of deception in their lives and keep the lines of communication with them as open as possible. Be encouraged, people are being delivered from the cults. God specializes in what we consider impossible!

43. Win people in other religions.

There are a lot of different religions around the world, it is not majorly Christian. We should care that all people, regardless of what their background is, have an opportunity to hear the Gospel. When we enter Heaven's gates, we will be met by many people originally from other backgrounds who accepted Jesus Christ as their Lord and Savior.

Missionaries have done a wonderful job overseas. It is interesting, however, to observe that God brings people from other nations and backgrounds into our area of influence. My personal conviction is that God is bringing people from all nations to the United States to introduce them to Christians who will share their faith with them. College students from around the world come here to learn our language and customs. We should be alert for opportunities and speak up for Christ. We can reach out to them and share how God has provided a way of salvation through Jesus Christ. Do not be fearful of witnessing to people with a different religious background. Christian love is the key to unlocking hearts.

Realize that the power behind both cults and other religions is Satan. Demon possession and demonic influence are both realities. But remember, *"Little children, you are from God and have overcome them, for he who is in you is greater than he who is in the world"* (1 John 4:4). We do not have to be fearful of Satan and his demons, but we do need to be respectful. I have heard Christians flippantly challenge Satan-acting like they were capable of giving him orders. We have no power against Satan or his followers. Christ does, not us. We can hide behind Christ and agree in prayer for Christ to rebuke Satan.

God sees the hearts of people throughout the whole world. There are people longing to know how to "die right." He can make the path of searching hearts and willing messengers to connect. We must care and be in step with God on this. There is a series of fifteen messages called ***The Pineapple Story*** by veteran missionary to Indonesia, Otto Koning. It exercises one's heart to see the good news of salvation through Jesus Christ shared with waiting hearts! (Available through Institute in Basic Life Principles, Box 1, Oak Brook, IL 60522-3001; iblp.org)

For years, God has asked individuals and families to go to other countries to proclaim the good news of salvation. **"How then will they call on him in whom they have not believed? And how are they to believe in him of whom they have never heard? And how are they to hear without someone preaching?"** (Romans 10:14). Have you considered going?

CHAPTER 21

Tips for Soul-Winning 44-51

Various Observations

44. Use available time.

Some opportunities provide sufficient time to share the Gospel; others allow only a short window of time. We may be able to provide considerable details if there is no need to hurry, but we should also know how to present the Gospel concisely. Being aware of the time available to us is part of being sensitive to the situation. We need to be prepared to be flexible. Additionally, if we have raised their curiosity, giving them a Gospel tract gives them information they can continue to consider.

For example, avoid causing someone to miss their bus connection to listen to you, unless they choose to do so. It may be that someone would choose to catch a later bus because they want to know more. But it should be their decision and not something we have caused that would make them angry.

45. Pray for the unsaved.

Pre-written prayers or spontaneous prayers, both must come from the heart. Sometimes prayers are written that can be repeated. Deciding what needs to be included in the prayer ahead of time helps us not to forget important items. Some specific, written prayers are especially helpful for spiritual warfare. For example, in Ephesians 6:10-18, Paul instructs believers to put on the whole armor of God and to pray. Jesus Himself provided a pattern for us to follow using "The Lord's Prayer." (Matthew 6:9) One fact is certain, prayer is powerful! Through communicating with the Lord, believers can claim ground for Christ in their own lives as well as in other lives.

In his book *The Adversary*, Mark Bubeck has shared a number of prayers for spiritual warfare that can be adapted to each situation. The author graciously freely gives permission for these prayers to be shared. One such prayer:

FRIEND OR LOVED ONE

Heavenly Father, I bring before You and the Lord Jesus Christ one who is very dear to You and to me_____. I have come to see that Satan is blinding and binding (him or her) in awful bondage. (He or she) is in such a condition that (he or she) cannot or will not come to You for help on (his or her) own. I stand in for (him or her) in intercessory prayer before Your throne. I draw upon the Person of the Holy Spirit that He may guide me to pray in wisdom, power, and understanding.

In the name of the Lord Jesus Christ, I ask you to loose _____ from the awful bondage the powers of darkness are putting upon (him or her). I ask you to bind all powers of darkness set on destroying (his or her) life. I ask you to bind them in the name of the Lord Jesus Christ and forbid them to work. I ask you to bind up all powers of depression that are seeking to cut _____ off and imprison (him or her) in a tomb of despondency. I bring in prayer the focus of the Person and work of the Lord Jesus Christ directly upon _____ to his/her strengthening and help. I bring the mighty power of my Lord's incarnation, crucifixion, resurrection, ascension, and glorification directly against all forces of darkness seeking to destroy_____.

I pray, Heavenly Father, that You may open _____'s eyes of understanding. Remove all blindness and spiritual deafness from (his or her) heart. As a priest of God in _____'s life, I plead Your mercy over (his or her) sins of failure and rebellion. I claim all of (his or her) life united together in obedient love and service to the Lord Jesus Christ. May you, Spirit of the Living God, focus your mighty work upon _____ to grant (him or her) repentance and to set (him or her) completely free from all that binds (him or her). In the name of the Lord Jesus Christ, I thank You for Your answer. Grant me the grace to be persistent and faithful in my intercessions for _____, that You may be glorified through this deliverance, Amen.

46. Take people.

For years people took a horse drawn carriage around to pick up people for church. At that time it was not car exhaust fumes, but rather horse discharge that polluted the streets. D.L. Moody (1837-1899) was known for going to children's homes, waking them up Sunday mornings, helping them get ready and stopping to buy bread on the way to church so that his charges were not hungry. Later church buses and vans could be seen making their rounds.

Even in our timeframe, it would be appropriate to consider people that cannot provide their own transportation to church. Why not fill up cars and freely give rides to young people, handicapped, elderly no longer able to drive, or those who do not have transportation? We need to be aware that laws have changed, one used to be able to fill a vehicle to overflowing, but now everyone in the vehicle has to be securely seat buckled.

How sad to see cars pulling into church parking lots with empty seats. Why not fill up the vehicles! Jesus encouraged, **"Go out into the highways and hedges, and compel them to come in, that my house may be filled"** (Luke 14:23).

47. Watch for Satan's interference.

Have you ever wondered if Satan knows our thoughts? Satan is limited; he cannot necessarily know our thoughts, but we do have to give him credit for being an apt student of human behavior. His number one job is to keep people from getting saved. However, once a person is saved, Satan's next priority is to keep them from sharing their faith with anyone else. He would prefer it if we stayed in our own religious groups. We easily become keepers of the aquarium instead of fishers of men. Why is it so hard to win souls? Because Satan fights soul winning with a passion!

Satan may not know our silent prayers, however, if we pray for someone out loud or he is able to discern our intent from observing us, we can be sure that he gives his demons and followers charge to interfere. But our God is greater than the enemy! *"Those who trust in the LORD are like Mount Zion, which cannot be moved, but abides forever. As the mountains surround Jerusalem, so the LORD surrounds his people, from this time forth and forevermore"* (Psalm 125:1, 2).

As a speaker recently pointed out ignoring Satan will not make him go away. We need to be alert and be aware of our enemy, but we do not have to be fearful. God the Father, the Son and the Holy Spirit are way more intelligent and powerful than Satan. But Satan is much smarter and stronger than we are. We need to hide "in Christ" and have God defeat him. We can be on the defensive as well as the offensive in the battle for souls for whom Christ died. When God is at work bringing men, women, boys, and girls to salvation, He will prevail!

48. It's all about God.

Beware of considering one's self more spiritual than others because of things that are cultural or personal taste. The goal is to be Biblical. The length of a person's hair does not make one person more spiritual than another. Nor does the way one dresses necessarily determine that judgment.

How will God be able to have complete unity in eternity with people from every generation, beginning with Adam and Eve to the last? For instance, my parent's taste in music is different from my children's taste in music, and I am somewhere in between. Just a three generational span of Christians reflect a difference of taste in musical expression.

There will be music in Heaven—whose taste will it be? Remember when the church was young, it grew out of a Jewish foundation? The early church leaders wanted to apply the rules that God had given to Israel to the church; circumcision and avoiding the eating of food that had been offered to idols. Paul had a battle on his hands when God called him to go to the gentiles and not to add converts to the Jewish synagogue, but rather to the Church of Christ! (Acts 10:45-11:26) We are not to burden converts with our rules, but rather they are to follow Christ. In Heaven it will be God's taste in music, along with everything else. His rules will be expressed and followed, and all will enjoy it! Even the angels express,

"Holy, holy, holy is the LORD of hosts; the whole earth is full of his glory!"And the foundations of the thresholds shook at the voice of him who called, and the house was filled with smoke. And I said: 'Woe is me! For I am lost; for I am a man of unclean lips, and I dwell in the midst of a people of unclean lips; for my eyes have seen the King, the LORD of hosts!'" (Isaiah 6:3-5).

Eternity will be all about God, not about us. We will worship Him just how *He* wants to be worshipped, not how *we* want to worship Him. Wouldn't it be nice if such were the case here on earth now? Let us not limit our ability to reach people by having unimportant differences separate us from being able to share the Good News of salvation!

49. Use names.

"My name is Gloria. What is your name?" Sharing my name first when opening a conversation, makes people more comfortable to share with me their name. Knowing their first name is sufficient since some people are guarded about giving their last name. Since all of us appreciate hearing our name, using a person's first name helps conversations to be friendly. We are showing interest in others by using their names, especially when coupled with good eye contact.

50. Consider the age of accountability.

The age of accountability is reached when one realizes that they have sin in their life. If individuals are not mature enough to recognize that they have sinned and that the consequence of sin is separation from God, then they are not yet ready to accept Christ.

Usually, mature individuals know they are sinners and can identify with the fact that they are separated from and uncomfortable in the presence of a Holy God. When they are not ready to admit their sinful condition, they are either lying, not being convicted by the Holy Spirit of sin, or they are not ready. Wait until they are ready! Paul states, *"For all have sinned and fall short of the glory of God,"* (Romans 3:23). Most people are already aware that they are sinners; they simply need to know how to escape from the sin trap.

51. Build a strong foundation.

In effective communication, one must reach people where they are. Avoid assuming that people know more than they do when talking with them about Christ. Some are familiar with religious terms and Biblical accounts—others are not. Including necessary background and definition of terms takes time, but provides a solid basis upon which a decision can be made. Even if people do not understand what you are saying, they may not want to seem ignorant or may hesitate to ask questions. Few honestly say, "No, I don't know what you mean."

By asking questions as one shares the Gospel and by watching their expressions, we often can see when there is a lack of comprehension or understanding. This interaction helps one to assist others to make decisions when they are ready to make them.

Some individuals do have a Biblical foundation and can relate easily to what we are saying. Others have little or no church background, or worse, have been taught falsehoods or false doctrine! One of the greatest challenges anyone faces is unlearning what was thought to be true, but is not! An excellent book for laying a thorough Biblical foundation is <u>The Stranger on the Road to Emmaus</u> by John R. Cross. It is translated into a variety of languages including

Arabic, and it is used by a number of missionaries on various fields. *(Cross, J.R. (2003) The Stranger on the road to Emmaus. GoodSeed International.)*

CHAPTER 22

Tips for Soul-Winning 52-62

※

Different Methods

52. Make the Gospel clear.

Whatever the method used, making the Gospel message clear is the goal. People need to be able to follow and understand what we say. Also, it is easy to make our presentation of the simple plan of salvation more complicated then it is. Stick to the Bible and what Jesus Christ presented; prayerfully fight against making the Gospel unnecessarily complex!

Jimmy DeYoung is a well known preacher who lives in Jerusalem. During a television interview, he was asked to present the Gospel to the audience. He stated that it was as simple as ABC: Admit you're a sinner, Believe Christ died for sin, and Call upon Jesus to pay for your sin.

The Apostle Paul gave us "the Gospel in a nutshell:" *"Christ died for our sins in accordance with the Scriptures, that he was buried, that he was raised on the third day in accordance with the Scriptures, and that he appeared to Cephas, then to the twelve. Then he appeared to more than five hundred brothers at one time"* (I Corinthians 15:3-6). He also said, *"Everyone who calls on the name of the Lord will be saved."* (Romans 10:13).

Another approach is the "bad news, good news" illustration. The bad news is that we all have a terminal disease of sin; the good news is there is a cure! The prescription which brings a cure is the blood of Christ applied to our sin. Just as medication does not help when it sits unused, every individual needs to apply God's remedy. One must take the prescription Christ died to give. *"For God so loved the world, that he gave his only Son, that whoever believes in him should not perish but have eternal life"* (John 3:16).

Any effective approach in sharing the Gospel includes certain basic doctrines or ingredients. 1). Understand that we are sinners separated from God. 2). Believe that Jesus Christ is God. 3). He came and died to pay for sin. 4). He was resurrected and now is at home again in Heaven. 5). One needs to personally call upon the name of the Lord in order to have the blood payment applied. Many adhere to 1-4 but neglect the 5th which is vitally important!

Different circumstances can call for different approaches. We need to be sensitive to the leading of the Holy Spirit! A complete listing of soul-winning approaches would be too numerous to try to cover here. However, the majority of Christians' style of witnessing is that they do not have one.

As individuals begin to care about lost souls, they develop a style of witnessing that works best for them. The method I like to use, that works best for me, is Jesus' explaining to Nicodemus how a person needs to be born again. Chapter 1 of this book shows that presentation. The plan of salvation, however, is interwoven throughout the entire Bible, Old and New Testament and can be found about anywhere one looks!

53. Use "The Romans Road."

As one is in the process of developing their own witnessing style, they need to start somewhere. "The Romans Road" has been used by many, including myself, as a starting point while gaining confidence in witnessing. Eventually, one comes to use a method more extensively than others, but not necessarily exclusively. With various people and circumstances, different methods may be used.

The "Romans Road" uses Scriptures from a neighborhood of verses in the New Testament book of Romans.

1). *"As it is written: 'None is righteous, no, not one'"* (Romans 3:10)
2). *"For all have sinned and fall short of the glory of God"* (Romans 3:23
   "Therefore, just as sin came into the world through one man, and death through sin, and so death spread to all men because all sinned" (Romans 5:12),
3). *"For the wages of sin is death, but the free gift of God is eternal life in Christ Jesus our Lord"* (Romans 6:23).
4). *"But as for the cowardly, the faithless, the detestable, as for murderers, the sexually immoral, sorcerers, idolaters, and all liars, their portion will be in the lake that burns with fire and sulfur, which is the second death"* (Revelation 21:8).
5). *"But God shows his love for us in that while we were still sinners, Christ died for us"* (Romans 5:8).
6). *"Because, if you confess with your mouth that Jesus is Lord and believe in your heart that God raised him from the dead, you will be saved....For everyone who calls on the name of the Lord will be saved"* (Romans 10:9, 10, 13).

Some soul winners find it helpful to mark in the margins of their Bible, next to each verse, the location of the next verse. This makes it necessary to only have to remember the location of the first verse.

If individuals are interested in using "The Romans Road," Larry Moyer with EvanTell (www.evantell.org) has an exceptional ministry of training people in this method.

54. Use Jesus' conversation.

I appreciate the John 3 approach because it allows what they call "cold contact" witnessing. Warm contacts are people that you are already acquainted with. In witnessing there needs to be a trust factor established that makes the person or persons trust that you know what you are talking about. The whole drawback of a cold contact is building a beginning foundation of who you are and establishing confidence that you know what you are talking about. People wonder, "Why should I listen to your opinion when I have my own concepts or belief?" "My religious training is as valid as yours." Or, "There are many opinions out there, why should I be interested in yours?"

With the John 3 method, I just have to arouse curiosity as to what it was that Jesus said in the matter. He has the credentials that will allow people to believe what is being said. I do not have to build the confidence that I know how to get to heaven. Rather, I perk someone's curiosity as to what Jesus said about it.

It also allows me to deal with established religious people. It isn't what I am saying, but rather what Jesus is saying. He commands more confidence than I do. It allows me to be in a third party position with the situation being between the person and the Holy Spirit. I am simply connecting the two and observing the results. Comparisons with what people have been taught do not demand that they make a choice between what they have been taught and what I am saying, but rather what Jesus says. How beautiful it is to see the light of understanding go on as the verses flow together and explain what the original problem is and what needs to be done. The conscience is stirred and the Holy Spirit will continue working on their spirit to consider the claims of Christ. Even if one is not able to follow through with them to a conclusion, the Holy Spirit will.

Some people are resistant to the concept of skipping around from one text to another to present a theory. Many religious persuasions build a case picking verses randomly to present a concept that they want to prove. They start first with what they believe and search to find proof to support their chosen theories. With John 3, one is simply explaining what is written in the Scriptures, letting it flow and explain itself. I personally have the desire to understand what the Scriptures teach and what the author had in mind when it was written- rather what someone could make it to say. I find people are more comfortable when there isn't a lot of turning pages back and forth.

When I first began witnessing, I used the Romans road which is an excellent method. But for me personally, John 3 fits better. The

Way of the Master approach presents the Ten Commandments and challenges one to consider where they stand and that they are guilty. If they are judged guilty, they deserve the punishment of sin. The good news is someone volunteered to pay the penalty for that sin. This again is an excellent method. The John 3 approach, however, goes back earlier than the Ten Commandments and explains the origin of sin and how we got into the position that we are in to start. I explain that we all have sinned, including me, and our need of the blood payment of Jesus Christ to meet the obligation of a Holy God.

I have yet to find anyone who thought they were without sin and good enough on their own: one who didn't need the sacrificial payment Christ made. I also like the idea of presenting the opportunity for people to "right now" make that decision before God. If they are not ready, then I like to make sure that they know how to when they are ready. Ask their permission to pray for them, requesting that God will bring them to the point of trusting Christ. Finally, I like to ask if they will let me know after they do so that I can rejoice with them.

I try to avoid pressuring people to do something they are not ready yet to do. It could be a false confession. It is said that the majority of Christians we believe to be backsliding are in fact, not actually a Christian yet at all. How tragic it would be to think that one had made a decision that was not completed.

This method makes it easy to transition from a normal conversation into a spiritual topic. One can say, "I ran across something that is really exciting! A conversation recorded in the Bible, between Jesus and a man named Nicodemus. He asked Jesus how one gets to Heaven. Jesus answered him and the answer is recorded in the Bible for us to study. That is a topic I personally am interested in. I certainly do not want to go to the other place. Everything I've heard about it makes me not want to go there." Can I share with you what Jesus said?" My enthusiasm and their curiosity often open the door, and I pull a Bible out of my purse, open it to the passage and away we go!

When we get to the part of being a sinner, I explain, "I am a sinner, we all are." Rather than saying, "You are a sinner." This helps people identify themselves without causing them to become defensive. People know that they fall short. The difference between born again believers and lost people is that Christians are sinners saved by grace, while unbelievers are sinners without Christ.

After explaining the conversation between Jesus and Nicodemus, one should conclude by inviting the individual(s) to pray. If they are unwilling, ask if you can pray. In that prayer, include a simple and short synopsis of the plan of salvation. Pausing in the prayer, ask them again if they would like to pray. If they would, then have them. One can tell people generally what to pray, "Just tell God what you want Him to do, to apply Christ's shed blood to your account right now," can be helpful. Try not to lead them word by word through a prayer. They should be able to put it in their own words if they understand and actually trust Christ

After an individual has received Christ as Savior, they should be shown Scripture verses that give assurance of salvation such as, *"And this is the testimony, that God gave us eternal life, and this life is in his Son. Whoever has the Son has life; whoever does not have the Son of God does not have life. I write these things to you who believe in the name of the Son of God that you may know that you have eternal life"* (1 John 5:11-13).

In addition, young Christians should be encouraged to share publicly their new relationship in the Lord. Sometimes, if there is someone else close by, you can ask them if they would be willing to share with that person what they just did.

Also important is encouraging new believers to become members of a Bible-believing church as instructed, *"Not neglecting to meet together, as is the habit of some, but encouraging one another, and all the more as you see the Day drawing near* [Rapture]*"* (Hebrews 10:25). The local church is God's design for raising new Christians to maturity, providing backing and fellowship. Satan works hard to divide and separate. There is strength in Christian fellowship and instruction from other Christians! Of all the Christians I have met, those who were willing to follow the Lord in baptism and joined a fellowship of believers are the ones who have grown and became successful in their Christian lives.

To see a complete presentation of the conversation between Jesus and Nicodemus you can refer back to Chapter one of this book.

55. Distribute tracts.

Many people have come to know Christ through the use of tracts. Tracts are written testimonies or instructions designed to attract someone to read them. Whether short, long, colorful, or creative, all are designed to present spiritual truths to the reader. Not only are tracts designed to be interesting to read, they record Scriptures and thoughts that can be studied and mulled. Some are read right away while others are tucked away and read at a later, more convenient time.

A list of the various ways tracts that have been distributed would probably be impossible to record. Most are distributed directly from person to person or mailed with correspondence, payment of bills, or Christmas cards. They can be placed in various locations to be picked up by curious people. Tracks can be given to sales people who come to the door or handed out when you purchase items Churches put in tract racks for people to pick up to distribute.

Prayerful imagination has been used in getting tracts to potential readers. Among other creative ways, they have been sealed in bottles and set afloat in oceans to be carried by currents until they have washed upon land, discovered and read. Some have been inserted in balloons that were released to float wherever the wind would take them. Upon popping, they dropped and were picked up.

Although Halloween is not a Christian holiday, it provides an opportunity to distribute tracts, along with candy, to children as they come to the door trick-or-treating. Others give their children tracts to take with them as they go trick-or-treating to give as a thank you for the candy given to them.

A friend traveled to the Philippines to visit her family and place of birth. She took a large number of tracts I gave her to give to her family and acquaintances. She distributed all of them. Reading materials were scarce there and the children, most of whom spoke and read English, were especially delighted to have something to read.

Traveling to a wedding on the East Coast, I offered $20.00 to the youngsters traveling with us who would distribute the most tracts. We left tracts at restaurants, rest stops, tucked inside state road maps, inserted into telephone books, added to literature racks, placed in restrooms, as well as given personally to individuals.

A particularly striking true testimony of God directing the path of a tract was of a missionary on the boarder of a closed country. He passed out portions of the Gospel of John. A native, unable to read, used one to line the sweat band of his hat. Much later, while traveling over remote mountains, he was invited to stay a night in a home. The pieces of paper fell out and the host gave him fresh lining for his hat. Later, noticing writing on the discarded papers, the host read the literature. He believed its message, shared it with others and built a place of worship for the God of creation rather than a god fashioned by human hands. Another missionary traveling through the area at a later time discovered the worshiping group and gave them further instruction and Bibles.

A friend of mine, Hal Miller, was handed a variety of different tracts regularly at his workplace by a coworker he respected. Hal and later his wife, Patty, trusted Christ; he went to a Bible college, became a pastor and then a missionary. He established Campus Bible Fellowship and worked successfully many years on college campuses starting in Iowa. CBF spread across the states becoming global. College students were reached with the gospel and many went into full-time Christian service themselves. I had the privilege of working in the college ministry with Hal and Patty for seven years.

God knows who has hungry hearts, and He is able to direct pieces of paper to a desired destination. There is no place in this world that God cannot somehow deliver His message of salvation to seeking hearts. He keeps His promise, *"Seek the LORD your God and you will find him, if you search after him with all your heart and with all your soul"* Deuteronomy 4:29). *"I love those who love me, and those who seek me diligently find me"* (Proverbs 8:17). *"You will seek me and find me, when you seek me with all your heart"* (Jeremiah 29:13).

Be sure that there is information on your tracts or literature for the reader to be able to make contact with someone for further information or to answer questions. It can be a church, your name and contact information, or someone else's. Tracts are like seeds scattered over different types of soil, just as Jesus illustrated by the parable about the sower of seeds. Some seeds fell by the wayside, some on stony ground, some among thorns, others on good ground (Mark 4:3-9). Those seeds need to be watered and cultivated and harvested. The first drops of watering can be your tears as you pray over your tracts and literature-asking God to direct them to the heart of someone who will receive them.

Through the use of tracts, we will see people in Heaven whom we have never met in person. There are casual tracts while others are more detailed. Each has its special purpose. For those who are interested in a tract that goes in-depth, chapter one of this book is available in pamphlet form.

56. Utilize the internet.

The World Wide Web has opened the door for Christians to witness to individuals around the world. Although Satan has been quick to use the internet, it is not the web itself that is evil but the use of it by people seeking to do wrong. I believe God opened the internet to be a tool used for His honor and glory. The web can take His message of salvation and Christian growth literally throughout the world!

Early history records that Rome built roads to move its armies throughout the known world to conquer nations and kill multitudes. The same roads were traveled by the early Christians to take the Gospel-bringing spiritual freedom and life through Christ to the ends of the earth. The roads were not good or evil but rather a method to give access.

Google tells us that every day, two million people are making spiritually-related searches on the internet. A former Apple executive, Wilson, said "by 2015 there will be WiFi everywhere on earth." This was reported by Allan Beeber, the Orlando director of Global Media Outreach ministry which is Campus Crusade for Christ's media arm. (www.Globalmediaoutreach.com /always_ready.html) For years now, GMO has sponsored an Internet Evangelism Day as a time for churches and individuals to take time to explore new ways to reach people near and far for Christ through the internet.

God's Appointment

Campus Crusade for Christ's media arm "Global Media Outreach" ministry reports that in one year, 66 million people visited one or more of their 100-plus websites to search for information online about Jesus and the hope He brings. Of that, more than ten million indicated a decision to follow Christ and nearly two million initiated discipleship lessons and requested more information about Jesus and Christianity through GMO's 4,000 online missionaries.

Building from this momentum, they are poised to touch even more lives. "GMO's Web sites allow online spiritual seekers to directly knock on the 'electronic' front doors of participating volunteers, who can guide them in their faith." As more and more people gain access to the internet and visit GMO sites requesting for more information, more and more "mature" believers are needed to respond.

Needed are workers who will reap the harvest. To meet the demand, GMO says it needs at least 10,000 online missionaries. They are encouraging believers everywhere to join the effort by devoting just 15 minutes of their day to help with responding to the e-mail inquiries received. 80 to 90 percent are reportedly sent from outside of the United States. To get more churchgoers involved in their Web effort, GMO launched "GmoAlwaysReady," an online missions program available to all churches. Presently, Christians participating in the ministry typically spend a few minutes a day responding to e-mails while holding another full-time job. Volunteers come from a wide range of professional backgrounds, often recruited from evangelical churches and recom-mended by their pastors. For further information, go to http://www.christianpost.com/.

As the Web outreach booms, the need for "Online Missionaries" is rising. This presents a fascinating opportunity for Christians to witness to people around the world. People otherwise restricted by health, age, family restrictions and resources can reach out and lead people to Christ around the world from their home. For the first time in history, geographical boundaries and closed doors cannot restrict us.

Horizon International Schools uses retired missionaries who work on formatting and proofreading courses and graphics to make current educational courses suitable for global use. The courses then are available to be translated into any language for nationals worldwide to have educational training available without having to leave their homes other than to locate a computer on which to download and upload lessons and assignments.

The ministry of Ray Comfort and Kirk Cameron, *The Way of the Master*, is seeking to "equip leaders to reach our world." A host of other ministries are using the internet to advance the Gospel. Increased technology only broadens the possibilities for those eager to take ad-vantage of this vast open door.

More than likely, the Internet will be useful to you in your soul winning ministry.

57. Share your personal testimony.

In Jesus' last moments with His disciples, He said, ***"You will be my witnesses"*** (Acts 1:8). If we have received Christ as our Savior, we have a personal testimony. Our eyewitness account of what Christ has done for us, can be shared showing others what Christ can do for them. Our own personal testimony is a very effective tool for sharing Christ.

Write out your personal testimony, edit it to be as short as possible, and select the main details. In witnessing situations you should try to keep the testimony less than a minute in length. However, in a situation in which you are asked to give a testimony, you can determine the time desired and add more details. Your testimony is unique and the Holy Spirit can use it to touch people that others cannot touch. One day, someone might say, "God used your testimony to bring me to Christ."

One's personal testimony can turn a conversation to spiritual things, allowing people to consider the claims of Christ in their own life. Whether sharing our testimony before an audience or a single person, be clear on the issue of "how" one trusts Christ.

58. Avoid hypocrisy.

All of us have probably heard Christians referred to as "hypocrites." We continually need to examine our lives prayerfully, making certain that we are not being self righteous. In the New Testament, Jesus gave an illustration of a hypocritical Pharisee, standing by himself praying, *"God, I thank you that I am not like other men, extortioners, unjust, adulterers, or even like this tax collector I fast twice a week; I give tithes of all that I get"* (Luke 18:11-12). Rather, Jesus praised the humble man who prayed, not even lifting up his eyes to Heaven, but beating his breast, saying, *"God, be merciful to me, a sinner!"* Jesus went on to say, *"I tell you, this man went down to his house justified, rather than the other. For everyone who exalts himself will be humbled, but the one who humbles himself will be exalted"* (Luke 18:13-14).

Though I find a Pharisaical attitude hateful, sometimes I wake up to the fact that such an attitude is creeping into my own life, and I have to get my heart right! We all need to be diligent and begin each day prayerfully, making certain that our hearts are cleansed by our Lord. He earnestly gave instruction concerning this sin, *"You blind Pharisee! First clean the inside of the cup and the plate, that the outside also may be clean"* (Matthew 23:26). It is the Holy Spirit which gives testimony of sincerity; if we are not sincere, He will not confirm our witness. We cannot control other people's attitude, but we can control our own.

Some people use the argument of hypocrisy to justify not going to church. Hypocrites will surface in all facets of life. If someone is going to stay away from going to a church to avoid hypocrites, perhaps they also need to consider avoiding restaurants, banks, stores and schools for the same reason! Jesus was not a hypocrite, and we are responding in our church attendance to Him, not men.

A child went to church, upon returning home commented, "God was not there." Sadly not all churches uplift Christ. There are things that go on in churches that make one just shake their head in bewilderment. A leader in a Midwestern church left when the Bible was declared no longer approved literature for the Sunday school. He moved his membership to a church that taught the Bible. Try to teach those you influence how to avoid churches which are just social institutions. A church must teach people how to get to Heaven. Discernment is needed in the choice of a church. I have met

Church leaders that are not themselves born again! Churches can be a doorway to Hell instead of Heaven!

God can help Christians find the church He wants them to go to if they will ask Him. A popular saying goes, "If you do find a perfect church, don't join it because then it no longer will be perfect." There is no perfect church; just as no person is perfect! Imperfect, yet the local church is God's design to accomplish His work in the world today! The church will not be perfect until we get to Heaven. Only there will we be in a perfect environment. My question isn't if a church is perfect, but if it is preaching the Word of God and knows how to bring people to Christ.

After helping people become born-again Christians, we should help them obey Jesus' instruction to seek out a church where they can grow in the Lord and serve Him. Teach them how to recognize a Bible preaching church. Family and friends going to church with them will then also hear the Word of God taught and possibly also get saved.

59. Be careful of tricky emotions.

When we are dealing with people, realize personality differences. Some people are more emotional than others. Emotions can be wonderful; however, emotions can also be tricky. Seek to establish those you are working with in a firm foundation of Scripture without becoming legalistic and cold! Though we have feelings, we are not saved by feelings nor are we saved by faith-but rather by the object of our faith, The Lord Jesus Christ!

We are not saved by receiving; we are saved by receiving Jesus Christ. Jesus warns, *"See that no one leads you astray. For many will come in my name, saying, 'I am the Christ,' and they will lead many astray"* and, *"Many false prophets will arise and lead many astray"* (Matthew 24:4, 11). More than once I have come up against a demonic situation involving a lying spirit impersonating Christ. The Lord Jesus Christ warns us, *"Beloved, do not believe every spirit, but test the spirits to see whether they are from God, for many false prophets have gone out into the world"* (1 John 4:1). Before coming to Christ, one woman described to me how she had seen and talked to Jesus. I told her it was not The Lord Jesus Christ! That response helped her to eventually realize that she was experiencing an imposter that was seeking to fool her.

In the 1960's-1970's, a Jesus movement was popular, especially with young people. One young man in Colorado told me that he had tried Jesus already, but Jesus had not worked for him. He considered himself spiritually beyond Jesus. He stated that he had evolved past the spiritual plane that I was in and was experimenting with other religions. When I inquired who Jesus was to him, he explained that Jesus was a good man, a teacher and a prophet. I replied that when he had tried Jesus, that Jesus was not my Jesus—who was, is, and will always be the Christ, the Lord of Lords, and King of Kings! No wonder he felt believing in Jesus didn't work; he had not met the real Christ!

More than one individual has described to me how a beautiful spirit appeared to them. At first, they thought it was Jesus—but the spirit changed before their eyes when challenged. A beautiful dream can be just that—a dream, or worse, an imposter. The Lord Jesus Christ did make genuine appearances after His resurrection, some of which have been documented in the Bible. (Matthew 28:9,17-20; Mark 16:9,12,14; Luke 24:15-31,36-49; John 20:14-17,19-30;21:1-25; Acts 1:3-9; 7:55-56; 9:4-17; 11:7-9; 18:9-10; 22:7-21; 23:11;26:13-18; Revelation 1:11-3:22). How can you tell the difference between an impostor and the real Jesus Christ? You can tell by your reaction. A feeling of peace, contentment and love is not enough. If the response is not a deep realization of the Holiness of God and the desperate sinful nature of self, a genuine repentance of sin-such as when Isaiah fell down before the Lord, then the interaction with Jesus may not genuine:

Holy, holy, holy is the LORD of hosts; the whole earth is full of his glory! And the foundations of the thresholds shook at the voice of him who called, and the house was filled with smoke. And I said: "Woe is me! For I am lost; for I am a man of unclean lips, and I dwell in the midst of a people of unclean lips; for my eyes have seen the King, the LORD of hosts." (Isaiah 6:1-8)

A girl assured me once that she was saved. In fact, she described to me the feeling of exquisite pleasure as she ran her bare feet through the warm sand and was aware of God. For her, that may have been a religious experience, but that experience did not reunite her with God for eternity. When dealing with a person that has been involved in satanic worship, in magic and folk beliefs, one has to be especially guarded. When Moses tried to convince the Pharaoh of Egypt to let the Israelites go, Moses performed the signs as dictated by God to convince Pharaoh. The magicians of Pharaoh duplicated the plague signs. Satan can do many powerful things that resemble the power of God. As well, He can heal, cause speaking in tongues and give interpretations.

We are up against a tricky foe whose main thrust is to use any means to keep us from becoming reconciled to God. A religious "experience" can be a tool to keep one from repentance and faith. Be careful! If we believe in God, we must also believe God when He tells us that we have an enemy, Satan. As much as God loves us, Satan hates us; and Satan wants us destroyed. As believers in Jesus Christ, we are sternly warned, ***"Be sober-minded; be watchful. Your adversary the devil prowls around like a roaring lion, seeking someone to devour"*** (1 Peter 5:8).

Jesus Christ went to the Cross and died to pay the ransom for our sin. But after His death and successful payment for sin, He arose! He is no longer dead on the Cross or in the grave—He is alive and well in Heaven, VICTORIOUS! God is not threatened by Satan. There is no contest; God is by far the most powerful. But Satan can get back at God by hurting man. One of his effective tools is mankind's emotions. If he can just keep us from becoming redeemed by the blood of Christ, he keeps us from Heaven which means eternity in Hell for us! Reunion with God is absolutely necessary for eternity in Heaven.

60. Use courtesy on the job.

In a survey asking what or who was responsible for their coming to Christ, the majority responded "a friend or relative." Extended members of family, personal friends and co-workers are our most effective outreach source in soul winning. Making cold contacts (people we do not know) are not as fruitful as warm contacts (people we are acquainted with). But above all, we need to be patient: sowing and nurturing seeds takes time. As God gives direction, we need to build relationships that will give opportunities to present Christ.

On the job, we often have opportunities to make friends and contacts for witnessing. By our living a Christian life, co-workers may come to appreciate that testimony, even asking for our prayers. We ought not to have to hide our faith at work. If we are persecuted, may it be for the cause of Christ, not because of personal shortcomings.

For example, let us avoid stealing, (even our labor hours) from the boss. We need to do our work to the best of our ability since we are paid to do that work! If, however, it is permitted to talk as we work, since others talk about their interests and such—then we should have the freedom to talk wisely about subjects of our choosing.

61. Know the evidence.

Our faith is defensible and we can with confidence search for truth! A skeptic, college student Josh McDowell was challenged to examine the claims of Christ. His research to refute Christianity centered on Jesus' resurrection. After more than 1,000 hours of studying the subject, he found Jesus' resurrection a well documented historical fact. The more he studied the historical-Biblical Christian faith, the more he realized that Christianity is a thinking person's faith. The proof is there for anyone seriously honest in their questions.

Jesus said, *"You will know the truth, and the truth will set you free"* (John 8:32). Josh has a burdened to help Christians know what they believe and why. Individuals wanting to read a book that presents a fine defense of the faith can get his book, *Evidence that Demands a Verdict.*

During the time of Rome, lions were tethered at the entrance to buildings where sometimes hecklers would taunt the lion. It was suggested that instead of trying to protect the magnificent animal, it should just be turned loose to protect itself. The same is true of

Scriptures; we do not have to defend the Bible, but rather turn it loose. The Bible's words are capable of defending itself.

62. Repeat often.

It has been suggested that it takes hearing something seven times before it sinks in. Teachers in classrooms go over and over materials for review. How many grasp algebra the first time or know how to diagram a sentence or how to take a car apart and put it back together again?

When talking to someone about the Lord, we don't know what point they may be at in their spiritual understanding of how to get to Heaven. It could be their first exposure or seventh or anywhere in between. In an unhurried conversation, we can go over the plan of salvation more than once. Each time we can build on the foundation of the time before.

First can be when we give an explanation of the Gospel. **Second,** if we ask them where they feel they are at spiritually. "Where do you place yourself in your spiritual journey; before the point of birth, at birth, or after birth?" **Third,** when asking "Do you want to call upon the Lord to be to your personal Savior and have His blood applied to your sin and be born again?" **Fourth** if they are not ready make a decision. If they are not ready right now ask, "When you are ready to trust Christ, how will you go about doing it? If they know how great, if not—you can explain it once again so that they know how to do it when they are ready." If they can accurately explain, we can have confidence that the Holy Spirit will continue to work in their lives. **Fifth** we can seek their permission for you to pray specifically that God will bring them to the place that they will be ready to invite Jesus Christ into their heart and life and be their Savior. By the end of a contact, the plan of salvation can be stated a number of times.

Repetition is not always necessary, sometimes people do come to Christ based on only a short exposure to the Gospel. The Bible gives many examples: Paul the Apostle (Acts 9:1-22), the woman at the well (John 4:4-42), the Philippian jailer (Acts 16:27-34), the Ethiopian eunuch (Acts 8:26-39), as well as others.

We can claim the Lord's promise, ***"And I am sure of this, that he who began a good work in you will bring it to completion at the day of Jesus Christ"*** (Philippians 1:6). Concern for someone's salvation is reason enough to see just how far you can go to discover where they are spiritually. I believe if a burden is from the Holy Spirit, it indicates that God is working towards their coming to know the Lord as Savior.

CHAPTER 23

Tips for Soul-Winning 63-75

❋

Bringing to a Conclusion

63. Expect results.

Expect people to get saved. I remember knocking on doors and praying that no one would open the door. It took me awhile to gain confidence. Jesus complimented a woman, ***"O woman, great is your faith!"*** (Matthew 15:28). He also said to a centurion soldier, ***"Truly, I tell you, with no one in Israel have I found such faith'"*** (Matthew 8:10). So just how does one develop "great faith?" Physical exercise = physical muscles. Spiritual "faith" exercise = great faith.

A discouraged ministerial student sought counsel of Charles Spurgeon. "And do you expect that the Lord is going to save souls every time you preach?"

"No, sir," the student replied.

"Well, that is why you do not get souls saved, if you had believed, God would have given you the blessing."

A positive attitude, expectation, gets one further than being negative. William Carey said, "Attempt great things for God; expect great things from God." The Holy Spirit is hindered by our inability to believe that He can win souls through us. I believe that one of the reasons that God blesses me with the opportunity to lead people to

Christ at fairs is because I feel that I am in the witnessing situation in obedience to His will and leading, and anticipate people will make a decision.

After all this is not a game or a hobby, it is serious business! There is absolutely no access to Heaven without a proper passport. No one will be an *illegal alien* in Heaven. The passport must be prepared in advance of the trip; it is not available at the gate at the time of arrival. There is only one gate to Heaven. Access to that gate is not by walking, by car, by boat or by plane. It is by escort only. The passport must have the blood of Jesus Christ's stamp of approval on it. Without the blood applied, there is no access. Let us help people prepare for their trip into eternity. This same tragedy happens often in our circles today. For example how many times at a Christian's funeral have we heard an excellent message, but there was no opportunity given to make the decision that would enable an unsaved person to go to Heaven, eventually to join the departed? How fitting it would be to simply pause during the funeral and invite those in the audience, right there in their seat, to trust Christ as Savior and Lord. How sad when such a vital detail is not mentioned. My husband preformed a funeral for a lady whose granddaughter shared with us that it was at her grandmother's funeral she made her decision to trust Christ. Sadly there are many opportunities that are missed.

When dealing with individuals, let us not leave them at the point of only understanding the plan of salvation, but invite them to receive it. So many times, we stop short of actually bringing people to a decision. If we do not expect individuals to trust Christ, they probably will not. Furthermore, if we are negative, "You don't want to trust Christ right now, do you?" They more than likely will say, "No." However, if you in a positive manner say, "You would like to do this right now, wouldn't you?" You would be surprised how many will say, "Yes," and do it. Sometimes seeing people make a decision for Christ is more about our level of faith than theirs. If we do not seek to bring people to a salvation conclusion, we may be allowing our lack of faith to keep them from exercising their own faith in Jesus' saving work.

Jesus used the phrase, *"The harvest is plentiful* **[great]***"* (Luke 10:2). Do we believe that there is a great harvest? If we do, then that means there are a _lot_ of people for us to lead to Christ. Why are we surprised when someone wants to be saved?

64. Follow through to a conclusion.

If, after witnessing to individuals, we leave them wanting to trust Christ without knowing how to, we may have lost an important opportunity. D. L. Moody, the famed evangelist of the nineteenth century, shared how he preached a strong salvation message in his church in Chicago. Many raised their hands, acknowledging that they were unsaved and were headed for Hell. Overwhelmed by the great number, he sent them home, instructing them to come back the next week so that he could reveal to them the path of salvation. That week, the tragic Chicago fire took place. That same congregation never gathered again. That event haunted Moody the rest of his life; he decided never to give the Gospel message without concluding with a chance for individuals to make the decision.

Similarly, how many times at a Christian's funeral have we heard an excellent message, but no one gave the opportunity to make the decision that would enable them to go to Heaven, eventually to join the departed? How fitting simply to pause at a funeral, inviting those in the audience, right there in their seat, to do what the deceased had done and trust Christ as Savior and Lord. How sad when that vital detail is not mentioned. A granddaughter of a lady my husband performed the funeral for, years later shared with us that it was at her grandmothers' funeral she made her decision to trust Christ.

History tells us that a preacher counseled Abraham Lincoln after the death of his son. When Lincoln realized that he would be able to see his son again in eternity if only he would trust Christ as his Savior, he did. Before his assassination, it is recorded that Lincoln had planned to follow the Lord in believer's baptism and had talked of going on a tour of the Holy Land. Instead of going to the land where Jesus once walked, Lincoln went to the Heavenly place where Jesus now walks!

If someone willingly takes time to listen to Jesus' instruction on how one becomes His child in the Bible, we should help them to go ahead and make a decision. If they are interested enough to listen, it is likely that, given the opportunity, they would choose to trust Christ, without waiting. If we neglect to provide the opportunity for them to pray, telling Jesus what they want Him to do for them, we are failing them. Whenever a person understands and is willing to accept Christ, that is the best time for them to do so.

After an opportunity to explain the plan of salvation, and the person understands, I ask them if it would be all right if I pray. Usually, they respond, "Yes." They do not mind if I pray, but they may not feel comfortable praying yet themselves. Often I begin by addressing God in the following manner: *"Thank you Heavenly Father for the opportunity to visit with _____ (insert name). I feel in my heart that _____ (insert name) understands, and I would like You to work in (his/her) heart right now to make this decision."* Then I pause, look at them directly, and ask, "Why don't you talk to God, as I just now did, and tell Him that you would like to trust Jesus Christ to pay for your sins and give you a home in Heaven?" My praying first often helps them have more confidence talking to God themselves.

It can be helpful to ask individuals after they trust Christ, if they would mind sharing what they just did with others. The very act of confessing to someone verbally is strengthening, as Paul writes, **"if you confess with your mouth that Jesus is Lord and believe in your heart that God raised him from the dead, you will be saved"** (Romans 10:9).

Writing down their name, age, address, phone and e-mail will help as you pray for them and enable you to contact them in the future in order to fulfill the rest of the ministry set forth in the Great Commission.

65. "Get ready."

When concluding an explanation of the Gospel, I like to ask individuals, "On the basis of Jesus saying, *'Truly, truly, I say to you, <u>unless one is born again he cannot see the kingdom of God</u>'* (John 3:3), where would you place yourself in your spiritual journey? Would you consider yourself before being born again, at the point of being born again, or having already been born again?" (Giving people the opportunity to identify where they feel they are at is better than my trying to convince them !)

Amazingly many times they answer; "I guess I am before birth."

My reply, "On the basis of your evaluation of being before "born again," are you ready right now to talk to Jesus and tell Him you know you are a sinner and that you are in trouble and recognize that He is the only one who can help you and ask Him to apply His blood payment to your sin personally?"

If they say yes, I ask them to go ahead right now and talk to Jesus and tell Him what they want Him to do. I bow my head and wait for them to pray. If they are shy and want to do it quietly rather than out loud, that is fine. Hearing them pray or their telling me what they prayed allows me to know if they understand and are addressing the situation. When they indicate they are finished, I ask them what they said. Normally they have no problem sharing, and I can be assured they knew what they were doing. If they are vague, I tell them that was fine but that they still should specifically invite Jesus Christ to apply His Blood payment to their sin. I encourage them to add this on to their prayer. If they know what they are doing, they should be able to share it.

Ask them, "If you just now received Jesus, believed in Him ,what happened?" *"But to all who did <u>receive</u> him, who <u>believed in</u> his name, <u>he gave the right to become children of God</u>"* (John 1:12). Pointing to the words receive and believe and then the phrase "child of God" ask, "Does God call you a son or daughter? If God calls you a son or daughter, then what are you? If I claim to be a son or daughter, it is not the same as God saying it. If God says, based on your receiving Christ Jesus and believing on Him, you are His child, that is a fact! Right now, having received Jesus Christ, makes today your spiritual <u>birth day</u>!" Encourage them to write the date down in their Bible or somewhere so that they will remember it. Every year I celebrate both of my birthdays.

If they say they are not ready yet, thank them for being honest and comment that unless they are ready, it would not do any good to just mouth the words. God knows if one has a genuine heart desire. Let them know that they do not have to ask God to save them right that moment. They should wait until they are ready, but it is important that they know how to trust Christ when they *are* ready; in the car, at home, in bed, anywhere at any time.

Do not condemn them to Hell if they do not make the decision at this time. Leave the door open for the Holy Spirit to continue the work in their hearts that He has started. At the same time, it is good that they understand that it is dangerous to wait. We never know what can happen and since they are undecided, they are not "born again." They therefore are not ready to go to Heaven should they die. You could say, "God brought our paths to cross and we looked together at John 3 in the Bible. Once you understand that you are not 'born again' and put it off you are like the fellow who asked his girl friend to marry him. She did not say 'yes' or 'no,' but 'I'll think about it.' That is where you are right now. You've understood the invitation of Jesus for you to open the door of your heart. You have Jesus on 'hold' do not put it off for very long—get back to Him on it as soon as possible. The best time to make a decision is when you first understand. Are you sure that you are not ready? Can I encourage you again to do it right now?" They may have reconsidered and want to go ahead and say "yes" to Jesus.

If they are still not ready you can ask, "When you are ready, can you tell me how you will go about trusting Christ to be your Savior?" To verbally explain the steps they would take to be saved when they determine they want to, shows they know how. If they are hesitant, repeat in a nutshell that they need to talk to Jesus and tell Him they are ready and now want to call upon Him for His Blood payment. Ask a question, "May I have your permission to pray specifically that God will bring you to that point of being ready soon?" I have never yet had anyone say no. Finally, ask them to do you a favor, contact you and let you know after they do it so that you can rejoice with them. Everyone so far has promised to do so. On a number of occasions, people have contacted me at a later date to share that they "did it!" They had received Christ. Rejoicing, I ask— when, and how, and encourage them to grow in their spiritual lives.

When they say they are not ready ask them to explain *how* they will go about trusting Christ when they are ready. If they cannot explain, summarize the instructions once again. The door to their heart may be only *temporarily closed;* the Holy Spirit may continue to work in their lives (Philippians 1:6). I often ask individuals if I may pray for them that God will bring them to the point of being ready to accept Christ. I have yet to have a person say, "No." I also request that they inform me when they make their decision, so that I can rejoice with them. Thus I am building a bridge to a time when they maybe will get saved!

66. Prevent "pleasing you" decisions.

Because many people desire to please others and may be persuaded to make a surface decision, let us be careful and not pressure people to make decisions. Rather let us pray that people will respond to the conviction of the Holy Spirit. Coming to know Jesus Christ as personal Savior is not reciting magical words. It takes a heart connection with God. This consideration is especially important with children.

67. Reconfirm commitments.

Some respond to the Gospel to the best of their ability but do not fully comprehend it. In such cases, we can claim the Lord's promise, *"And I am sure of this, that he who began a good work in you will bring it to completion at the day of Jesus Christ"* (Philippians 1:6).

Others tentatively follow Christ, gradually growing to the point that they realize who Christ really is. With the majority of Christ's disciples, it took the reality of the Resurrection of Christ to go from believing *about* to believing *on* and *in* as stated, in several passages of Scriptures: *"For God so loved the world, that he gave his only Son, that whoever believes in him should not perish but have eternal life"* (John 3:16); Also, *"Whoever believes in him is not condemned, but whoever does not believe is condemned already, because he has not believed in the name of the only Son of God"* (John 3:18); *"Whoever believes in the Son has eternal life; whoever does not obey the Son shall not see life, but the wrath of God remains on him"* (John 3:36); and, *"But to all who did receive him, who believed in his name, he gave the right to become children of God"* (John 1:12).

Many times, young children brought up in a Christian home find themselves later in life, reaffirming their commitment to Christ. Perhaps they, like the eleven Disciples of Christ, heard and accepted His teachings but didn't fully grasp the reality of Christ until a certain point later in their lives. It is important to allow the Holy Spirit control in every witnessing experience, as only God truly knows the heart and what is necessary to complete salvation in each spirit. It is dangerous for us to assume that we know better than God. It is God, working through us, who reaches out to bring people to full salvation.

People from a strong religious background, but unsaved, may be open to doing a prayer of recommitment. There may be a fear that we are trying to get them to change churches, denomination or religion, but that is not the case. We are talking about deepening one's personal relationship with God. It involves talking with God, acknowledging the fact that one is a sinner and deeply appreciates the work that Jesus Christ did on the Cross to pay for sin, even their sin. They want to affirm the fact to God that they indeed want the Lord Jesus' blood applied to their sin and express their thanks to Him for the gift of everlasting life. Note the similarity between this recommitment and the Romans Road plan of salvation. It does not matter what you call it as long as the ingredients are present for salvation.

After such a confirmation, individuals have remarked to me that they identified this point as being when they became "born again." The idea of recommitment builds on their previous attitude towards God and clarifies what is necessary for their sins to be forgiven and united with God. The first time I used this method was with a man on his death bed. He was walking through the valley of the shadow of death, and his wife was on high alert to keep him from straying from his religious denomination. He wanted peace for his journey, and he received it. But, we had to go around the wife's presence in the room to accomplish it. This is a way to side-step people who are controlling who otherwise would not allow you to help the individual. How sad it is when a person wants a right relationship with God, and there is someone that will not allow them to do such.

How comforting to know that if we are faithfully obedient in witnessing opportunities, the soul's salvation is not in our hands but in the Lord's hands.

68. Use a salvation prayer.

Is it necessary to say a prayer to get saved? No, I do not believe the prayer is necessary for salvation. We are saved by "faith," "by grace," "believing in," and "receiving," not by a prayer. A prayer is simply verbalization of what is going on in the heart of the individual. As stated, *"For by grace you have been saved through faith. And this is not your own doing; it is the gift of God, not a result of works, so that no one may boast"* (Ephesians 2:8, 9).

The prayer just provides a glimpse inside the individuals' thoughts. If the people with whom we're dealing about salvation pray saying, "Now I lay me down to sleep," we can know that they do not understand what they need to do. We can then give a few words of clarification, suggesting that they continue their prayer, including the necessary step of "receiving" Christ. A vague prayer shows what needs to be done to clarify their connecting with God. It may be more the confusion of *how to pray* than a lack of wanting to be saved. Often, the second time as they verbalize their prayer, individuals will go directly to the Cross and receive the blood payment for their sin.

If people understand the Gospel message, they should be able to pray without our leading them word-by-word; we can instruct them to "Just tell Jesus Christ what you want Him to do." It is beautiful to hear the sincere prayer of a heart reaching out to God.

Sometimes people are too shy to pray out loud, preferring rather to pray silently. In that case, we can simply ask them, after their silent prayer, "What did you ask God to do?" "Did He hear you?" "What did He say, 'Yes or No?'" If they can explain their thought process, we can better understand what happened. If they say they asked God to help them be a better person, we know they missed the connection. My concern is that when individuals bow to pray, they do not only mouth the words, but actually receive Jesus Christ as Savior and Lord.

For some, they have all the ingredients to salvation except they had an unwillingness to surrender control of their life to God. When that last barrier is removed, salvation comes. For others it is acknowledging that Christ is indeed the Son of God and the only way of salvation. Not everyone has the same blockage or hindrance to salvation that must be overcome.

69. Avoid just saying the words.

If people do not consider themselves unsaved or sinners, they are not ready to take that step of faith in Christ's work on the Cross. If they understand their status as sinners and are ready to accept Christ's free gift of salvation, then it is easy for them to take the step. At times, though, it is possible for people to understand the choice that needs to be made, yet still not be ready to take that step. Forcing someone to say words that are not heartfelt does not produce salvation. There is nothing magical about saying the words; it is the yearning of the heart and receiving Christ that counts. It would be better for them to wait until they are ready.

70. Give control to God.

Sometimes people want to accept God's gift of salvation, but do not want to give Him access to their life and decisions. They want the ticket to Heaven, but do not want to give up smoking, drinking, immorality, drugs, self-control over their own life decisions or whatever. Perhaps the following example can be useful. If people want to buy a house, they can present an offer to purchase that house. But if they state in the contract that they do not want to make any payments, the home-owner will not accept the offer. God does not enter into a salvation contract with anyone who has a "but" clause in their heart. He simply will wait until they lose the "but" and are ready to accept Christ on HIS terms, not theirs.

A lady once shared that when she first felt God working in her heart, she was afraid that if she trusted Christ, God would ask her to be a missionary to Africa. She tried to say "Yes, but I will not be a missionary to Africa." It was not until she was willing to give up control that she experienced salvation. God never did call her to be a missionary. It was not that she had to be a missionary to get God's salvation; He simply didn't accept her heart attitude of saying, "No."

Jesus spoke to an individual who wanted to follow Him, but could not, *"If you would be perfect, go, sell what you possess and give to the poor, and you will have treasure in heaven; and come, follow me. When the young man heard this he went away sorrowful, for he had great possessions"* (Matthew 19:21-22). We are not expected to give up all of our sins in order to be saved, but we need to be willing to. The Holy Spirit helps us change after we are saved. It is dangerous to say "no" to God. We must be willing to let God be in control and not trying to retain control of our lives ourselves.

When I was a teenager, a cousin came to visit us for a length of time and attended church and activities with us. Our hearts were thrilled one night when he went forward at an invitation to trust Christ. As we congratulated him, he made it clear, yes, he wanted a free ride to Heaven, but in no way, did he want anything beyond that. As far as we could tell, there was a lack of spiritual interest, growth or fruit in his life. Getting saved is not repeating a magical set of words; it is a genuine heart commitment.

71. Beware rejection of the messenger.

When people seemingly reject the Gospel, sometimes they are rejecting the messenger, not necessarily Christ! People have to understand the Gospel before they are able to reject it! It may be that they are rejecting the messenger or the approach rather than actually rejecting Christ. If there is to be offense, let it be the offense of the Gospel not dirty fingernails, uncombed hair, messy dress or other avoidable personal concerns. We need to be conscious of our appearance, be well-groomed, teeth brushed, and have clean hands.

There are other ways to offend others, such as attitude or unscriptural requirements. We need to try to be inoffensive to the best of our ability. When individuals are not receptive, do not try to force them. We should just say what God leads us to say and then pray for them. Often when they see us, the Holy Spirit will remind them of what was said.

Furthermore, if people do not respond to the Gospel, we should not damn them to Hell. We need to leave a door open for another opportunity. Let us avoid leaving a person with the thought that they are rejecting Christ. Instead, let us build a bridge for the future. Perhaps that individual is not ready to receive Christ that day; it is their decision. Still, we can emphasize that when they are ready, they can talk to God, anytime, anywhere. They need to know that choosing to accept God into their lives is a serious decision to make—the sooner the better! I have come across many that I had previously talked to about the Lord, who were not ready at the time, but made a personal decision for Christ later! Continue praying for those who balked to yet choose Christ.

The Gospel in a nutshell is, *"For I delivered to you as of first importance what I also received: that Christ died for our sins in accordance with the Scriptures, that he was buried, that he was raised on the third day in accordance with the Scriptures"* (1 Corinthians 15:3,4).

72. Take step to future.

It is impossible to lead others to the Lord without the Holy Spirit's preparation in their lives. Jesus asked Peter, *"'But who do you say that I am?' Simon Peter replied, 'You are the Christ the Son of the living God.' And Jesus answered him, 'Blessed are you Simon Bar-Jonah! For flesh and blood has not revealed this to you, but my Father who is in heaven'"* (Matthew 16:15-17).

A business acquaintance shared with me that his wife had died, and he was having a difficult time adjusting. The Holy Spirit sporadically laid it on my heart to pray for him. One day, I had a strong burden to talk to Dennis about trusting Christ as his Savior. We visited for awhile in his store. He explained, while he appreciated my intentions in talking with him, he was *"good enough,"* and didn't need to be born again. Strangely, God had directed me to talk to him, but Dennis was not ready. This may just be a step towards something in the future. God may have another opportunity for Dennis yet! When Jesus was here during His earthly ministry, not everyone with whom He spoke believed.

When individuals say that they are not yet ready to make a decision, we may need to let them know that they do not have to ask God to save them right that moment. They should wait until they are ready, but it is important that people know how to trust Christ when they *are* ready; in the car, at home, in bed or anywhere at any time.

When people say they are not ready, we can ask them to explain *how* they will go about trusting Christ when they are ready. If they cannot explain, summarize the instructions once again. The door to their heart may be only *temporarily closed;* the Holy Spirit may continue to work in their lives (Philippians 1:6). I often ask individuals if I may pray for them that God will bring them to the point of being ready to accept Christ. I have yet to have a person say, "No." I also request that they inform me when they make their decision so that I can rejoice with them. This enables the building of a bridge to a time when they maybe will get saved!

On a number of occasions, people have contacted me at a later date to share that they "did it!" They had received Christ. Rejoicing, I ask—when and how, and then encourage them to grow in their spiritual lives.

73. Come just as we are.

Talking with people, some will say that they want to change their lives before they trust Christ; they want to "turn over a new leaf." It is not possible to change our lives and be acceptable to Him. They need to understand that we cannot fix ourselves or earn our way into Heaven by changing. The best person in the world is still under the curse of sin and falls short of being acceptable to God. God gave the Mosaic Law, which includes the Ten Commandments, to show us that it is impossible to please Him by our own works. We can only come just as we are.

It is hard for us to understand how we look to God without the blood of Christ being applied to our sin. God declares, **"We have all become like one who is unclean, and all our righteous deeds are like a polluted garment. We all fade like a leaf, and our iniquities, like the wind, take us away"** (Isaiah 64:6). The reason it was necessary for Christ to die was that it is only His blood sacrifice and the acceptance of it that makes us acceptable to God. In our own strength, we may be able to clean ourselves up, but we cannot make ourselves into a new person.

God will work the changes in our lives through His Holy Spirit, *after* we receive Christ! Paul says, *"Therefore, if anyone is in Christ, he is a new creation. The old has passed away; behold, the new has come"* (2 Corinthians 5:17); John points us to Christ who is the source of our change, *"The next day he saw Jesus coming toward him, and said, "Behold, the Lamb of God, who takes away the sin of the world!"* (John 1:29).

Choosing to hold onto a sin rather than choosing to trust Christ is to allow something to have the power to keep us from eternity in Heaven—how foolish. If we miss Heaven, the only other choice is Hell. Even if we cling to these pleasures now, eventually we will have to give them up! Eternal separation from God is terrible torment with no sinful pleasures at all. Partying with friends, drunkenness, smoking, drugs, immoral sex and other sins do not take place in Hell. Jesus gives this account of a certain man's entrance into Hell,

> *"The poor man died and was carried by the angels to Abraham's side. The rich man also died and was buried, and in Hades, being in torment, he lifted up his eyes and saw Abraham far off and Lazarus at his side. And he called out, "Father Abraham, have mercy on me, and send Lazarus to dip the end of his finger in water and cool my tongue, for I am in anguish in this flame." But Abraham said, "Child, remember that you in your lifetime received your good things, and Lazarus in like manner bad things; but now he is comforted here, and you are in anguish."* (Luke 16:22-25)

Often sin has such a strong hold on us, we know we cannot give it up by ourselves. When we trust Christ—He gives the power to change.

74. Avoid coercion.

When we are involved in soul-winning, we are not on a commission basis, paid for every decision "we can rack up" such as in sales, nor are we in competition with anyone else, seeing who will lead the most souls to Christ. Instead, soul winning involves the teamwork of the body of Christ!

God does promise a reward for our obedience and faithfulness, but not on the basis of our results. The results are HIS work. The Apostle Paul's attitude was, *"I planted, Apollos watered, but God gave the growth. So neither he who plants nor he who waters is anything, but only God who gives the growth"* (1 Corinthians 3:6, 7).

History records times when people of various religious persuasions have tried to spread their influence by force. There are times one would like to make people do what they should do, but this is not God's way. He wants individuals to make a choice on the basis of their own free will. Paul taught that Christians are to be representatives for Jesus Christ. *"Now then we are ambassadors for Christ, as though God did beseech you by us: we pray you in Christ's stead, be ye reconciled to God"* (2 Corinthians 5:20).

75. Realize "No" can change to "Yes."

When people decide to say, "No," consider building a bridge towards a future opportunity. Sometimes one does need to be persistent in seeking a decision for Christ; it does not hurt to remind the individual that now is the best time for them to make a decision. Late may be too late; no one knows when we will check out of this life and enter eternity. Gambling on another chance truly is foolish and can prove eternally tragic!

Since we do not really know the hearts of people, as Jesus does, some whom we press to make a decision for salvation may say it without really meaning it. Yet, at a later time, they may really choose to trust Christ as their Savior! Be careful when pushing for a positive decision. The current situation may only be one link in a chain of events designed by God for them in understanding the Gospel. Their decision may change with the passing of time.

Many times the Holy Spirit will burden one to pray again for those who were not previously ready to make a decision for Christ. Experiencing a burden to pray for someone is an indication that God is in the process of working. He wants us to agree with Him, before the Throne in prayer, thus enabling the power of God to be released.

Planting and watering the Gospel seed is necessary, but the goal is for harvest. A good gardener checks the plants frequently to determine when they become ripe. Just because the harvest is not ripe today does not mean it never will be ripe. Keep checking back if you can, or if you can't, pray that God will use someone else. A piece of literature, song, memory or flashback can bring the soul to harvest. Consider revisiting past contacts.

We can earnestly pray that God will direct the steps of our life to bring us into contact with the individuals that He has been preparing for salvation. Our challenge is to recognize those opportunities and to be diligent.

CHAPTER 24

Tips for Soul-Winning 76-84

After a Decision

76. Introduce assurance of salvation.

In the little book of 1 John, the word "know" is used thirty-six times: *"And this is the testimony, that God gave us eternal life, and this life is in his Son. Whoever has the Son has life; whoever does not have the Son of God does not have life. I write these things to you who believe in the name of the Son of God that you may <u>know</u> that you have eternal life"* (I John 5:11-13). After having talked about "eternal life," and "everlasting life," it is helpful to review what "everlasting" means. It means never ending. If it "never ends," then we are still His child a day later, a year later, ten years later! If we have "everlasting life", then lose it—then it was not everlasting! God uses words that He means; He does not lie. If He says that life is everlasting, then it does last forever!

Of course, Christians still have a problem with sinning. So what do we do when we sin? God tells us we need to confess sin, not in order to be born again, but to have cleansing from daily sin, *"If we confess our sins, he is faithful and just to forgive us our sins and to cleanse us from all unrighteousness"* (I John 1:9). In the physical realm, we need to frequently wash our hands. When we get dirty and soiled by sin in our daily lives, we need to confess that sin to God; thus finding forgiveness and cleansing.

Experiencing lack of assurance can cause individuals to be discouraged and backslide. Truthfully, attempting to get to Heaven by our good works does not work! We are never good enough nor strong enough to defeat the devil in our own strength.

> *"Whoever believes in the Son of God has the testimony in himself. Whoever does not believe God has made him a liar, because he has not believed in the testimony that God has borne concerning his Son. And this is the testimony that God gave us eternal life, and this life is in his Son. Whoever has the Son has life; whoever does not have the Son of God does not have life. I write these things to you who believe in the name of the Son of God that you may <u>know</u> that you have eternal life"* (I John 5:10-13).

We do not want to leave anyone with a false assurance of salvation. If I had a choice between (1) falsely believing that I was saved and on my way to heaven, and (2) believing that I was saved but had lost my salvation when I had not; I would without a doubt choose the second scenario! It would be better to arrive pleasantly surprised in Heaven than to have the gut-wrenching experience of waking up in Hell. But still, there is joy and peace in knowing our place in Christ *now*. If "everlasting" means "never ending" then it is a fact that we cannot lose our Salvation once we truly have it.

77. Encourage Christians to grow.

Having accepted His rich gift of salvation, we need to grow in our Christian lives. The following will help individual Christians to achieve spiritual growth. Not only does the Lord tell us how to be saved, He also instructs us how to grow.

Pray: Prayer is simply talking to and listening to God. Christ wants to lead us, to direct us in things we should or should not do, and tells us to, *"Pray without ceasing"* (1Thessolians 5:17). The

Bible calls believer's sheep; Jesus observes that *"the sheep follow him: for they know his voice"* (John 10:4). His voice is an inner voice which we learn to recognize and follow.

Bible Reading: As we prayerfully read the Bible, we will grow in our understanding. A person could pray something like this: "Lord Jesus, as I read the Bible now, help me to understand what it says and apply it to my life. Thank you."

In the New Testament, the Apostle Paul encouraged Timothy, *"Do your best to present yourself to God as one approved, a worker who has no need to be ashamed, rightly handling the word of truth"* (2 Timothy 2:15). We can ask Jesus to help us understand the Bible. When considering doing something that contradicts the Bible, prayerfully choose rather to follow the Bible. It is to be the final authority for what we believe and do. God empowers the Christian who prays and obeys God's teaching.

Baptism: Baptism has nothing to do with being saved or obtaining eternal life, but Scripture consistently includes the practice of believers being baptized as an outward sign of their salvation. Jesus obeyed God and was baptized (Matthew 3:13-16). Baptism is included in Jesus Christ's last instruction to His disciples as part of the Great Commission: *"Go therefore and make disciples of all nations, baptizing them in the name of the Father and of the Son and of the Holy Spirit"* (Matthew 28:19).

A letter by the Apostle Paul to believers in Rome explains the meaning of baptism, *"We were <u>buried</u> therefore with him by baptism into death, in order that, just as Christ was raised from the dead by the glory of the Father, we too might walk in newness of life. For if we have been united with him in a death like his, we shall certainly be united with him in a resurrection like his"* (Romans 6:4, 5). Consider the fact that it takes more than three spoonfuls of dirt to be buried. Sprinkling and pouring do not portray the same picture as immersion does. God wants us to tell the world by public baptism that we have received Christ as our Savior and are not ashamed of Him. We need to be obedient in baptism, showing our submission to God.

Attending Church: In the Bible, God says that He wants us to go to church regularly, *"Not neglecting to meet together, as is the habit of some, but encouraging one another, and all the more as you see the Day drawing near"* (Hebrews 10:25). Ask for His direction about which church the Lord wants us to attend. Some churches play religious games while others really mean business for Christ. In churches, people should bring their Bibles and know more about the Scriptures when they leave than when they came. They often get together recognizing the importance of studying together as well as fellowshipping—including rejoicing together and bearing each other's burdens. The church should be a place full of love for God, for His word, for each other, and sharing with others how to get to Heaven.

Certainly no church, pastor, or denomination is perfect, but going to church is God's design and command. God instructs Christians to search the Scriptures and discern truth from error. God wants us to individually understand and obey the truths of Scripture rather than blindly follow what others may expect of us. Paul gives praise to the church in Berea who *"were more noble than those in Thessalonica; they received the word with all eagerness, examining the Scriptures daily to see if these things were so"* (Acts 17:11). We need to do likewise.

Sharing: Someone shared with us, and as God leads, we should tell others how to get to Heaven. Jesus said, *"I am the way, and the truth, and the life. No one comes to the Father except through me"* (John 14:6). He *is* the only way to Heaven. Everyone must come the same way, through Jesus Christ, "the Lamb of God who takes away the sin of the world" (John 1:29). Let's not go to Heaven alone—let's take others with us! Jesus promised His disciples, *"Follow me, and I will make you become fishers of men."* (Mark 1:17). We can love others as God loves us and spread the good news.

Lordship: Appreciating what Christ has done for us, we need to give Him control of our lives everyday as our Lord. After all He has done for us, the least we can do for Him in return is to give Him our faithful service. Paul exhorts,

"I appeal to you therefore, brothers, by the mercies of God, to present your bodies as a living sacrifice, holy and acceptable to God, which is your spiritual worship. Do not be conformed to this world, but be transformed by the renewal of your mind, that by testing you may discern what is the will of God, what is good and acceptable and perfect" (Romans 12:1, 2).

God promises many blessings and rewards in this life, and in the life to come for those who serve Him. *"Each one's work will become manifest, for the Day will disclose it, because it will be revealed by fire, and the fire will test what sort of work each one has done. If the work that anyone has built on the foundation survives, he will receive a reward"* (I Corinthians 3:13-14). Psalm 23 teaches, *"Surely goodness and mercy shall follow me all the days of my life, and I shall dwell in the house of the Lord forever"* (Psalm 23:6). But regardless of the benefits we may or may not receive, He is worthy of our full-hearted love and service.

A suggested prayer: **"Lord Jesus, I want you to be Lord of my life. Please take control. I give you your rightful place as King, Lord, Master, and God in my heart. Take the pieces of my existence and put them together, as only You can. Make something beautiful out of my life, to bring honor and glory to Yourself."**

78. Share helpful literature.

After leading individuals to the Lord, give them a tract or literature. This documenting of verses that were shared with them permits reviewing what they just experienced. This assists them to be able to share with others that they have trusted Christ and gives them information on how to make contact with you (your name, address, phone and or e-mail). It may even aid them in leading others to the Lord. I try to encourage the new Christian, "Now that you know how to get to Heaven, don't go alone; take someone with you!"

79. Do multiplication.

One person led to Christ, in turn leading someone else, and that one leading another—the possibilities are endless! How blessed are the individuals who led D.L. Moody, Billy Graham, and others who have influenced great numbers of souls to Christ. Multiplication is the goal. I know that some I have led to Christ have, in turn, led others to Him. To be a soul winner is a blessing, but an even bigger one is training and encouraging others to do soul winning.

We are in debt to those who, through the years, have shared the Gospel with us. We are their fruit, and our fruit is also theirs. Only eternity will show the full extent of our soul-winning efforts.

80. View results.

It is impossible to know how many people I have really led to the Lord. When the Holy Spirit has burdened me to talk to individuals, afterwards that burden is lifted. Even if not a single person sincerely was saved, my obedience to the Lord in speaking to them as He led is what is important. I am confident that many sincerely did trust Christ as Savior, but God alone knows the heart; He is the judge. Sadly, I have also missed opportunities to speak to people.

Someone observed to D. L. Moody that one of his converts was walking in sin. Moody replied that obviously it must indeed, have been his convert, and not the Lord's. Jesus made reference to *"disciples of John"* and *"disciples of the Pharisees"* (Luke 5:33) as well as to *"His disciples"* (Luke 9:14). He refers to his disciples as wheat, "For now, the wheat and the tares are together, but God will separate them in the future: *"Let both grow together until the harvest, and at harvest time I will tell the reapers, Gather the weeds first and bind them in bundles to be burned, but gather the wheat into my barn"* (Matthew 13:30). Let us focus on following Christ, and He will make the Gospel seeds grow. One of these days the harvest will come, and then, we will know who really came to know Christ!

The Great Shepherd is Christ, (Hebrews 13:20). As a Christian, we are one of His sheep, and should not think that other sheep belong to us but rather Him. The body of Christ (Christians) should nurture and help one another. Sheep are supposed to reproduce. However, it is the Holy Spirit that was with the individual both drawing them to cross our path and burdening us to witness to them. It is He that is with them and will continue to be with them, even when we cannot. Yes, we are to disciple and mentor as much as we are able, but where we can't, He can.

81. Acknowledge the help of others.

A lot of people have helped us to be where we are today. We have not succeeded on our own. We all owe a debt to others and need to exhibit a sense of gratitude. Paul considered that he had an obligation to others. (Romans 1:14)

Charles Plumb shared the following true life account. He was a US Navy jet pilot in Vietnam. After 75 combat missions, his plane was destroyed by a surface-to-air missile. Plumb ejected and parachuted into enemy hands. He spent six years in a communist Vietnamese prison. Surviving the ordeal, he eventually returned home. One day, when Plumb and his wife were sitting in a restaurant, a man at another table came up and said, "You're Plumb! You flew jet fighters in Vietnam from the aircraft carrier Kitty Hawk. You were shot down! I packed your parachute. I guess it worked!"

Plumb assured him, "It sure did. If the chute hadn't worked, I wouldn't be here today." Plumb could not sleep that night. He thought of the many hours the sailor had spent at a long wooden table in the bowels of the ship, carefully weaving the shrouds and folding the silks of his chute, holding in his hands Plumb's fate. Plumb reflected that he had needed many kinds of parachutes when his plane was shot down over enemy territory—he needed his physical parachute, his mental parachute, his emotional parachute, and his spiritual parachute before finally reaching safety.

As we go through life, we need to appreciate people who packed our parachutes. I would like to take this opportunity to say thank you to all those who had a part in packing my parachute. I hope you will be mindful of those who have helped pack yours! Paul had a spirit of appreciation and he stated, *"I do not cease to give thanks for you"* (Ephesians 1:16).

82. Enjoy the harvest.

The song, *"Thank You for Giving to the Lord"* tells of a man entering Heaven and being approached by different individuals thanking him for helping them get to Heaven. A young person from the Sunday school class that he had taught came to him and said, "Thank you," for helping him pray the salvation prayer. Another man from a mission field thanked him for sacrificially giving so that the Gospel message reached his corner of the world. One individual after another thanked him for touching their lives.

How special it will be when we see the results of choices we made during this lifetime, affecting the eternity of others! God has blessings for those who win souls and serve Him. It is a good thing to look at the events of this life with eternity in mind.

The following are some of the verses that have been an inspiration to me.

> *"And those who are wise shall shine like the brightness of the sky above; and those who turn many to righteousness, like the stars forever and ever."* (Daniel 12:3)
> *"The fruit of the righteous is a tree of life, and whoever captures souls is wise."* (Proverbs 11:30)
> *"Let him know that whoever brings back a sinner from his wandering will save his soul from death and will cover a multitude of sins."* (James 5:20)
> *"He who calls you is faithful; he will surely do it."* (I Thessalonians 5:24)
> *"Jesus said to them, 'My food is to do the will of him who sent me and to accomplish his work. Do you not say, 'There are yet four months, then comes the harvest' Look, I tell you, lift up your eyes, and see that the fields are white for harvest. Already the one who reaps is receiving wages and gathering fruit for eternal life, so that sower and reaper may rejoice together. For here the saying holds true, one sows and another reaps. I*

sent you to reap that for which you did not labor. Others have labored, and you have entered into their labor." (John 4:34-38)

"Those who sow in tears shall reap with shouts of joy! He who goes out weeping, bearing the seed for sowing, shall come home with shouts of joy, bringing his sheaves with him." (Psalm 126:5, 6)

83. Follow up.

Leading someone to the Lord is just the beginning of a new life for them. They need help to grow and mature. Seek the Lord's guidance in doing whatever can be done to help them in that growth. Jesus Christ designed the local church to be the organization to mature people from being spiritual infants to maturity.

When Satan has lost the individuals' soul, he does not give up. He goes into full throttle to keep them from growing in the Lord, and to keep them from, in turn, reproducing in other's lives. We are warned, *"Be sober-minded; be watchful. Your adversary the devil prowls around like a roaring lion, seeking someone to devour"* (1 Peter 5:8). In the wild, when a lion is hunting, it goes first for the straggler to separate it from the others. When a herd takes a stand against the enemy, facing it defiantly with the young and vulnerable protected in its ranks, that herd will survive and grow. There is strength in numbers. Let us prayerfully protect our spiritual babies!

In Scripture, new Christians are described as a new creation, *"Like newborn infants, long for the pure spiritual milk, that by it you may grow up into salvation"* (1 Peter 2:2). It is important that they be nurtured. We are also instructed, *"Not neglecting to meet together, as is the habit of some, but encouraging one another, and all the more as you see the Day drawing near"* (Hebrews 10:25).

There are times when we personally are not able to do the follow-up with a new convert. Be careful not to use that fact as an excuse for not witnessing. Remember that we are only the third party in the situation. The Holy Spirit that initialized the meeting and brought it to a point of salvation, will also continue to be with them! If they are obedient to Him, He will make certain that they are nurtured. They will never be in a situation beyond God's reach! We are comforted in the assurance,

> *"If I ascend to heaven, you are there! If I make my bed in Sheol, you are there! If I take the wings of the morning and dwell in the uttermost parts of the sea, even there your hand shall lead me, and your right hand shall hold me. I say, 'Surely the darkness shall cover me, and the light about me be night,' even the darkness is not dark to you; the night is bright as the day, for darkness is as light with you."* (Psalm 139:8-12)

84. Be cautious.

A person can pray a prayer and "go through the motions" of being born again without actually connecting with God.

People in life can date without getting married. Some people have a religious experience without truly seeing themselves as lost, without repenting, without changing. No one who truly meets God can walk away and not be changed. Being born again is not the result of words; it is a heart responding to God genuinely and becoming a new creation. In His great love, Jesus Christ reaches out to us; we must respond honestly and sincerely.

My mother's life changed so beautifully after she found Christ that I wanted what she had found. The night I trusted Jesus Christ as my Lord and Savior, my life also changed. I began a personal relationship with God as my Heavenly Father and Jesus Christ as King of my life. I talked with Him, read His Book, talked about Him, and tried to obey Him. As well I followed the Lord in believer's baptism and became a member of a local church. This is normal; there should be a change.

Just as the Gospel of John chapter 3 tells us *to be* born again, the Epistle of 1 John explains how we can know *if we have been* born again. If there has not been a change in our life, more than likely something is missing. The Bible clearly states that it is the fruit produced in our life that shows what our position truly is. Paul tells us, **"But the fruit of the Spirit is love, joy, peace, patience, kindness, goodness, faithfulness,"** (Galatians 5:21-23). We can know what our relationship is with God. When reading 1 John, if there has not been a change in one's life, one should be very concerned and pray—asking God to make any necessary changes!

> *God is light, and in him is no darkness at all. ⁶ If we say we have fellowship with him while we walk in darkness, we lie and do not practice the truth.* (1 John 1:5b, 6).
> ¹⁵ *Do not love the world or the things in the world. If anyone loves the world, the love of the Father is not in him. ¹⁶For all that is in the world— the desires of the flesh and the desires of the eyes and pride in possessions—is not from the Father but is from the world. ¹⁷And the world is passing away along with its desires, but whoever does the will of God abides forever… ²⁸And now, little children, abide in him, so that when he appears we may have confidence and not shrink from him in shame at his coming,"* (1 John 2:15-17, 28).
> ³*And everyone who thus hopes in him purifies himself as he is pure".* (1 John 3:3).
> ¹⁸*We know that everyone who has been born of God does not keep on sinning"* (1 John 5: 18a).

Apparently it is impossible for a born-again Christian to continue to be comfortable living in deliberate sin. I remember hearing about a man who trusted Christ but continued to return to the bar night after night. When asked about why his life had not changed, he replied that it had changed. Previously, he had enjoyed drinking, but now the enjoyment was gone. Eventually, his life did change, and he did quit drinking. Change is from the inside out and may take time to gain strength. After being born again, we are newborn babies in Christ, and we should grow. That growth is produce, *"Like newborn infants, long for the pure spiritual milk* (the Scriptures)*, that by it you may grow up into salvation"* (1 Peter 2:1-3). We learn to walk and talk and mature through the milk of the Word of God. If we do not, there is something wrong! We need to examine ourselves.

The truth of the old saying, "You can lead a horse to water, but you can't make him drink," is applicable in winning souls for Christ. You can lead individuals to Christ, but you can't make them accept

Christ so that they become born again. Individuals themselves must connect with the power of the Holy Spirit—with a spirit of repentance. Then there is new life. God expects us to bear fruit—the fruit of the Spirit as spoken of in John 15.

If we plant a tree and there are never apples on it, probably is not an apple tree. Jesus said,

> *"Beware of false prophets, who come to you in sheep's clothing but inwardly are ravenous wolves. You will recognize them by their fruits. Are grapes gathered from thorn bushes, or figs from thistles? So, every healthy tree bears good fruit, but the diseased tree bears bad fruit. A healthy tree cannot bear bad fruit, nor can a diseased tree bear good fruit. Every tree that does not bear good fruit is cut down and thrown into the fire. Thus you will recognize them by their fruits."* (Matthew 7:15-20)

According to those verses, the following should be true. (1) There should be spiritual fruit in our lives. If fruit is not evident, then we should be concerned as to the reality of our salvation. (2) We should consider the Bible to be God's love letter and instructions for our lives. (3) We should talk to God. (4) We should listen to and follow Him. *"My sheep hear my voice, and I know them, and they follow me"* (John 10:27). If these factors are not present in our lives, we need to consider if we really are born again.

I am glad it is God's responsibility to know who is and who is not a true Christian. But, it is interesting that no matter where you go in the world, you meet some people that you just know are born again Christians. Your spirit gives testimony with their spirit that you are one in Christ. There are many people who claim to be Christians, with which your spirit does not have that same inward testimony with their spirit. [24] *"by this we know that he abides in us, by the Spirit whom he has given us"* (1 John 3:24).

Not everyone would be happy in Heaven. For some, to see Jesus Christ face-to-face would be awkward. For them to enjoy singing praises to God would be unnatural. For them, to enjoy the fellowship of born again believers—from Adam and Eve, the Apostle Paul, on down to the martyrs who will be beheaded for their stand for Christ during the future tribulation—they would be uncomfortable. For them to serve the Lord forever in eternity when they didn't want to serve Him here on earth would be impossible. They could not enjoy Heaven without their hearts being changed. Sadly, they will not be happy in Hell either, for no one is happy there—for all eternity! Their only hope is Christ! Will you be there? If you are not sure—MAKE SURE!

Consultation and coaching is available by appointment for individuals and groups.

Contact Gloria Goering
P.O. Box 4185, Waterloo, IA 50704;
gloriagoering@hotmail.com
Web page: familyaltarbroadcast.com